The Northern Shamanic Herbal

Raven Kaldera

The Northern Shamanic Herbal

Raven Kaldera

Hubbardston, Massachusetts

Asphodel Press
12 Simond Hill Road
Hubbardston, MA 01452

The Northern Shamanic Herbal
© 2010 by Raven Kaldera
ISBN 978-0-9825798-4-8

Printed in cooperation with
Lulu Enterprises, Inc.
860 Aviation Parkway, Suite 300
Morrisville, NC 27560

For Mengloth, who was willing to teach me.
For Gerda, bride of Frey, who watches over my herb garden.
For Frey, who guards my farm.
For all my green friends who have given me so much.
For all my flesh friends who help weed.
For sun and earth,
for moon and water,
for flesh and blood,
for how you've helped keep me alive,
I am grateful.

Contents

Part I
Northern Shamanic Herbalism

Introduction: The Greenwights

When I was a child, I talked to plants.

I didn't have any wise old family members who held old herbal knowledge and taught it to me, as so many famous herbalists have recounted. I did have a grandmother who was into gardening, but she tended towards pansies and pachysandra. My family were middle-class American suburbanites who saw everything in terms of the latest scientific theories, and would have found my practice of talking to plants fanciful at best and ridiculous at worst. Gardening was all right—for a few years my father grew some vegetables in the back yard, and my mother put in a few small trees and some chrysanthemums—but plants weren't medicine, and they certainly weren't people that you could talk to.

I knew better. I was one of the outcast children at school, poorly coordinated and oddly behaving, picked last for gym teams and exiled to far left field for many phys-ed classes. Sometimes an hour would go by without a ball coming my way (not that I could have caught it, anyway), or anyone noticing that I was sitting down in the tall grasses at the edge of the recess field, touching weeds. Sometimes I would pick leaves and fold them, pull them apart. Sometimes I just stroked them like a pet. (I wasn't allowed pets at home due to the allergies of other family members.) Sometimes the plant would communicate with me, not exactly in words, but I could tell that its consciousness had responded to me. A clump of Plantain read about like a mouse to me in terms of consciousness sophistication, although one was mobile and one sessile. Like one might talk to a mouse in a box, I would talk to it, and it would respond in some small way that did not include physical movement. I'd long ago learned that I could see the glow of life force in a living thing, and I could see it in plants just as strong as animals. As I petted it, it glowed brighter. That Plantain was just as alive as an animal, although it wasn't very bright.

But there was something else present that was. Sometimes when I talked to plants—on the recess grounds, in the back yard, at my grandmother's house—I sensed a larger presence looming behind the plant like a parent standing over me and watching my interaction with their child. Whenever I sensed this sort of presence, my heart would pound and the hair would stand up on my neck, and I would be careful not to pull off any leaves while they were there. I convinced myself that I couldn't see them, largely because I didn't want to look. Besides, I sensed that whatever it was, was very old, and as a child I felt that I oughtn't to associate with my elders. The little clump of Plantain was just about my speed.

As an adult, I ended up in the city and all my dealings with plants ceased for years, caught up in a cycle of poverty, single parenting, chronic illness, and general scrambling for a living in the concrete jungle. However, somewhere along the line a friend drove me some hours away into the country, and we visited an herbfarm. I was captivated, wandering around in a daze. The herbs seemed so much more alive, somehow, than the over-fertilized tame hybrid vegetables or plastic-colored bedding flowers or scraggly weeds that I'd known in my youth. (I had no idea, at that time, how isolated I was from nature, how isolated most modern people are.) They called out to me with those voices that were not voices, and I ended up frantically buying a dozen of them to bring home and keep in pots. The herbs weren't timid; it was as if they sauntered up and demanded my attention. From that day on, I would never again live without live herbs in or around my house.

I read everything that I could find about them, ransacking the public library for books. As I read, something echoed in me again and again: I'd done this before. Not the reading, but the growing of them, the talking to them, the harvesting and preparation and ... dosing? Yes, giving them to people who were ill. I'd known what to do then, although I got the feeling that while some of the information I got out of those rather general library herbals was common knowledge I'd had before, some of it wasn't. I'd known things that weren't written there, scraped up through trial and error and the advice of those who had taught me. I also noticed that while there were many herbs who would call out to me, there were many more who wouldn't. It was the European herbs that drew me in with those memories, and specifically ones from northern latitudes, or that had been naturalized there. I also felt that from some of the local North American plants in the ecosystems where I lived, but those seemed to be less about "I remember you—don't you remember me?" and more about "Hey, I saw you when you were a kid, talking to that Plantain. Want to talk to me?"

I learned, now that I was older and wiser and no longer afraid to look large spirits in the eye (in fact coming to terms with the fact that I could see human ghosts helped me face the spirits of nature), that the Presences looming over me were the overriding spirit of that sort of plant. Devas, some New Age folk called them. I called them Grandmother Mugwort and Grandfather Plantain, Mother Dill and Father Comfrey, Master Fennel and Mistress Hyssop. They sometimes looked human in my mind's eye, but I never assumed that this was anything more than the way that my mind interpreted their energy. Some didn't look human at all. Some were simply undelineated Beings. Some seemed to like me, some were indifferent or even hostile. Some helped me, offering advice. I found that when the Grandparent spirit was standing over them, the little plant spirit didn't mind giving up its leaves, and even the sacrifice of its entire being was not accompanied by negative feelings. The Grandparent spirit simply gathered it in, and I took its body to make medicine with.

For medicine they were. I was poor, and had no health insurance, and was chronically ill. Taking herbs saved me from wasting my meager money on doctors often enough to make it definitely worth my while. It was quite satisfying, too—I was getting one over on the Man. Every time I fought off a cold with Garlic and Elderberry, I was robbing a pharmaceutical company, a doctor's office, and the entire medical industry. I was walking in the ways of my ancestors, some of whom might have once been me.

The story of how I became a shaman, how the Northern gods and wights came for me, killed me, brought me back, and trained me in the other parts of my job is a path that runs parallel to my dealings with the plants ... or Greenwights, as I began to call them after the cultural context of my practice congealed around me. When most people think of shamans and spirits, they think of animal spirits—the shaman's allies are Wolf, or Bear, or Eagle. (You'll also notice that the popular stories all have large impressive animals; you rarely hear of famous shamans using Rat or Sparrow.) While I did eventually get introduced to a handful of animals, it was always plants first for me. Instead of Wolf, I got Agrimony. Instead of Bear, I got Burdock. The stories also tended to refer to the shamans as only having one or two allies; instead, I was expected to make some kind of alliance, however tentative, with every sort of plant that would talk to me.

Two plants in particular dogged my footsteps, and I began to refer to them as my watch-wights. Before I had learned that term, I just made sure to look for one or the other of both whenever I found a new apartment, even in the city. If I saw one or the other, it was a sign that this place would be important or useful to me. One was Belladonna, the other Elder. They were the first Grandmother spirits that I ever faced. Lady Belladonna was dark and sleek, languid and sardonic, sorceress and Black Queen, sharp and dangerous as a stiletto, the Mata Hari of the plant world. Even though she told me that she had been set to guard me by my patron goddess Hela, I have always been careful to treat her with respect and never turn my back on her. Dame Ellhorn, on the other hand, was a dignified grandmother, a wisewoman of noble blood who expected me to treat her with courtly manners. At first I thought that she had been set to guard me as well, but she told me that she had merely seen me once as a child and had taken a liking to me, which suggests that all my talking to weeds paid off.

The Northern Tradition religions are at bottom animistic, seeing soul and life and the force of Wyrd in all living things, and some things that do not appear to be alive to the naked eye. Animals, plants, trees, stones, even the very land has wights that one can (and ought to) communicate and work with. Probably the best known wights are land-wights, the indwelling spirit of a particular piece of land. In most Northern Tradition practice, offerings are made to any land-wight whose space you will be using for worship, sacrifices to deities, magic, hunting, gathering, or anything else that has the potential to upset the balance of their land's energy.

As I touched on earlier in this introduction, the first thing to understand in dealing with plant-wights (and animal-wights too, for that matter) is that a distinction must be made between the spirit of a particular sort of plant or animal (Comfrey-wight, Dog-Spirit, etc.) and the wight of a specific plant or animal (the Comfrey plant outside your side door, your pet dog, etc.). You'll deal with the first sort, the overarching Calendula-wight or Vervain-wight, when you are doing the charms themselves. You'll deal with the second sort if you are actually growing and/or gathering your own live plant material. For large plants, it's good to ask permission of the specific plant spirit to allow you to take some of their leaves. (Generally, I've found that nearly all are fine with it if you are using them for purposes of healing. If they aren't fine with it, sometimes appealing to the overarching spirit can get you an override.) For taking a whole bunch of small plants, it's better to ask permission of the land-wight, who may tell you if taking so many will mess with the ecological balance of that area.

While you can use any plant and get some good from it—the alkaloids will work no matter what—it is by contacting the plant spirit and making it your ally that your healing efforts are made significantly stronger. With the aid of the plant-wight behind you, those alkaloids have a better chance of going where they need and getting the job done. This is where the job of the Leike clearly evolved from part of the job of the ancient shaman, whose powers lay not only in wortcunning and the knowledge of plant properties, but in wightcunning and a battery of spirit helpers. Many of the charms of the Anglo-Saxon herbals seem to be charms of this nature, although perhaps poorly dictated by country healers who had either forgotten their original use or weren't talking about it to the (perhaps Christian) herbal-writer sitting with suspicious and scholarly pen in hand.

After a few years of urban container gardening, I couldn't stand it any more and my new wife and I bought a small piece of land in the country. We both wanted to homestead, but the biggest draw for me was the thought of a big herb garden. It started small, just a couple of beds in the front yard holding the transplanted herbs I'd brought with me, but it grew as steadily as I could manage to dig up the dry matted turf and replace it with beds of goat and rabbit manure. Soon there was no more front yard, and eventually no more side yard, either, just herb beds. As my garden grew, so did my relationship with the two Norse goddesses who would teach me how to use them.

One was Gerda, the wife of Frey the god of agriculture, the Sacred Corn King. My wife is descended from Frey's festival-got children—her mother's maiden name was Ingerson—and we both called on his blessing when we began our small farm and the first vegetable beds went in, the first goats and sheep and chickens found their pens. It would be later that I met his wife. Gerda is a giantess-goddess, quiet and dark and heavy where Frey is golden and bright and laughing. Her name means "guard", and she came to me as the Lady of the Walled Garden. Frey oversaw our farm, but the herbs were Gerda's place. Indeed, as the garden grew, she claimed more and more of it until the whole area within the stone walls and fences became her sacred place. She would come to me while I was weeding or digging—conveniently already on my knees before her—and talk to me about the herbs, telling me their stories. (They weren't stories I'd ever read, and I don't know if they have ever been written down. The shamanic tradition of my ancestors was lost while they still had an oral culture.)

Gerda introduced me to plant spirits that I didn't yet know. Some who had previously been indifferent to me stood up and took notice when I followed in the wake of her quiet dark-cloaked figure. She specifically introduced me to certain types of greenwights—the Wisewomen like Mugwort and Yarrow, the Magicians like Fennel and Speedwell—who knew the gossip about other greenwights, and who ought to be used for what, and might be willing to teach. To this day, when I meet other herbalists, they invariably ask me who I've studied with. I know that this is their way of determining my credentials and methodology, but I always have to be honest and say, "The plants taught me." Some raise their eyebrows, smile fixedly, and move away. Some smile more deeply, and nod; there's really nothing else to do about it.

For years, I read books and talked to the greenwights, and treated my friends, and learned. Then I began to treat other people, mostly low-income friends of friends who had no money and no insurance, and were willing (or desperate enough) to be experimented on. I learned at least as much from these experiments as I did from reading about herbs in books. Even so, I didn't think of myself as a healer, or even a herbalist. I was a shaman who worked with herbs, no more than that. I didn't have any psychic healing abilities; in fact, my particular set of talents was completely resistant to such things. To me at that time, the word "healer" meant, on a religious/spiritual level, someone who had "the healing gift", who could lay on hands and do something special. I, on the other hand, couldn't even learn Reiki—I was "wired" differently.

In spite of this, somewhere along the line my patron goddess Hela told me that I would have to learn to do something with the H-word. "But I'm not—" *Do it anyway. Go talk to a healer-goddess and see what she can do for you.* My first thought was Eir, the healer-goddess of Asgard, handmaiden of Frigga, whose very name means "healer". I prayed to her and she responded, with a brief, terse message that was more of a memo. *You're not for me. Talk to my colleague.* This came accompanied by an image of a mountain somewhere in the Norse-cosmology world of Jotunheim, the home of the Giants. On top of that mountain, a giantess-goddess stood, robed in white and bedecked with jewels, surrounded by her own group of handmaidens. Not knowing what else to do, I looked up references to mountains in Jotunheim until I suddenly ran into the saga of *Svipdagsmal*, the story of the hero Svipdag who won the heart of the healer-giantess Mengloth. She lives, according to the story, on the top of Lyfjaberg Mountain, surrounded by a bevy of handmaidens, and women in need of healing made offerings to her. Her name means "necklace-glad", and she knows all the secrets of healing from many races and places.

My next step was to make a shamanic journey to her mountain, where I asked for her aid in many things. She told me the story of her courtship with Svipdag from her perspective, and after a time of scrutinizing me, agreed to take me on as a student. My work with Gerda stood me in good stead there; one of Mengloth's handmaidens is Gerda's mother Aurboda. Still, she warned me that I would have to work very hard, that it was a great deal of knowledge, and that she would expect me to take on clients professionally as soon as I was able.

"But I'm not ... talented in that area." *I know. I can see that from here.* She was clinical but kind in her assessment of me. *But in the times of your ancestors, one never knew what sort of shaman one was going to get in any given generation. Some might have the healing gift, some might be better at other things. Yet if you can make alliances with enough spirits, they will do the work that you cannot. That's what it is to be a shaman, foolish one. And you already have the spirits.*

I did, indeed; I had the greenwights whom I'd met and learned to love, and I had the rune-spirits who agreed to help direct the efforts of the greenwights in healing *galdr*. (This technique, as well as the many other things that I've since learned in Mengloth's Med School, as I call it with my tongue planted firmly in my cheek, will be delineated in the next book in this series, *Northern Shamanic Healing.*) Much of this book comes from my years under the training of Mengloth and Gerda.

If you, the reader, are interested in herbalism and healing from a Northern Tradition perspective, I encourage you to initiate contact with (read: start praying to) Northern deities who might help you with this work. While I learned herbs from Gerda, I am sure that other earthy deities such as Jord or Nerthus might have something to teach about them as well. Frey, the god of agriculture, is the resident expert on food plants and nutrition. For those who are more Aesir-focused, there is no better teacher than Eir the healer of Asgard. If you're not Northern Tradition but are simply interested in this technique of herbalism, go straight to the greenwights themselves. You might consider doing *utiseta* with a particular plant. *Utiseta* is a skill outlined in detail in my *Pathwalker's Guide to the Nine Worlds* book, but in short it is a matter of "sitting out" for a long period (usually overnight) while putting yourself into a trance in order to speak with a spirit. When it comes to greenwights, this works especially well with trees because you can get your back up against them, but it will also work with any wild plant you can sit next to, or any domestic herb that has a sitting-sized space next to it. My personal method of plant *utiseta* is to take a bit of the plant and put it in my mouth, lie down with my eyes closed, breathe and hum myself into a light trance state, and ask it to talk to me. If I get a good connection with the plant-wight, and it agrees to aid me in the future, I swallow the plant bit as a kind of sealing the deal. Obviously, this method doesn't work well with poisonous plants; for that I generally have to go out and lay down in the grass next to the plant, as close as possible without getting its oils on my skin, and talk to it there.

Has there been a price for my involvement with the greenwights? Of course there is. In all worlds, there's no such thing as a free lunch. Some greenwights (like the Ancestral Fathers and Mothers) are bound to us as a species and are obligated to help us. Others simply like humanity and have a close relationship with it, or are healers of such power that they are spiritually obligated to heal when asked under the right circumstances. Still others are indifferent to humans and must be convinced to aid us. The greenwights have demanded that I be more aware of what I eat, especially plant matter; they would prefer it if I only consumed organic food, a deal that I can't fully consummate yet but I am sincerely working toward. Genetically modified food is out of the question, and overly processed food is also an abomination to them. I have had to be mindful of what I harvest in the wild and how; what I feed to my livestock; what I throw out and where it goes. A picnic at a park may become waylaid by a greenwight who wants to talk to me, right now in the middle of the sandwiches.

Another strange taboo they've laid on me, which will probably upset a good number of people, is that I cannot be a vegetarian for reasons of principle. If I required that sort of diet for health reasons, that would be one thing, but my body likes meat protein and does well on it. To the greenwights, saying that it is wrong to kill animals but right to kill plants would be privileging animals over plants, and a plant shaman can't do that. The carrot has as much reason to live as the cow, and is as necessary and worthy of respect when sacrificed so that we may live. Ironically, my involvement with plants has therefore also led me to support organic and cruelty-free livestock farming. (If you don't think that the two are related, go have a talk with Master Clover, or better yet, Frey.)

You don't need to be able to talk to plant-wights in order to be a competent herbalist. The plants will work in their own ways, regardless of whether you are aware of them as spiritual beings. However, our ancestral practice of spell-healing can provide valuable insight and aid, if you have the talent and ability and patience. In this herbal, we have provided descriptions of our impressions of the plant-wights we and other herbalists have worked with. Think of it as sort of an introduction, like handing you a phone number. Whether you pick up the phone and make the call is your choice.

If you're looking for a scholarly treatise on herbs or shamanic magic or the Norse Gods, complete with footnotes and references, this isn't your book. (Some of the books in the bibliography might be, though.) This is a practical manual of herbalism that happens to concentrate on herbs native to and anciently imported into northern Europe, and a spiritual and magical manual on working with their spirits. The herbal information is partly my own experience and partly the work of many great herbalists before me. The religious information is nearly all my own experience and those of a few friends who spoke of greenwights I hadn't yet met. It's a window onto my world, not a book of academic theory. Take it and use it; the spirits are there, and all we have to do is to reach out to them.

Shamans and Healers

As there is no written and very little archaeological evidence for the ancient shamanic traditions of northern Europe, our only choices are to either look beyond that area to other similar areas, or to consult the Gods and wights directly. The second option is difficult—you have to be a spirit-worker of some might to get anything useful—but the first option can give us clues. We can also look at the later traditions and see the vague threads of the original shamanic knowledge.

In northern Eurasian cultures where shamans still practice, or where they did until recently, the position of herbalist might be part of the shaman's job, or it might be separate. There are many different types of shamans, differentiated partly by each one's innate talents and partly by the sorts of spirits that they made alliances with. (Those two factors are related, as certain spirits are drawn to certain types of people.) For some, the plant-spirits and their healing work were an integral part of their practice; others concentrated on calling game, divining, aiding tribal warfare, religious ritual, or many other things depending on proclivities and spirit allies.

Simultaneously, a psychically talented herbalist might also gain the aid of plant spirits, and could certainly learn the lore of healing plants, without actually going down the long and tumultuous road of being a classic shaman. These healers likely worked alongside shamans in many situations, and were probably the first line of defense for the sick, as the shaman would be called in for more serious cases than the healer could handle. Both shamans and herbalists might or might not have energy-healing talents such as curing through laying on of hands. One could never know, from generation to generation, who would be born with what talents.

As the culture changed to a more civilized ideal with heavier population centers, the shamanic traditions slowly waned. The spread of Christianity wiped out the last tattered remnants, but people still needed healers. While the early Church was suspicious of any kind of healer—not only might they be in league with the Gods of old, the original Church doctrine was that healing should be achieved only with spoken Bible verses and the power of their God—practicality won out and the tradition of the Leike, or healer, lasted for a good long time after the onslaught of Christianity.

The word *Leike* (lay-keh) is Old Norse, and is cognate to the Anglo-Saxon *Laece* (laa-cheh), which eventually gave rise to our word leech. Most people think of the small bloodsucking parasite when hear that word, and few know that it originally meant, simply, healer. As the medieval period passed, health care personnel began to put more emphasis on those bloodsucking parasites as bloodletting came into favor. As a joke, people began to refer to the parasites as "healers", and when bloodletting fell out of favor the word was abandoned as being too closely associated with it. To come up to that another way, imagine if modern doctors faddishly decided to go back to regular use of little black parasites, and people began to humorously call them "doctors" ... and a thousand years later, everyone "knew" that the word "doctor" meant a small swamp parasite, not a respected human profession.

The Modern Leike

Today in the Pagan and New Age communities, there are a lot of people calling themselves healers, with a huge variance in skills and credentialing. Some have modern medical experience—physician, nursing, or EMT— and some have trained in psychic healing skills such as Reiki or Ch'i Gong. Some know herbs, to one extent or another. Some seem to have as their credentials merely the fact that they are "very sensitive" people.

I am not arguing that everyone who calls themselves a healer should have modern medical certification— certainly I'm no medical doctor, nor will I ever be. On the other hand, there is currently no course of healing in Pagan religious circles that both takes earth-centered spirituality into account and gives a strong practical grounding for basic fixing of broken people. I'd like to see one created, perhaps on a Guild-style model with individual study and group testing. I'd like to see a word besides the nebulous "healer" to indicate someone you could go to in order to fix a stomachache, a cut finger, or a spiritual imbalance. In other words, I'd like to see the trained Leike make a comeback. As a shaman, I'd love to see the Leike as the first line of defense, before they have to call me in with the heavy voltage.

While the training and skills of a Northern Tradition shaman is beyond the scope of this book, the skillset of a Leike (or its modern equivalent) is appropriate to explore here. I feel that it is crucial that those might choose to call themselves a Leike within their community should actually be expected to have a certain baseline level of training. To take on the title of healer means that sooner or later, someone will show up and ask you to take charge of their health in some way. This is an awesome responsibility, and to fail in that responsibility can have severe consequences for the individual who has placed their trust in you. Because of this, I believe that the Leike ought to be held to a higher standard than some of the other, less crucial community roles.

To this end, I am suggesting a curriculum and skillset whose structure is based as closely as possible on that of the original Leike. While there are some things that the medieval Leike would have had to do that are obviously better done by medical professionals (such as major surgery) and allowances have to (and should) be made for modern medical knowledge and technology, the original division of healing is still surprisingly useful and accurate.

Tripartite Course of Healing

The Germanic peoples lived in a society divided into three parts—commoners who were farmers and craftsmen, warriors who defended and seized land, and priests who interceded with the Gods and wights for the community. All parts of their society revolved around this ideology, and the job of the Leike reflected this. A Leike was in his or her own way a farmer (whose crops were primarily herbs, both raised and gathered), a warrior (who fought against disease and injury in order to protect the tribe) and a priest (who used charms and prayers as part of healing).

Healing, in the tradition of the Leike, was therefore also a threefold process: herbal healing or "wyrtcunning"; knife healing or surgery; and healing by charm and prayer. Each of these areas can be learned by the aspiring Leike who wants to be a healer to their community and tribe, and ideally all three should be given in-depth study. To call oneself a Leike should not be something that is done casually. This book will attempt to create a thorough and complete guideline for the training of a Leike; it is up to the Northern Tradition communities in general to hold their healers to a high standard of training and competence.

In each of the three divisions of healing, the basic skills are necessary to ensure a ground level of competence; one ought to be able to master all of them in order to formally take on the title of Leike. The skills marked "Optional/Advanced" would ideally be taken on by the Master Leike, who would have responsibility of overseeing and judging the training of the other Leike, perhaps in a Guildmaster position, perhaps simply as a respected elder of the community.

I. Wyrtcunning

Herbal healing, which is the main focus of this book, is the "agricultural" part of the tripartite healing system. Ideally, a Leike who has mastered wyrtcunning ought to be able to do the following:

Required:

1. Have a basic working knowledge of as many herbs as possible. A "basic working knowledge" is defined by knowing a herb's appearance (not just dried bits from the store, either), active parts, medicinal uses, household and culinary uses (though one need not be a gourmet cook, just know which parts of which herb are used in cooking), and have used it in some way, if only for their own healing. For example, a working knowledge of Valerian would mean that the Leike knows what Valerian looks like, and could pick it out in a garden; knows that the root is the active part; knows that it is used in tinctures and tea for a sedative; and have used it at least once on themselves or another for insomnia or the like.
2. Have grown at least a few herbs, if only in pots in an apartment. If the Leike lives where there is absolutely no space even for potted herbs, they should make a point to volunteer in someone else's herb garden. There's no such thing as a gardener who doesn't need extra hands to weed, and this can be a good lesson in how to identify herbs in the field.
3. Have a working knowledge of at least a few wild-grown herbs that are local to their area, and have gathered and used them.
4. Know how to make a poultice, an infusion, a decoction, a tincture in alcohol, vinegar, and glycerine, an infused oil, a syrup, a medicinal candy, and an ointment/salve.

(*Raven's Note:* While I considered discussing how to make these herbal media in this book, I decided against it because it would take up so much space, and there are far better books out there on the subject. For the serious student, I highly recommend James Green's *The Herbal Medicine-Maker's Handbook*, which should give you all the information that you might need on the subject.)

Optional/Advanced:

1. Have an extensive herb garden, and have a working knowledge of how to grow most of the domestic herbs that one works with.
2. Have access to wild areas—woods or meadows—and a regular conservation relationship with local wild herbs.
3. Know about the active alkaloids in the herbs that are used, which would require some study in organic chemistry.
4. Know how to make more advanced herbal delivery methods, such as powders, creams, pastilles, candied flowers, extracts, distillations, suppositories, and moxa.
5. Be aware of and regularly researching current medical trends and testing of herbs in the rest of the world.

II. Knife Healing

Knife healing, in the days of the Leike, included such things as simple surgery—wound cleaning, removal of foreign objects, etc.—and perhaps more advanced techniques such as cauterization, amputation, and trepanning after serious battle injuries. In other words, knife healing dealt with mechanical dysfunctions of the body. Today we would consider the knife healing part of the Leike's training to be study of the functions of the body, and the ability to deal with some basic things going wrong. You need not be a medical doctor or a nurse to be a Leike—and such things as major surgery are best left to experts—but you should be able to deal with smaller medical injuries easily.

Ideally, the knife healing segment of Leike training should include the following courses of training:

Required:
1. A college-level course in Anatomy and Physiology
2. Some kind of official training in the following areas: Basic First Aid. CPR. Bloodborne pathogens and sterile procedure. In the US, the Red Cross takes care of many of these, but Red Cross programs can be variable in their quality and how hands-on they are. The military also gives classes in these subjects, as do local community colleges. In non-US countries, you'll have to research where you can find such training.

Optional/Advanced:
1. EMT training and certification
2. Midwifery training, for those who feel called to be midwives
3. Training and/or certification in therapeutic massage, acupressure, or other forms of bodywork
4. Nursing or medical training (obviously not an option for the average lay Leike, but everything that you can learn about how to deal with actual mechanical bodily dysfunction will help, especially in figuring out when a problem is beyond your scope of practice and should be referred to a physician)

III. Spell Healing

Spell healing in the Northern Tradition is and was an important part of the job, as can be seen in all the old herbals and treatises on disease. While modern folk may be a bit uncomfortable at the idea of spell healing, seeing it as superstitious, backward, and possibly dangerous, we feel that it should be emphasized just as thoroughly as the more mechanical forms of healing. This is a tradition of religious healing, not a historical-reconstruction role-playing game; if we do not include the Gods and wights in our work, it might as well be secular.

This is also one of the main differences between Northern Tradition magical healing and other magical systems: the Gods and spirits are involved, the line between magical charm and prayer is vague and perhaps nonexistent, and the understanding of the body and the world is strongly animistic, not mechanical. The charms in this book are designed to work with the herbs and their attendant wights. While oil of Comfrey will certainly work without magic, a prayer-charm dedicated to its affinitive goddess Eir along with it lends energy, direction, and intent, and brings the blessing of Eir onto the endeavor.

A Leike skilled in spell-healing ought to have mastered the following skills:

Required:
1. A working alliance with the wights of at least some of the plants that one works with as part of wyrtcunning. This means doing some *utiseta* with at least a few plants in order to get a feel for their energy and spirit.
2. Knowledge of at least some useful prayers and charms for the mainstay herbs that you work with. This book will try to combat the dearth in that area.
3. Knowledge of healing deities, and some kind of votive relationship with at least one of them.
4. Knowledge of the magical properties of the herbs that you work with medicinally, so as to be able to incorporate them into non-medicinal charms, recels, etc.

Optional/Advanced:
1. A strong relationship with more than one healing deity, and knowledge of which deities favor which plants.

2. Ability to create your own healing charms and prayers when necessary.
3. Ability to use charm and prayer for nonphysical kinds of healing—mental illness, emotional problems, spiritual despondency, elf-shot, and disorders of the *hame* (energy body).
4. Knowledge of the anatomy of the energy body, and how to work with it.
5. Acupuncture. While this is not taught as a Northern Tradition skill at present, keep in mind that Otzi the Iceman had acupuncture tattoos dating from two millenia before the Chinese supposedly invented it. Northern Tradition acupuncture is currently being reconstructed and reinvented; until it is ready to be taught as a separate skill, learn the Chinese style and remember that energy meridians are the same on any body from any ancestry.
6. Some kind of energy-healing system, such as Reiki, Ch'i-Gong, the newly invented Run-Valdr, or a non-name-brand system.

That's the ideal structure; the next step is for folks to pick it up and go with it. I leave it in the hands of the community-minded healers who read this, and hope that they will take it and run.

The Northern Shamanic Herb Garden

One of the great things about northern European herbs is that they are tough. They've stood the test of millenia of bad weather, poor soil, grazing by livestock and wild animals, general neglect, and in some cases sub-zero temperatures and many feet of snow. This means that they are transplantable nearly everywhere, and will grow without much help in conditions that would blight vegetables. This is much of why they have lived on for so many centuries and continue to be popular today.

The perennial herbs, especially, can be tenacious and live year after year in some unfertilized corner of your garden. Some will self-sow wildly, or spread rapaciously, which the keepers of small orderly gardens have trouble with, but I think that's a great trait. If you are actually going to be harvesting your herbs on a yearly basis, rampant behavior is not a bad thing. It means less work for more plant matter. When they spread or sow themselves randomly all over the garden, you just harvest extra that year.

When I created my list of herbs, I considered which plants could be considered "native" to an area of Norse/Germanic religion, and which were imports. To start with, there is a great climatic difference in a garden on a Norwegian fjord or on a Bavarian mountain, and one in southern England. When the Saxons conquered England and pushed the Britons into Wales, they got themselves a far warmer area than their homeland. (It was even warmer than it is today, as the Little Ice Age of the medieval period hadn't yet occurred; wine grapes could be successfully grown all over England at that time.) Similarly, when the Franks moved south into Gaul, they came into contact with warmer-climate plants that had been naturalized from Mediterranean Europe via Roman invasion, such as Rosemary, Bay, Myrtle, and other Greek and Roman herbs. The authors of the Saxon herbals certainly used these plants, some of which could be carefully garden-grown in southern England or pot-grown elsewhere.

While one could technically argue that anywhere the Germanic-language peoples settled and planted gardens could be considered a northern-religion area, and that any plant known and used by northern herbalists would also count, we felt that it was important to draw the line somewhere. After all, the Saxon herbals also speak of Ginger and Zedoary (white turmeric), and we know that those were never anything but dried imports. Some northern herbalists had only heard of these herbs via Greek and Roman texts. With this in mind, we have created this herbal around those plants that were either native to the northern parts of Europe, or became naturalized there before the Scandinavian migratory period.

The first big plant-exchange contact with Germanic-speaking peoples was the bringing of the Teutonic tribal territories into the Roman Empire. To this day, some of the Latin-based words in our language stem from the time of Roman occupation camps along the German river borders. They introduced such herbs as Lovage, Lettuce, Horehound, Fenugreek, Onions, and Rosemary. Germanic tribesmen were recruited as soldiers into the Roman army, went to Rome after their triumphs, and came home with new plants for their wives' gardens. Romans who built villas in the outlying areas brought their gardens with them, as many plants as would grow in the more violent climate. New plants were eagerly sought—they were medicine, they were food, they were flavoring for other foods. No one would pass up an opportunity to expand their palate variety and their ability to heal. As they came into the North, the Northern Gods snapped them up by affinity, and so we have folkloric associations of Northern Gods with Mediterranean plants.

During the early medieval period, trade picked up again and more new plants came up from the south, some having been introduced from as far away as Persia, India or even China. We did include a few of those, because they quickly became part of the "classic" herb garden. After Charlemagne made his famous proclamation in *Capitulare de Villes* that certain herbs should be grown wherever possible in noble and monastery gardens, the medicinal herb garden took on a more formal nature. While Charlemagne and his era were well past the time of Christian conquering and conversion, many of these herbs also seem to have affinities with the Northern Gods, who were not quite as asleep as we might think.

We don't know what ancient northern herb gardens might have looked like, if indeed they looked like anything besides a plot of stick-fenced land near the hut or cottage planted randomly with whatever herbs the Leike was able to grow. The idea of beautifully laid-out gardens was a much later concept, in the eras of large estates and urbanization, an inheritance from Mediterranean civilizations. Monastery gardens were carefully laid out to reflect the sense of order that Jehovah had visited on the world and all living things. Most of our ideas of what an herb garden "should" look like come from those aesthetic concepts; the likelihood is that the ancient Leike—or even more ancient shaman—leaned entirely toward the utilitarian. If the rabbits couldn't get in and the plants weren't too crowded to grow, that was good enough.

People who live in cities have similar problems. I spent years doing urban container growing, a practice which adapts reasonably well to the growing of herbs. (If you live in a cold climate, some herbs are going to have to be confined to pots and brought inside in the winter no matter how much open land you have.) At one point, I had my tiny asphalted back yard laid wall to wall with trashpicked plastic flowerpots and cracked white restaurant buckets, growing vegetables and herbs as best I can. If you're reduced to this kind of thing, do your best, just don't put the pots by the street or anywhere that car exhaust can blow on them. City air is bad enough. If the plants are brought inside in the winter—and they will probably have to be if you have cold winters, as pots don't provide the insulation of the ground—you might want to invest in UV lighting attached to shelves. There's not always a lot of light in the winter. If you have friends who garden in the country, it may be possible to convince them to let you plant a plot of perennial herbs on their land, especially if you offer to trade weeding labor for the privilege. There's no such thing as a gardener who doesn't need help weeding.

Those of us with a little of our own land may like the idea of planting an herb garden, both for beauty and the wonderful energy one gets from walking through it, and for a regular supply of medicinal plants. They can be laid out like a tradition medieval garden if you love the look of that, or purely utilitarian in easy-to-care-for beds. I prefer raised beds myself, if only a couple of inches, as it allows me to control the soil entirely and better contains plants that spread by root runners (like Mints and Oregano). I like to have one bed just for annuals that gets cleared and refertilized every winter, and the perennials are usually split up into categories of size and use.

One can, of course, plant an herb garden on the basis of what looks attractive, or what fits in that space between the path and the fence, or what's tall or short, or annual or perennial. However, it can be both interesting and magically useful to make specific garden plots for deities, or for purposes. One possibility for garden plots is to make a garden for a specific deity, perhaps centered around a tree of a type sacred to them (if it's not so large as to block out all the light) or a god-post or shrine. For example, a Freya garden might contain plants both traditionally sacred to her and ones that she has shown interest in today: Cowslips, Primroses, Daisies, Columbines, Snowdrops, Strawberries, Lily of the Valley, Pimpernel, and ornamental Beans such as Scarlet Runners. (Columbines, for example, were attributed to her in Swedish folklore, and Snowdrops were said to be the tears that she shed during her first spring as a hostage in Asgard, upon seeing the bleakness of the landscape when compared to her fertile home of Vanaheim.) One could also position a Linden tree far enough behind so that it wouldn't overshadow everything, perhaps with benches under it where one could sit in blessed shade and contemplate her garden and shrine.

Another sort of garden might be purpose-specific. For example, a protection garden might be planted close to the street in a long strip, putting the might of the greenwights between your house and the world. It might include Mustard, Onions, Leeks, Garlic, St. John's Wort, Agrimony, Cinquefoil, Tormentil, and perhaps a few carefully placed Nettles. A love garden might contain flowers sacred to Freya and Lofn, and a garden planted to bring peace and plenty to the home could use plants sacred to Holda and Frigga. Herbalists might choose to plant a healer's garden—not just a garden of medicinal plants, but a smaller plot within that of plants sacred to Eir and/or Mengloth, in order to ask for a blessing on their work.

If you have the room to work with trees as well as herbs, it's possible to make a Norse/Germanic sacred grove (stafgarðr in Old Norse, Anglo-Saxon hearg or frithgeard) with a circle of sacred trees ringed with a hedge and with a sacred herb garden laid out in the middle. While the Norse/Germanic folk don't have a set of sacred grove trees as detailed as the Celtic sacred trees, there are still plenty of references, and such a grove might have Oak for Thor or Angrboda; Rowan for Thor; Ash for Odin or Ask, along with Elm for Embla; Birch for Frigga; Holly for Tyr or Frau Holle; Linden for Freya, Cherry for Frey, Apple for Iduna, Spruce for Skadi, Yew for Ullr, Beech for Saga, Maple for Hlin, Aspen for Mani, Fir for Nerthus or Jord, Alder for Loki, Willow for the World Serpent, and Sycamore for Hela. (Sycamores used to grow in Europe, but are now nearly extinct there; they still grow abundantly in America and are referred to as "ghost trees" for their patchy bark which almost looks like stylized rot. In Europe they are known as "plane trees" and are associated with poverty; both aspects are right for Hela, who does seem to like these somber patchy trees.) The hedge around the outside of the sacred enclosure (the Germanic root word haga is cognate to later words for hedge, witch, and holy) was traditionally Hawthorn and Blackthorn, perhaps with Raspberry brambles thrown in. The perimeter might also be marked with Hazel staves holding up ropes. In the middle could be god-posts marking each tree, and a garden laid out with a plot for each deity.

Most herbs can be grown from seed, although some are trickier than others. Rosemary, for example, is persnickety enough that it's easier to get cuttings sometimes. More modern herbs such as French Tarragon are propagated almost entirely from cuttings, as they don't produce much viable seed. Many seed catalogs have at least a few standard culinary herbs, but a few have a wider selection, and Richter's out of Canada is truly amazing. I've listed good mail-order herb seed sources in an appendix in the back. Another good source is other herb growers; some have email lists where people can share their love of herbs, and many will swap or just give away plants. I've certainly given away quite a few in spring, when I'm weeding out volunteers and hacking back vigorous spreaders.

With all this said about gardens, I cannot neglect the issue of wildcrafting. I get a lot of plants from my 12-acre woodlot, many of them endangered local plants that I have formed relationships with. Part of my responsibility to them is to refrain from overharvesting them, so that they will never be endangered here. This means that I can't sell them commercially, even though it would be profitable ... I just can't take enough to make that worth my while. My personal practice is to never take more than a tenth of the plants I can see in visual range in any one area. If there are only two or three plants and I need the whole thing, or the root, I just give it a pass and ask the greenwight to spread and have more babies, if possible. If I need the bark of a tree, I will take only a small vertical strip from a large tree (remember that horizontal stripping kills the tree), or if there are many small saplings or suckers from a tree's roots, I will thin them out and peel them.

I've watched popular herbs become endangered from overharvesting, and it's one of the great sorrows of the rise of alternative medicine. While I love that people are going back to herbal healing, I wonder if, with our modern overinflated population, if there will be enough plants to do for us all, especially the ones that don't do well in captivity. When Goldenseal started to look thin on the ground, herbalists recommended Oregon Grape. Now Oregon Grape is starting to look thin. What's to be done? I don't know, but I am being careful with my own small patch of land, which grows Lady's Slipper and Bethroot and other ecologically delicate plants.

If you wildcraft, I suggest talking to the land-wight first, before you pick. It knows better than you do what plants are in danger. I also suggest making an offering to it afterwards, if it's not your own land. Keeping the earth happy is part of keeping the plants happy, and we have the knowledge to do that directly.

The Nine Sacred Herbs

The original Song of the Nine Sacred Herbs that was discovered by the Northern Tradition God Woden is listed in an 11th century manuscript called the Lacnunga. By the time I ran across it, I already had an herb garden. Reading it struck me with the force of a blow; I knew that this would be an important part of my practice, if I could just find the herbs! Fortunately, as I counted them off, I realized that I wouldn't have to be acquiring them. They had already found me.

Mugwort was the first of the Nine that I read about. Since I'm not allowed, by the order of the spirits that I work with, to use techniques from cultures other than the ones they specify, I'm always looking for European or Eurasian alternatives to practices that most Americans have borrowed from Native American practices. Smudging with White Sagebrush was one of those practices, but when I discovered Mugwort as the first of the sacred herbs, I knew that this was my alternative. For years, the Mugwort plant in my garden had been spreading itself everywhere; I had to continually hack back and pull up new Mugwort seedlings. In my garden, it grew six feet tall. "This is all very nice," I would say as I looked at its enormous silvery bushiness, "but what do I do with all of it?" Once I discovered its purpose, I knew why it had been growing there in abundance, waiting for me to figure it out.

Some of the other herbs, like Plantain and Nettles, were local weeds that had colonized my garden from the outside. I'd pull them up, and they'd come back again. There were Crabapples on my farm from long before I'd bought it, planted by old Finnish farmers of a century ago. Fennel and Chamomile were annual herbal basics that I planted every year. Watercress had been brought to me in a pot by a friend, who told me that she saw the plant and suddenly knew that it needed to come to my house. At the time, I thanked her and didn't think much of it; later I was to remember that with some wonder.

There is some argument over the last two herbs. One is generally translated as "Chervil", but the Chervil that we use today in gourmet cooking is actually French Chervil, and it is a later development. The plant that the English people knew as Chervil in the 11th century is occasionally still called "British Chervil", but we generally know it as Sweet Cicely. Like Fennel, it is slightly licorice-flavored, and its greatest bounty is its seeds. Since the two are considered to be a pair, it makes sense that they would taste similar and both be seed plants as well as foliage plants. Besides, I had a huge clump of it in my garden.

The last herb is referred to as "Atterlothe" in the song of the Nine Herbs, and there is a huge amount of disagreement on what it refers to. Some suggestions have been Betony, Bistort, Cock's Spur Grass, Sainfoin, Belladonna, or Viper's Bugloss. Rather than just be stumped like everyone else, I resorted to talking to the actual plant spirits, which I followed up with runic divination. According to the plants themselves, Atterlothe is Viper's Bugloss (*Echium vulgare*).

I'd read about Viper's Bugloss, but I didn't know what it looked like, so I looked it up first in my herb books and then in a wildflower book ... Oh. So that's the name of that big prickly blue-flowered plant that grew up in the middle of my garden. Well, there we were: nine herbs already on the property and ready to be used. Now I just had to figure out what they were good for. I looked up folk research on their magical uses and listed them, but except for Mugwort, I had no clue on their shamanic uses. So I did it the old-fashioned way; I sat with the plant and let it speak to me. I ingested them, I let them move through my body, I asked them to tell me their stories, and they did. The uses that I have listed here are the results of that communication with these nine powerful plant spirits.

Part of what was strongly communicated to me when I read it was that I should learn to sing it properly, even though there was no music left to reference. So I studied the Old English words slowly, over a period of months, and a tune began to form behind them line by line. It didn't come from me, it came *through* me, bit by bit. I don't know how close it is to the original, but it is acceptable to the Gods, and that's what counts.

I did move the words around a bit, to make it more coherent. The song itself reads like something remembered from an oral tradition, and scribbled down without quite knowing all the lines. Parts of it seem to be moved out of place; I took the liberty of moving them back into a more coherent form. The poem calls three of the four directions at the end, and stops at a half-line; I added in the fourth one, which nicely fills out the line.

I also cut the line about Christ watching over things, near the end. I didn't do this out of any animosity towards Christianity, although it does seem a bit inappropriate as Woden is the main star deity of this poem. However, the Christ line is the only line in the whole song that is only one line long. It has no alliteration, and it is not connected to the lines before or after it, while they are connected to each other. It looks jarringly like someone stuck it in randomly during the writing-down process, in order to put a little bit of Christianity into a pagan charm, perhaps to make nice with the authorities. It doesn't feel like it belongs there, and when it is cut, the verse flows better.

I really would have preferred to learn the song in modern English, but as I tried to sing it that way, I realized that it wasn't going to work. Part of the power of charms in the old Germanic-descended languages is in their alliteration, and translating it ruined that, and it just didn't have the same power. When I painstakingly began to learn it in Old English, it revealed its beauty and power to me. If you decide to try it in the old tongue, don't be discouraged. The pronunciations aren't as hard as they look, and you don't have to get your accent perfect in order for the alliteration to work. English departments in local colleges may have someone who might be able to help with pronunciations as well.

According to the charm, one is supposed to sing the song three times over each herb, and then twice at the subject that you're trying to heal, once in each ear. I've found that it's enough to sing the verse that applies to the herb in question three times when you harvest and prepare it. You can also sing that verse when you use the herb by itself in some way; for example, you can sing the Mugwort verse while purifying an area with Mugwort smoke. Of course, the nature of the song is such that singing one verse makes me want to sing the whole thing, and I often do.

A file of me singing the song is available in the online version of this herbal, on my website (www.northernshamanism.org), for people to hear and learn themselves. However, even if learning a long piece in Old English is not in your repertoire, anyone can grow and use the Nine Sacred Herbs themselves. They are listed in the Materia Medica, with all the others.

You will notice, as you read the entries for the herbs, that like the worlds, their uses line up in complementary pairs with a single center. Mugwort is central, the purifying herb; Viper's Bugloss and Crabapple are like unto the surgeon's knife and the post-surgery healing salve, respectively; "fille and finule", the "mighty two", are for seeing the light and the dark; Watercress and Nettles are for watery shaping and fiery boundaries; and the powers of Chamomile bring you up into the light while those of Plantain take you down into the darkness.

My version of the Old English:
Gemyne ðu, mugwyrt, hwæt þu ameldodest,
Hwæt þu renadest æt Regenmelde.
Una þu hattest, yldost wyrta.
ðu miht wið þre and wið þritig,
þu miht wiþ attre and wið onflyge,
þu miht wiþ þam laþan ðe geond lond færð.

Modern English Translation:
Keep in mind, Mugwort, what you made known,
What you laid down at the great denouncing.
Una your name is, oldest of herbs,
Of might against three, and against thirty.
Of might against venom and the onflying,
Of might against the vile foe who fares through the land.

Ond þu, wegbrade, wyrta modor,
Eastan openo, innan mihtigu;
Ofer ðe crætu curran, ofer ðe cwene reodan,
Ofer ðe bryde bryodedon, ofer þe fearras fnærdon.
Eallum þu þon wiðstode and wiðstunedest;
Swa ðu wiðstonde attre and onflyge
And þæm laðan þe geond lond færð.

Stune hætte þeos wyrt,
    heo on stane geweox;
Stond heo wið attre, stunað heo wærce.
Stiðe heo hatte, wiðstunað heo attre,
Wreceð heo wraðan, weorþeð ut attor.

þis is seo wyrt seo wiþ wyrm gefeaht,
þeos mæg wið attre,
    heo mæg wið onflyge,
Heo mæg wið ðam laþan
    ðe geond lond færð.
Fleoh þu nu, attorlaðe,
    seo læsse ða maran,
seo mare þa læssan,
    oððæt him beigra bot sy.

Gemyne þu, mægðen, hwæt þu ameldodest,
Hwæt ðu geændadest æt Alorforda;
þæt næfre for gefloge feorh ne gesealde
Syþðan him mon mægðan to mete gegyrede.

þis is seo wyrt ðe wergulu hatte;
ðas onsænde seolh ofer sæs hrygc
Ondan attres oþres to bote.
Stond heo wið wærce, stunað heo wið attre,
Seo mæg wið þre and wið þritig.
Wið feondes hond and wið færbregde,
Wið malscrunge manra wihta.

Fille and finule, felamihtigu twa,
þa wyrte gesceop witig drihten,
Halig on heofonum, þa he hongode;
Sette and sænde on nygon worulde
Earmum and eadigum eallum to bote.

þær geændade æppel and attor,
þæt heo næfre ne wolde on hus bugan.

ðas nygon magon wið nygon attrum.
Wyrm com snican, toslat he man;
ða genam Woden nygon wuldortanas,
Sloh ða þa næddran, heo on nygon tofleah.

Nu magon þas nygon wyrta

And you, Waybread (*Plantain*) mother of herbs,
Open from the east, mighty inside.
Over you chariots creaked, over you queens rode,
Over you brides cried out, over you bulls snorted.
All of them you then withstood, you withstood them,
May you likewise withstand poison and the onflying,
And the loathsome foe roving through the land.

Stune (Watercress) is the name of this herb,
    it grew on a stone,
It stands up against poison, it stands against pain,
Stithe (*Nettles*) this one is called, it withstands poison,
It wrecks the wrathful one, it casts out poison.

This is the herb that fought against the snake,
It has power against poison,
    it has power against the onflying,
It has power against the loathsome foe
    roving through the land.
Put to flight now, Venom-loather (*Viper's Bugloss*),
    the great poisons you are less than,
The lesser poisons you are greater than,
    until the cure for both be with him.

Remember, Maythen (*Chamomile*), what you made known,
What you accomplished at Alorford,
That never a man should lose his life from infection
After Maythen was prepared for his food.

This is the herb that is called Wergulu (*Crabapple*).
A seal sent it across the sea-right,
A vexation to poison, a help to others.
It stands against pain, it dashes against poison,
It has power against three and against thirty,
Against the hand of a fiend and against noble scheming,
Against the spell of vile creatures.
Chervil (*Sweet Cicely*) and Fennel, two very mighty ones.
They were created by the wise one-eyed Lord,
Holy in heaven as he hung on the tree;
He set and sent them to the nine worlds,
To the wretched and the fortunate, as a help to all.

There the Apple accomplished against poison
That it would no more dwell in the world.

These nine have power against nine poisons.
A worm came crawling, it killed nothing.
For Woden took nine glory-twigs,
He smote the adder that it flew apart into nine parts.

Now there nine herbs have power

wið nygon wuldorgeflogenum,   against nine fleers of glory,
Wið nygon attrum and wið nygon onflygnum,   Against nine poisons and against nine onflying:
Wið ðy readan attre, wið ðy runlan attre,   Against the red poison, against the foul poison.
Wið ðy hwitan attre, wið ðy wedenan attre,   Against the white poison, against the blue poison,
Wið ðy geolwan attre, wið ðy grenan attre,   Against the yellow poison, against the green poison,
Wið ðy wonnan attre, wið ðy rudenan attre,   Against the black poison, against the dark poison,
Wið ðy brunan attre, wið ðy basewan attre,   Against the brown poison, against the crimson poison.

Wið wyrmgeblæd, wið wætergeblæd,   Against worm-blister, against water-blister,
Wið þorngeblæd, wið þystelgeblæd,   Against thorn-blister, against Thistle-blister,
Wið ysgeblæd, wið attorgeblæd.   Against ice-blister, against poison-blister.

Gif ænig attor cume eastan fleogan   If any poison comes flying from the east,
oððe ænig norðan cume, oððe ænig suðan cume,   Or any from the north, or any from the south,
oððe ænig westan ofer werðeode.   Or any from the west among the people.
Ic ana wat ea rinnende   I alone know a running stream,
þær þa nygon nædran nean behealdað;   And the nine adders beware of it.
Motan ealle weoda nu wyrtum aspringan,   May all the weeds spring up new herbs,
Sæs toslupan, eal sealt wæter,   The seas slip apart, all salt water,
ðonne ic þis attor of ðe geblawe.   When I this poison from you blow.

(This next part isn't sung; it's not part of the song but the directions on creating the healing salve. There is a lot of speculation on what it's for on a medicinal level, from smallpox to hemorrhoids. Should you want to try it, it's pretty harmless.)

Mugcwyrt, wegbrade þe eastan open sy, lombescyrse, attorlaðan, mageðan, netelan, wudusuræppel, Fille and Finule, ealde sapan. Gewyrc ða wyrta to duste, mængc wiþ þa sapan and wiþ þæs æpples gor. Wyrc slypan of wætere and of axsan, genim finol, wyl on þære slyppan and beþe mid æggemongc, þonne he þa sealfe on do, ge ær ge æfter. Sing þæt galdor on ælcre þara wyrta, III ær he hy wyrce and on þone æppel ealswa; ond singe þon men in þone muð and in þa earan buta and on ða wunde þæt ilce gealdor, ær he þa sealfe on do.

Mugwort, Plantain open from the east, Lamb's Cress, venom-loather, Chamomile, Nettle, Crabapple, Chervil and Fennel, old soap; pound the herbs to a powder, mix them with the soap and the juice of the Apple. Then prepare a paste of water and of ashes, take Fennel, boil it with the paste and wash it with a beaten egg when you apply the salve, both before and after. Sing this charm three times on each of the herbs before you prepare them, and likewise on the Apple. And sing the same charm into the mouth of the man and into both his ears, and on the wound, before you apply the salve.

Angelica and Elder:
The Road Up And The Road Down

Two other herbs that are of special worth in Northern Shamanism are Elder and Angelica. According to Saami tradition, the hollow tubes of these plant stalks are used in trancework as tunnels to the upper world (in the case of Angelica) and the underworld (in the case of Elder). While Norse/Germanic cosmology technically has nine worlds, they are all arranged around a central World Tree/Universal Pole with a Sky World at the top (Asgard) and a Death Realm at the bottom (Helheim). It's not that different from any number of shamanic upper/middle/lower world combinations; in fact, it's hardly different at all. Therefore, it stands to reason that these two plants would be used in the same way.

Folklore associates Angelica with Heimdall, the Watchman of the gates of Asgard. This makes a great deal of sense, considering that if one were to travel to Asgard unannounced, the first deity you'd run into would be Heimdall at the gate, asking you what your business was in the Land of the Aesir. In a sense, the Angelica stalk/tunnel is equivalent to Bifrost, the Rainbow Bridge, with Heimdall's hall Himinbjorg at the top of it.

On the other side, Elder is associated both with Hela, Queen of the Dead, and with Frau Holle/Holda. Holda is a Germanic goddess whose fairytales feature a young girl who falls down a well into an underground realm ruled by Frau Holle, so she also is a type of underworld goddess in her own way. Its association with Hela is obvious, given this system. As the equivalent of the Hel Road, Elder could also be associated with Mordgud, the armored giantess who guards the gates of Helheim; she is very much Heimdall's opposite number on the way Down.

Old accounts continually refer to Angelica as being one of the two "tubular" plants that Eurasian shamans used to travel to the Underworld, along with Elder. Some say that the roots of these plants were burned and inhaled; others speak of breathing through the tubes for trance states. Either way, there is another point that outsiders have overlooked: Angelica and Elder have very different affinities. Elder is a plant of the Underworld itself, and is used by shamans with Underworld and Lower World alliances. Angelica is a heavenly plant of the High Worlds, and is used by shamans with Upper World alliances and affinities to visit the Underworld—which, being a dangerous place for them, would require the special protection of this light-bearing plant.

Elemental Herbal Energetics

When I first started studying the art of herbal remedies under the instruction of Mengloth, Gerda, and a lot of plant-spirits, much of the information—especially about energetics—was garbled and difficult to understand. Images would come into my head, but I couldn't quite understand the depth of them. Plants who shared the nature of fire? Of stone? Of mountains, even if they didn't grow there? I struggled on for some time by myself, and then finally began to run into books and articles on herbalism that discussed the elemental energetics of plants.

Most of the information was from the Chinese Five Element tradition, and I had to weed that out. Mengloth's attitude toward it was, "That's all very well and good, but it's not what you're doing." (She had that attitude about most of Chinese medicine; although she insisted I learn the acupuncture points, she felt that the theories underlying Chinese medicine were fine in their own right, but not relevant to me. This meant that when I tried to study it, I'd forget everything that I'd learned by the next day, until I got the message and quit.) Ayurvedic medicine got the same treatment. Finally I ran into writings on the Galenic elemental system, and the nineteenth-century tissue states, and it got her approval. "Yes. That's the system you're to be working with. Well, more or less." The more I read, the more I realized that it described in words I could understand the vivid imagery I was being fed. I am indebted to Matthew Wood, among other people, for reconstructing this information in a format that is understandable to modern people, and in which I could recognize much of Mengloth's energetic system.

When I was fourteen, I got involved with a Gardnerian Wiccan coven of the British traditional variety (without the knowledge of my parents, a situation that would never happen today) and I was drilled in the various meanings of the pentagram, the five-pointed star found all over Europe and the Near East as a religious symbol. One symbolism of the five points was the four basic elements of Earth, Air, Fire, and Water, with the fifth point being Aether or Spirit. The four "lower" elements and their various associations were also drilled into me. In a sense, I was steeped in it. So was every person of the European ancient world who was educated in religion, magic, or philosophy. To one extent or another, the four elements—with or without the cap of Aether/Spirit—were a basic human truth in the continent of my ancestors. This system also works with those basic elements in describing pathologies and treatments.

A lot of herbalists have tried to line up the European elements with the Chinese five elements, in an attempt to create a "universal" system. Having scrutinized it (and compared things with practitioners of Chinese medicine), I don't personally feel that this works. For one thing, they're just different. Some are similar—Fire, for example—but Air is not Wood and Aether is not Metal. To attempt to crunch them into a syncretized box does a disservice to both systems, which are workable and consistent within their own spheres.

One change you'll find below is that one of the elements is divided into two categories. That's Water, and it is divided into River and Swamp for purposes of useful diagnosis. This brings us to six states of energy, in bodies and in plants. So, to begin with the elements as they appear in the body:

Fire

Fire is the easiest of the elemental states to understand, because it's Heat, pure and simple. We require Fire in our bodies to stay alive, but when it's overdone it can kill us—as a high fever, for example. While there are many different kinds of fevers, all partake of the energy of Fire. Any condition with an associated fever has Fire in there somewhere. Fire drives away Water, one of its two opposing elements, as we can see through fevers bringing sweat (and their associated toxins) to the surface of the body. Another obvious Fire condition is inflammation, where tissues become hot and red; its very name means "to flame". People with Fire conditions (or with bodies that tend to be hot) may have very red tongues, sometimes even pointed like flames. Like changeable Fire, the mental state that often comes with physical Heat conditions is restless and unfocused. Some refer to this state as "excitation" or "irritation", but I think Heat is pretty clear.

Fire herbs are carminatives and stimulants—warming, pungent or spicy aromatic plants full of volatile oils, and act best on Cold Earth conditions. One of the first herbs whose spirit I made friends with wasn't a Northern plant at all, but the tropical Ginger, a perfect example of a Fire plant that warms the stomach, lungs, throat, and overall metabolism. (I still have a great weakness for Jamaican Ginger beer.) Examples of Northern warming herbs are Garlic, Onion, Leek, Mustard, Cumin, or Rosemary. Air is the most compatible element with Fire, and Fire herbs tend to be drying as well unless they have Water affinities.

For a Fire/Heat condition in the body, you bring on cooling herbs such as Wood Sorrel or Hawthorn, or fruit such as Apple or Cherry. Coolants tend to be sour. Matthew Wood suggests thinking of citrus fruits on a hot summer day. You also use sedatives (Stone herbs), in some cases, such as Broom or Willow. Both types are Earth plants.

Earth

The element of Earth is Cold. This is not only the case for our ancestors, who lived in the colder areas of the Earth, but from a natural perspective as well. When things die, they return to the earth (assuming nothing else interferes), where they become Cold and then rot. When an organism develops an Earth pathology, everything slows down and becomes more sluggish and chemical activity is depressed. In the worst cases systems quit working and putrefaction sets in, and the organism actually does begin to rot. Earth is the final stage of all organisms. This condition is sometimes referred to as "depression", but this is an older term used before that word came to be entirely associated with mental illness. In Earth conditions, the tissues can darken and the tongue can be pale or dark.

The Earth category has more types of herbs than any other, not surprising considering that plants themselves are more Earth than anything else. I count four basic types in this system: coolants, sedatives, relaxants, and nutritives. For purposes of defining them quickly and clearly in my head through symbolism, I refer to them as Earth herbs (cooling) , Stone herbs (sedative), Mountain herbs (relaxant), and Harvest herbs (nutritive). I don't divide the entire element in two, like Water, because there is really only one Earth pathology, which is Cold. There are just a variety of Earth-affinity herbs which reflect other aspects of Earth. Earth is a complicated element, with many different manifestations. These categories are pictures, visions, stories that are told about and that the plants themselves tell about how they interact with the world, including the Inner World of the human body. The stories help me to understand and place them properly.

The ones I refer to as Earth herbs are cooling, and are used to treat Fire conditions. There are generally two types—refrigerants, like the sour cooling plants, and cyanogenic bitters. These are one of the three types of bitters, and they cool the body by acting on the chemical reactions of cells. Examples are Plantain, Chicory, or Rose.

Sedatives are Earth herbs which calm overheated bodily action. Narcotic herbs, as a subset of these, are also considered Cold as the state of unconsciousness is by definition "colder" (less active) than a conscious state. These are also used for Fire conditions. I refer to them as Stone herbs, because they calm you into a slower condition. Some Northern Earth herbs used for this purpose are Lemon Balm, Cowslip, and Betony.

Relaxant herbs tend to be acrid. When you taste them, your body automatically shivers, thus showing their affinity to Cold, in another way. According to Matthew Wood, that also indicates that they work on the nervous system. These are used on Storm conditions. Relaxants work by chilling and slowing the muscular contractions of Storm's violent fluctuations. I call them Mountain herbs, because the Mountain grounds the Storm and is unhurt. Examples of these are Valerian, Chamomile, Elder, Elecampane, and Mistletoe.

Other Earth-affinity plants are nutritive and nourishing, and carbohydrate-based; they tend to be sweet. A lot of plants that we would consider vegetables fall into this category, but according to the Green World, there's no silly arbitrary line between a "vegetable" and an "herb". (I was sternly lectured about this by the Celery-wight once.) It's all medicinal in some way. Nutritive Earth plants are used to treat Air conditions, like laying down a layer of humus over the desert. I call them Harvest herbs, because "field" was too easy to confuse with plants that grow in a field, and they are often part of our food harvests. Examples of these are grains such as Oats or Barley, nourishing herbs such as Borage and Lambsquarters. Nettles, and various mushrooms, are examples of "meaty" rather than sweet nourishers, which is indicative of their high levels of protein.

For an Earth pathology in the body, you want herbs that will Wake The Dead. That means aromatic, strong-smelling warming herbs full of volatile oils—the Fire plants, like Mugwort, Angelica, and Thyme. I sometimes picture the ancient Egyptians wrapping dead bodies in aromatic unguents in preparation for their rebirth.

Air

The element of Air is Dry. Deserts don't exist merely because of heat; there are lush jungles just as hot. For a desert to exist, there has to be a lack of water and lots of wind blowing all the useful topsoil away. Think Dust Bowl, or Air-Drying. Dryness is necessary to keep all our many fluids in their proper vessels, and for that matter from leaking out of the body itself, but too much dryness causes cracking and atrophy. Plants can't absorb nutrients from soil if they are too dry, and neither can we absorb our food properly if our tissues are too dry. It's no accident that nervousness and restlessness are an Air condition, just like the constantly moving breezes; in conditions of overall dryness, the nervous system ramps up. Astrologically, it is the Air signs which are the most nervous and restless. In Air/Dry conditions the tongue is often long, thin, and perhaps withered in extreme cases. This condition is sometimes referred to as "atrophy", but I find that's a bad word to use with clients, as it disturbs them. In general, if the function of an organ system is "drying up"—meaning that it is slowing down and stopping and there are no obvious signs of Swamp or Cold Earth, assume that it is an Air condition and give remedies that nourish the system.

Air herbs are astringent, meaning that they tighten up tissues and encourage them to properly hold their fluids. They clear up Water conditions, of either type. Air herbs don't so much have a taste as an action; they pucker the mouth when you taste them. They often contain tannins, which create astringency. Examples are Bistort, Agrimony, Cinquefoil, Oak, and Sorrel.

Air conditions need two different sorts of treatments; they need moisture, and they need nourishing because the tissues have not been absorbing nutrients. The moisturizing has to come first. Moisturizing herbs are Water herbs, including River herbs such as Parsley, Comfrey, or Marshmallow; also oily Swamp herbs such as Milk Thistle. Nutritive herbs are Harvest herbs, like Clover and Roseroot. Imagine what one needs to rehabilitate a desert: you need moisture, and you need to replace the wind-eroded topsoil that will nourish plant growth.

Water

Water is the most common substance in the human body; we're about three-quarters water by volume. Because of this, Water does a variety of different things in the body, and it's useful for us to differentiate at least two separate Water conditions. I call them River and Swamp, because those are the images that I got from Mengloth. Earth is the most compatible element with Water, and Water herbs tend to be cool as well unless they have Fire affinities.

River

Rivers flow in their banks, but sometimes they overflow. Many rivers of different sorts of fluids run through our bodies, and sometimes that flowing gets out of hand. In a River condition, the fluids are attempting to leave the body at a high rate of speed, producing dehydration in the worst cases. Examples are diarrhea, hemorrhage, and the kind of runny nose or overflowing, phlegmy lungs where you wonder how one body can possible produce that much mucus. This condition is sometimes called "relaxation", because the vessels relax, but I find that this term will also confuse most clients.

River herbs are water-based moisteners that bring water to dried-out parts of the anatomy. Examples are Marshmallow, Comfrey, Mullein, and Viper's Bugloss

River conditions are treated with Air astringents to dry up the excess fluid, strengthen the vessels, and make sure that the rivers are forced to stay within their banks.

Swamp

Swamp conditions occur when the fluids stagnate and back up, sometimes partially solidifying. In the outside world, swamps are places of much varied growth of organisms, and in a Swamp condition, all sorts of interesting bacterial growth can set in, and toxins can build up, especially in the bloodstream. Examples of a Swamp condition might be stuck mucus in the lungs, hemorrhoids, varicose veins, or rheumatism. This is sometimes called "stagnation" or "torpor". Swamp conditions are slow to change and difficult to clear up—draining a Swamp isn't easy. When the body is Swampy, immunity is low and there is a lot of exhaustion. The individual often feels—and looks—slow and sluggish. The lymphatics slow down, and the backed-up toxins show in the skin with lesions and oiliness.

Swamp herbs are oily moisteners like Milk Thistle and Flaxseed. Oil moves slower than water, just as the swamp moves slower than the river. However, a great many substances in the body—including all its hormones—are lipid-based rather than water-based, and require enough lipids to carry them from one place to another. This is where the oily, slow-moving Swamp herbs do well.

Swamps need to be cleansed and purified, and it's the second group of bitters—the purifying ones—that do the job. These include Rue, Wormwood, Gentian, and Celandine.

There are other herbs that work on Swamp conditions as well; they tend to be various detoxifiers that don't fall into any one elemental category.

Storm

The four basic elements are the four cornerstones of the world, but when you move one step up to "action" rather than "being-ness", there is usually a fifth point which embodies the four of them working together in some violent motion. The ancient Greeks called this Aether, the living, moving force that imbued the otherwise inert elements and made them combine and work together. Wiccans use the cauldron as their metaphor—the Fire beneath, the iron of Earth, the herbs of Earth, the Air and Water making violent exchanges in bubbles and steam. The imagery that Mengloth gave me was Storm—the Fire (lightning) leaping from Earth to Water-Filled cloud, Water falling from the sky and Air moving violently, all circling in a whipped-up dance.

A Storm condition is one of violent change and motion, too fast for the body's rhythms. It is characterized by a rapid on-off pattern, constriction and relaxation and constriction again. Examples might be fever and chills, racking coughs, muscle tension, and any kind of painful cramping. The body is tense, often from pain or clenching.

Storm herbs are purifying bitters that "clear the air" in stagnant conditions, such as Swamp problems. These are usually called "alteratives" in that they cleanse the blood and slowly work permanent change throughout the system. They are almost always bitter-tasting (like Gentian, Wormwood, Horehound, and Centaury), and it's important to actually taste them, because that taste signals to the brain via the mouth that it is time to release digestive enzymes. The Storm, in its elemental sense, is movement and change created by the confluence of all four of the other elements working together, and alteratives move, change, and cleanse.

Storm conditions are treated with herbs that relax and alleviate tension. Some relax muscles, some vessels, some the entire central nervous system—nerviness and narcotics. These generally come from the third group of bitters—the acrid ones, which are Earth plants of the Mountain variety. What stops a storm? Fire (heat) will only give it more energy. Water will add to its density and heavy rains. Air will whip it up. Only grounding Earth, and Coldness, and the "solid", mountainous hills of high pressure fronts, can disperse it. The Storm expends itself on the highest point, and if that is unmoving and steady, it dribbles off. Acrid Mountain herbs include antispasmodics like Catnip, Chamomile, and Dill.

When dealing with herbs and their energetics, the important thing to remember is that herbs don't each fall nicely into one of these categories. Some certainly will, but others will fall into two or more elements. The really useful polyvalents—the real herbal multitools—will have several elemental affinities. A single herb may contain "opposite" elemental affinities, meaning that it can do opposite actions. One affinity/action may be dominant and the other subordinate, or it might be either depending on the situation. One example of this would be Catnip; this is primarily an earthy relaxant herb working on Storm conditions (cramps and tension), but it can be either fiery and heating or show earthy cooling depending on what it deems best in the body of the afflicted human. Similarly, earthy cooling Plantain is both an astringent and a mucilage, and can be either drying or moistening depending on the needs of the situation. Elder is a true master (mistress?) at regulating and normalizing temperature and can be either heating or cooling as needed. Hemp can stimulate or sedate, depending on the metabolism of the ingester. Vervain contains both cleansing bitters and acrid bitters, and can either bring Storm energy to a Swamp or alleviate Storm energy.

In the Materia Medica, the elemental affinities are listed as to their potency in any specific plant. While this is a matter of debate—some might say that Caraway is primarily hot, others that it is primarily oily—I've listed them as I've seen them act. This means that actions which are at the end of the queue may be the weakest ones. A plant that is primarily nourishing and emollient, but a little bit astringent, would still work perfectly well on a dry Air condition because the moistening actions are stronger.

How to diagnose which herb(s) to use? Quiz the client on their symptoms. If necessary, check the elemental associations with the runes, a system I'll go into next. Then take the client's pulse. Put a drop of tincture on their skin at that wrist point, or rub a bit of leaf into their skin. Wait five minutes, then take their pulse again. If it it acting strangely—speeding way up or slowing way down or being irregular—don't use that herb. If there's not a lot of change, that's at least acceptable. If it was already irregular and the application of the herb helped to calm it down, that's extra good. Use that one. If it seems to come right up to the surface and thrum rapidly like a taut guitar string under the skin, that's the immune system kicking up and it indicates an allergic reaction ... don't do it.

Runes for Elemental Energetics

Runes are a wonderful multipurpose toolkit, and I wish I had more time to go into their healing uses. In the next book in this series, *The Northern Shamanic Healer*, I will be going into the runic system of organ affinities—what runes correspond to what body part and what bodily function—and the use of rune-galdr in healing. For now, however, I will simply point out those runes that have an affinity to the elements and that can be used to divine the primary elemental problem in a particular bodily issue. I use the Anglo-Saxon Futhorc, because it is dear to my heart and gives a much broader range of possibilities. However, for a quick elemental draw, pull the runes Kenaz, Ansuz, Jera, Laguz, Isa, and Hagalaz out of either a Futhark or Futhorc rune set, put them in a separate bag or container, and pull from there. These six are good at communicating about the elemental conditions of Fire, Air, Earth, River, Swamp, and Storm respectively.

If you want an overall picture of the elemental issues of the body, you can hold those six runes with both hands over a flat surface with edges (like a tray or flat dish) and drop them, lithomancy-style. Look to see which one is closest to the middle, and what's closest to that. For example, I just did such a divination for a hot, inflamed infection, and got Jera in the middle, with Kenaz close to it. The next one out was Isa (Swamp, although Isa is ice, it's still blocked-up Water) right behind Kenaz. Kenaz—Fire—was obvious from the heat and inflammation, and if I knew nothing else I might be treating only with coolants. However, the Jera (Earth) in the center indicated that this inflammation had arisen from a condition of Cold (sepsis from infection, and infection probably from a Cold-induced state of low immunity, as this was an ear infection occurring in the middle of an especially cold winter). Earth caused Fire which then caused Swamp from stagnant fluids in the swelling which refused to go down. This meant treating with pungent Fire herbs as well as cooling Earth herbs and astringent Air herbs, in turns rather than all at once.

Combining for Herbal Formulas

When you're putting together a herbal formula, you want to take into account the following correspondences, in the following order:

1) Organ affinity. What organ system is the problem affecting? If it's a respiratory problem, you're going to look for respiratory-affecting herbs; a liver problem will require liver herbs, etc. This will give you a very long list, of course. Let's say your problem is respiratory; which of the 70 or so herbs in this book that could be used for the lungs (and that's only the ones in this book!) should you use?

2) Elemental condition. What's going wrong with the problem area? Is it Hot, or Cold, or Damp, or Dry? Figure out the elemental condition of the area and then select out the herbs that specifically act on that element. For example, let's say that the lung problem is a constant dry cough with a scarce amount of stuck mucus, with some nervous exhaustion and dry membranes. That's an Air condition, so you're going to narrow down the list to the herbs that work on Air conditions. This will still give you about 20 or so, but it's a smaller list.

Also be careful to note if there is a secondary elemental condition, and remember that sometimes the apparent primary condition is actually the secondary one. For example, does the problem look like heat but is actually arising from dryness? What caused what? Here I will sometimes do a rune draw to figure out what was the initial problem. Once you figure this out, you can narrow down the elemental affinities. In the example above, Fire coming from Air, that's a classic indication for Marshmallow.

3) Specifics. Does one or two particular symptoms stick in your head? See if there are any herbs that are especially for that sort of thing. Sometimes the specifics are actually elsewhere in the body; make sure that you ask about other problems that might be going on at the same time. While they may not be causing or caused by the initial problem, they might be additional examples of an overall problem.

4) Talk to the Greenwight. Sometimes when I can't think of anything else, I'll walk through my herb garden (or my pantry of dry herbs when it's winter) and just ask, "Is there anyone here who would really like to help with this matter?" Sometimes this is the way that I find the primary herb for the problem. See if anyone jumps out on this.

5) Delivery method. Some herbs work best in the same delivery methods; some don't. If you've got a primary herb that works best with a root decoction, like Angelica, you might want to stick to secondary supportive herbs that can be made up in tea separately and mixed with the decoction. If you're making a vinegar tincture for your primary herb, don't use resinous barks as your secondaries, as they don't do well in vinegar. This step has a lot to do with your client. Some clients love tinctures and hate teas; some vice versa. If they won't take the remedy, it's a waste of everyone's time. Ask them, "What is most convenient for you?" Sometimes it's gelcaps full of herbs, which can be sorted into a med-minder and popped like pills without dealing with long preparations. Whatever it is, try to choose herbs that will go with their preferred delivery method.

6) What have you got on hand? This sounds ridiculously obvious, but not everyone has a well-stocked pantry with hundreds of herbs in various forms. Rather than bemoaning the fact that you don't have one rare herb, see what can be done with what you actually have.

In Traditional Chinese Medicine, there is an elaborate procedure for deciding which is the primary herb in a formula and which are supporting herbs. In much of modern Western cookbook-style herbalism, it seems to be a matter of randomly listing a handful of your favorite organ-affinity herbs without discussing why you chose those. (Maybe you had them on hand the first time, and it worked, and so you're using them again?)

In the examples below, the primary herb is starred. You can omit others, but it's the one that the formula is based on. Some people have referred to that one as the Mother and the others are Daughters. I generally use twice the amount of the Mother herb to equal parts of the Daughter herbs, except for very strong ones like Garlic which only get a couple of crushed cloves. (That's for tea; if you're combining tinctures, just use double the Mother herb.) While the Mother herb is extra important, one can use any number of combination of the Daughter herbs, more or less. When in doubt, ask the plants.

If you are combining formulas because you have more than one condition—for example, hot and dry—it's all right to have two Mother herbs so long as they are not in opposition to each other (for example, a strong astringent herb opposite a strong moistening herb, a very hot herb opposite a cooling one, etc). If in doubt, sit for a moment with one in each hand and ask them if they will lead the team well together.

These are by no means the only herbs one could use in these combinations; they're just examples using the herbs listed in this book. I often use herbs not listed here, as I had to sadly stop at 150. However, once you figure out the elements of other herbs, the same theory applies. I also didn't have space or time to list herb combinations for every organ affinity. I suggest that as you work with these herbs and remedies, you slowly put together your own personal clinical manual, with your favorites in combination for various things. What's below will get you started, though.

Example Combinations for Specific Organ/Elemental Conditions

Lungs/Respiratory

Fire Lungs: (*Hot, raw cough with fever (no chills) or active infection, pleurisy*) Elder*, Coltsfoot, Mint, Cowslip root, Lemon Balm, Marshmallow.

Earth Lungs: (*Cold-burned, weak, stagnant mucus, congestion, old lingering infection*) Angelica*, Costmary, Elecampane, Garlic, Horehound, Horseradish, Hyssop, Thyme.

Air Lungs: (*Constant dry cough, stuck dry mucus, with weakness and exhaustion, poor oxygenation*) Mullein*, Marshmallow, Coltsfoot, Garlic, Horehound, Iceland Moss, Old Man's Beard.

River Lungs: (*Constant mucus flow, wet cough*) Elecampane*, Costmary, Elder, Herb Bennet, Speedwell, Sage.

Swamp Lungs: (*Stuck mucus, but damp; unproductive cough*) Hyssop*, Elecampane, Birch, Coltsfoot, Horehound, Horseradish, Thyme.

Storm Lungs: (*Asthma, whooping cough, uncontrollable spasms, bronchitis with fever and chills alternating*) Agrimony*, Cowslip root, Elder, Elecampane, Thyme, Sage, St. John's Wort.

Gastrointestinal

Fire Guts: (*Overstimulated GI tract, excess salivation, excess appetite, acidic heartburn, gastric reflux, inflammation, colitis, Crohn's disease*) Yellow Dock*, Mint, Pennyroyal, Catnip, Meadowsweet, Marshmallow, Chamomile, any cold fruit.

Earth Guts: (*Lack of appetite, lack of saliva, lack of digestive juices, no enjoyment of food, food sits and rots, generates acid reflux and general indigestion, constipation, sluggishness, diverticulitis with putrefaction*) Fennel*, Sweet Cicely, Mugwort, Mustard, Dill, Cumin, Caraway, Alecost, Ash Leaves.

Air Guts: (*Lack of secretion, gas, constipation, dry hard stools*) Angelica*, Flaxseed, Parsley, Marshmallow, Lovage, Caraway, Chickweed, Fennel, Good King Henry.

River Guts: (*Easy vomiting, lots of mucus in the stomach, gastric bleeding, diarrhea, bloody flux, food poisoning*) Cinquefoil*, Yarrow, Tormentil, Alecost, Raspberry Leaf, Oak, Lady's Mantle, Speedwell, Bistort.

Swamp Guts: (*Lack of digestive juices, poor nerve reflexes, nausea but no vomiting, bloating, gas*) Meadowsweet*, Vervain, Speedwell, Gentian, Centaury, Lovage, Rue (half amount) .

Storm Guts: (*Cramps, spasms, alternating diarrhea/constipation*) Chamomile*, Centaury, Vervain, Mint, Fennel, Dill, Catnip, Periwinkle, Betony.

Liver/Gallbladder

Fire L/G: (*Jaundice, liver infection, active hepatitis*) Yellow Dock*, Chicory, Milk Thistle, Calendula, Strawberry Leaf, Apple Vinegar.

Earth L/G: (*Liver insufficiency, hardening, sluggish, making gallstones*) Carline Thistle*, Parsley, Celandine, Wormwood, Mugwort, Marshmallow, Vervain, Fennel.

Air L/G: (*Hepatic atrophy, wasting, deficient immunity*) Burdock*, Chicory, Dandelion, Milk Thistle, Centaury, Fennel.

River L/G: (*Hepatic hemorrhage*) Milk Thistle*, Sage, Horehound, Tormentil.

Swamp L/G: (*Fatty liver, stagnation, edema, ascites, congestion*) Dandelion*, Burdock, Celandine, Centaury, Gentian, Carline Thistle, Ash Leaves.

Storm L/G: (*Gallstone cramps, liver pain*) Agrimony*, Centaury, Gentian, Mugwort, Fennel, Vervain.

Kidney/Bladder

Fire K/B: (*Inflammation, cystitis*) Cleavers*, Pellitory, Meadowsweet, Lady's Bedstraw, Fennel, Plantain, Crabapple, Strawberry Leaf, Marshmallow, Willow.

Earth K/B: (*Kidney sluggishness, old low-grade infections, dark urine, stones*) Goldenrod*, Heather, Ground Ivy, Nettles, Mugwort, Rue, Lovage, Madder.

Air K/B: (*Painful scanty urination, weak kidneys*) Lady's Bedstraw*, Fennel, Strawberry Leaf, Mugwort, St. John's Wort, Celery Seed , Lovage, Marshmallow, Burdock.

River K/B: (*Bedwetting, urgency, too frequent urination*) Plantain*, Celery Seed , Speedwell, Cleavers, Crabapple, Rue, St. John's Wort.

Swamp K/B: (*Edema, waterlogged atonic tissues, swelling*) Parsley*, Juniper, Nettles, Elderflowers, Cleavers, Fennel, Goldenrod, Centaury, Broom, Heather, Speedwell, Madder, Ground Ivy.

Storm K/B: (*Cramps, spasms*) Agrimony*, Elderflowers, Hops, Mistletoe, Cowslip, Centaury, Heather.

Heart/Circulatory

Fire Heart: (*Superficial elevated pulse, heart palpitations, high blood pressure*) Hawthorn*,, Horehound, Mistletoe, Linden, Motherwort, Sweet Woodruff.

Earth Heart: (*Clogged arteries, sluggish circulation, stagnant blood*) Sage*, Ground Ivy, Burdock, Nettles, Sweet Woodruff, Rosemary, Motherwort, Bugle.

Air Heart: (*Pale weak circulation, purple extremities, sticky platelets, drying and hardening of arteries, low blood pressure*) Rosemary*, Angelica, Clover, Nettles, Linden, Hawthorn, Sage, Flaxseed.

River Heart: (*Floppy loose heartbeats, cardiac edema*) Elder*, Woadwaxen, Bugle, Hawthorn, Sage, Motherwort.

Swamp Heart: (*Hypertrophy of the heart, edema in the extremities, cardiorenal edema*) Broom*, Garlic, Ground Ivy, Clover, Nettles, Dandelion, Motherwort, Lovage, Bugle.

Storm Heart: (*Angina, emotionally induced high blood pressure*) Motherwort*, Linden, Mistletoe, Valerian, Lavender, Willow.

Female Reproductive

Fire FR: (*Infection, inflammation, hot menorrhagia*) Yarrow*, Raspberry Leaf, Strawberry Leaf, Lady's Mantle.

Earth FR: (*Cold sluggish bleeding, slow delivery contractions, dead baby, damaged uterus, menopause*) Angelica*, Calendula*, Mugwort, Motherwort, Yarrow, Goldenrod, Juniper, Sage, Caraway.

Air FR: (*Amenorrhea, lack of lactation*) Motherwort*, Flaxseed, Angelica, Borage, Parsley, Caraway, Fennel.

River FR: (*Hemorrhage, leucorrhea, yeast infection*) Shepherd's Purse*, Yarrow, Lady's Mantle, Calendula, Periwinkle, Bistort.

Swamp FR: (*Sluggish, swollen, adhesions, prolapse, congestion before period, cysts*) Lady's Mantle*, Broom, Calendula, Vervain, Juniper, Goldenrod, Raspberry Leaf, Hops.

Storm FR: (*Cramps, dysmenorrhea, violent labor*) Vervain*, Mugwort, Hops, Motherwort, Periwinkle.

Fever

Fire Fever: (*High, roaring, acute fever*) Elder*., Catnip, Chamomile, Cinquefoil, Crabapple, Lemon Balm, Linden, Meadowsweet, Willow, Mint, Pimpernel, Sorrel, Strawberry Leaf, Viper's Bugloss, Pennyroyal, Yarrow.

Earth Fever: (*Low-grade fever, low-grade infection with "incomplete" fever that never gets high or goes away*) Calendula*, Thyme*, Herb Bennet, Elder, Feverfew, Black Horehound, Hyssop, Mint.

Air Fever: (*Baking, drying fever*) Linden*, Calendula, Sorrel, Elder.

River Fever: (*Fever with oily sweating*) Cinquefoil*, Herb Bennet, Black Horehound, Meadowsweet, Yarrow, Wood Sorrel.

Swamp Fever: (*Stagnant fever with bloating*) Hyssop*, Chamomile, Cinquefoil, Feverfew, Black Horehound, Meadowsweet, Yarrow.

Storm Fever: (*Alternating fever and chills*) Chamomile*, Agrimony, Hops, Vervain, Elder, Catnip.

Skin (in salve, tea, or tincture)

Fire Skin: (*Active inflammation, hot allergic rash, eczema, burns*) Houseleek*, Cleavers*, Beech Tar, Burdock, Chickweed, Chicory, Crabapple, Dock, Elder, Linden, Marshmallow, Purslane, Rose Petals.

Earth Skin: (*Old sores that don't heal, suppurating sores, old bruises, hematomas, scarring, fungus, athlete's foot, blisters, gangrene*) Burdock* (if internal), Watercress* (if external), Alder Leaves, Angelica, Beech Tar, Carline Thistle, Elder, Feverfew, Nettles, St. John's Wort.

Air Skin: (*Dry itchy flaky skin, cracking, eczema, dry scalp, psoriasis, diaper rash*) Chickweed*, Angelica, Burdock, Chicory, Cleavers, Clover, Comfrey, Elm Leaves, Linden, Mallow, Marshmallow, Nettles, Purslane, Sweet Violet, Viola.

River Skin: (*Freely bleeding wounds*) Yarrow*, Lady's Mantle, Comfrey, Dock, Elm Leaves, Bugle, Mallow, Speedwell, Rose Petals.

Swamp Skin: *(Oozing wounds that won't close, oily skin, acne)* Burdock* (if internal), Sweet Violet and/or Viola* (if external salve), Carline Thistle, Chicory, Dock, Elm Leaves, Feverfew, Lupine seeds, Nettles, Speedwell.

Storm Skin: *(Rashes from stress)* Elder*, Cowslip, St. John's Wort.

Skeletal (external poultices and salves)

Fire Bones: *(Inflamed arthritis, rheumatoid arthritis)* Willow*, Aspen bark, Cowslip, Hyssop, Lavender, Teasel (tincture)

Earth Bones: (Cold arthritis with cold extremities, better with movement and warmth) Juniper oil*, Fir resin, Hyssop, Nettles, Rosemary.

Air Bones: *(Dry, creaking joints)* Clover*, Comfrey, Nettles.

River Bones: *(Broken bones that need bonesetting herbs)* Comfrey*, Mullein, Burdock, Teasel, Bugle.

Swamp Bones: *(Edema around joints, gout)* Birch*, Clover, Fir resin, Hyssop, Juniper oil, Nettles, Teasel (tincture) .

Storm Bones: *(Severe spinal or joint pain)* Cowslip*, Comfrey, Lavender, possibly Aconite in very tiny amounts, but check the dosage with a professional.

Part II
Materia Medica

Northern Tradition Herbal Materia Medica

How To Use This Herbal

Herbs in this Materia Medica are listed alphabetically by common name. We certainly acknowledge that we have by no means included every piece of information about each herb; our space is limited, and besides, others have already gone over that ground far better that we ever could. For further information on (especially) the medicinal, culinary, and dye uses for each plant, please see the Recommended Reading section in the back of this book.

Name: While herbs are usually known by many names, we have chosen the one that we are most familiar with, and that seems to be the most popular. In some cases, this was not an easy choice.

Botanical Name: For the scientifically minded. Sometimes it's impossible to identify a herb among all those folk names unless you find it by botanical name.

Anglo-Saxon, Old Norse, Old Germanic Names: We searched for these as best we could. In some cases, the word is entirely lost to us. In other cases, one plant might have several names, or one name might refer to several plants. For good discussions of how this happens—given several centuries and many isolated dialects—we refer to you Stephen Pollington (*Leechcraft*. p. 88) and Carole Biggam (*Haewenhnydele*, entire article) to learn the difficulties of nailing down one specific name for each plant.

Modern German, Swedish, Danish, and Norwegian Names: These are included partly as an interesting contrast to their ancient root languages, and partly because I've found that when making verbal charms for plants, it helps to have many names to work with, and some folks might find these useful. The names were given to me by friends living in those countries. (Thank you, Michaela, Anneke, and Thista!) In the Scandinavian countries, there are no surviving herbals of the antiquity of the Anglo-Saxon herbals; the first herbals were imported from southern countries during the later medieval era and were usually in Latin, and thus the names of many herbs were Latinized among the educated classes and the older names died out unwritten. Kjell-Erik Andersen of the Norsk Farmaceutisk Selskap reports that the first herbals printed in Scandinavia were *En nøttelig Legebog* in 1533 by Christian Pedersen, and *Een skøn loestig, ny vrtegaardt* in 1547 by Henrik Smit, both of Malmö, Sweden. These came after the arrival of the printing press in Denmark; no pre-printing herbals have survived. By the time of these books, all herbal information was coming from an amalgam of Latin, Greek and Arabic medicinal knowledge; northern folk medicine never made it into Renaissance pharmacy.

Deity Association: In some cases, the deity association is traditional, and in some cases it has made itself known to modern Northern Tradition herbalists and practitioners that we have interviewed.

Height: For those looking to plant this herb in a garden. It's best to group taller plants together, with shorter plants to the sunnier side of them.

Season: We have found that it is easier to keep annuals and perennials separate, unless there is a special-purpose garden. Annual beds can be turned under and refertilized in the fall, whereas with perennial beds you don't want to disturb the plants too much. Biennials are their own problem; some, like Angelica, will grow up "daughters" and act like perennials, others should perhaps get their own bed that gets turned over every two years.

History: We have not included the entire history of any herb, due to space considerations and relevance. This entry tells whether a herb was native to northern Europe, and thus familiar to our ancestors from the beginning, or whether it was imported, and if so, during approximately what era. It may also include interesting anecdotes.

Medicinal Uses: While a particular herb may have been prescribed for many different uses (including those in ancient herbals), we have decided to limit ourselves to those medicinal uses which are generally accepted as correct and useful to modern herbalists. This has further informed our decision to list only the medicinal uses for those herbs where we have modern corroboration for their safety, dosage, preparation, and effects, and where we have some familiarity with the plant and its application. This section also tells you whether the plant is an alterative, a specific, or both.

Household Uses: We probably didn't get all of them, but we tried to get most of them. Remember that any plant used for an around-the-home craft can also be used for a magical purpose or propitiating a divine blessing.

Culinary Uses: While we did not focus on culinary recipes in this herbal, for the most part, we invite you to look to the Recommended Reading section for such inspiration. Besides, we've found that including herbs in your food is a matter of taste and experimentation.

Magical Uses: Traditional magical charms and spells, coming down to us from a variety of sources but mostly medieval English.

Shamanic Uses: Here we have gathered information from interviews and personal experience; this section is unabashedly the personal gnosis of various folk who work with the northern herbs and the northern gods and wights. This information is especially useful to seidhr-workers, Northern Tradition shamans, and other spirit-workers, but it is also simply useful to the average Northern Tradition practitioner who wishes to know what to put into a votive incense for Heimdall, for example.

Affinity: This explains the elemental affinities and characteristics of each herb, and what sort of elemental problem it works on. The first element listed is the primary one, and the others secondary. If an herb is used as the main plant in a compound formula, one should be using its primary element.

Point: This is something that will probably appear jarring in a Northern Tradition herbal. You can blame Mengloth for that; I worked closely with this Goddess of healing during the formation of this book, and She insisted that all humans have the same meridians and energy points that are used in Chinese medicine, regardless of where they were born. She directed me to information about Otzi the Iceman, who had tattoos on acupuncture points appropriate to his reconstructed ailments, in the Swiss Alps two thousand years before it was supposedly invented by the Chinese. She also informed me that there were plants associated with each point, varying with the geography and climate, and that I should get busy and ask the plant spirits which were which, so I did. (That same year, a woman who works with Celtic deities informed me that she got the identical message from the goddess Airmid, without knowing that Mengloth had told this to me. I consider this to be a case of PCPG—peer-corroborated personal gnosis.) So, jarring or not, I include what the plant spirits have told me about these points. According to them, the appropriate plants were burned to ash and tapped into small tattoos on the points for long-term ailments. The full list of European herbs for the acupuncture points will be listed in my next book on Northern shamanic healing.

Plant-wight's Nature: This information was gathered from healers and spirit-workers who do *utiseta* with plant spirits and work directly with them, rather than simply using the medicinal aspects of the plant. It will give the average herbalist a more intimate familiarity with each herb; even if you have not contacted the Rowan spirit, knowing what she feels like to others can help you when you speak her charm.

Magical/Medicinal Charms: There are many examples of verbal charms to be said over herbal concoctions in the old northern herbals. The charms and prayers that we have listed to be said over each preparation are created in similar style, and with (we hope) similar intent to those of our ancestors, but are modernized for our own language and understanding of the herbs and the Gods. Some are healing charms to go along with medicinal remedies, others are purely magical charms utilizing the energy of the plant and its attendant wight. For multiple-herb-formula charms, see the following chapter.

Agrimony

Botanical Name: *Agrimonia eupatorium*
Folk Names: Church Steeples, Cocklebur, Garclive, Philanthropos, Sticklewort, Stickwort, Egrimoyne
Anglo-Saxon Name: Garclife ("Spear-Cleavers")
Modern German Name: Odermenning
Modern Swedish Name: Småborre
Modern Danish Name: Agermåne
Modern Norwegian Names: Akermåne, Monkelus
Deity Association: Angrboda
Height: 4'
Season: Perennial
History: Agrimony, as far as we can tell, is long native to all parts of Europe, and has long been used as a medicinal herb, as well as burned or carried for protection. It has been one of the most-praised herbs in the medieval herbal lexicon for its versatility in treating a wide variety of ills. The ancient Greeks drank it in a spring tonic for renewal.
Medicinal Uses: A strong astringent, Agrimony is a good tonic for the gastrointestinal tract, to ease indigestion, mild intestinal bleeding, and colitis, and sometimes for gallbladder and liver problems such as jaundice. The leaf infusion is a gentle remedy for diarrhea that is safe for children, and can be taken by nursing mothers to dose infants, and tea or tincture treats bronchitis (especially in drying up excess phlegm) and UTIs. Eyewash is good for conjunctivitis. Gargle is used for sore throats, and is good for nasal irrigation. May inhibit tuberculosis bacterium. Medieval war wounds were treated with a wash of Agrimony and vinegar. Poultice of leaves has been applied to soothe migraines. Don't take Agrimony if you're constipated, as it will make the problem worse.

A lesser-known property of Agrimony is that it is a painkiller of sorts, in that it helps tension throughout the body, but especially in the organs where constriction of the liver and kidneys can cause pain. Tense, uncomplaining, inwardly tortured people in general are helped by it, as are those with organ pain (gallstones, kidney stones, dysmenorrhea, bronchial inflammation, etc). If the organ pain is bad enough that the client is holding their breath, this is an indication for Agrimony. It is very good at relieving a muscle spasm; hold a fomentation of the tincture against the spasming muscle.
Household Uses: Plant has an apricot scent and is added to sachets and potpourri. Flowers were once added to mead. Entire plant yields a yellow dye when gathered in summer; fall-gathered plants produce a darker yellow. Drunk as a tea and made into a shampoo for thinning hair.
Magical Uses: Agrimony has long been considered a strongly protective and purifying herb. As an incense it has a more intense and aggressive feel than Mugwort, and can be planted by doors for protection. It was said that someone who slept with Agrimony under their pillow would not wake until it was removed. This herb is a warrior plant, and can give "spine" to the weak, stiffening their resolve and helping them to leave bad situations. It is said to work on hierarchical relations such as those in jobs or public interactions, clearing the way of obstacles and protecting one from the ill will of those in positions of power.
Shamanic Uses: Agrimony is an important herb used in banishing unwanted spirits, including those that might be taking up residence in someone against much of their will. It can be drunk in tea or burned

and the smoke blown at them. It is also used in incense for a protective circle against unwanted astral intruders. It is much liked by Angrboda, the Hag of the Iron Wood, and can be used to invoke her protection, although her price is usually rather steep.

Affinity: Air (astringent), Earth (cooling). Use on Storm, River.

Point: LV 2

Plant-wight's Nature: Grandmother Agrimony appears to me as a lean female warrior of middle age with close-cropped grey hair and a lined, weathered, narrow face. She moves like an athlete and is the sort that could be easily mistaken for male at first glance. Her gaze is penetrating and intense, and she counsels against impulsiveness. "Think about what you are asking for," she says. "Is it clear? How can a wight help if you don't really know what you want? Think through how this should go before you run out and cry for aid." When she is engaged as a protector, her work is swift, spare, and economical of movement; there are no flourishes to waste her energy, and she cleanses in a tight radius that nonetheless creates firm, tight boundaries of protection and a very clean area. She endows people with the will to change, to break out and make new changes in their lives.

Medicinal Charm: Angry Guts Agrimony Tea

When there is pain and overflowing of any organ, finely chop the aerial parts of Agrimony, and pour a pint of boiling water over a handful of the herb. While you do it, say or sing the following charm:

> *Garclife calm the cramp and flow,*
> *May nourishment come fair and slow.*

Then drink as a tonic, daily, in order to slowly convince your guts to avoid diarrhea and digest thoroughly, and to quiet the pain of angry organs.

Magical Charm: Purifying Smoke

To protect and ward an area—perhaps after it has already been recaned with Mugwort or Juniper for cleansing—tie many twigs of Agrimony together and bind them with plant-fiber thread, let dry thoroughly, and then light the end of the Agrimony recaning stick and recan the area. Another possibility is to burn the herb as incense, but dry it thoroughly first—Agrimony does not like to be burned green. While burning, speak the following charm:

> *Agrimonia, Garclife,*
> *Spear that cleaves the veil sealed,*
> *Sticklewort and Cocklebur,*
> *High Protector of the Field,*
> *With the blessing of the Hag,*
> *May all who would attack me yield.*

Alder

Botanical Name: *Alnus glutinosa*

Folk Names: Scottish Mahogany, King of the Woods, King of the Rivers, Fearn

Anglo-Saxon Name: Alor

Old Norse Name: Elrir

Old High Germanic Name: Elira

Modern German Names: Schwarz-Erle, Rot-Erle

Modern Swedish Name: Klibbal

Modern Danish Name: Elletræ

Modern Norwegian Names: Svartor, Orer

Deity Association: Loki

Height: 80'

Season: Perennial tree

History: Alder trees are native to all of Europe. An Alder grove is actually one enormous tree that spreads by root runners, so that the entire grove is actually one entity. The Alder is Fearn, the fourth Celtic tree month; in British folklore it is known as the "King of the Rivers", with the Willow as its queen, due to its love for marshy land and riverbanks. In Germany, the *Erlekonig* or Alder-King was a faery chieftain who tended to steal children. The inner bark was supposedly used in the flying potions of witches, but as it has no discernable hallucinogenic effect (and quickly induces vomiting), we must assume that they were being affected directly by the Alder-spirit, through some kind of alliance. Today, oddly enough, Alder has become the wood of choice for wood-bodied electric guitars due to its weight and resonance.

Medicinal Uses: Leaf infusion is a refreshing footbath; Alpine peasants were known to treat extensive rheumatism by being covered in hot soaked Alder leaves. The yellow inner bark infusion is used as a gargle for sore throats and enlarged throat glands. Tinctured in vinegar, it has been used to treat gallbladder congestion and jaundice, as well as gangrene, skin inflammations, and eczema, and various other itches.

Household Uses: Alder has a long relationship with the element of fire because it makes the best charcoal, and was once a mainstay in smelting ore. It is burned to smoke and flavor meats, especially salmon. It is also long enduring under water without rotting, so it was often used for troughs, sluices, pipes, etc. The bark gives a dye that varies from red to yellow to black with different mordants. The young shoots give a yellowish-grey dye; new shoots give a Cinnamon color; fresh wood makes a pink dye and catkins make a green dye. The leaves have been used for tanning leather, although it turns it a reddish color.

Magical Uses: First wood laid on a sacred fire in some traditions. Vampire stakes were fashioned of Alder wood.

Shamanic Uses: The Alder, as the tree of Fire, is much liked by Loki. You could use it to call him, but whether he came would be entirely up to him. Make an Alder-wood talisman with the rune Ken/Kaunaz on it to help with skill in starting fires, and with discerning truth from lies. This is something that, ironically, Loki can help you to learn.

Affinity: Storm (bitter alterative), Air (astringent). Use on Swamp.

Point: ST 41

Plant-wight's Nature: The Alder-Man is mysterious and a little scary. He appeared to me as a thin, angular man, pale parchment skin stretched over the odd-shaped bones of his face, with piercing red eyes. His chin and nose and forehead protrude, almost like a man-in-the-moon face. He dresses in skins and is tattooed (or painted, I couldn't tell) with red-ochre-color glyphs and patterns; bone earrings hang from his lobes. A knife and a bow hang on his back, and he carried a little bowl of red paint with which he touched me, still with that wide-eyed half-crazy stare. "Blood and fire," he said. He speaks in short cryptic phrases like that, and you have to interpret what he means as if it was an oracle. He is very conscious of the fact that he is a sacred tree, and becomes violent if disrespected.

Medicinal Charm: Traveler's Feet

Boil a double handful of Alder leaves in water, while saying the following charm:

> *Alor, alor, Alder-man,*
> *Fire-sap flow through footsore steps,*
> *Blood-sap soothe the seeker's soles,*
> *Elrir, catch me as fast I fall.*

Then soak tired, swollen feet in it for an hour

Alecost

Botanical Name: *Tanacetum balsamita*
Folk Names: Costmary, Costmarie, Bible Leaf, Balsam Herb, Mace, Balsamita
Anglo-Saxon Name: Cost
Modern German Name: Balsamkraut
Modern Swedish Name: Balsamblad
Modern Danish Name: Balsam
Modern Norwegian Name: Balsam
Deity Association: Aegir
Height: To 30"
Season: Perennial
History: Costmary is native to southern Europe and Asia; its name is derived from its Latin name, Costus. It was introduced into continental Europe in Roman times and spread to England and Scandinavia during the early Middle Ages; it was already known to the writers of the Anglo-Saxon herbals. It became a traditional strewing herb, and was carried in Bibles to Mass as a bookmark; tired churchgoers could nibble on the leaves while endeavoring to stay awake.
Medicinal Uses: Costmary is antiseptic and a wash is used to soothe burns and stings. The tea treats colds and phlegm, upset stomach, cramps, dysentery and was once taken to ease childbirth. It is a mild emmenagogue, contraindicated for pregnant women.
Household Uses: As its name implies, Alecost was used in brewing before Hops were available, to clear, flavor, and preserve ale. Also a popular "strewing herb" and used to make a scented water with which to rinse linens. Costmary was often combined with Lavender for sachets.
Culinary Uses: Fresh leaves were made into conserve. They give a sharp tang to game stuffings and fruitcakes. As a preservative, they can be put into a sauce for meat that must stay out all day.
Magical Uses: Peace in the home. Costmary was given to wanton women in order to make them chaste and modest, or to womanizing men in order to make them settle down. It was also carried in fidelity charms.
Shamanic Uses: One of the herbs much liked by Aegir, the undersea brewer. Make ale with Alecost and pour it out as a libation to him, or carry it if you are traveling on the sea.
Affinity: Fire (pungent stimulant), Air (astringent). Use for Earth and River conditions
Point: ST 41
Plant-wight's Nature: Costmary appears to me as a rotund female plant-wight, disheveled but sweet and a bit naïve. She is one of the Homemaker wights who will bless a house, if the homemaker sprinkles some crumbled Alecost about. She is a homebody and will wilt if forced to move; she prefers a small, warm, orderly world where she knows everything that might happen.
Magical Charm: Brewer's Blessing

To bless the work of a home-brewer, or to make your own alcoholic beverages for sacred purposes—such as for ritual usage, or for a libation to a God—use a pinch of Alecost in the making of the brew (if you're a brewer, you'll be able to figure out where and how much) and sprinkle the bottles or cask in which the brew ferments with crumbled dust of Alecost, while saying the following charm:

> *Alewife of the garden, bless my brew,*
> *Venerable not , hallowed not harsh,*
> *Fermented fair as Costmary can do.*

Angelica

Botanical Name: *Angelica archangelica*
Folk Names: Archangel
Old Norse Name: Hvann-njoli ("hollow-stalk")
Modern German Names: Echte EngelwurzErzengelwurz, Arznei-Engelwurz, Angelika
Modern Swedish Name: Kvanne
Modern Danish Name: Angelik
Modern Norwegian Name: Kvanne
Deity Association: Heimdall
Height: To 7'
Season: Triennial

History: Angelica originated in the Near East, but it spread to all of continental Europe with the Roman invasions, eventually even to the subarctic regions of Lapland. Angelica was praised as both a healing herb and a tonic vegetable; it was carried in singing procession when there was an epidemic attack of disease, in order to purify the village. Associated with Heimdall the guardian of Asgard, its dedication was switched to the Archangel Michael, another guardian wielding a sword and great horn, with the advent of Christianity. It did not, however, reach the British Isles until well into the Middle Ages, so there is no mention of it in Anglo-Saxon herbals.

Medicinal Uses: Angelica is a gentle but very powerful alterative. The leaves are a general vitamin tonic, and are infused for indigestion and bronchial problems and put into salve for skin irritations. It is one of the best all-over long-term digestive stimulants, and is good for thin, dry, pale people with little willpower who seem to droop constantly. The roots are tinctured for bronchial infections, phlegm, digestive problems, rheumatism, or as a uterine stimulant for delayed labor. Use the tincture in a compress for rheumatic joints, or use Angelica oil as a massage oil for the same issues. An infusion of the powdered root will help flatulence, and is a stimulating expectorant. Angelica should not be given to diabetics, as it can cause an increase of sugar in the urine. Pregnant women should avoid it, unless they need to give birth immediately. The oil, used externally, can cause photosensitivity, so be careful about going outside in the sun with it on your skin.

Household Uses: Seeds are burned as a fragrant incense, and can be used in liqueurs—Angelica gives Benedictine its distinctive taste. The root is dried as a fixative in potpourri. Crushed leaves freshen the air in a car and help prevent carsickness; they can also be used in a relaxing bath and stewed with acidic fruits in order to reduce the sugar requirement.

Culinary Uses: The stems are sliced and candied as a winter vitamin tonic pill. The greens and chopped stems can be eaten raw in salads or stews. The seeds can be dried and baked into cakes.

Magical Uses: Used in spells of protection and exorcism. In the bath, Angelica tea removes hexes and curses. During the Middle Ages, it was said that the Archangel Michael had revealed it as a cure for the Black Plague, and it was used to commune with him. Angelica has strong radiant energy that can be tapped into if it likes you, and you're the right sort of person.

Shamanic Uses: Angelica is associated with Heimdall, the guardian of the gates of Asgard, and is an excellent herb for warding magics, as long as one is doing it for honorable reasons that Heimdall would approve of. See also the chapter on Angelica as the Road Upward.

Affinity: Fire (stimulant), Swamp (oily), Harvest (nourishing). Use on Air and Earth.

Point: GB 21

Plant-wight's Nature: Angelica is a radiant being of light. Sometimes she is kind and protective, sometimes she is stern, but always she casts drying light through you, taking up dampness and opening dark places. She is the enemy of all damp darkness, and that includes your psyche. Angelica is hollow inside, and that is somehow one of her mysteries—she is Filled not with flesh but with invisible light. She is a good helper for people who are also hollow, who have no substance to them due to long-time depression, ill health, poor constitution, and fear. She fills them up with light and health. I see her as very classically angelic in her way—tall, slender, hair that flows out in all directions like her seedheads, hands outstretched. She sings like the sound of a flute, or a violin—high and pure.

Medicinal Charm: Sweetness and Light

For a fine winter tonic for the whole family, cut the stalks of Angelica in early summer, before the seedheads go to seed, but when the lower stalks are large enough to nearly put a small finger through. Strip off the leaves and the small stems, chop them fine, and mix them with honey until you have a thick paste. Chop the large hollow stalks carefully into one-inch sections and gently stuff the paste into them without breaking the sides. Then dip the whole pieces in honey, or if you like, egg white and white sugar, or a thick syrup of white sugar and water. (If you use the egg white version, you will need to keep them in the freezer rather than on the shelf.) Let them sit out and dry thoroughly, until they are quite hard to touch. These sweet lumps should be taken out as eaten as vitamin pills (sweet enough for any child to bear!) at various times during the winter, especially when there are coughs and colds going around and the constitution needs protection. As you eat them, say the following charm:

> *Rainbow Guardian, Angel's Light,*
> *Hollow horn, Heimdall's fair wight,*
> *Lend my limbs thy strength and might.*

Ash

Botanical Name: *Fraxinus spp.*
Folk Names: Nion
Anglo-Saxon Name: Aesc
Old Norse Name: Ask
Old High Germanic Name: Asc
Modern German Name: Esche
Modern Swedish Name: Ask
Modern Danish Name: Ask
Modern Norwegian Name: Askeslekten
Deity Association: Odin, Woden
Height: To 65'
Season: Perennial tree

History: The Ash tree is so strongly linked to Northern Tradition religion that the central core of the Nine Worlds cosmology—Yggdrasil, the World Tree—is said to be an Ash. Certain species of Ash trees exude a sugary sap, much like Maple or Birch trees, which the Greeks called *meli* or "honey". This gave the Ash tree extra value in the eyes of the ancients; it is said that mead flows in the branches of Yggdrasil, and that honey rains from its leaves. As far south as Iran, the World Tree is referred to as a "mead tree". A surviving Finno-Ugric ritual, observed and recorded in 1911, combined the themes of Ash and honey in a similar way. (The exudates of Ash trees were fermented and sold under the name of "Manna" as a medicine in Western countries until the early 20th century.)

This "tree honey", at least in the case of Yggdrasil, was said to have been sprinkled on it by the Norns at Urda's Well. Up until the 19th century in Germany and Scotland, imported Manna-resin from Ash trees was the first non-milk food given to infants. There is even some conjecture that the mysterious Indo-European "soma", the sacred drink that falls from a ruddy mountain tree, is Ash-tree sap; another conjecture is that the magical mead drunk by Odin is fermented Ash-Manna. The Ash tree is *the* sacred tree of the Indo-Europeans, paralleled only by the Oak.

However, ironically enough, the "Manna Ash" species (*Fraxinus ornus*) is not native to northern Europe; scholars suggest that the Manna Ash associations were carried by Indo-European travellers to their newer homes and the sacred memory applied to the native species of Ash tree. While the Manna Ash will grow in some northerly climes, such as Britain, it is not hardy above Zone 6.

Medicinal Uses: Ash bark is a bitter astringent, and the decoction was used to remove obstructions of the liver and spleen, and as a wash for scalp rashes. The leaves are laxative, diuretic, and purgative, and decoctions have been prescribed for water retention and dissolving kidney stones. The leaf tea is good for constipation.

Household Uses: As one of the toughest and most elastic timbers in Europe, Ash was used for spears and bows, and it still said to be best for axe-handles, ladders, etc. American Black Ash is traditionally split for basketmaking. It is so elastic that an Ash joist will bear more before it breaks than any other tree.

Culinary Uses: Ash keys have been pickled and eaten like capers. While any of the *Fraxinus* species will work for the uses above and below, only *Fraxinus ornus* gives forth the Manna sap, which can be used like honey.

Magical Uses: Ash is a counter-spell tree, used to return hexes from whence they came. Ash is often associated with water, and an equal-armed cross of Ash wood is protection against drowning at sea. The Ash tree is strongly protective, and supposedly repels snakes. Ash staves ward off evils, and Ash wands are used for healing. The leaves are scattered to protect an area. Injured children were sometimes passed through a split Ash sapling for a cure. Placing Ash leaves in your car will keep you protected on journeys. An Ash branch, held up to the wind, is used for divination—ask the winds your question, and see which way they blow.

Shamanic Uses: Ash is the tree most strongly associated with Yggdrasil, the World Tree. While I would not say that Yggdrasil is an Ash tree per se, the Ash seems to resonate well with its nature. A piece of Ash wood, especially one carved with the rune Gar, can be used to contact Yggdrasil itself ... but be warned, Yggdrasil is large and old and lives at a slower pace than you. It may be weeks before it gets around to responding, and it does not respond in words. Ash wood can be used to find your way to the boundary of any world that is closest to Yggdrasil. As Ash is also the name of the first man—Ask—it can be used in workings to honor the ancestors. It is also special to Odin, as he hung on the Tree, and when used in conjunction with his name (or on an Ash staff) it should be used with the rune Ansuz/Aesc.

Affinity: Storm (bitter alterative), Air (astringent). Use on Swamp.

Point: UB 36

Plant-wight's Nature: Ash Tree came to me robed in silver-grey, leaning on a staff. There was always a sense of wind and rain about him—either a salt breeze from the ocean, or a brisk riverside rain, but always that sense of wind and water. He had nobly chiseled features and brown hair to his shoulders;

his eyes were grey as wind and water. Ash is a Magician Tree, and he is choosy whom he speaks and works with. He can give the gift of eloquence, but not so much in performance as in everyday diplomacy. "Those whom I love," he said, gesturing fluidly, "I cast my cloak of protection over them. It is a rare gift to be chosen by me." Then he left, politely, as I was obviously not one of those chosen ones.

Medicinal Charm: Loosening The Knots

Boil two ounces of crushed Ash leaves in a quart of water until the water has changed color, and then let simmer for an hour and strain. Sweeten to taste and drink for constipation, saying the following charm:

> *Ask, whose name the new man bore,*
> *Brought forth through earth and cold and grief,*
> *All these obstacles I would thee take*
> *As Yggdrasil's branches once did shake*
> *Odin's blessed blood from its trembling leaves.*

Aspen

Botanical Name: *Populus tremula*
Folk Names: Quaking Ash, Old Wives' Tongues, Craobh Chrithinn, Eadha
Anglo-Saxon Name: Æspe
Old Norse Name: Ösp
Old High Germanic Name: Espin
Modern German Names: Zitter-Pappel, Espe, Aspe
Modern Swedish Name: Osp
Modern Danish Name: Asp
Modern Norwegian Name: Asp
Deity Association: Mani
Height: To 100'
Season: Perennial tree
History: Aspen trees are native to all of northern Eurasia. Their strongly flattened stems allow the leaves to twist and turn in the slightest breeze, and as such they were said to be constantly speaking to the winds. Aspen is Eadha, one of the sacred trees of the Celts.
Medicinal Uses: Aspen bark contains salicylic acid and is a mild painkiller for arthritis.
Household Uses: Yellowish and black dye is obtained from the leaves, and brown from the bark. Aspen wood was used for shields due to its strength and flexibility.
Magical Uses: Aspens were always strongly associated with the wind and wind-wights due to their flexible bending in strong breezes. Its round leaves were used in anti-theft spells, and placed under the tongue for eloquence.
Shamanic Uses: The Aspen tree is much loved by Mani, the god of the Moon, and is used in his worship. Mani often takes an interest in the people he sees as he rides through the sky, and sometimes interferes with their lives if he thinks that they are being mistreated. To call on his aid, your message can be hung on an Aspen tree, or burned at night with Aspen leaves while the moon is overhead. Aspen leaves under the pillow can be used to communicate with him in dreams or *utiseta*.
Affinity: Earth (coolant), Stone (sedative). Use for Fire conditions.
Point: SI 14
Plant-wight's Nature: The Aspen tree-wight is thin, delicate, androgynous, and vaguely sad, in a nostalgic way. Aspen spends a lot of time singing songs of maudlin sorrow; it is easy to understand why the

lonely Basque shepherds transplanted to the American southwest were moved to carve doleful drawings into the bark of the Aspen groves in Nevada. It likes to be sung sentimental songs.

Magical Charm: Leaves On The Wind

To send a message to someone who is unreachable—perhaps they are far away and incommunicado, perhaps they will not speak to you or listen to what you say, perhaps they are unconscious—gather a handful of Aspen leaves and sing to them. First, sing the following charm—with any tune, or tunelessly monotonous—and then sing all the things that you want that person to hear or know. Then go outside and release the leaves into a strong wind.

> *Tree of the Wind, Friend of the Moon*
> *Lonely Traveler's tale on the track,*
> *Sing to the one that my voice cannot reach,*
> *Bring all my words to them, bring their mind back.*

Barley

Botanical Name: *Hordeum spp.*
Folk Names: John Barleycorn, Barleykerne, Aleseed
Anglo-Saxon Name: Bere
Old Norse Name: Bygg
Old High Germanic Name: Bariz
Modern German Name: Gerste
Modern Swedish Name: Korn, Bjugg
Modern Danish Name: Byg
Modern Norwegian Name: Byggslekten
Deity Association: Frey, Ing
Height: 3'
Season: Annual
History: Barley was first brought into cultivation in the Near East during the Mesolithic era. By the Neolithic era, it was a staple food all over Europe and northern Africa. The cult of the Sacrificed Grain God is most associated with Barley; although beer and ale can be made from many grains, it was Barley that took the crown.
Medicinal Uses: Vitamin-rich brewer's yeast is a byproduct of Barley malting. The cooked grains can be applied to sores, and Barley water aids convalescents. Barley enhances the ability of the body to pass on waste through the bladder, and is excellent as food for a recovering patient, as it is rich in nutrients.
Culinary Uses: Cereal grain, breads, malt for beer and ale.
Magical Uses: Barley is one of the great grains of the world, and the one most closely associated with the sacrificial grain god. It is a Lammas plant, planted late and harvested early, and used in Lammas altar sheaves. Mark an Ing rune on any Barley bread.
Shamanic Uses: Barley is sacred to Frey in his aspect as Ing, the sacrificial Corn god. All Barley products, especially the liquid ones, are appropriate to use as libations for him, and to ask his blessing in sorrowful places. As he is one of the Bright Guys, he is especially good to call on when one is depressed and unhappy. Barley is associated with the Ing rune; for centuries bags of grain were labeled with the double X (a broken-apart Ing), and Dos Equis beer continues this association.
Affinity: Harvest (nourishing), Fire (stimulant), River (moistening). Use on Air and Earth conditions.
Point: CV 9
Plant-wight's Nature: Barley is one of the Ancestral Fathers. Ancestral Father and Mother plants are the ancient food plants of our ancestors, and unlike most of the herbs (who will cheerfully ignore us if we

ignore them), the Ancestral Parents are very bound up with humanity and concerned for our well-being. They give of themselves selflessly to see that we are fed, and Father Barley is no exception. He is a broad farmer of a man, muscled and fair-haired, with a paternal ambience. One expects him to pat you on the head and tell you that it's time for dinner, so go wash up. He is firm but caring, and he will often inquire, bringing his thick awn-spiky blond brows together, as to whether you are eating properly. Seeing that people are fed is important to him.

Magical Charm: Fasting Nourishment

If it is necessary for you to fast for any length of time, ask for Father Barley's blessing and carry a handful of Barley in your pocket, tied up in a cloth with an Ing rune marked on it. Every day, untie the cloth and hold the Barley grains in your hand, and ask for Father Barley to pass some of the potential nourishment of those grains into you, without having to eat them. If he approves of your fasting—if you're doing it for good reasons and not self-indulgent or self-destructive ones—he will help you out and let you absorb some of the nutrition from the grains. Ideally, you should plant a couple of them in dirt each day, if they're still viable. If they spill when you're removing them from the cloth, it means it's time for the fast to end, regardless of what agreement you've made with yourself. Father Barley knows best what you body can endure.

Bean

Botanical Name: *Vicia faba*
Folk Names: Poor Man's Meat
Anglo-Saxon Name: Bean
Old Norse Name: Baun
Old High Germanic Name: Bona
Modern German Name: Bohne
Modern Swedish Name: Böna
Modern Danish Name: Bønne
Modern Norwegian Names: Hestebønne, Bondebønne, Fababønne
Deity Association: Freya
Height: To 3'
Season: Annual
History: The Beans that were a staple crop for the peoples of ancient Europe are known as broad Beans, or Fava Beans, from the Indo-European root word *faba*, their word for Bean. Their history goes back several thousand years. However, traditional European Beans have been mostly replaced by American Beans, which come in many more varieties, thanks to the centuries of effort of Native Americans. Fava Beans are more cold-hardy than American Beans, can be planted earlier, and will withstand frost.
Medicinal Uses: As a nourishing alterative, Bean pods help reduce high blood pressure and regulate blood sugar metabolism, which makes them good for diabetics. The husks increase weight loss in diet plans, and eliminate the insulin swings that lead to increased fat deposits. Cloth soaked in the cooking water from Beans makes a good ulcer-healing poultice.
Household Uses: Cooking water from Beans is used to clean woolen fabrics. Growing Beans in the garden will add nitrogen to the soil.
Culinary Uses: Soaking Beans overnight in water, and then changing the water out, will help cut down on their tendency to flatulence. Use the water for the above purposes.
Magical Uses: Dried Beans were traditionally used as a charm against evil sorcerers. If you think someone might be trying to hex you, put a Bean in your mouth and spit it at them. Stringing dried Beans and hanging them over the bed can smooth out marital difficulties. Supposedly they can help with impotence when eaten. One old love spell suggested planting a circle of seven Bean plants and then

inducing the love object of your choice to walk over them. Beans were also used magically to enhance male fertility.

Shamanic Uses: Beans have always been sacred to the fertility goddesses of every European tradition, be it Demeter, Gaea, Cardea, Ceres, or Freya. Their flowers are usually white, and a wreath of flowering beans or Peas can be made in spring and given to Freya as a gift. Grow flowering runner Beans over an archway for her, and stand under it to speak to her.

Affinity: Harvest (nourishing), River (moistening). Use for Air conditions.

Point: ST 4

Plant-wight's Nature: Bean-wights have different natures depending on what variety they are, but the Fava-wight is one of the Ancestral Mothers. Standing tall and proud in her simple garment, her long hair—streaked black and white like her flowers—cascading around her twined with beads and carved bone, face lined and weathered but wise and caring, Mother Fava is a Matriarch. Her body is lean and muscled, except her belly which is rounded from bearing many children. She was once sacred to Goddesses, and remembers it. Like all the plants who are Ancestral Parents, she is concerned for

humanity, and our feeding and nutrition, about which she (rightfully) worries. If she can help, she will; humans matter to her. (I also met her shorter, rounder sister Mother Pea, who does not have an entry here, but is fatter and merrier—and equally worried about us. We had a conversation about the violations and depredations being done to their distant Asian cousin, the Ancestral Mother Soya.)

Magical Charm: Favomancy

Yes, favomancy—divination with Beans—is an actual term, and was actually done. It's very intuitive—dried Beans of different colors (and yes, you can use Mother Fava's American cousins, as most of the Beans eaten in America and Europe are actually American Beans, but try to have at least one Fava in the lot) are given meanings such as Good Fortune, Bad Fortune, Birth, Death, Marriage, Plague, Journey, etc. It's very archetypal and each Bean should be consulted to find out what it is. You might look for especially old heirloom Beans, to have one each of those—check with the Seed Savers Exchange, and/or seed catalogs that specialize in heirloom seeds. Then you take your handful of Beans, draw a small circle in the dirt, and toss them. Those that land in the circle and stay there are relevant to the question; the nearer the center they are, the more crucial an answer. If nothing stays in the circle, the Gods aren't talking. "That means that you should be able to figure that out for yourself," says Mother Fava tartly.

Beech

Botanical Name: *Fagus sylvatica*
Folk Names: Bok, Boke, Buche, Buke, Fagio, Fagos
Anglo-Saxon Name: BeceBoc
Old Norse Name: Bœkr, Bók

Old High Germanic Name: Buohha
Modern German Names: Rotbuche, Blutbuche
Modern Swedish Name: Bok
Modern Danish Name: Bøg
Modern Norwegian Name: Bøk
Deity Association: Saga
Height: To 150'
Season: Perennial tree

History: The name of the Beech-tree comes from the same root as the word for book, and the Beech was the "book-tree", because its bark was supposedly fine to write on, and there was a possibility that runic tablets were made of Beechwood. Its Latin name comes from the Celtic name Fagus, who was supposedly the spirit of the Beech tree.

Medicinal Uses: Beech tar has been used to treat skin diseases. The inner bark has been used as a stimulating expectorant for coughs.

Household Uses: Nuts are traditional food for both people and animals. They can be roasted as a coffee alternative or pressed for a nondrying oil that is particularly good for lamp oil and making soap. Beech ash is used as a blond hair dye.

Magical Uses: Carve wishes onto Beechwood and bury them. Carry the leaves for creativity. Burned Beechwood ash is sprinkled on garden paths as an offering to the plant-wights.

Shamanic Uses: The word "book" comes from the Anglo-Saxon word for this tree, since rune markers were traditionally carved from it. As such, it is much liked by Saga, goddess of lore. Use a Beech marker carved with her name to guide you to uncovering old lore; you can bring it with you on research trips or put it under your pillow at night for finding her wisdom in your dreams. (There are many ways to recover old lore.) Eat the nuts for her wisdom.

Affinity: *Bark/Tar:* Fire (stimulant), Earth (cooling). Use for either Fire or Earth conditions; Beech will know which affinity to use. *Nuts:* Harvest (nourishing), Swamp (oily). Use for Air conditions.

Point: LI 17

Plant-wight's Nature: Mother Beech is solidly built, broad and round, and is usually found seated and thoughtful. She appeared to me as a middle-aged woman dressed in shades of beige, tan, and sand, forehead wrinkled in concentration. She is a deep thinker and does not often like to be interrupted, unless you are hungry and need her nuts. Her favorite interaction with someone is to have them sit under her tree and read; she seems to be able to absorb what they are reading through their presence.

Magical Charm: Lore Seeking

Carry Beech leaves, or your Beechwood tablet with Saga's name on it, when you visit the library. As you cross the threshold, quietly say the following charm, and then go in search of your precious knowledge.

> *Hail Saga! This seeker comes in silent respect*
> *For whatever gifts are given by these tattered texts;*
> *With Mother Boekr in hand, I welcome*
> *Whatever road would guide me next.*

Betony

Botanical Name: *Stachys officinalis*
Folk Names: Bishopwort, Lousewort
Anglo-Saxon Name: Betonice
Modern German Name: Heil-Ziest, Gemeiner Ziest
Modern Swedish Names: Humlesuga, Läkebetonika

Modern Danish Name: Betonik
Modern Norwegian Name: Legebetonie
Deity Association: Vara
Height: To 3'
Season: Perennial

History: Betony is native to the European continent, having come to the British Isles some time later; it is known to the writers of the Anglo-Saxon herbals, but under several names, many of which are also applied to other herbs. On the Continent, it was much valued as a multi-dimensional healing herb. It was said that even wounded wild animals would seek out Betony and eat it to be cured.

Medicinal Uses: Betony is a mild sedative, used traditionally for headaches, neuralgia, tension, and other problems of the head and nervous system. It encourages circulation in the head and brain, and has been used to treat brain damage and coma, and gives improvement if administered directly after strokes. The dried herb has been smoked to relieve headaches. As a diuretic, it stimulates and cleanses the system, and a poultice of Betony encourages wounds to knit and make scar tissue. A strong infusion of Betony may be drunk during a hard labor, both to speed up uterine contractions and to calm the birthing woman. Matthew Wood says that Betony acts on the solar plexus, the "brain of the stomach" which is a large nerve center bringing the proper information to the digestive and hepatic system, as well as physically helping us to determine "gut" instincts from unreal fears. As such, it has long been used to calm a nervous stomach and aid digestion.

In general, Betony helps people become grounded and brings them back into their bodies; it has had a certain amount of use as a mild, gentle, slow-acting drug for people with low-grade reality disorders, bringing them away from their unreal fantasies and anxieties and back into line with earth's reality. Spiritually, it also drives away evil spirits when burned or, even better for the nature of this herb, is used as a wash or asperging. What about when it's hard to tell what's an evil spirit and what's a mental sock puppet? Ask yourself: In this case, does it really matter? If whatever they are were just to go away, would the problem be solved? Betony can help with that, regardless of which you're dealing with. (If it does really matter, for more than merely ego or curiosity's sake, then it's best to call in someone who can tell ... and then use the Betony anyway.) Use Betony to treat the spacy, somewhat forlorn types who ignore the world and neglect their bodies, and the paranoid sorts who imagine bad things all the time.

Magical Uses: Purification and protection—of the soul, not the body. Betony was carried to keep one safe against demons, and was thrown onto Midsummer bonfires so that people could jump through the purifying smoke. It was said to shield one against evil visions and dreams, which suggests that it can be consumed by those who are troubled by unwanted out-of-body nocturnal experiences, or plagued by dream visitations. It is also a counter-magic herb, turning hexes and curses. Betony was planted around graveyards to keep the Dead from bothering people.

Shamanic Uses: Betony is a protector of the astral body. Before journeying or pathwalking, wash in an infusion of Betony, and drink some of it. Sprinkle it on the bed before laying down if you are journeying; carry it if you are pathwalking. Having Betony in your system, and being on good terms with the greenwight, is an excellent way to prevent being possessed by outside spirits without your consent. As a herb favored by Vara, it can be carried whole or sprinkled dried at weddings or other oath-taking ceremonies.

Affinity: Stone (sedative), Air (astringent), Fire (stimulant). Used a on a variety of conditions, as Betony is an anomalous herb. Look to more specific uses above.

Point: GV 16

Plant-wight's Nature: Master Betony is a warm, friendly, service-oriented sort. When I first plucked a leaf to speak to him, he apologized that it was insect-holed, and assured me that he would try to keep things tidier in future. I believed him. Master Betony likes tidiness and is made distraught by mess; he enjoys gardens planted in neat rows with no weeds about them. He is firm and personable, and eminently dependable. His name translates to "Goodhead", referring to his salutary effect on headaches, but he does indeed have a good, quick head on his shoulders. He is curious without being prying, and very perceptive while still remaining discreet, as a good servant should. If he says that he will help you, he will do it to the best of his ability; if he says that he can't, he will be excruciatingly polite about it, and perhaps direct you to someone more helpful.

Medicinal Charm: Headache Tea

Make a weak infusion of Betony with one pint of water to every ounce of dried herb. Drink two cups per day to relieve chronic headaches. As the water boils, say the following charm:

> *Betonica, Betonica, my head it is besieged,*
> *Surrounded by the screams of silent pain,*
> *Drive the dreadful demons from my brain.*

Magical Charm: Guarding the Door

If you are doing any magical or shamanic working where there is a chance of you being possessed by some malign outside force, Master Goodhead can be your ally. His acupuncture point is at the base of the skull, a particularly vulnerable area when it comes to spirit possession. "I guard the door," he said to me. Make a strong tea of his leaves—about twice the leaf-to-water ratio of the recipe above—and pour it over the back of your head, from crown to well down your back, saying the following:

> *Master Goodhead, guard my head's door*
> *From dark deception, from evil invasion,*
> *Bolt swift the beam, o sacred servant,*
> *And none shall pass your patient eye.*

Birch

Botanical Name: *Betula spp.*

Folk Names: Beth, Beithe, Bereza, Berke, Bouleau, Lady of the Woods

Anglo-Saxon Name: Beorc

Old Norse Names: Berkana, Birka, Bjarkan

Old High Germanic Name: Birka

Modern German Name: Birke

Modern Swedish Name: Björk

Modern Danish Name: Birk

Modern Norwegian Names: Bjørk, Bjerk, Birk

Deity Association: Frigga

Height: To 100'

Season: Perennial tree

History: Birch trees have been used for their paper-bark in northern and central Europe since Mesolithic times; we know because we've found it in archaeological sites. In every culture that reveres the Birch, she is associated with mother goddesses of some sort. To the Germanic folk, she was the tree of Frigga, the rune Berkana/Beorc which symbolizes growth and is a pictograph of woman's breasts. Birch was also associated with purity, due to its light color, and beginnings, as it is the first tree to "step out" into a burned area and start the reforestation process. Birch is the first of the Celtic tree-months, Beth.

Medicinal Uses: Birchleaf tea has been recommended for rheumatoid arthritis and fibromyalgia; it clears waste material from muscles and joints. The leaves are antibacterial, diuretic, and lower cholesterol; they are good for dry coughsfrom inhaling woodsmoke. The extracted bark oil is used in soaps for eczema. Birch leaves are antiseptic and can be used in wound poultices. Among the Saami people, Birch trees are frequently used in folk medicine: the spring Birch sap was drunk as a preventative medicine and applied to rashes and burns; the thin inner bark was used as a temporary antiseptic bandage; the leaves were made into a tea to be drunk for blood purification and helping the kidneys. It is one of the few kidney diuretics that is safe even for people with severe kidney disease.

Household Uses: The extracted bark oil is used to condition leather, and put into medicated soaps. Books bound with Birch-oiled leather are less likely to become moldy. Birch makes an excellent hair rinse, making the hair fuller and shinier.

Culinary Uses: Birch beer is made from the bark extract, and wine and vinegar can be made from the sap, which can also be boiled down into a syrup.

Magical Uses: A cradle of Birchwood protects babies. The traditional witches' broom was often made of Birch twigs. As Birch is a strong but gentle purifying tree, Birch limbs have been used to strike possessed people or animals as a way to exorcise them. A Birch tree hung with red and white ribbons outside a stable was believed to protect the animals inside from being hag-ridden, or bothered by faeries. Sprigs of Birch twigs hung around the house prevented burned food or kitchen accidents. The Saami people would lay a person with chronic pain on a bed of fresh (or, if dried, soaked in warm water) Birch leaves, and cover them with the leaves as well.

Shamanic Uses: Birch twigs are traditionally used for the ritual flogging between rounds of the Finnish sauna. The flogging (which can be as hard or as gentle as one wishes) both ritually purifies one and gets blood circulating to the skin. As Frigga's tree, a talisman with her name carved in runes can be used to take you to her private hall, Fensalir, assuming that you have prior permission to be in Asgard. Birch leaves can be burned in a fire in order to send her a messsage. Birch is the tree of the Berkana/Beorc rune.

Affinity: Storm (bitter alterative), Air (astringent). Use on Swamp conditions.

Point: CV 2

Plant-wight's Nature: Grandmother Birch is a tall white woman—skin like old ivory, hair the color of rich cream, breasts that overflow with milk. She is an extremely motherly plant, treating those who come to her like children who need to be coddled. While she is usually a fountain of overflowing nurturing, once in a while she may turn Fey and become the Lady With The White Hand, whose touch upon the brow leaves a white scar that causes madness. It is unclear what causes such a change in her; perhaps it is the attitude of those who approach. Some say that it is because the individual is in such a bad way that all she can think of to do is to reduce them to a babe's wits, where they will be more likely to be taken care of, at least as she sees things. Usually she is loving and willing to help as she can.

Medicinal Charm: White Hand's Relief

If you are plagued with pain, especially rheumatic pain of the joints and bones, Birch can help. Take the inner bark of the Birch tree (do not peel it off of a living tree, as that will kill it; take it from one that has been cut down), dry and crumble it, and make an infusion of it—one ounce of bark to one pint of water, steeped for half an hour. As you drink it, say:

> *First foot forward into the field,*
> *Birka, Berkana, to your touch I yield,*
> *Bark of Beorc, give me sweet rest,*
> *I am a babe at thy loving breast,*
> *White dove bed me in your nest.*

Bistort

Botanical Name: *Polygonum Bistorta*

Folk Names: Snakeweed, Adderwort, Serpentaria, Columbrina, Serpentary Dragonwort, Bistort, Oderwort, Easter-Mangiant, Easter Giant, Easter Ledges, Patience Dock, Passions, Twice-Writhen

Anglo-Saxon Name: Nædderwyrt

Modern German Name: Schlangenwurz

Modern Swedish Name: Stor Ormrot

Modern Danish Name: Slangeurt

Modern Norwegian Name: Ormerot

Deity Association: Jormundgand

Height: To 2'

Season: Perennial

History: The Serpent-Plant is native to nearly the entirety of Eurasia, being found as far north as Siberia, as far east as Japan, and as high as the Himalayas. It was, however, later in coming to the British Isles, where it had naturalized by the time of the Anglo-Saxon herbals. The roots were often soaked and roasted and eaten in cold-climate areas such as Russia, Siberia, and Iceland. It tends to cluster in patches, which are almost impossible to eradicate due to its creeping rootstock.

Medicinal Uses: Bistort root is one of the strongest herbal astringents available, and highly styptic; as such it is used to stop bleeding on external conditions such as cuts and nosebleeds, and internal conditions such as stomach ulcers, colitis, uterine hemorrhage, and hemorrhoids. It was a standby in snakebite, keeping the poison from liquefying tissue. Shoots and soaked rhizomes are cooked as a nutritive tonic, especially for diabetics. Infusion is used as a gargle for mouth sores and bleeding gums, up to and including severe rot in the mouth and throat. When nothing will stay in the stomach due to vomiting, an enema infusion will treat diarrhea.

Household Uses: Rootstock is used in tanning leather.

Culinary Uses: Rhizomes can be used in soups and stews. The young shoots have been used with young Nettle-tops, Oatmeal, Barley, and eggs for a healthful spring pudding.

Magical Uses: Burn to improve psychic powers. Sprinkle a tea to drive out poltergeists.

Shamanic Uses: This is the plant of the Midgard Serpent, and it can be used to mark boundaries for protection. The Serpent is also good for invoking in order to make sense of strange nonverbal images that come to you; s/he speaks in a language without words. As the Big Snake is hermaphroditic, Bistort root carved with a Ior rune is a good charm for third-gender spirit-workers.

Affinity: Air (astringent), Fire (pungent). Use on River and Earth conditions.

Point: SP 3

Plant-wight's Nature: Bistort is indeed very snakelike and cold; it seems to have no gender and not much similarity to humanity. It writhes and twists, and then stays completely still for a time, and then darts off again. Its harsh action is like a serpent biting on; you don't so much talk to it as send it pictures of what needs to be done, and hope that it responds. If it does so, it will be immediate and not gentle.

Medicinal Charm: Black Dragon's Cave Ointment

For treatment of hemorrhoids, combine one part powdered Bistort root, one part powdered Marshmallow root (one for the stanching and one for the healing), and if you can get it, one part powdered Horse Chestnut. Mix with melted lard and olive oil in a ratio of 1 ounce powder to 4 ounces lard to 1 ounce olive oil. Simmer gently for an hour, and say the following charm:

> Hail Serpentwort, Hail Dragonwort,
> The blood runs from your brother's cave,
> The dragon dark must aye be stanched,
> Twice-Writhen, mountain's root you save.

Let the salve cool and apply as needed. This can be used prophylactically if it is a chronic condition, but watch out for drying things up too much and creating cracks

Blackthorn

Botanical Name: *Prunus spinosa*
Folk Names: Sloe, Sloeberry, Straif, Draighionn, Draighean
Anglo-Saxon Name: Slahþorn ("Sloe-thorn")
Old Norse Name: Slaaen
Old High Germanic Name: Sleha
Modern German Name: Schlehedorn, Schwarzdorn
Modern Swedish Name: Slån, Slånbär
Modern Danish Name: Slåen
Modern Norwegian Name: Slåpetorn
Deity Association: The Alfar and Dokkalfar
Height: To 20'
Season: Perennial tree
History: A traditional native hedgerow plant, Blackthorn was planted to keep livestock from straying, as it creates a twelve-foot thorny wall when planted in rows. Also known widely as the sloe or sloeberry, its bitter fruit was eaten by ancient Europeans as a tonic. Sloes were archaeologically found to have been eaten as early as the Mesolithic. In England, a long hard winter was known as a "Blackthorn winter", as the earlier-blooming tree-berries might not make it, and there would be only sloes to eat.
Medicinal Uses: Flower infusion has mild diuretic and laxative effects, and is used as a gargle for laryngitis and tonsillitis. The berries are tonic bitters.
Household Uses: The astringent berries are used to make sloe gin.
Culinary Uses: The sloe-fruits have been used in preserves.
Magical Uses: Blackthorn trees were traditionally used to makes staves and clubs. Blackthorn is traditionally a tree of dark magic, of cursing and wounding, of keeping secrets. A Blackthorn stang is used for blasting and cursing; the thorns were thrust into poppets, and string was tied around the trees for binding.
Shamanic Uses: Blackthorn trees, also known as The Mother Of The Woods, are associated with the Alfar of both types, dark and light. A Blackthorn staff or shillelagh will supposedly keep them off, or at least make them like you; if you have already offended them, it may break under your weight. Blackthorn is a traditional staff or wand wood for those who work with the Alfar (or Dokkalfar), and can be used to call them. The thorns have been used in a particularly dangerous practice, for people who have deep-rooted mental illness from nasty invading energies that refuse to budge by gentler means. The thorns are thrust under the skin and allowed to become septic, and then the evil spirits are called into them and yanked out, and the wound healed by the means of other herbs. (This practice is only for highly experienced shamans who are in close connection with Mother Blackthorn.)
Affinity: Air (astringent), Earth (cooling). Use on River and Fire conditions.
Point: CV 23

Plant-wight's Nature: Mother Blackthorn looks at you darkly under heavy-lidded eyelids, suspicious and untrusting. If she is in a generous mood, she may gift you with berries, but she always seems as if she'd like your blood, smeared on her bark from the prick of her thorns, as payment. She is tall and thin, with purple-black hair that falls in long ringlets, and long nails and teeth. When she sings, it is dangerously lulling. When she shrieks, it is all you can do to keep from fleeing in panic. She clutches a midnight mantle about her thin form, and gestures in a foreboding manner as she speaks. If she takes a liking to you and decides to help you with magic, be grateful ... and don't take her for granted. She will want regular offerings for her trouble.

Magical Charm: Secrets Kept

When you hold a secret, and telling it would do no one good and many harm, but it burns within you, call upon Blackthorn to silence the temptation. Find three thorns from a Blackthorn tree. Pick up the first one and say:

> *Sloe-Thorn, stop my tangled tongue,*
> *My words shall not wiggle from where I have chained them.*

Pick up the second one and say:

> *Sloe-thorn, stop my tangled tongue,*
> *My chains have no chink for my folly to flee.*

Pick up the third one and say:

> *Sloe-Thorn, stop my tangled tongue,*
> *My need is nailed by the Wood-Mother's will.*

Wrap the thorns in purple cloth and tie with black thread, and then find a swamp deep in the woods, and sink the package into deep waters there.

Borage

Botanical Name: *Borago officinalis*
Folk Names: Star Flower, Corago, Bugloss, Euphrosinum, Burrago
Modern German Name: Borretsch
Modern Swedish Name: Borag
Modern Danish Name: Hjulkrone
Modern Norwegian Name: Agurkurt
Deity Association: Frigga, as Lady of the Hall
Height: 2'
Season: Annual
History: Borage originated in the Persia/Syria area and spread throughout the Mediterranean, and is not mentioned in any of the Anglo-Saxon herbals, meaning that it was not likely known in England during that era, and I almost didn't include it in this herbal ... but Borage insisted, saying that she had indeed come to the Germanic people by that time, anyway, and came to England not much later. Borage gives courage, and Borage flowers were floated in the cup of wine given to knights as they rode out to battle.

Medicinal Uses: Borage nourishes the adrenal glands, and is the best possible adrenal alterative, gently bringing them back into line. Borage tea is given for stress, depression, and for people on corticosteroid treatments. The leaves are mineral-rich and can be added for food flavoring for people with salt-free diets. It reduces fevers, helps dry coughs, stimulates milk flow (especially when combined with Fennel), and can be drunk in infusion for depression and grief. The pressed seed oil is used for menstrual and irritable bowel problems, eczema, and hangovers, and lowers cholesterol. It has Omega-9 oils in it, which are good for autoimmune disorders. The flowers can be added to cough syrup, especially with Marshmallow flowers. Borage is a deep nervine that helps exhausted, overrun, depressed people to come back to life; it was used for "melancholy" in medieval times, but it seems to do best with stress-induced depression.

Culinary Uses: Borage has beautiful blue edible flowers that don't last unless you candy them with egg white and sugar (and even then they're so fragile that they don't last long) so eat them while they're around. They can be frozen in ice cubes. The leaves can be put into salads, although they are kind of furry to eat.

Magical Uses: Courage spells. Flowers enhance psychic powers when eaten. Leaves are burned as incense for meditations that strengthen the inner warrior.

Shamanic Uses: Given as a gift when you visit the hall of any deity.

Affinity: Harvest (nourishing), Earth (cooling), River (moistening), Swamp (oily). Use on Air and, surprisingly, Swamp conditions.

Point: SI 1

Plant-wight's Nature: As Borage brings courage, I expected a warrior, but I was wrong. Lady Borage appeared to me as a tall, beautiful maiden with her hair in two long braids, wearing a gown of blue like the princess in an Arthurian romance. She is the Lady of the Hall who girds the sword on the warrior, who brings him the last cup when he leaves, who sees him off with a kiss. She is the one that he remembers when he fights, whose memory stiffens his spine in battle. She is the Roman mother who says to her son, "Come back with your shield or on it." She has an affinity with the Valkyries, who watch for the most courageous.

Magical Charm: I, Borage

This is the traditional charm, in Latin: Pour yourself a cup of wine, and float a few Borage flowers in it, or steep some of the dried herb in it. Toast to yourself, and speak as if telling your virtues to a great hall; do not be afraid to boast, even if you must do this spell alone in your kitchen. Then toast to Borage, and say: *Ego Borago Gaudia Semper Ago.* Quaff the wine and go on to the frightening thing that you must face.

Broom

Botanical Name: *Genista scoparius* or *Cytisus scoparius*
Folk Names: Besom, Bizzom, Planta Genista, Scotch Broom
Anglo-Saxon Name: Brom
Old High Germanic Name: Bram
Modern German Name: Besenginster
Modern Swedish Name: Harris
Modern Danish Name: Gyvel
Modern Norwegian Name: Gyvel
Deity Association: Holda, Loki
Height: To 6'
Season: Perennial

History: Broom is a weedy shrub native to wastelands all over northern Europe and northern Asia. It was the badge of the Plantagenet dynasty of England. It was, indeed, used to make brooms, and gathered for the purpose as well as its medicinal uses.

Medicinal Uses: Broom is both an alterative and a specific, safe to give over a long period of time. A strong diuretic and kidney cleanser, Broom should not be used in cases of extreme kidney inflammation. It is a uterine contractor and should not be given to pregnant women, but can be used to bring on menstruation. Broom is a mild cardiac sedative and has been used to slow rapid hearts.

Household Uses: Making brooms, of course. The roots bind earth together, making it a useful shelter for game and more delicate shrubs. It has been used for making baskets, building huts, thatching cottages, and heating bakers' ovens. The bark fiber has been made into rope, and the fibrous shoots into paper. The bark contains tannin and has been used for dyeing yarn a yellow-green.

Culinary Uses: Pickled Broom buds were a delicacy in Elizabethan times.

Magical Uses: Raising the spirits of the Air. Purification through sweeping. This is one of the traditional plants for witches' brooms. While indigenous European belief systems considered Broom to be purifying and sacred, Christian lore held it to be cursed, saying that it had alerted Herod's soldiers to the fleeing Mary and Joseph. Since Broom was known to be popular among the peasants for creating temporary sacred space, it is not unlikely that this was a deliberate smear campaign. It is still used to bless weddings. Supposedly the yellow Broom-flowers should not be picked for no reason, or one's fortune will wane.

Shamanic Uses: Traditionally attributed to Holda, Broom plants can be used to purify a home via the sweeping, bringing her blessing. Broom plants make good aspergers for purifying an area or a person with water. They can also be used dry, as the plant's name suggests. The plant does have a connection of some kind with the : and weather, so they can be waved to propitiate the wind spirits, although the weather gods have the final say over major weather changes.

Affinity: Stone (sedative), Storm (bitter alterative). Use on Fire and Swamp conditions.

Point: HT 7

Plant-wight's Nature: Master Broom is a tall, lean, stiff wight with a stern face. He is not forbidding, though, just a pessimistic sort who worries a lot. He likes being a household implement, and enjoys being useful. He remembers proudly that he once went into battle on the hat of Geoffrey of Anjou, and was the badge for the Plantagenets. His face softens when he recounts all the women with whom he has danced across a kitchen floor, and actually smiles when he is reminded of Broom's reputation of flying with witches, but he will not tell tales, being too polite and discreet—although he will sometimes refer to them as his "wives," and one can see that he is proud to have "flown" with even the oldest and ugliest of crones, and considered her beautiful. "There's more to beauty than meets the eye," he admonishes. "Actually, that's the least part of it."

Medicinal Charm: Against Too Much Water

When the body suffers from retaining too much water, make the following potion: Boil one ounce of Broomtops and half an ounce of Dandelion roots for each pint of water until it is down to half its amount; at that point add half an ounce of Juniper berries and boil for five minutes more, while saying:

> Holda, the floor is full of water; with Besom sweep it away;
> Sunna, the field is fairly flooded, dry it with golden rays;
> May the river run freely from me to the four quarters of the day.

Let the decoction cool and strain it; take a cupful three to four times a day.

Bugle

Botanical Name: *Ajuga reptans*
Folk Names: Thunder-And-Lightning, Carpenter's Herb, Middle Comfrey, Sicklewort
Anglo-Saxon Name: Ðunorclæfre
Modern German Name: Günsel
Modern Swedish Name: Revsuga
Modern Danish Name: Læbeløs
Modern Norwegian Name: Krypjonsokkoll
Deity Association: Thor
Height: 3"
Season: Perennial
History: The creeping Bugle plant is a hardy native weed all over Europe, from the Mediterranean to the Arctic. Medieval herbalists said that having it around was better than a surgeon. The Saxons called it "thunder-clover" in honor of Thor; by the thirteenth century it was still referred to as "thundreclovere".
Medicinal Uses: Bugle is astringent, containing tannins, and will stop bleeding when applied to wounds as a poultice or tincture, as well as drying up open sores. It is also used to stop internal bleeding and hemorrhage and is a diuretic. Good as a lung dryer when there is coughing of blood. Bugle has a mild digitalis-like action and works on the heart, regularizing it and equalizing circulation, but should only be used in this capacity by a trained herbalist. It is a very mild narcotic and gentle sedative, and has been used for hangovers. It is said to be one of the "bonesetting" herbs, with the wisdom to help knit a broken bone in place when poulticed.
Magical Uses: Carry the leaves as a charm against accidental injury during carpentry or other building projects. Growing Bugle in your yard will protect your home from storm damage by falling trees or lightning.
Shamanic Uses: You can use it as an offering to Thor. It's unclear why this tiny creeping plant was sacred to Thor ... well, as an astringent plant, it is drying and thus air-associated, in spite of its low growth habit.
Affinity: Air (astringent), Fire (pungent), Storm (bitter alterative). Use on River, Swamp, and Earth conditions.
Point: HT 4
Plant-Wight's Nature: The Thunderclover-wight showed up as a wizened little man, only a few inches tall, glaring at me crankily. He seemed rather peevish when I spoke to him. Yes, he has many virtues, although you wouldn't know it to hear folk speak today! "They all consider me useless!" he muttered. He is very sensitive about his height and doesn't like it being spoken of. It's best to get down on the ground next to him if you want any communication at all. I asked about his cardiac properties, and he just looked at me and said, "The heart is where the thunder rolls."
Medicinal Charm: Blood and Thunder
When you have cut yourself during work, take up a few of the Bugle's flat leaves, plaster them over the wound, and say: "Thunder stop the flow, lightning seal the blow, Thunor strike my woe."

Burdock

Botanical Name: *Arctium lappa*

Folk Names: Lappa, Fox's Clote, Thorny Burr, Beggar's Buttons, Cockle Buttons, Love Leaves, Philanthropium, Personata, Happy Major, Clot-Bur, Herrif, Aireve, Airup, Klettenwurzel

Anglo-Saxon Name: Clate ("Clout", as in breechclout)

Old Norse Name: Klutr, Haevindl

Middle Germanic Name: Klute

Modern German Name: Große Klette

Modern Swedish Name: Stor Kardborre

Modern Danish Name: Burre

Modern Norwegian Name: Storborre

Deity Association: Farbauti

Height: To 4'

Season: Biennial

History: Burdock is native to all parts of Eurasia and North America. The Japanese claim that the root is an aphrodisiac; many cultures eat it as a vegetable. The burrs have always been a bane to sheepherders, as they can ruin a fleece. (They have been used to hold fabric together, in a pinch.) In general, people who are not herbalists tend to think of Burdock as a noxious and annoying weed, and even some herbalists can be upset when they have to pick painful burrs out of their skirts. Like Nettles, there is a strong component of the fire-thurse in Burdock, which accounts both for its tenacious, annoying nature and its ability to burn impurities from the blood. Also like Nettles, the rune Cweorth can be used with Burdock.

Medicinal Uses: This annoying weed is a powerful healer. The roots of first-year plants are dug, dried, and powdered. Excellent as a blood purifier for toxicity and liver ailments, Burdock is one of the safest standbys in body purification and clearing the system. It is good in a liver formula with Yellow Dock and Dandelion, two of its best friends. Burdock is especially good for chronic illness, when the sickness has dragged the body down and cluttered it with random problems, including the waste products of a lot of medications. It has a strong affinity for the skin; Burdock creates healthy skin from the inside out, as well as the decoction being used as a wash for scaly skin, eczema, boils, sores, and fungal infections. Bruised Burdock leaves are applied as a poultice to burns, Poison Ivy, sores and blisters on the feet. The root tea has been taken for uterine prolapse and swollen prostate glands, including prostates damaged from weight training. Burdock increases kidney activity, clears out the urinary tract, and helps to pass stones. In some tests it has been shown to be a mild cancer inhibitor. For skin problems, Burdock works well with Viola. The seeds make the tongue tingle, and have been chewed for toothache.

Culinary Uses: Young Burdock root is considered a delicacy, called *gobo*, by the Japanese. It is especially good for diabetics, cooked as a vegetable, as it contains inulin.

Magical Uses: Burdock root was cut into slices and strung like beads on red thread to keep away evil spirits. The burrs were used as curse-bearers. The seeds were said to improve memory if eaten regularly, as the clinging burrs would cling to thoughts and facts and help you to hold onto them.

Shamanic Uses: Burdock seeds, while largely a pain, can be used whilst adventuring in dangerous otherworlds. Sprinkle them behind you as you go, and they will foul the footsteps of pursuers. Burdock is favored of Farbauti, the lightning-giant who is the father of Loki, and can be carried as a token to gain his blessing.

Affinity: Storm (cleansing alterative bitter), Swamp (oily), Harvest (nourishing). Use for Air and Swamp.

Point: LI 11

Plant-wight's Nature: Burdock-wight is grumpy, tenacious, and a bit difficult to please. He is both aware of people's general distaste for him, and completely unwilling to concede that their attitudes are anything but unfounded. He is rather like the grouchy, cynical old man who shakes his cane at the passing, laughing children; there is sometimes even a sly meanness to him. On the other hand, when he is aroused to fight, his healing abilities are immense, especially his ability to burn toxins out of the blood and off of the skin. He is harsh, but skilled. If you have a Burdock plant on your property that you use regularly, greet it as you go by, and if its burrs catch you, don't get too upset about it, at least not where he can hear you.

Medicinal Charm: Blood Burning

For skin inflammations of any kind (including infections that are too much for gentle Calendula) or if the blood is laden with toxins from living in this "civilized" world, make a strong infusion of Burdock leaves, or the root if you can get it and can afford to dig up a whole plant. You can combine it with equal parts Comfrey if there are no active or past liver problems, as the two are old friends and work well together, and Comfrey adds a strong healing touch to Burdock's harshness. For skin inflammations: Strain the green matter out and poultice the affected area with it. Of the remaining infusion, pour off a cup's worth to drink (you can add other herbs for taste if you like) and put the rest in a cool bath to soak in. For detoxifying, make it into a tea and drink it. As you soak, and/or sit with the poultice, and/or drink the tea, say the following charm:

> Fire's friend, cling fast the foe,
> Burning burr, burn clean the blood,
> Sly fox's clout, though you we curse,
> From blood to skin, from skin to bone,
> We beg ye now, ye child of thurse,
> Forgive our slight, and see us home.

Magical Charm: Memory Clinging

For those with poor memory, or who are currently doing a lot of memorization study, go out in the evening and collect burrs from a Burdock plant in the fall. Then next morning, make yourself a tea of them, strain, and drink. Repeat this every day for one turn of the moon. As you drink, recite the following charm:

> Hedge-Ruffian, run off all worries
> And mend my mooning mind, O Lappa,
> Airup, clear the clouds and cling fast
> All facts that fly into my hands.

Calendula

Botanical Name: *Calendula officinalis*
Folk Names: Caltha, Golds, Ruddes, Ruddles, Mary Gowles, Pot Marigold, Marygold, Oculus Christi, Fiore D'Ogni Mese, Solis Spousa, Solsequia, Jackanapes-On-Horseback, Bride of the Sun, Marybud, Holigolde, Husbandman's Dial, Summer's Bride
Anglo-Saxon Names: Meargealla, or Ymbglidegold ("it turns with the sun").
Modern German Name: Garten-Ringelblume
Modern Swedish Names: Ringblomma, Solsocka
Modern Danish Name: Morgenfrue
Modern Norwegian Name: Ringblomst
Height: 12"
Season: Annual

History: Associated with both the Sun and with calendars, due to its daily opening and closing, Calendula is native to southern Europe and brought to northern Europe by the Romans and Greeks. It was said by them to bloom on the "kalends", or first day, of every month.

Medicinal Uses: Calendula is herbal sunshine. It is one of the most important wound-healing herbs, keeping open wounds clean and bacteria contained until they can heal. It is especially good for wounds in dark crevices of the body, bringing sun to where it never shines, as it were. The flowers are made into an ointment to smear on cuts, inflammations, burns, sore nipples from breastfeeding, bruises, wounds, and vaginal inelasticity. The essential oil is a potent antifungal for yeast infections. An infusion is used for fevers, as it gently brings on perspiration; as a compress for varicoseveins, and as a gargle for gum disease and inflammation of the esophagus. It shrinks swollen glands, helps to heal damaged livers, and brings on sweating during deep bone-aching fevers. Calendula is a gentle cleanser of the lymphatic system, and as such is a mild immune stimulant; Calendula petals were floated on soup in the cold, dark season by northern Europeans as a way to stave off colds and fight the winter blahs. As a woman's herb, Calendula brings life to the female system and combats dysmenorrhea. This herb's affinity for the "calendar", meaning natural cycles, is real; it will bring a woman's menstrual cycle gently back to a regular time and season.

Household Uses: The infusion is used as a hair rinse to bring out red tones in the hair.

Culinary Uses: Flowers are eaten in salads, used to color soups, to dye cheese yellow, to replace Saffron in rice, and made into conserve.

Magical Uses: The petals, picked at noon in bright sun, were used in sachets to strengthen the heart and lift the spirits. The dried petals were scattered across doorways for protection, scattered under beds for prophetic dreams, and carried in the pockets to trials for favorable justice. Placed in the shoes, they supposedly help to understand the language of the birds.

Shamanic Uses: As the plant of Daeg, god of the Day who follows Sunna, Calendula is ingested during *utiseta* to speak to him, usually to ask him what he has seen on his rushed travels. It can also be used by trance-workers who spend so much of their time out of the world that they lose track of the natural physical cycle.

Affinity: Fire (warming), Storm (bitter alterative), Air (astringent), Harvest (nourishing). Use on Earth and Swamp conditions.

Point: SP 10

Plant-wight's Nature: Calendula is a pampered but wistful girl-child, or sometimes a young maiden just past puberty. She is no wild thing—her medieval name, Pot Marigold, reflects her domestic garden-nature—and she lives happily in sheltered gardens, her golden hair reflecting the Sun. She enjoys counting games, and nursery rhymes with counting or memory-repetition involved. Her healing touch is like that of a child, full of innocent goodwill and hope for mending.

Medicinal Charm: Sunshine Salve

To make Calendula salve, warm a cup of olive oil on the stove. It can get to a mild simmer, but nowhere near a boil. Stir in 3 cups of Calendula petals, fresh or dried. (The jury is out on which is better—fresh are more potent, but contain more water which may separate out later and need to be poured off.) Stir gently at this level of low heat for an hour, while singing:

> Sun Seeker, Summer's Bride, Lover of the Day,
> Holigolde will heal me hale, Meargalla light the way.

At this point, many herbalists will stop and strain out the petals. I leave them in. I'm not looking for remedies that have a ten-year shelf-life, as I'm not a phamacist or commercial remedy maker, and I like having the actual body of the plant in what I'm going to smear on my skin. However, if you want to stop and strain and reheat, go ahead. After that, stir in ¼ cup of grated beeswax, very slowly. Pour it into a shallow, wide-mouthed jar, and let cool. Scrape the rune Dagaz into the cooled salve. Use for any of the above external problems.

Caraway

Botanical Name: *Carum carvi*
Folk Names: Karawya, Alcaravea
Anglo-Saxon Name: Cymen (due to confusion with Cumin)
Old High Germanic Name: Kumil
Modern German Names: Echter Kümmel, Wilder Kümmel
Modern Swedish Name: Kummin
Modern Danish Name: Kommen
Modern Norwegian Name: Karve
World Association: Material-realm plant, no divine or ethereal association
Height: To 2'
Season: Biennial
History: Caraway was originally native to the Mideast and Central Asia; its first known usage is among ancient Arabs. It came from there to Greece and thence to Rome, and northward with the Roman conquest. It was known vaguely to the writers of the Anglo-Saxon herbals, but they confused it with Cumin, another southern herb, which suggested little contact with Caraway at that time. Caraway spread over the northern continent enthusiastically, however, taking root especially in Germany and Finland.
Medicinal Uses: The seeds are antiseptic and used to expel worms. Caraway tea is good for flatulence and indigestion, and is a mild stimulant. It breaks down greasy fats and tones the digestion overall. It tightens up the intestines and has been used for menstrual cramps, as it has a warming effect on everything down below.
Household Uses: Essential oil distilled from the seeds is used to flavor gin and the liqueur *Kummel*, as well as mouthwashes, soaps, and aftershaves.
Culinary Uses: The seeds are a popular spice in breads, cakes, pork, goulash, sauerkraut, cheese, pickles, and cabbage. They reduce the smell of strong brassicas. Chopped leaves can be added to soups, and the roots can be cooked as a vegetable.
Magical Uses: Caraway serves as protection against all manner of "evil spirits", and any object which holds some Caraway seeds cannot be touched by them. (Unfortunately, it cannot be used in any endeavor that involves world-traveling or contacting most spirits, either; see below.) The seeds are said to have the gift of making animals, people, and things stick around; items sprinkled with Caraway will not be stolen, and if there is attempted theft, the thief will find himself unable to leave the premises. In keeping with this idea of retention, Caraway is said to strengthen the memory and induce fidelity. It is thrown at weddings to enhance marital bonding, and kept in bags with sacred tools to bond them to their owners.
Shamanic Uses: Caraway is a very human-loving herb, and it tends to dislike non-human species, with the possible exception of Earthbound elementals. Indeed, Caraway is the seed to scatter if you want to drive off entities from other worlds, or shut otherworldly doors, or in general create a space that is limited to our very material plane. People with nonhuman blood in them—Alfar or faery blood, Jotun blood, etc.—sometimes may have an allergy to Caraway, depending on how strong the blood is in them. It should go without saying that no offering to anyone in the Nine Worlds should contain Caraway.
Affinity: Fire (pungent), Storm (bitter alterative), Swamp (oily), Air (astringent). Use for Earth, Air, and River conditions.
Point: SP 15
Plant-wight's Nature: Caraway is thin, dark, Gypsylike, and hard to pin down. Like Grandfather Plantain, he is a travelin' man, always on the road, but unlike Plantain he is generally quiet and unobtrusive, irritated by those who bother him (to which he responds with a sharp remark, a turned-up collar, and

a hasty retreat) and conversely generous and kind when invited in to the occasional feast. He is like the worn traveler at the door who will bless your house if you take him in, or curse it if you turn him away. He doesn't like foreign wights in general, although he gets along well with the "little people" of the natural world, and most of the other plant spirits seem to know him and like him. He will help your stomachache with a touch if he's a good mood; reward him for his help by eating a fine meal with Caraway somewhere in it, so that he can enjoy it through your body and blood.

Magical Charm: Down to Earth

When, for whatever reason, you want to close all otherworldly influences out of an area and allow the energies of the natural world to have their way, sprinkle a handful of Caraway seed in all directions, saying the following charm:

> *Caraway, close thee all gates,*
> *Shut out all wights not here by birth,*
> *Block out all hands that manipulate,*
> *And bring this road right down to earth.*

Carline Thistle

Botanical Name: *Carlina acaulis*
Folk Names: Dwarf Thistle, Stemless Thistle
Anglo-Saxon Name: Eoforþrote ("boar's throat")
Modern German Name: Stengellose Eberwurz, Große Wetterdistel, Silberdistel
Modern Swedish Name: Silvertistel
Modern Danish Name: Sølvtisdel
Modern Norwegian Name: Sølvtistel
Deity Association: Frey
Height: 12'
Season: Perennial
History: Carline Thistle is a native of southern and southeastern Europe, spread to the northern areas during the early medieval period. Carline Thistle gets its current name from "Charlemagne's Thistle", which tells part of its history; the Emperor Charlemagne supposedly, by one account, dreamed of it as a plague cure. Another account suggests that he was influenced in its use by Italian and Greek healers. At any rate, he demanded that it be grown all over Europe as part of his long list of favored medicinal herbs.
Medicinal Uses: The roots macerated in wine are a stomach tonic; a root infusion is diuretic, mildly laxative, an antiseptic gargle and wound wash, good for eczema and skin rashes, a liver tonic, and a worm expeller.
Household Uses: The leaves can be used to curdle milk, and promote appetite in cattle. The leaves close as rain approaches, making it traditional humidity gauge for farmers.
Culinary Uses: The flower receptacle can be eaten like an artichoke.
Magical Uses: Carried against plague, snakebite, and for general protection.
Shamanic Uses: Straw-yellow instead of purple, the Carline Thistle was called "boar's throat" and was used in magical incantations involving Frey, the boar-god. It is used to invoke Frey in his boar form, which is strongly protective and fairly aggressive.
Affinity: Storm (bitter alterative), Fire (warming). Use for Swamp and Earth conditions.
Point: LV 13
Plant-wight's Nature: Carline Thistle appeared to me shifting in and out of boar-form—sometimes a male boar, sometimes a great wild sow, but always silver-white. I remembered the stories about sacred white pigs who were used as oracles during the interaction. Carline Thistle settled down to being a

humanoid being with a shock of spiky silver hair and a snoutlike face. Strongly protective, this wight is drawn to those that it considers nobility, by its own rather unclear standards, and will offer to protect them if it is grown to flowering stage on their property.

Medicinal Charm: Gut Bug

When the evil spirits have infested your gut, take four ounces of the roots of Carline Thistle and simmer them for an hour in a half gallon of water or wine, depending on which you prefer. As it is simmering, say the charm below. Strain, drink a cupful, and repeat every 12 hours until it is gone.

> *Gullinbursti's hearty herb, I beseech thee,*
> *In the name of the Golden One's sweet steed,*
> *Beat this brimstone from my bowels,*
> *Hear my plea this night of need.*

Catnip

Botanical Name: *Nepeta cataria*
Folk Names: Catnep
Anglo-Saxon Name: Nepte
Modern German Name: Echte Katzenminze, Silberminze
Modern Swedish Name: Kattmynta
Modern Danish Name: Kattmynte
Modern Norwegian Name: Kattemynte
Deity Association: Beyla
Height: To 3'
Season: Perennial
History: Native to all of Eurasia, Catnip was used by northerners long before they had cats. It is a member of the Mint family.
Medicinal Uses: Infusion of the leaves treats colds, relaxes the muscles of upset stomachs, reduces fevers, and soothes headaches. A wash soothes scalp irritations. Catnip has a very mild sedative action, milder even than Chamomile, and thus is used for colicky babies. It is good for older children of the quiet type who hold their emotions in and then develop stomach problems.
Household Uses: Used to intoxicate cats and repel rats and flea beetles.
Culinary Uses: Brewed as a tea substitute.
Magical Uses: Used in love sachets, along with Rose petals. Given as friendship spells for friends who are moving and wish to keep in touch. Used for general luck-attracting.
Shamanic Uses: Beloved of Beyla, farm-servant of Frey and Gerda whose name means "Bee", Catnip is used in charms to keep livestock safe and close to home, be they bees, pigs, cattle, or even cats and dogs. Catnip is said to help the skin-swift who wish to go about at night shapeshifted into cats.
Affinity: Mountain (relaxant), Earth (cooling), Fire (stimulant), River (moistening). Use for Storm, Earth, and Fire conditions, especially Storm.
Point: UB 64
Plant-wight's Nature: Master Catnip is bald, rotund, and complacent, and naps a lot. He prefers animals to people, and you can actually get on better with him if you come to him pretending to be an animal who needs his help. It's not that he's fooled, but your willingness to act like a cat or dog or horse amuses and entertains him, and makes him more likely to work with you. He speaks in a high, squeaky voice that is often difficult to make out, and there is something of the slightly demented child in him.
Medicinal Charm: Baby Belly

When the baby cries and brings his legs upwards in pain, may run a fever, and may have explosions in the diaper, it is time for Catnip. Use a half dose—half an ounce in a pint of hot water—and make sure that you strain it well. Mix it half and half with breast milk or formula, and coax it into the little one with a bottle. As you feed the baby, sing: "Catnip, cure my kitten, keep the cruel claws from the belly," preferably in a funny voice, because that will amuse Master Catnip. The baby will probably enjoy it too.

Celandine

Botanical Name: *Chelidonium majus*
Folk Names: Greater Celandine, Swallow Wort, Swallow Herb, Celidoyne, Chelidoninum, Devil's Milk, Kenning Wort, Tetterwort, Wartwort, Wenwort
Anglo-Saxon Name: Cilðenige, Celðenie, Celeðonie
Modern German Name: Schöllkraut, Schellkraut
Modern Swedish Name: Skelört, Svalört
Modern Danish Name: Svalurte
Modern Norwegian Name: Svaleurt
Deity Association: Loki
Height: To 4'
Season: Biennial
History: Greater Celandine was originally an import from southern Europe, and its northern names are mostly variations on the Greek name, which means "swallow plant", as it blooms and dies with the coming and going of the swallows in southern European areas. Introduced into Europe in the early medieval period, it was confused with the native Lesser Celandine (*Ranunculus ficaria*), also known as figwort or pilewort, which is not related to it and has entirely different properties.
Medicinal Uses: Celandine's bile-yellow sap marks it as a herb of the liver and gallbladder, and this is indeed its most common usage. The aerial parts have been used to stimulate the gallbladder and liver, thin the flow of bile, relieve jaundice, and treat hepatitis. It is especially good for conditions where the gallbladder is sluggish and the bile thick from underuse, which can manifest as swelling and pain in the liver area (just below the right scapula), jaundice, yellow stools and urine, stomach bloating, and migraine headaches on the right side. (The swollen liver and gallbladder pain can move up the nerves into the head.) It is also used in the treatment of gallstones, and for livers damaged by long-term drug use. Weak Celandine infusion is a good eyewash for dry and reddened eyes. Celandine's caustic purgative orange sap has been used to burn off warts, corns, ringworm, and skin cancers. Celandine is mildly toxic in large doses, and terribly bitter in tea, so the safest use for it is to make tincture of it and then treat with only one or two drops per day.
Magical Uses: Celandine is the herb of escape from imprisonment and entrapment; wearing it is a charm against getting caught in a tight spot. It was often worn to trials, and is said to cure depression if carried. Some see it as a solar victory herb, from its yellow solar flowers, and use it in spells to win against an enemy.
Shamanic Uses: As one of Loki's plants, a bag of dried Celandine can be used as a charm to ask Loki's aid in escaping from any situation where you are held against your will. Those who are on the best terms with the Celandine plant spirit have been known to use it to walk through walls on other planes. Emotionally, it is used to treat the twin conditions of dull, depressed lethargy, and guilt over having done some elusive wrong. This gallbladder plant also bestows the kind of audacious courage one can only refer to as, well, gall. It can be useful for when you need to do something that will bring public disapproval. Ask Loki all about that.
Affinity: Storm (bitter alterative), Fire (warming). Use for Swamp and Earth.

Point: UB18

Plant-wight's Nature: Celandine-wight is a narrow, twiglike, stick of a creature with a head of high-swept hair that may actually be roots or leaves, mischievous eyes, a toothy vertical grin, and a hyperactive dance. He enjoys playing tricks and laughing at people's mistakes, and it is best to work with him in conjunction with other herbs if you are using his plant for important internal purposes such as liver and gallbladder function, which he excels at. Celandine-wight is whimsical with the occasionally seen hard edge to his trickery and hard glint in his eyes. In spite of all that, he is quite powerful in his own way, a power which I am still at a loss to nail down, but which struck me anyway.

Medicinal Charm: Free Flow of Gall

That's a Loki-sounding term, isn't it? Like its patron, Celandine herb needs to be handled with care. Fill a jar with the chopped aerial parts and cover it with alcohol; seal and shake daily for one turn of the moon, saying the following charm:

> Swallow Wort, make free the burning flow,
> The Salt Springs rise by Devil-Wort below,
> By Flame-Hair's hand, the Well of Plenty freely goes.

After a month of this, strain and rebottle the tincture. If you are worried about it being too caustic, combine it with Dandelion tincture, using twice as much Dandelion—the two work well together and cheerful Dandelion can settle out Celandine (she has that effect on many other difficult spirits, including Burdock); or do the same with Yellow Dock, whose saturnine nature can keep the trickster in line. Or use all three in a 2:2:1 ratio with Celandine last, and take 5 drops per day for no more than one month at a stretch. Then take a month off before doing it again.

Centaury

Botanical Name: *Centaurium erythraea* or *Erythraea centaurium*

Folk Names: Bitterwort, Fel Terrae, Earthgall, Felwort, Filwort, Red Centaury, Christ's Ladder, Isiphon

Anglo-Saxon Name: Curmealle, Feferwort

Modern German Names: Eines Tausendgüldenkraut, Echtes Tausendgüldenkraut

Modern Swedish Name: Klint

Modern Danish Name: Tusingylden

Modern Norwegian Name: Skjermgyllen

Deity Association: Mountain Jotnar

Height: 12'

Season: Annual

History: Centaury is native to central Europe and Siberiabut was introduced to other areas of Europe during the medieval period. It was named by the Greeks after Chiron, the famous centaur healer of myth.

Medicinal Uses: Alterative tonic effect on the liver, kidneys, and gallbladder; take prophylactically for problems in these areas. Good digestive; encourages appetite. Used for anorexics to stimulate eating. Eases heartburn when eaten after meals. Good for convalescents or the elderly with no appetite due to stomach troubles and slow digestion. Used externally as a compress on varicose veins.

Magical Uses: Centaury has been burned to drive off snakes. The Celts considered it to be a lucky plant, and medieval peasants carried it to ward off evil spirits. Medieval magicians claimed that Centaury, mixed with the blood of a female lapwing or plover and burned in lamp oil, would convince all who breathed the smoke that they had magical powers, and that it would cause the very stars to fight with each other. It has also been used as a countermagic herb.

Shamanic Uses: Centaury is a powerful banishing herb when used in recels. It has been known to confuse one's enemies and make them turn on each other. It is beloved of the mountain-etins and cliff-thurses of Jotunheim, where it grows freely and has somewhat more powerful properties than it does here. Using Centaury can lend you their strength and stubbornness in holding their ground.

Affinity: Storm (bitter alterative), Mountain (relaxant), Fire (stimulant), Harvest (nourishing). Use on Storm and Swamp.

Point: LV 14

Plant-wight's Nature: Centaury-wight is a woodland spirit, even after centuries of being grown in gardens. He crouches at the edge of the woods, eyes flicking about and taking in his environment, periodically pouncing on small game to pop it in his mouth and crunch it down. There is something very troll-like about him, with his sharp-toothed grinning mouth and his inclination to eat anything that moves. He is friendly enough, although he demanded that I grow him from seed, and when informed that I'd tried and the seeds didn't sprout, shrugged and said that I hadn't tried hard enough. (The seeds are a bit tricky to get to germinate in potting soil; I had to go to the woods and get leaf-mold to make it work.) Being as one uses his plant as an alterative, if you'll be using him, you'll be using him regularly, so it's best to make friends even if he seems a bit barbaric.

Medicinal Charm: Slow Eater Tea

For those with sluggish digestion and lack of appetite, pour a quart of boiling water over an ounce of dried Centaury, with another ounce of some bits of other more tasty herbs to alleviate the bitter taste. While it steeps, say the following charm:

> Bitterwort, Felwort, help this one to hunger
> For food more filling than thy bitter binding,
> Give guts good fortune as they wend a-winding.

Take a cupful half an hour before each meal for appetite and good digestion.

Chamomile

Botanical Name: *Chamomilla matricaria* or *Matricaria recutita* (German Chamomile), *Anthemis nobile* (Roman Chamomile)

Folk Names: Maegthen, Maythen, Mayweed, Ground Apple, Heermanschen, Manzanilla, Chamaimylon, Baldersbrow, Whig Plant

Anglo-Saxon Name: Mægðen

Modern German Name: Echte Kamille

Modern Swedish Names: Kamomill, Kamill, Komenteblomma, Sötblomster, Sötkulla, Söttuppa, Sötros, Sötört, Surkulla, Tyskentopp

Modern Danish Name: Kamille

Modern Norwegian Names: Kamille, Kamilleblom

Deity Association: Baldur

Height: 12"

Season: Annual (German); perennial (Roman)

History: There is some variety of Chamomile to found everywhere in Europe, north Africa, and most of Asia. As the most gentle and safe of sedatives, it is still one of the most popular commercial herb teas today. The most authentic form to the Northern Tradition herb garden is the annual German Chamomile (*Chamomilla matricaria* or *Matricaria recutita*), as the perennial Roman Chamomile (*Anthemis nobile*) came north from the Mediterranean. The two have identical medicinal properties. Chamomile was associated with the newborn Sun on the winter Solstice, and has been used modernly as a bath for the man portraying the Sun before a Solstice rite.

Medicinal Uses: Sedative, antifungal, antimicrobial, antispasmodic, anti-inflammatory. Relieves gas, heartburn, stomach upset, and is used to treat irritable bowel syndrome. Applied externally in teabags to heal burns and rest eyes; used as gargle or packed in around teeth for toothache. Ointment is used for eczema, insect bites, and genital and anal irritation. Mouthwash heals mouth inflammation. Inhalation of steam is good for phlegm and hay fever. Tincture dissolved in warm water is a good eyewash for conjunctivitis. Chamomile treats fevers (especially recurring low-grade fevers), flus, earaches, and as a reliable sedative is excellent for insomnia and night terrors—in the latter case, drink before going to bed rather than waiting to wake up.

The Sun is also associated with the innocence of children, and Chamomile is the safest possible herb for them, easing the pain of colic when a mild tea is mixed with mother's milk and giving them rest without the aid of allopathic drugs. If the child (or adult, for that matter) cannot keep food down, they can soak in bathwater with a strong infusion of Chamomile added to it. In general, it is good for people who are feeling whiny, annoyed, loudly sharing their discomfort with everyone within range. If they are acting like two-year-olds, it's time for Chamomile tea. It is also good for prolonged pain that makes the body oversensitive, or for necessary pain in sensitive people with low thresholds. Chamomile may get an allergic reaction from some people.

Household Uses: Known as the "plant's physician"; grow near ailing plants to perk them up. Make into an antifungal spray for tree diseases. Spray infusion on seedlings to prevent "damping off disease" and on compost to activate decomposition. Boil the flower for a yellow-brown dye. Wash blond hair with infusion for lightening. Use in potpourri and herb pillows.

Magical Uses: A solar plant, associated with the sun and the god Baldur. It is used to attract money, and a handwash is used by gamblers. Use in sleep incenses (and tea!); makes the best sleep potion. Removes curses and hexes when sprinkled around the property. As a "plant healer", it can also be used as a focus to protect the garden.

Shamanic Uses: This is the plant of Asgard, the land of the Aesir. Its English name Maythen was originally spelled *Maegthen*, as can be seen from the *Lacnunga* poem, and *maeg* is cognate to mage, and *maegen*, both words about power. Chamomile is a solar plant, and it harnesses the power of the Sun. As the plant of golden Asgard, it can be burned in recels or scattered as a way to send your words straight to the Aesir and have them hear you. I suspect few of them would ignore you if you were holding Maegthen in your hand. It burns away the darkness and the creeping negativity, as its medicinal nature as an antifungal demonstrates.

Affinity: Mountain (relaxant), Earth (cooling), Stone (sedative), Harvest (nourishing), Storm (alterative for GI when dried). Use on Storm, Fire, and Swamp conditions.

Points: PC 5 (German), PC 6 (Roman)

Plant-wight's Nature: Many years ago, when I was a child, my parents took us to Europe for some years while my father worked overseas. We spent years in Germany and Austria, among other places, and I remember the elaborate festivals of Christmas there, so different from the over-commercialized celebrations in America. One character in the German Christmas iconography was the Kristkindl, which literally meant "Christ Child" but didn't seem to actually have much to do with the infant Jesus. The Kristkindl was sometimes a little boy but just as often a little girl, ethereal and wreathed in light, holding out chubby hands in blessing. Sometimes the child had wings; sometimes they were clad in traditional embroidered folk costume, male or female. I was confused by the figure until later when I learned that the Kristkindl was a holdover from the old Pagan Solstice rites, symbolizing the newborn Sun that is born in the winter darkness.

When I went out to meet the Chamomile wight, two small children approached me hand in hand as I sat in the garden. My first thought was how amazingly similar they appeared to the Kristkindl figures that I remembered—golden-haired twins, a boy and a girl, dressed in traditional costume and wreathed in light. Granted, one's subconscious often fills in associative details when faced with something you're only "seeing" with your inner eye, but I still think that there's some real connection there. They were definitely the Children of Light ... and there were definitely two of them. At first I thought that they might be one of those wights that changes gender, but then they communicated that they were two separate beings, brother and sister. The little girl was the spirit of German Chamomile, and the little boy was Roman Chamomile, both of which I grow in my garden. I tend to use them interchangeably and think of them as the same plant, which they chided me about: "How can you confuse a tall annual with a short perennial? Why, just see how different we are?"

The Maythen Children are two of the wights who have sworn to aid humanity, and as their appearance suggests, they are particularly fond of children and babies, and those who are momentarily having an attack of babyish need. Safe enough to feed to an infant, the Maythen Children lullaby the whiniest soul to sleep and fill their soul with ethereal, calming light. They will almost never refuse to give their gentle aid, although their power may fail against serious pain or refusal to let go of whirling anxiety.

Medicinal Charm: Day And Night

Used magically, Chamomile can be a powerful antidepressant. Why, then, does it cause sleep? One of the symptoms of depression is actually a lack of good, solid, peaceful sleep, and Chamomile is the best plant for this purpose. There is also that finding a way out of depression is a long, slow journey that may require changes in brain chemistry, a finicky business at best. This sort of thing is best done slowly and quietly, over time, preferably on a sleeping person. To bring the Sun into someone's life, give them tea made from charged and hallowed Chamomile that has been asked to slowly purge the depressing chemicals from their brain, every night when they go to sleep, for a long time, perhaps months. One day they may find that they no longer need it, but if it does nothing after three turns of the moon, there is something going on that even this herb cannot cure, and you can discontinue it. To properly hallow the tea, hold the cup to your heart and either sing the Maythen verse from the Song of the Nine Sacred Herbs, or say the following prayer:

> Maythen, may the morning come
> Bright and blessed with smiling skies
> May world be white and high and fair
> And shadows flee the Sun-song's rise.

Cherry

Botanical Name: *Prunus spp.*
Folk Names: Various—Sweet Cherry, Chokecherry, Black Cherry, depending on variety.
Anglo-Saxon Name: Cyrse
Old Norse Name: Heggr
Old High Germanic Name: Keresjo
Modern German Name: Kirsche
Modern Swedish Name: Glanshägg

Modern Danish Name: Kirsebær

Modern Norwegian Name: Kirsebærslekten

Deity Association: Frey

Height: 20-30' depending on variety

Season: Perennial tree

History: Cherry trees seem to have originated in southern Europe, and the Germanic peoples got them from the Romans during the occupation of the Empire. They quickly spread north into all areas of Europe.

Medicinal Uses: The inner bark of the Cherry, while containing hydrocyanic acid and thus mildly poisonous, is safe in small amounts soaked in water. This is used to clear throats and treat coughing. Only small amounts of fresh bark should be used. Never consume any wilted Cherry leaves, as the cyanide concentrates in wilted leaves.

Culinary Uses: Pies, jellies, jams, syrups, and anything else you can think of to make.

Magical Uses: Love spells, too many to recount here. Cherry juice is also used as a blood substitute in some rituals.

Shamanic Uses: Cherries of any kind are beloved of Frey, and they are one of the Vanaheim plants. In fact, while the Crabapple is a Vanaheim plant, the bred northern cultivars of Apple are all sacred to Iduna, and thus Asgard plants. Cherries, however, are pure Vanaheim. They are also found in Ljossalfheim, spread by Frey who has a hall there. Make an offering of Cherries to him when they are in season.

Affinity: Earth (cooling), Air (astringent), Storm (bitter alterative). Use on Fire, River, and Swamp conditions.

Point: CV 20

Plant-wight's Nature: Cherry-wight is a dancer. Cherry-wight is sometimes a slender laughing maiden, and sometimes a slender laughing youth, both with rosy complexions. Cherry-wight loves dancing, romance, and sex—ask Cherry for luck in love and then make sure that you seduce someone under a Cherry tree. Some of the Cherry varieties put a different slant on things—Chokecherry is wilder and more mischievous, Black Cherry more passionate, etc. Take hold of Cherry's branches and dance with the wight, even if only for a moment—Cherry will enjoy it.

Magical Charm: Love Renewal

For those who have been hurt in love, and have turned their eyes from it because they cannot bear to be hurt again, let them wait until the healing is done and then come to Cherry-wight for aid in believing again in love. For those who are ready, take three dried, pitted cherries, three Cherry pits, three dried Cherry leaves, and a scant spoonful of wild Cherry bark, which is boiled in an ounce of water and drunk warm. First they must crumble the leaves in their hands, saying,

> *Wilt has walled me, pain has poisoned me,*
> *I wash away the past dead and dried.*

Then let them wash the bits of dried leaf from their hands in a bowl of clean water, and fling it out onto the earth. Then they should taste the warm Cherry-bark tea, and pour it out on the earth, saying the following:

> *Bitter bark, this lesson I learned,*
> *All things run again to renewal.*

Then they should eat the three dried pitted cherries, saying:

> *Love left me slack and empty,*
> *But still there is sweetness in life.*

Then they should take the three Cherry pits and bury them in the ground, saying:

Fair Frey, lift me from this fear,
I face the future holding my open heart,
Golden Lord, let me fall only into gladness,
Let me love again.

Chickweed

Botanical Name: *Stellaria media*

Folk Names: Starwort, Starweed, Adder's Mouth, Passerina, Satin Flower, Tongue Grass, Stellaire, Winterweed

Anglo-Saxon Names: Cicena Mete ("Chicken's Food"), Æðelferðingwyrt

Old Norse Name: Arfi

Modern German Name: Vogelmiere

Modern Swedish Names: Våtarv, Natagräs, Nate, Våtnarv

Modern Danish Names: Fuglegræs, Hønsetarm, Skovstjerne

Modern Norewgian Name: Vassarve

Deity Association: Nott

Height: 16"

Season: Annual

History: Chickweed is a common weed that is native to all of Europe and Asia. In ancient Norse, Chickweed was used to refer to something common and valueless; a meager inheritance was referred to as "no more than a heap of Chickweed".

Medicinal Uses: Chickweed is a slow, safe, and incredibly nutritive alterative. While it comes into its own as a specific in a poultice—Chickweed poultice (or Chickweed cream) is used to soothe inflamed skin, eczema, psoriasis, and helps to pull out splinters—taken internally over a period of time, it cleanses the entire lymphatic system and almost all the organs. It helps to dissolve fats, which is why it is used for weight loss and poulticed for lipomas, and it regulates water absorption. It is drunk as a cleansing tonic for chronic cystitis and constipation.

Culinary Uses: Leafy stems are edible, although they don't taste great.

Magical Uses: Carried to bring fidelity to love relationships, and to bring new love to a flagging romance.

Shamanic Uses: Strangely enough, Chickweed is a talisman for astrologers, especially the sort who do actual star-gazing. Chickweed also has an affinity for birds, so those who work with bird spirits might want to make friends with it. Feeding it to a bird in your care is a bonding activity.

Affinity: River (moistening), Earth (cooling). Use on Air and Fire.

Point: UB 28

Plant-wight's Nature: Chickweed appears to me as a wild adolescent girl, the sort who grew up half-wild in poverty and knows more about running through the woods and fields than anything to do with manners and education. Her hair is disheveled, with a myriad of leaves and starry white flowers in is, sticking out at all angles; her dress is frayed and ill-fitting, her feet are caked with manure. She isn't shy at all—more the type to seize the hand of a total stranger and enthusiastically pull him off into a field to look at some interesting mushroom she's found on a dungheap, with no thought as to whether he might not find that just as fun and fascinating as she does. She isn't the deepest of plant-wights, but for some reason she has a naïve innate knowledge of the skies, from laying out on hills all night when decent folk are in bed, and staring at the stars. Nott likes her a great deal, and can help you keep her calm.

Medicinal Charm: Star Cleanse

Earthy little Chickweed's head is always in the stars. This cleanse is top to bottom, earth to sky. If you can fast during it, great; if you can't fast due to medical or personal reasons, eat a diet of natural organic whole food, no junk or processed things, during the six days you are on it. Basically, eat the equivalent of a double handful of Chickweed per day. You can pour boiling water over it and make tea, you can juice it if you have it fresh, you can put it in capsules and eat it (in which case don't fast, you need other food to digest capsules). The dosage is not so important. Just do this for six days. When you take your morning dose, say:

> Starwort, I am seeking cleansing,
> Make me the Maypole, earth to sky,
> From star to seed, all grime shall fly.

Chicory

Botanical Name: *Cichorium intybus*
Folk Names: Succory, Clock Flower
Anglo-Saxon Name: Eofola ("Endive")
Modern German Name: Wegwarten
Modern Swedish Name: Cikoria
Modern Danish Name: Cikorie
Modern Norwegian Name: Sikori
Deity Association: Mani
Height: To 4'
Season: Biennial

History: Chicory is a weed common to nearly the entire world. Its usage is so old that its name comes from an ancient Egyptian word, which is the root word for the name of that plant in almost every language. Its other name "succory", comes from a Latin word referring to its spreading underground roots. Its German name, *Wegwarten*, means "road warden", which was an actual police-type job in the medieval period.

Medicinal Uses: Chicory is another gentle cleanser—of the digestive system, the liver, and the spleen. It gets things moving, and is used for sluggish organ performance, atrophied limbs (internally and externally) and delayed emotional development. The juice of Chicory or its cousin Endive is used for cataracts. The leaves are poulticed for skin inflammation. The root is the strongest part and is often roasted.

Household Uses: The root is roasted for a coffee substitute. Magdeburg Chicory is specially bred for this. The leaves yield a bluish dye.

Culinary Uses: One carefully-selected form of Chicory is Endive (also called escarole if it has ruffly leaves), which has been a popular salad herb and cooking green since before written records. The blue flowers can be eaten in salads.

Magical Uses: Chicory is carried to remove obstacles that crop up in your life.

Shamanic Uses: As it is a "clock" flower, meaning that its blossoms open and close with the sun's hours, it can be used in spells to speed up or slow down time during pathwalking, but be careful with this sort of thing. The safest "time shifting" use for it is to sprinkle it as part of a spell as you move from one world to another, willing the time gap on the two worlds to line up together. This may help the time distortion problem when the other world is strongly different from ours time-wise. (Niflheim is the biggest culprit of the lot when it comes to radically different time-measurements.) Mani the Moon-God is the most knowledgeable Northern deity when it comes to calendars and time (with the possible exception of Unn the mermaid, and Mani is more approachable and makes more sense), and he can help you with Chicory charms.

Affinity: Earth (cooling), River (moistening), Harvest (nourishing), Storm (bitter alterative). Use on Fire, Air and Swamp conditions.

Point: GB 34

Plant-wight's Nature: Chicory-wight is thin and oddly-shaped with a mop of bright blue hair. She moves like a wind-up toy made of sticks, folding herself into the grass at odd angles. She tends to tilt her head and look at you with wide, almost blank eyes, as if she is never quite here in the same world with you. She speaks in disjointed phrases which sound like the magical equivalent of a physics professor ... indeed, I found myself thinking the phrase "if Einstein had been a plant..." as I spoke to her. She knows a great deal about the "cosmic clock" of the Universe, but it is almost impossible to get the information out of her, as there seems to be a meat-brain language barrier between us and her mode of expression. Occasionally, though, she will say something that you know would be brilliant if you could only understand it, and sometimes, on further thought, you might find that you can.

Magical Charm: Brain Harmony

There are no words for this little charm. If you are either a left-brained analytical sort who lacks imagination, or are a right-brained creative sort who lacks organization of thoughts, pull the blue petals off of a blooming Chicory plant. Work them into your hair along the midline of your skull, where the two hemispheres come together, and wear them like that all day. After an hour or so, if Chicory-wight is willing, you will start to have some changes in mode, moving you more towards a middle ground. It won't last, unless you were to work hard with Chicory-wight for a long time, but it can help for a short while.

Cinquefoil

Botanical Name: *Potentilla reptans*

Folk Names: Crampweed, Five Finger Blossom, Five Finger Grass, Goosegrass, Goose Tansy, Moor Grass, Pentaphyllon, Silverweed, Sunkfield

Anglo-Saxon Name: Hræmnes Fot ("Raven's Foot")

Modern German Name: Kriechendes Fingerkraut

Modern Swedish Name: Revfingerört

Modern Danish Name: Potentil

Modern Norwegian Names: Krypmure, Kryptepperot

Deity Association: Odin

Height: 12"

Season: Perennial

History: The European Cinquefoil is a common field and meadow plant all over Europe, naturalized in North America where it is almost indistinguishable from the native species there, *Potentilla simplex*. As its leaves are shaped like a hand, it was attributed with a great variety of magical uses. The Saxons called it Raven's Foot, which it also resembles.

Medicinal Uses: A powerful astringent, the flowering tops are used for bleeding and inflammation, and to bring down fevers. Culpeper claimed that three "fits" or doses of Cinquefoil would cure any fever with chills. The rootstock is boiled as a decoction to bring down fevers, as well as for cramps and diarrhea. In fact, Cinquefoil tea is your best first line of defense for dysentery and most other sources of diarrhea; the sole exception would be food poisoning, when you really do want everything out as fast as possible. It has been used post-partum to remove afterbirths, and for various sorts of internal bleeding. A mild infusion is used to rinse the sinuses during infection, and the tea can stop an asthma attack in an emergency. Some herbalists have used it to treat epilepsy.

Culinary Uses: The rootstock was cooked as a vegetable by the Celts.

Magical Uses: As this plant is shaped like a hand, so it was said to convey all the magic of the uplifted hand. It turns away the "work of evil hands", preventing theft and manipulation by those with ill will. Like Agrimony, it is said to work on hierarchical relations, clearing away obstacles from one's professional and public life. Cinquefoil was hung in doorways or placed in beds for protection, and can be carried as a charm into any situation where people with power over you might wish you ill or try to meddle with your life.

The five points of Cinquefoil supposedly represent love, money, power, health, and wisdom, and carrying it was said to bring all five of these. It was also carried for eloquence in public situations, especially court cases. Associated with the fishing harvest, it was carried by fishermen and thrown into the sea for a good catch. A perfect five-fingered leaf, gathered under the full moon and pressed into a book, is a protection charm for travelers crossing over water. Washing one's hands in Cinquefoil water was said to eventually cure the shaking of palsy. Cinquefoil was tied to fishing nets as a charm for a strong catch, and it was said to draw frogs.

Shamanic Uses: Cinquefoil has a strong connection to Huginn and Muninn, the two ravens of Odin that represent Thought and Memory, as its Anglo-Saxon name "Raven's Foot" shows. It can be drunk in tea in order to work with Odin for the increase and clarity of mental powers.

Affinity: Air (astringent), Earth (cooling). Use for River, Swamp, and Fire conditions.

Point: UB 25

Plant-wight's Nature: Master Cinquefoil is a Magician herb. He appeared to me as a short, small-boned man robed in gold with a wide mane of yellow hair and large eyes, alternately serious and charming. His short-fingered hands are always moving—gesturing, pulling things out of nowhere, sending them off again with a snap and a wave. There is something of the stage magician's attitude in him, as he smoothly shows off his skill and rapidly chatters about all the magical things one could do with him. The patter makes you think that he's sharing great secrets with you, but I got the feeling that he was only giving me things that he knew I could easily find out anyway, and the real secrets were closemouthed behind the showiness. "Love, money, power, health and wisdom!" he said with a flourish, but more lurked behind his wide tawny eyes and slightly self-satisfied smile that I didn't think I'd be able to access without a lot more time working with him.

Medicinal Charm: Dysentery Tea

Chop Cinquefoil rootstocks finely, being careful not to scrape off the root bark, as that is the most potent part. Boil for about half an hour, then add the chopped fresh or crumbled dried aerial parts and simmer for another half hour. (If you can't get the roots, just simmer the aerial parts for a half hour and work with that; it will still be fine.) Cool, strain, and drink, reciting this charm:

> *Crampweed catch the culvert,*
> *Five Fingers stop the flow,*
> *Cinquefoil dry me down the dell.*

Magical Charm: Five Fingers

When those in direct power over you—your boss, social worker, parole officer, etc.—are acting unfairly and you need the situation changed, tie up some Cinquefoil in a bit of cloth and recite the following charm over it. Then carry it with you when you meet with them, and, ideally, secrete it in the place where they carry out their power.

> *Raven's Foot, twin ravens*
> *Fare forth for my good;*
> *With Woden's blessing,*
> *They blaze the way for my will;*
> *What five fingers hath done,*
> *O Pentaphyllon,*
> *Five Fingers shall undo,*
> *O Pentaphyllon.*

Cleavers

Botanical Name: *Galium aparine*

Folk Names: Goosegrass, Barweed, Hedgeheriff, Hayriffe, Eriffe, Grip-grass, Catchweed, Scratweed, Mutton Chops, Robin-Run-In-the-Grass, Love-man, Goosebill, Everlasting-Friendship, Click, Clitheren, Clithers, Heyryt, Cosgres, Tongebledes

Anglo-Saxon Name: Hegerife ("Hedge-Reeve")

Modern German Names: Kletten-Labkraut, Klebkraut

Modern Swedish Name: Snärjmåra

Modern Danish Name: Burresnerre

Modern Norwegian Name: Klengemaure

Deity Association: Gerda

Height: 1-3', depending on whether it has a place to climb

Season: Perennial

History: An abundant weed everywhere in the northern hemisphere, Cleavers springs up in many fields and meadows. Its English name "Hegerife", actually the name for a tax collector, comes from its habit of tangling itself in the wool of sheep who lean against it and pulling out some of their wool. Its other name, "Love-man", comes from this same habit of clinging.

Medicinal Uses: This common weed is a powerful cleanser. An infusion of Cleavers is a mild sedative, and gives a restful sleep; it is also used for head colds. It is an excellent urinary tract herb, doing a good job on UTIs and kidney stones. In a salve, it has been used for burns and skin rashes. Cleavers is a cooling lymphatic cleanser and is used as a safe, nourishing, long-term detoxifying tonic for hot conditions. Like its cousin Lady's Bedstraw, it has been used by pregnant women to prevent miscarriages. It has also been used for cancer treatment, especially in the mouth or facial region, and is useful for prostate problems and cystic breasts. It also has an affinity with the throat, and has been used for goiter and thyroid problems.

As a nervine, Cleavers is good for people who are easily irritated by small things, or who have gotten into that kind of irritable, picky mood due to stress or illness. It is also a nerve medicine for any sort of neuroma or neuralgia, poorly healed nerves or oversensitive skin, especially where there is also a rash. As it is a powerful diuretic, care should be taken when giving it to diabetics.

Household Uses: Cleavers seeds are a good coffee substitute when dried and ground; they taste vaguely like coffee and they have all the caffeine. The stalks were often used as a rough sieve, especially for straining milk. Poultry especially love this herb, although too much given to chickens will make their eggs taste like Cleavers. A hair rinse treats dandruff and itchy scalp.

Magical Uses: Cleavers is given to friends in order to keep their friendship, especially over long distances.

Shamanic Uses: Cleavers is a protective herb for a small space—lay the long stems in a circle, or at the base of a small room or area. Gerda, as Lady of the Walled Garden, will protect you, if only by making sure that you aren't noticed.

Affinity: Earth (cooling), River (moistening), Harvest (nourishing). Use on Air and Fire.

Point: UB27

Plant-wight's Nature: Cleavers-wight is the archetypal merry shepherd lad, broad-faced and grinning, lazy and irreverent, pulling his sisters' braids mischievously. He's invasive, and likes to touch people, but all in good fun. If you can keep it in the same spirit of good fun, you can get away with a lot of similar behavior—slapping his hands away, etc.—and still keep his friendship. If you anger him, he'll simply ignore you. Since Cleavers is a long-term alterative, it's best to have a good relationship with him if you are going to be using him regularly. If you have trouble with him, ask Gerda to step in; she has clout with him, although he'll still try to weasel out of things.

Medicinal Charm: Cool And Clean

Regardless of the problem, Cleavers works by cooling things down and cleaning them out. It loses all its properties when dried, and heating it will do the same thing, so you either have to use it fresh, or make a tincture or cold water infusion with the fresh herb. To make a cold water infusion for any of the problems listed above, pick many handfuls of Cleavers in the spring, before it flowers. Chop the plant finely and mash it in a mortar until is is green paste and fibers, and then put it in a jar of cold water in a dark place overnight. Before leaving it to steep, say the following charm. In the morning, strain and drink. The infusion will keep for a couple of weeks in the fridge.

> *Hail Hedge-reeve, my tax of labor paid,*
> *Click and Clitheren clear and clean me,*
> *Catchweed, Scratweed, strain and drain me,*
> *Goosegrass run the rivers shy in shade.*

Clover

Botanical Name: *Trifolium pratens*

Folk Names: Red Clover, Honeystalks, Trefoil, Meadow Trefoil, Trifoil, Shamrocks

Anglo-Saxon Name: Clæfre

Old Norse Name: Clafre

Old High Germanic Name: Kle

Modern German Name: Klee

Modern Swedish Name: Klöver

Modern Danish Name: Kløver

Modern Norwegian Name: Rødkløver

Deity Association: Huldra

Height: 2'

Season: Perennial

History: Native to the entirety of Eurasia, from the Arctic Circle on down.

Medicinal Uses: Red Cloveris a nutritive, alterative tonic that carries estrogen and is drunk daily for breast, ovarian, and lymphatic cancer prevention and treatment. It is a blood thinner and is used for arthritis and arteriosclerosis. It is cooling and moist, and good for dry skin conditions; it acts on the lymph glands and is especially good for mumps. Red Clover is an anticoagulant, helpful for those with heart disease. A well-strained infusion is used as an eyewash for conjunctivitis and as a vaginal douche. The flower petals have been added to cough syrups. Red Clover is good for breaking up cysts;

although in large doses it can make them. While it does not cure cancer, it has been used to encyst cancerous tissue to keep it from spreading.

Household Uses: Good for planting around beehives.

Culinary Uses: The petals of White Clover were once dried and made into "fairy-bread".

Magical Uses: Much has been said about those carrying four-leaved Clovers being able to see faeries (or Huldrefolk), which means that one can see through their glamour. Clover was also used to determine whether the person you were speaking to was a witch or sorcerer. Even three-leaved Clovers were said to help with that. Four-leaved ones were used for divining one's future mate by putting it under the pillow and dreaming, and for consecrating tools made of copper. White Clover was used in spells for fidelity, and given as a sign of that intent. It is associated with the spring Equinox.

Shamanic Uses: Clover is much liked by Huldra, the handmaiden of flocks and herds, and making an offering to her of Clover blossoms will propitiate her to help your wealth and resources increase. It also has an affinity with the rune Fehu/Feoh, and can be laid out to form that rune, or a pouch of it can be marked with a rune talisman.

Affinity: Earth (cooling), River (moistening), Harvest (nourishing). Non-Storm alterative. Use for Air or Swamp.

Point: TH 17

Plant-wight's Nature: Master Clover is a herder-wight by nature. Millennia of association with domesticated animals have made him a special protector of livestock. He came to me as a lanky farmer in a green shepherd's smock, wearing a cloak of woven reeds as French shepherds have done for thousands of years. Wide-faced and wide-mouthed with twinkling green eyes and a shaggy mop of hair, Master Clover chewed on a straw and made comments about my sheep and goats. In a way, just as the Ancestral Mother and Father plants have been bound to help human beings, Master Clover is bound to aid cows, sheep, goats, pigs, and any other animals that humans have pressed into service over the last few millennia. This means that he will always take the side of an animal over than of a human, and of a domestic sheep over that of a wolf. "Someone needs to speak for them," he says. He seems to have no trouble with them being eaten by humans so long as they are treated well during their lives, but seeing livestock kept in inhumane circumstances saddens him. Master Clover is wise in the ways of the soil, and can tell a farmer a lot about his dirt, should he be asked.

Magical Charm: Huldrefolk's Luck

If your animals are sickly and your land is not as fertile as it could be, assuming that you're already doing what you can to alter those things, call on Huldra and the Huldrefolk, the maidens with cow's tails who look after these things. In the evening, as the sun is setting, place out a plate of food (especially sweet breads and butter) and a mug of milk, and lay eight Clover blossoms on the plate also. Say the following charm:

> Master Clæfre, call the cow-footed maidens,
> Honeystalks hie them hither to help us,
> Lady of Labor, lend me your ladies
> To aid this land and heal this homestead.

Then go into the house, and make sure that no member of the household leaves the house until dawn breaks, and no guest arrives until the next day. Repeat this charm for three days, again staying inside at night—leave the night to the Huldrefolk. Your land and herds should improve if you've managed to get their attention, but you should keep giving them food and milk periodically.

Coltsfoot

Botanical Name: *Tussilago farfara*

Folk Names: Hallfoot, Horsehoof, Horsefoot, Foalswort, Ass Foot, Bull's Foot, Coughwort, Pas d'ane, Sponnc, Son-Before-Father

Anglo-Saxon Name: Clite

Modern German Name: Huflattich, Brustlattich

Modern Swedish Name: Hästhov

Modern Danish Name: Følfod

Modern Norwegian Names: Hestehov, Leirfivel

Deity Association: Frey

Height: 12"

Season: Perennial

History: Coltsfoot is native to all of Europe, western and northern Asia, and northern Africa. It has been used as a sovereign cough remedy for thousands of years.

Medicinal Uses: The cough herb. Coltsfoot flowers reduce phlegm and bronchial inflammation, and help the system. Leaves are used in cough medicine, and applied to boils and abscesses, as they have high levels of zinc which is an anti-inflammatory. There are small amounts of toxins in Coltsfoot, but these seem to be destroyed by boiling. Coltsfoot breaks up phlegm so that it can be coughed or blown out, and is drunk in tea for sinus congestion.

Household Uses: Smoked for herbal tobacco. It is useful for asthma in this way.

Culinary Uses: Can be eaten young and tender in soups and stews.

Magical Uses: Protective charm for hoofed livestock.

Shamanic Uses: Much liked by Frey, this plant is associated with the rune Ehwazand can be used as a fast-travel charm. The leaves, when smoked, are said to cause visions. This plant has an affinity for the runes Ehwaz and Fehu—horses and cows.

Affinity: River (moistening), Earth (cooling), Air (astringent). Use on Swamp, Fire, Air.

Point: KD 26

Plant-wight's Nature: Coltsfoot-wight always comes shaggy and with hooves, but always upright and on two legs. Sometimes he looks like a shaggy mountain pony, sometimes as if he is half Highland cattle, sometimes half donkey. His face is an amalgam of humanoid and horse/cow/donkey. He does not speak in words, but can communicate in images and body language. If he likes you, he will puff and blow on you, or perhaps try to nuzzle you. It is important not to eat meat from cruelly-farmed hoofed livestock while using Coltsfoot medicinally—shell out for locally-grown organic meat whose treatment you can vouch for during that time.

Medicinal Charm: Lung Clearing

When the respiratory bugs have set in and you are coughing up nasty stuff, boil an ounce of Coltsfoot in a pint of water, add some Mint to steep, and drink. Repeat as needed. As you drink, say this charm:

> *Horsehoof, Foalswort, pearly print*
> *Of sacred stallion, blow my breath*
> *Like wind in wild mane, clear and clean,*
> *Son and Father I stand between.*

Comfrey

Botanical Name: *Symphytum officinale*
Folk Names: Consolde, Knitbone, Assear, Blackwort, Bruisewort, Knitback, Wallwort, Yalluc, Gall-Apple
Anglo-Saxon Name: Galloc
Modern German Name: Gemeiner Beinwell, Wallwurz
Modern Swedish Name: Vallört
Modern Danish Name: Kulsukker
Modern Norwegian Name: Valurt
Deity Association: Eir
Height: 4'
Season: Perennial

History: Various varieties of Comfrey are native to everywhere in continental Europe, and they have long been revered as healers of wounds. While the first references we have to Comfrey in northern countries is the medieval herbals, we can guess that it was used from far earlier times, especially as it is one of the plants that livestock eat greedily, and look for when they are ill and in pain.

Medicinal Uses: Comfrey is the great regenerator of bone and tissue. Take internally in tea and externally as a poultice for bruises, swelling, arthritis, and broken bones, as its compounds speed cell renewal. Pick the fresh leaves, macerate into a paste, and apply. The poultice can also be applied to skin cancer, where it has been shown to do a remarkable healing job. Comfrey is also useful for healing internal gastric wounds, such as ulcers; take one cup of Comfrey root tea daily. Dosage is one-half ounce of chopped root bits boiled in one quart of water; this makes four one-cup daily doses. Comfrey tincture can also be used both internally and externally. Comfrey has been known to help brain injury, in some cases.

Comfrey roots, when wetted, are gluey and gummy, and they were actually used as splints for torn ligaments and sprains in medieval times. (They were also used this way for broken bones, but in this case, due to the difficulty of setting bones correctly, we suggest that casting broken bones be done by a doctor.) To do this, split the roots lengthwise into long, flat strips, soak them for a couple of hours, spread them on wet muslin, and then lash the while thing vertically around the limb and let them congeal and set up.

(Note: Much has been said about the dangers of Comfrey because some laboratory rats died after being given concentrated extracts of specific alkaloids; however, to get this kind of amount and concentration from the unextracted root or leaf, you would have to drink 4 cups of Comfrey tea a day for 140 years, or eat 20 bushels of Comfrey a day for a month ... or eat ridiculous amounts of comercially-made Comfrey extract. Four human beings have actually developed severe liver damage from long-term heavy Comfrey abuse; these were people who popped handfuls of commercially extracted Comfrey-pepsin tablets every day. There are no reports of anyone developing liver disease by ingesting the leaves or root via infusion or poultices, and all studies of livestock who eat large amounts of Comfrey note that they have no deleterious effects, and indeed are better for it. In other words, in order to create a toxic form and amount of Comfrey, you need the aid of modern technology. So I have no qualms about prescribing Comfrey, as long as you work with the actual plant matter and are reasonable about dosage. A cup of tea a day is a perfectly safe dosage, and poultices can be used with complete impunity. All I hear right and left is that herbalists shouldn't tell people to use Comfrey because they might get sued. Well, I'm not a commercial herbalist, I'm a shaman, and no one would ever be so stupid as to sue me, especially as I have no money worth speaking of. So I'll say it.

One warning that I have heard about overuse of Comfrey that I actually believe is that in particularly susceptible people, it can cause an overgrowth of bone or tissue after long use—fixing the problem and then going too far, as it were. Working directly with the greenwight and making your need clear can help with this. Actually, perhaps this is a good time to reiterate a much-repeated warning, especially with regard to the above-mentioned Comfrey fracas: If you offend the greenwight by misusing a plant—and I think that much of the commercial *"herbal" industry does just that—then you court disasters. It's not the plant, it's the Mind behind it. Remember that.)*

Household Uses: Extremely good fodder crop for animals. Soaked in water for a month, it makes an excellent fertilizer for potatoes and tomatoes. Boil fresh leaves for a golden-brown dye.

Magical Uses: Leaves are used in one's shoes as a travel charm and to make sure one's traveling belongings do not get stolen. They are also used as a charm for fertility in animals. Comfrey baths were thought to restore virginity; such a bath could be used by someone working towards sexual healing of rape or abuse.

Shamanic Uses: Another plant that is beloved of Eir the healer, Comfrey can be used to invoke her aid in healing wounds.

Affinity: River (moistening), Air (astringent), Earth (nourishing). As a mucilaginous astringent, Comfrey works on the combined River/Air problems of injuries.

Point: UB 11

Plant-wight's Nature: Father Comfrey is an immensely powerful healer. The Comfrey-wight is nurturing, but in a more paternal than maternal way. He loves animals and will usually willingly aid pets and livestock. He has an earthy, practical nature, but he can be immensely comforting in the same way. One is reminded of the loving father who says, "It's all right. We can fix that," and proceeds to do so with kindness and competence.

Medicinal Charm: Knitbone Oil

This is an oil to use externally. Pick clean dry Comfrey leaves and chop them coarsely into pieces. Pack them as tightly as possible into a jar of dark glass cleaned and sterilized with hot water. Apply a screw-top lid, and label this with a bind rune of Eir's name—Eihwaz Raido. Store this in a dark place for two years, never opening it. Take it out every three months and hold it in your hands, and say the following charm:

> Galloc, give mending to my breaks,
> Comfrey, come and cure my aches,
> Knitbone, to bruises be a balm,
> Sweet Eir, stitch me strong and sound.

After two years of this, open the jar. You will have a viscous amber liquid with some sediment. Decant the "oil" into a smaller container and add a drop of essential oil if the smell is not pleasant. Use on skin irritations, eczema, bruises, sprains, arthritis, broken bones, and larger wounds once they have closed over. Say the charm again as you apply the oil. If you want to make it into a salve, you can melt beeswax into it in a 1:4 ratio of beeswax to oil, perhaps adding Plantain oil and Vitamin E oil as well.

Medicinal Charm: Comfrey Poultice

For inflammations, bruises, sprains, or other problems of skin, bone, or muscle, make a strong infusion of Comfrey leaves. If there is an infected inflammation, mix with equal parts Burdock leaves; the two work well together. Strain out the green matter and sit with a poultice for at least half an hour, then pour off a cup of the tea and drink it. The rest of the infusion should go into a cool bath in which you will sit later in the day. While in the bath, and/or waiting with the poultice, say the following charm:

> Galloc, gift of earth's bedrock,
> Eir's Blessing, Fever flee,
> First forefinger of the Lady's Leike,
> Bone-Builder, flesh strengthen,
> Strong as Bruisewort, rooted deep.

Cowslip and Primrose

Botanical Names: *Primula veris* (Cowslip) and *Primula vulgaris* (Primrose)

Folk Names: *Cowslip:* Arthritica, Artetyke, Buckles, Cuy, Drelip, Fairy Cup, Frauenchlussel, Herb Peter, Key Flower, Key of Heaven, Lady's Key, Lippe, Paigle, Paralysio, Password, Peggle, Plumrocks. *Primrose:* Butter Rose, English Cowslip, Spring Primula

Anglo-Saxon Name: Cuslyppe, for both

Modern German Names: Echte Schlüsselblume, Frühlings-Schlüsselblume, Arznei-Schlüsselblume, Himmelschlüssel (*Cowslip*), Erd-Primel, Stengellose Primel, Garten-Kissen-Primel (*Primrose*)

Modern Swedish Names: Stor Gullviva, Gökblomma, Himmelsnycklar, Jungfru Marie Nycklar, Oxlägg, Sankt Pers Nycklar

Modern Danish Names: Kodriver

Modern Norwegian Names: Marianøkleblom, Kusymre

Deity Association: Freya

Height: 6-12"

Season: Perennial

History: Cowslip is a marsh plant, native to wetlands all over Europe, including England. Primrose is closely related to Cowslip, and many ancient herbalists considered them to be variations on the same plant. The largest difference is that Primrose is sometimes found in fields, where Cowslip is very much a waterside and wetlands plant.

Medicinal Uses: Cowslip petals are mildly sedative and antihistamine, absorb free radicals, and reduce inflammation. A tea soothes nervous tension headaches, provides a wash for acne and sunburn, and is drunk for chronic bronchitis. The essential oil is added to baths for insomnia and relaxation. The roots are expectorant, helping to expel phlegm, and contain aspirinlike compounds. Soak a poultice in strong root decoction and apply for arthritis. Primrose shares all the same qualities of Cowslip, in slightly less strength, and can be used in the same ways. The infusion is a good cough and headache remedy and mild sedative. Both have been used to treat epilepsy, vertigo, and palsies, and for bladder pains.

Household Uses: A wash of Cowslip water will improve the complexion, and the dried flowers and roots of both are used for potpourri. Cowslip wine is an old country favorite.

Culinary Uses: Cowslip is traditionally used in jam, wine, and pickles. Primrose flowers are edible and can be put into salads, made into jam, crystallized, or used in an ancient Roman dessert of rice, almonds, honey, Saffron and ground Primrose petals.

Magical Uses: Cowslip preserves youth and beauty, discourages visitors when placed beneath the front porch, and can be used as a dowsing sprig to find hidden treasure. Primrose protects the garden from adversity, attracts faeries, attracts love and lust, cures madness, and when sewn into children's pillows, makes them loyal to their parents. Supposedly, if they are sprinkled across the doorstep or placed in a bunch at the door, no magic-worker with evil intent can pass them.

Shamanic Uses: Is sacred to Freya, and can be used to lead you to her hall, Sessrumnir. It is said to be able to open the door to her hall, thus the names "Lady's Key" and "Password". Can be used for Vanir magic in general.

Affinity: Stone (sedative), Mountain (relaxant), Earth (cooling), Air (astringent). Use for Fire and Storm conditions.

Points: PC 8 (Cowslip), PC 7 (Primrose)

Plant-wight's Nature: I list these two together because I met them together, as a pair of sisters holding hands. It was actually the Maythen Children who introduced me to them, another pair of golden-haired siblings. They were clearly related, but just as clearly opposites. Primrose was neat and modest, her dress falling in buttercup folds and a wreath of flowers on her smooth blond braids. Cowslip, on the other hand, was a wild thing dressed in disheveled bits of cloth tied together, random wildflowers sticking out of her tangled mane. She didn't speak; Primrose did the talking for both of them while she beamed at me. The two of them, as a pair, work the mysteries between wild and domesticated—plants, animals, and passions.

Medicinal Charm: Primula Tea

While both the leaves and flowers of Cowslip and Primrose are medicinally useful, herb-wives used to use only the flowers because they were sweet and made a tastier tea, while the leaves were more bitter. If you use the leaves as well, add more honey. To make the tea, pour a pint of boiling water over a cup of flowers and let steep until drinkable. Add a tablespoon of honey, and as you stir it in, say:

> Fairy Cup, Key of Heaven,
> Freya's Password, find me peace,
> Nerve be calm and nothing bother,
> Lady's Buckles, bring me ease.

Crabapple

Botanical Name: *Pyrus malus*

Folk Names: Crab, Sour Apple

Anglo-Saxon Name: Wergulu, Wudusuræppel ("Wood Sour Apple"), Æppel (Apple, in general)

Old Norse Names: Apaldr (apple-tree), Epli (apple or tree-fruit in general)

Old High Germanic Name: Apful

Modern German Name: Apfel

Modern Swedish Name: Apel

Modern Danish Name: Æble

Modern Norwegian Name: Eple

World Association: Plant of Vanaheim. All cultivated Apples are dedicated to Iduna.

Height: To 30'

Season: Perennial tree

History: The Apple, in general, is a tree of northern zones, as it will not set friut properly unless the winter temperatures fall below a certain level of coldness. The Crabapple, or Wild Apple, is likely the earliest form of the Apple, and is found even further north, being even hardier. However, it may not have been found in the British Isles until it was brought by the Romans.

Medicinal Uses: The Crabapple, and Apples of any kind, are cooling and moistening and good for hot, dry conditions. The acidic nature revives and cleanses sluggish systems, especially in the morning. It is a diuretic for urinary tract problems, an antiseptic, and a tonic that is a rich source of various vitamins, trace elements, amino acids and flavonoids. Malic acid is the principal acid of the fruit, hence its Latin name. Apples neutralize greasy fats and as such are often eaten with them. During digestion, the acid fruit gives off alkaline substances; this is especially true for Apple cider vinegar. It is useful in the management of immunomediated diseases, and contains an antifungal constituent. It reduces skin inflammationand helps in removing dead skin fragments. The bark of the Crabapple tree has been used to reduce severe fever and chills in malaria and flus. However, the Crabapple's most-used remedy is ocular: fresh slices have been used for centuries as a compress on sore eyes, and it is said to actually improve vision over a period of time. Crabapple does seem to have an affinity with the eyes.

Household Uses: Used for its pectin, to set jams and jellies. Used to flavor mead, and make melomel.

Culinary Uses: Crabapples are generally made into jams with a large amount of sweetener, whereas the cultivated Apple has hundreds of culinary uses.

Magical Uses: Used for anything an Apple can be used for, which is tons of things.

Shamanic Uses: This is the plant associated with Vanaheim, the land of the Vanir. It can be used for any fertility charm, whether for people, animals, or the fields, as it carries all the fertility of Vanaheim behind it. It is also a powerful healer, and rubbing Crabapple slices on an afflicted body and then burying them in the Earth is a useful healing technique, as the clean, sharp energy of the Crabapple absorbs disease energy. It can also be charged with healing energy and eaten. Its wholesomeness makes it an inappropriate carrier for seek-and-destroy spells; use Crabapple as a follow-up after using other plants in this way, in order to strengthen the body's defenses.

Affinity: Earth (cooling), Air (astringent). Use on Fire conditions.

Point: UB 1

Plant-wight's Nature: This is the story that the Apple-Maiden told me.

The very first Apple in the Nine Worlds was the Crabapple, and it grew in Vanaheim, alongside many other fruits that the Vanir were breeding and cultivating. Few fruits grew in Asgard at this time, as the climate and land did not suit them, and few had the skill and talent to speak to greenwights as the Vanir did. Yet one day, not long after the war had come to an end and the hostages were exchanged, a former Valkyrie came ragged and hungry into Vanaheim, and asked for sanctuary on her way through to Asgard.

While the Vanir had no love, at this time, for Asgard or anyone who had come of those folk, the woman's story was piteous enough that they allowed her to stay for a few nights. She had been captured and imprisoned by Ivaldi, the Emperor of the Duergar, and been forced to bear children to him until he finally tired of her. She had only just been released, and held her two small daughters by the hand, equally tired and hungry. Her eyes were reddened from weeping; her sons had chosen to stay behind with their father. The hearts of the Vanir were moved to pity and they bade the Asa-woman and her daughters to rest and eat, although Nerthus commanded them to take nothing of Vanaheim with them to Asgard. Enough of Vanaheim's riches, she said, had gone to the White Realm already; no more would be given to them for free.

Yet while they waited on the shore, days later, for the ship of Njord's fleet that would take them to Asgard, the elder daughter of the Valkyrie broke an Apple-laden branch from a Crabapple tree and hid it under her clothing, and brought it with her across the ocean. She was a maiden so young that her breasts had only started to grow, and as she had spent her life in a cave, her marveling at the beauty of the red fruits, and her subsequent theft, might be sympathized with if not excused.

Once in Asgard she planted the seeds and sang to them, and so charmed the Apple-Maiden that she came forth and spoke to the young half-breed girl. Aye, the Apple-Maiden, with her round face and hair of scarlet and gold, with her skin as white as blossom, with the wafting of scent about her, with a smile so sweet that only the hardest of hearts would not fall in love. The Apple-Maiden, dressed in a gown of Apple-green and holding many secrets within her, who under her fair exterior is friend to the Norns, who understands Fate, who punishes with all the harshness of La Belle Dame Sans Merci, who is one of the oldest and most sacred of the greenwights. "If you will take it on yourself to devote your life to me, I will give you Apples such as no one has ever seen," the Apple-Maiden said, and the young girl agreed.

Thus the trees that sprouted were not Crabapples at all, but great golden creatures, and the Apple-Maiden taught the young girl how to enchant them in such a way that they would bring temporary immortality, health, and radiance to all who ate them. The girl begged that these Apples would grow only in her garden, and that for their lack of generosity to her family the Vanir should never have their secret, and nor should anyone else, and the Apple-Maiden granted this wish. So it is that the Apples grown in Vanaheim, for all their fineness and sweetness and sharpness and healing ability, are

never the great golden cultivated Apples that keep the Aesir immortal. And so it is that Iduna came to be the keeper of the Apples of immortality, and the only one in the Nine Worlds to know that secret. Or so the Apple-Maiden told me, with beauty and danger in her green-gold eyes.

Magical Charm: Fertility

To grant fertility to someone who is lacking in it, cut a Crabapple horizontally so that it shows the five-pointed star of seeds. Then take that half and rub it over them—on the belly if it is a woman, on the scrotum for a man—and say the following charm:

> I am a fertile field of the Green World,
> I am a seed sown in living loam,
> I am a doorway of the Apple-Maiden.

The Crabapple should be eaten afterwards. If she so chooses, the Apple-Maiden will grant you fertility and living children.

Cumin

Botanical Name: *Cuminum cyminum*
Folk Names: Cumino, Cumino Aigro, Jeera
Anglo-Saxon Names: Cymen, Suþerne Rind ("Southern Bark")
Old High Germanic Name: Kumil
Modern German Names: Kreuzkümmel, Mutterkümmel
Modern Swedish Name: Spiskummin
Modern Danish Name: Spidskommen
Modern Norwegian Name: Spisskummen
Deity Association: Heimdall
Height: 12"
Season: Annual
History: Cumin originated in the Near East and India, was highly valued by the Greeks and Romans, and was spread to the Germanic people during the Roman occupation. It is a delicate plant, difficult to grow in colder climates, so as it was much in demand during Roman and post-Roman times, Cumin seed was largely imported and a luxury item. It could sometimes be grown in carefully sheltered Northern gardens, but never in much quantity, so it is arguable whether it ought to considered a Northern Tradition herb ... but the Scandinavians associated it with Heimdall and included it in high-class grave goods, perhaps as a gift for the guardian of Asgard.

Medicinal Uses: Seeds aid digestion and are used to treat flatulence, colic, and diarrhea, and are a blood-purifier. A mixture of sea-salt and Cumin is an old-fashioned remedy for any kind of disease (and disease prevention) in poultry—chickens, ducks, geese and especially pigeons—and it is given as a blood-purifying remedy to other livestock. It is good for humans in the same way; generally only the strong taste prevents people from using it.

Household Uses: Cumin is made into warming liqueurs, such as *Kummel*. The essential oil is used in perfumes to enhance floral tones. It is an excellent massage oil for cellulite.

Culinary Uses: Use the chopped stems and seeds in spicy dishes, breads, cookies, curry paste, pickling mixtures, and yogurt.

Magical Uses: Cumin is put into bread to keep wood spirits from stealing it, which shows it as one of the herbs used against faery magic. It is a potent anti-theft spell; sprinkling Cumin on something or hiding a pouch of it inside the item will deter thieves. It is carried at weddings to ensure fidelity—another sort of theft—and carried in general to keep your peace of mind from being stolen. It has also been used in lust potions, mixed with wine and coriander and other love herbs, again for fidelity.

Shamanic Uses: One of the herbs found in the Oseberg burial, Cumin is much liked by Heimdall the guardian of Asgard. Use it to invoke his blessing on something that must not be touched or tampered with.

Affinity: Fire (stimulant), Earth (relaxant), Harvest (nourishing). Use for Earth.

Point: SP 17

Plant-wight's Nature: Cumin is a lover, not a fighter. Cumin has a strongly masculine nature, but it is highly sensuous, in a rather aggressive way. Cumin's energy is hot-blooded and enthusiastic, highly physical, and lusty. Work with this plant for sexual potions and spells. I could especially recommend Cumin to long-term partners who want to put spice back into their sexual relationship.

Medicinal Charm: Warming The Belly

Mix the following dry ingredients together: 1 part sea salt, 2 parts Fennel seeds, 2 parts Dill seeds, and 4 parts Cumin seeds. Grind to powder in a mortar, add to any savory bread recipe, and bake. As you knead the dough, say the following charm:

> *Cymen, cymen, keep warm the belly,*
> *Gift of the golden Gate-Guardian,*
> *No wind, no wound, naught but unfettered flow.*

Slice the fresh bread and keep it in the freezer; defrost and eat a warmed slice to help with colic, flatulence, and other stomach problems.

Daisy

Botanical Name: *Bellis perennis*
Folk Names: Bairnwort, Bruisewort, Day's Eye, Llygady Dydd, Maudlinwort, Moon of the Day, Goldens, Gowan, Dun Daisy, Poverty Weed, Priest's Collar, Moon Penny, Drummer Daisy
Anglo-Saxon Name: Dæges Ege ("Day's Eye")
Modern German Name: Gänseblümchen
Modern Swedish Names: Prästkrage, Kragblomma
Modern Danish Name: Tusindfryd
Modern Norwegian Name: Tusenfryd
Deity Association: Freya and Baldur
Height: 6"
Season: Perennial
History: The ubiquitous Daisy has been a meadow weed all over Europe and Central Asia for millenia. It is so common that almost no one thinks to notice it. The folk name "Drummer Daisy" supposedly comes from *Baldurs draumar*, the Norse name for the story of Baldur's death.
Medicinal Uses: Drink in tea for enteritis, diarrhea, coughs and colds. Crushed fresh leaves can be added to a poultice to heal wounds and sprains. May slow the growth of breast tumors. Care should be taken, however; the Daisy can provoke allergies.
Household Uses: An infusion can be added to a spring tonic bath to revive dull skinGood nectar plant for bees and butterflies. Hung in bunches around the house, it has been used to drive out fleas.
Culinary Uses: Young leaves and petals are edible in salad.
Magical Uses: When worn, helps in flirting. Brings love. Used in love divination. Protects a garden from damage via thunderstorms.
Shamanic Uses: Sacred to Freya, it can be used for protection during battle. Its protection extends especially to warriors who are women or nonheterosexuals, as these come under Freya's dominion rather than Odin's. It is secondarily sacred to Baldur and grows at Breidablik, his future domain.
Affinity: Earth (relaxant), River (moistening). Use on Storm and Fire conditions.
Point: ST 16
Plant-wight's Nature: For all that Daisies are said to be a symbol of innocence, this is a tough little plant. Daisy-wight's energy is like a rambunctious child, quick to laugh, quick to fight, and quick to dig in stubbornly when it doesn't get its way. Daisy finds it hilarious when it makes you sneeze; that's an example of its nature.
Magical Charm: Spring Daisy Bath

As soon as the Daisy blooms, assuming that you are not allergic to it, pick the flower heads and cast them into a bath of hot water. Then soak yourself in it, saying the following charm:

> *Eye of the Day, may my days and dreams lengthen*
> *Like the Sun in the sky, O merry moon-money,*
> *May my sleep soon be sound like bonny Baldur's Brow,*
> *May my fortune be fair like the Lady of Love,*
> *The Warrior Wench whose giving is golden.*

Dandelion

Botanical Name: *Taraxacum officinale*
Folk Names: Priest's Crown, Swine's Snout, Piss-The-Bed, Fairy Clock, Blowball, Cankerwort, Lion's Tooth, Wet-The-Bed, Puffball
Anglo-Saxon Name: Ægwyrt ("Egg Plant")

Old Norse Name: Fífill

Modern German Names: Wiesen-Löwenzahn, Gemeiner Löwenzahn

Modern Swedish Names: Maskros, Gubbaros, Gulgubbe, Gullborste, Gålbussen, Smörblomma, Stadeblomma, Svinaart, Svinört, Svinros

Modern Danish Name: Mælkebøtte

Modern Norwegian Name: Vanlig Løvetann

Deity Association: Sunna

Height: 6"

Season: Perennial

History: The Dandelion is common and indeed ineradicable all over the northern hemisphere. Its modern name comes from the French words meaning "tooth of the lion". Wherever Sunna shines, there the Dandelion shines back. It is another plant that wasn't thought much of by the makers of herbals—they don't bother to mention it until the 15th century, when they gave it its fancy French name, but it was a useful weed to the common folk and still is. I remember laughing when I saw a list of medicinal herbs that the government was thinking of controlling, and one of them was Dandelion—there's no way to control that one, I thought. Not all the "lawn care" poison in the world can do it.

Medicinal Uses: A powerful diuretic, Dandelion leaves are good for UTIs and water retention, as they don't deplete natural potassium levels like chemical diuretics; they are also a gentle treatment for gout, flushing uric acid. The root is a blood purifier, and one of the best liver and gallbladder herbs around, used for jaundice and gallstones. (The Shirley Temple of the green world, Dandelion plays well with many other liver plants, including grumpy Burdock, saturnine Yellow Dock and trickster Celandine; they all like her and she can pull together a liver herbal combination.) Dandelion root is good for infections that have gone into the bones, such as long-term sinus and tooth infections. If the infection has demineralized the bone, Dandelion can remineralize it (as can Oak). It is quite safe to use for a very long time; the one caveat for Dandelion is that it is very slow-acting and prefers to make changes over a period of many months rather than days or weeks. Dandelion can do amazing things given time; be patient and encourage your clients to do likewise.

Household Uses: The flowers are made into wine, or used to flavor beer and the roots yield a magenta dye.

Culinary Uses: The buds are pickled, and the young leaves are eaten in salads.

Magical Uses: The seedheads of Dandelions, blown at the wind, can carry messages to absent loved ones, or bring the winds. The long, sturdy roots of Dandelions were said to go all the way to the underworld, and were worn dried in chunks on a string as a spell to thwart Death.

Shamanic Uses: Dandelions are sacred to Sunna, and can be used as offerings to her. The root, ground and made into a tea, is said to draw spirits with its steam. Drinking it can aid in taking the spirits into you. Supposedly they will stay until you piss, which considering the effect of Dandelion, won't be long.

Affinity: Storm (bitter alterative), River (moistening), Harvest (nourishing). Use on Air and Swamp.

Point: UB 19

Plant-wight's Nature: Despite ragtop appearance, the Dandelion is brave and tough. She is a bit of a tomboy, marching into parts unknown, waving her golden flag about. She can pretend to be fierce, but it's just that—a pretense. Mostly she is resilient, pushy, and somewhat mischievous, the best friend of Daisy. She can appear to be anywhere from childhood to adolescence, but there is a sturdy boyish-girl innocence to her. She will sense right away if you aren't the courageous sort, and may try to drag you into difficult circumstances in order to make you braver. (The brave, of course, will be able to stand up to her more or less easily.)

Medicinal Charm: Spring Cleansing

When the Dandelion leaves have sprung forth, but before they get the bud in the center that heralds the flower stalks, pick them and make a strong tea of them, adding a little local honey in the process. Ideally, you should brew up enough for a week's worth of cups of tea. Stand outside in the spring air, breathe it in, and say the following charm over the tea as you drink it:

> Sunna's Spirit, I stand in the morning of the year,
> Yearning for cleansing in the cool of the spring,
> Fifill-Child, Fairy Clock, cleanse my body,
> My mind shall follow in the sun's dance.

Repeat this for seven days, reheating the tea or drinking it cold as desired.

Magical Charm: Sun and Moon

This is one of the oddest charms in the book, because it was told to me straight out by Dandelion-wight about a friend who was suffering from bipolar disorder. Dandelion told me that she cures bipolar disorder, and I got a strong image of this two-phase plant ... first bright, solar, enthusiastic, even overexuberant in the way that she springs up ... then becoming soft, white, lunar, and slowly losing all her petals passively on the wind until she withers and wilts. The cure, she said, would take a full year—one turn of Sunna—and during that time they would have to take her into their body every day in some way. (Capsules are a good thing here.) Ideally, they should start in the spring when the Dandelions erupt, but any time will do. When they are feeling manic, they should say, "Lion's Tooth, I fly too high, bring me down." When they are feeling depressed, they should say, "Blowball, I am blown, bear me back up." (Writing the two rhymes on opposite sides of a card drawn with a sun and moon that can be hung on a string and turned back and forth at will might be good, especially if it is hung in a commonly-seen place like the toilet or computer or refrigerator.) If the Dandelion-wight takes pity on them, she will heal them in a year's time.

Dill

Botanical name: *Anethum graveolens*
Folk Names: Dylle, Tille, Dulla, Anete, Aneto
Anglo-Saxon Names: Dyle, Dile
Old Norse Name: Dilla
Old High Germanic Name: Dill
Modern German Name: Dill
Modern Swedish Name: Dill
Modern Danish Name: Dild
Modern Norwegian Name: Dill
Deity Association: Hlin
Height: To 2'
Season: Annual
History: Dill is native to the Mediterranean area and to southern Russia; it spread to Germany in ancient times, to Scandinavia in the Viking era through settlements in Russia, and to England in the early Middle Ages.
Medicinal Uses: Dill seed or tea helps any kind of stomach disturbance, and promotes milk production in nursing mothers.
Household Uses: Seed decoction gives a nail-strengthening hand soak.
Culinary Uses: Seeds are put into herb vinegars, pickles, potato salad, bread, and many other dishes; weed is good in almost any savory dish whether fish, meat, or vegetable. Dill was traditionally combined with Fennel for many baked dishes.
Magical Uses: Stuffed in pillows for sleep, especially for children—the word "dill" is cognate to "dull", or sleepy. Dill is one of the traditional herbs gathered on the eve of the summer Solstice in England,

although it may be a bit early for it in more northerly climes. It is hung in bunches to bless a home, and put into cooking for peace in the house.

Shamanic Uses: Dill seeds, tossed onto burning coals and the smoke blown around, calm and pacify spirits that are agitated and angry. It won't stop homicidal ones who are determined to kill you, but it can make the general atmosphere less tense and adversarial.

Affinity: Fire (stimulant), Mountain (relaxant). Use on Storm and Earth conditions.

Point: SP 14

Plant-wight's Nature: There is a deep sorrow in Mother Dill that she will not speak of to anyone. She is quiet and calmly nurturing; she will rock the child to sleep, soothe the fevered brow, and silently do the healing and nursing that is required, but she never smiles. There is something of bereavement about her, and she understands loss and mourning; her way of dealing with it is to be a healer and an aid to others. She is the wounded healer whose own wound cannot be cured, but who gives of herself anyway, making a monument to her loss. Mother Dill sings all the time that she is not a silent, gliding robed figure; her voice is a crooning lullaby that soothes all who hear it.

Medicinal Charm: Mourning Belly

Sometimes when great loss comes to a person, the shock of grieving for many days reverberates through their body, and some of their systems stop working for a time. The stomach is one of the most vulnerable of these; grieving people will often have indigestion or simply feel the food settle dully without digesting, and the ensuing lack of nutrition over many days exacerbates depression. Even when someone is in the throes of terrible grief over some loss, they need to keep their body going and nourished. Part of this can be helped by support people making sure that easy food appears in front of them at regular intervals, and that they are encouraged to eat. Mother Dill can help with the internal part. She understands mourning, and will not try to interfere with the process going on above, which must take the time that it needs to pass on. She will simply help keep the body going as best she can in the meantime, because getting through grief requires a great deal of strength. So make the mourning one a half-cup of Dill (seed and/or weed) tea each day before the main meal, and see that they drink it. There is no charm of great words for this, but as it steeps you can croon her name—"Dilla, Dilla, Dilla..."—in order to bring her spirit into the cup.

Dittany

Botanical name: *Dictamnus albus*

Folk names: Burning Bush, Gas Plant, Hindhealth, White Dittany, Fraxinella

Anglo-Saxon Name: Hindhæleða, Hind Heoloða

Modern German Names: Diptam, Brennender Busch

Modern Swedish Name: Diptam

Modern Danish Name: Diptam

Modern Norwegian Name: Askrot

Deity Association: Surt

Height: 30"

Season: Perennial

History: White Dittany is not to be confused with Dittany of Crete, its southern and more tender relative. Both have similar uses, but White Dittany is not as ornamental, and Crete Dittany lacks the explosive nature. Both types were known to the ancient Mediterranean peoples, and White Dittany seems to have come north with the Romans.

Medicinal Uses: The leaves and flowering tops can be brewed into a digestive and nerve-tonic tea, and is a diuretic used for UTIs. The root is also a diuretic and causes the uterus to contract, but is mildly toxic and must be used with care. It is also a nerve-tonic, and has been used to sedate epileptics, combined with equal parts of Peppermint, and administered in a very small amount—one or two tincture drops per day. The Anglo-Saxon name comes from the myth that a deer (or in some stories a wild goat), when shot and then lost, would eat Dittany to put out the arrow and heal itself.

Culinary Uses: Dittany is bitter and considered inedible, but was one of the original ingredients in Absinthe, probably for its nerve-sedating value. It is associated with Samhain, and used in incenses to contact ancestors on that night.

Magical Uses: Dittany incense supposedly helps spirits to manifest in the smoke.

Shamanic Uses: All parts of the Dittany plant are covered with lemon-scented glands which exude sufficient vapor to ignite in hot weather; thus its folk names. Setting a live Dittany plant afire is a strong protection spell to drive off magical attacks, but it sacrifices the plant, and one must first gain permission from Grandmother Dittany. As a plant with Muspellheim energy, Dittany is beloved of Surt, and can be used in incenses to honor him. Dittany is also added to general incenses used for faring forth.

Affinity: Fire (stimulant), Storm (bitter alterative), Mountain (relaxant). Use for Earth, Swamp, and Storm conditions.

Point: LI 6

Plant-wight's Nature: Grandmother Dittany is a witchy woman dressed in skins and bone beads, carrying a torch. She speaks in a moaning sing-song that seems made for summoning spirits, dances in circles, and glows in the dark. She informed me that she was a doorkeeper, able to open the doors between worlds and then tightly close them again. Grandmother Dittany is temperamental, though, with a quick temper that might flare at the slightest insult, and then she will thrust her torch in your face and stun you, possibly knocking you out for a time. Handle her carefully and with great respect. She can also summon spirits into and out of someone's body, another weapon in her arsenal which could also be used to heal.

Magical Charm: Ancestor Night

On All Hallows' Eve, should you wish to speak to your ancestors—perhaps about any genetic diseases that you may have inherited—burn incense of White Dittany, put out an offering of food and drink, and ask the ancestors to tell you about your DNA. (This also works well for adopted folks who want more information.) Speak this charm as the Dittany burns:

> *Fire-Lord's Flower, light this dark night,*
> *And send thy spark to the Nether Realms,*
> *Where those who wove their lives that I*
> *Might live and walk, dream deep and sweet*
> *If they do not yet live again. Hail them, Hindhealer,*
> *I would have them map the red road for me,*

And answer my pleas, in the name of the blood bond
We share. Kin to kin, I call!

Dock

Botanical name: *Rumex crispus*
Folk names: Docce, Yellow Dock, Curled Dock, Curly Dock
Anglo-Saxon Name: Docce,
Middle Germanic Name: Tocke
Modern German Name: Krauser Ampfer
Modern Swedish Names: Krusskräppa, Krussyra, Svinsyra, Vanlig Krusskräppa
Modern Danish Name: Skræppe
Modern Norwegian Name: Krushøymol
Deity Association: Nerthus
Height: 2-3'
Season: Perennial
History: As a gentle alterative, the lowly Dock has been used for centuries on both sides of the Atlantic—being native to four continents—to help the body become more efficient over time in detoxifying itself and making bile. Today it is targeted as a noxious weed, along with its friend Burdock, which is really too bad.
Medicinal Uses: The roots stimulate liver bile, clear toxins, and are used for chronic skin disorders. Dock is one of the best liver plants around, ideally to be used in combination with Milk Thistle, Burdock, and Dandelion. It has also been used for cancer patients in order to keep their bodies eliminating toxins while they fight the disease. Dock dries up diarrhea and bloody fluxes, and is especially good when the stools are soft but difficult to expel. It treats colitis and removes excess acid from the stomach—in general, it clears heat from the digestive tract. Dock body washes were recommended for diabetics before the age of insulin. It also has the ability to extract iron from the soil, and thus become an iron tonic; old-time herbalists sprinkled iron filings into the soil around a Dock plant that they had earmarked for such a tonic. A vinegar tincture made from iron-enriched Yellow Dock is used for iron-deficiency anemia. (Use vinegar rather than alcohol for its mineral-extracting ability.) The leaves soothe Nettle stings, and the root, ground and boiled in vinegar and mixed with lard, has been used to soothe Poison Ivy.
Household Uses: The root yields a yellow dye when used alone, and has enough tannin to be useful in tanning leather. Mordanted with iron, it yields a rich dark brown dye. The young, fresh seeds mordanted with alum yield colors from amber to oxblood. The ground seeds are used in homemade toothpastes as an astringent, especially good for bleeding gums and tooth rot.
Culinary Uses: The ground seeds can be made into cakes or gruel. The iron-rich leaves can be cooked in one change of water and eaten.
Magical Uses: Seeds are used in money spells.
Shamanic Uses: Sprinkle Dock seed on or around the area before doing a reading about someone's financial situation. Feed them some of it as part of a money spell.
Affinity: Storm (bitter alterative), Earth (cooling), Stone (sedative), Air (astringent). Use for Swamp, River, and Fire conditions.
Point: UB 48
Plant-wight's Nature: Dock is tall, lanky, laconic, and saturnine. He comes across as a lean, almost dried-up, wrinkled stick of an old farmer who doesn't talk much, but is full of useful knowledge. Dock praises little and tends to heap on the sarcasm, or at least the tight-lipped frowns, but he will help as long as you are committed to working on your health. This is his biggest beef: you have to be willing

to put work into making yourself healthy. If you come to him with the desire for a quick fix, he will say something cutting and run you off. If you are willing to do your part, he is reliable and helpful, although never terribly friendly or outgoing.

Medicinal Charm: Nettle-Sting-Out

This traditional charm has come down to us through the centuries, and hardly needs any alteration in its simplicity. Boil some Dock roots in vinegar until they are soft, and make a mash of the root and enough of the vinegar to keep it soft. (The vinegar that is poured off is medicinal; jar it up and use it fairly soon.) Then mix with some lard to make it into a smooth salve. Put it through the blender if it is too lumpy for your taste. Keep refrigerated, and when you get hit with the Nettle-soldiers of Muspellheim, smear some of the salve on the burn, and say: "Nettle out, Dock in, Dock take the Nettle sting." This can be used for Poison Ivy as well.

Dyer's Greenweed

Botanical Name: *Genista tinctoria*
Folk Names: Dyer's Broom, Woadwaxen, Woodwaxen, Woodwax, Dyer's Weed
Anglo-Saxon Names: Wuduweaxe ("Wood-sinew"), Wede-wixin, Woud-wix
Modern German Name: Färber-Ginster
Modern Swedish Name: Färgginst
Modern Danish Names: Gulvisse, Farvevisse, Farvetrae
Modern Norwegian Name: Fargeginst
Deity Association: Holda
Height: 3-6'
Season: Perennial
History: A relative of Broom, native to northern Europe and also much loved by Holda, Woodwaxen was used both as a dye plant and a medicinal plant, although its actions are somewhat harsher than its cousin Broom. Along with Madder and Woad, it was found at the archaeological digs at Danish York.
Medicinal Uses: Dyer's Greenweed is a diuretic used for dropsy, ascites, and rheumatism, and in large doses it can be an emetic. It has a mild action on the heart.
Household Uses: The flowering tops are used as a yellow-green dye, and -dyed cloth is soaked in it in order to make a good strong green.
Magical Uses: Woodwaxen is used in spells to commune with forest spirits.
Shamanic Uses: More of the same. Bringing a spring of Woodwaxen with you while journeying can help you speak to recalcitrant forest spirits in faraway woods. They will tend to trust you more if you are carrying this plant, but don't push it.
Affinity: Air (astringent), Fire (stimulant). Use for River and Earth conditions.
Point: HT 4
Plant-Wight's Nature: Master Woodwaxen appears to me as a thin, fair, silent green-clad figure who hides behind trees and in bushes, watching. He says very little, but the right word can bring a faint smile to his face. While he has been cultivated in gardens for some time, he is still really a creature of the forest, and prefers to consort with those who love the woods and spend much of their time there. He is skilled in silence and silent walking, and can teach these things to those who are patient. His eyes are sharp in his thin face, and see much. He approves of being used as a green dye, because he assumes that it is for the purpose of hiding among the trees.

Magical Charm: Silent Strands

For hiding in the woods—whether for hunting, tracking, or any other purpose—make a dye of Dyer's Greenweed and dye some natural-fiber article of clothing, or even a skein of wool which can then be plaited into a bracelet or anklet. Wear it when you woodswalk, and you will blend in with the background. As the pot of dye boils, say the following charm:

> *Forest fair welcome me,*
> *Fleet my feet, silent my step,*
> *Woodwaxen, walk with me.*

Edelweiss

Botanical Name: *Leontopodium alpinum*
Folk Names: Everwhite, Noble-White, Queen's Flower
Modern German Name: Edelweiß
Modern Swedish Name: Edelweiss
Modern Danish Name: Edelweiss
Modern Norwegian Name: Edelweiss
Deity Association: Forseti, Hyndla
Height: 6"
Season: Perennial
History: One of the best-known Alpine flowers, Edelweiss is the national flower of Switzerland, where it is known as Queen's Flower, made famous by the song in *The Sound of Music*. It is native to mountain ranges all over northern Europe, growing even along the edge of glaciers. Its name literally translates to "Noble-White". It is associated with soldiers in some northern countries; Swiss generals have it as insignia.
Medicinal Uses: The flowers of Edelweiss have been used to treat diarrheaand dysentery via a water extract or infusion. Another folk remedy cooks the flowers in milk, butter and honey to extract fat-soluble compounds for respiratory disorders and tuberculosis, which is a better method than water or alcohol extraction. Edelweiss aids in removing free radicals from the skin and strengthens the walls of capillaries and veins, and as such has been used in cosmetics in Europe as a treatment for varicose veins.
Magical Uses: Worn in a wreath, Edelweiss supposedly confers invisibility and protects against daggers and bullets. To gain your heart's desire, plant and care for an Edelweiss flower, and it will help for as long as you care for it.
Shamanic Uses: Edelweiss is used as a token of friendship among frost-giants, and can be left as an offering for them, or carried when you travel in Niflheim or the northern mountains of Jotunheim.
Affinity: Air (astringent). Use for River conditions.
Point: LU 6
Plant-wight's Nature: Grandmother Edelweiss is the Wisewoman of the Snows. She appeared as an old woman hunkered down in the mountain snow, dressed all in white with her hair in many grey braids. Her claim to fame is that she is a fair judge of grievances, and I got the impression that she has this role often in the northern green kingdom. She is a wise counselor, but in spite of her friendly demeanor she is very impartial, and likely to tell you politely but coldly when you are being unfair ... in a cosmic sense, that is; we may find her system of judging to be somewhat less favorable to humanity than we would like.

Medicinal Charm: Edelweiss Custard

The good stuff in Edelweiss is fat-soluble, and for those who can eat dairy and eggs, custard is a smooth, cool dish that slides down sore throats well. For a good medicinal food for the family with respiratory illness, cook a few spoonfuls of Edelweiss flowers in 2 cups of milk, 2 teaspoons of butter, and a cup of sugar (or ½ cup of honey) for 20 minutes; do not let it boil. Strain the herbal matter out, and add 1 teaspoon of vanilla and 6 egg yolks slowly, stirring all the time. Pour it in a glass pie pan, and set the pie pan in a larger flat glass cake pan Filled with water to just below the level of the pie pan. Bake in this double boiler until the custard is solid, and serve to your family.

Now here's the embarrassing part. I asked Grandmother Edelweiss for a proper charm, and all that ran through my head, over and over, was that silly "Edelweiss" song from *The Sound of Music*. Apparently enough people sing it that she considers it a song of worship to her, and as long as it existed in my head, she wouldn't give me any other. You never know what wights are going to like. Anyway, if you have kids you can probably get them to sing it with you.

Elder

Botanical name: *Sambucus nigra*
Folk names: Ellhorn, Lady Ellhorn, Battree, Boure Tree, Eldrum, Frau Holle, Hildemoer, Hollunder, Hylder, Ruis, Old Gal, Old Lady, Pipe Tree, Sureau, Tree of Doom, Yakori Bengeskro
Anglo-Saxon Name: Ellen
Old Norse Name: Alri
Old High Germanic Name: Holantar
Middle Germanic Name: Ellern
Modern German Names: Schwarzer Holunder, Holder, Holderbusch, Holler
Modern Swedish Name: Fläder
Modern Danish Name: Hyld
Modern Norwegian Name: Svarthyll
Deity Association: Holda, Hela, Mordgud
Height: To 30'
Season: Perennial tree
History: Elder is native to all parts of Europe, and has been a popular medicinal plant since

prehistoric times. It is the thirteenth Celtic tree month, Ruis. The name Elder comes from Hylde or Holda, and it is associated with Frau Holde in her Germanic myth of the young girl who falls through the well in an underworld. The Elder tree was associated just as frequently with Hela, or other various unspecified Queens and Kings of the Realms of the Dead. In contrast to the earlier summer brightly fruiting trees and berries, Elderberries fruit last, in the autumn, and are purple-black. Elder wood should never be burned, as it is bad luck; in medieval days "Lady Ellhorn" was treated as a sentient being who should never be cut or burned. The Danes called her *Hylde-Moer*, or Elder-Mother. When Christianity took over, the story was changed so that Elder was supposedly the wood of Christ's cross and thus was bad luck to burn; it seems that making sure that Lady Ellhorn was not burned was more important than the reasons why. It should never be used for furniture; supposedly a child laid in a cradle of Elder wood will be pinched black and blue by invisible fingers. If an Elder tree grows on your property, leave it be; if you must cut it to make way for a building, propitiate the tree spirit with vigor.

Medicinal Uses: Elder was called "the medicine chest of the country people", and every part of this small tree is useful for something. The flowers, fresh or dried in tea, are used to bring down fevers and treat coughs, colds, hay fever, influenza, pneumonia, and as a gargle for sore throats and toothache; it reduces phlegm and is one of the best sweat-producers. Elder opens the lungs and helps any condition where people can't catch their breath. It is mildly sedating, and cools and purges heat. It is a good remedy for infants with breathing problems, and possibly a SIDS preventative. Elderflower water is good as an eyewash, especially during allergy season; taking Elder in early spring may reduce hay fever later. It is also a mild sedative and bathing in it before bed can reduce insomnia. The leaves are nasty-tasting and as such as used as a topical skin healer for hot inflammations. Ointment made from the flowers is used to treat burns; ointment made from the leaves treats bruises and sprains. The inner bark acts on the liver, opening its vessels, used for arthritic conditions and stubborn constipation, but causes vomiting in large doses and is a purgative in small ones. A syrup of the berries builds up the blood and helps anemia, and is regularly used to fend off flu viruses; it is a good winter cold treatment for children (and anyone else). The pith is used to purge water in cases of edema; the flowers and berries can be used for a lighter remedy in these cases. Elder treats colic and digestive cramps, as an antispasmodic. It can be summed up as acting on any problem where the "tubes" of the body are blocked and cooling air or water needs to come out of them.

Household Uses: Elderberries yield green, violet, and black dyes. Elderflower water was a classic skin-toner and freckle-remover for centuries. The Romans used Elderberries steeped in wine as a hair dye to darken the hair.

Culinary Uses: The berries are eaten in jellies and pies, being rich in Vitamin C, and were made into tonic syrups for winter nutrition. Wine has long been made from both the berries and the flowers.

Magical Uses: Elder is immensely protective and is hung over doorways and windows to protect a home from evil, snakes, and robbers. Hanging it in a barn will protect livestock. It supposedly has the power to release people from evil enchantments cast on them by sorcerers. Elder leaves or berries cast upon someone or some place are a blessing. Flutes or panpipes made of Elder will call nature spirits when played, and an Elder staff (as the plant of Hela) will allow one to see through glamour. Green Elder branches were laid in graves to protect the dead soul.

Shamanic Uses: This tree is sacred to Hela, the Death Goddess, and it was used in burial rites in many areas of northern Europe. All the way back to the earliest folkloric mentions, the Elder tree is one of the two plants (the other being Angelica) whose "tubular" nature wound them up in spells to slide through and visit the Underworld. The difference between them is that Angelica is the plant of Light, by which those shamans whose alliance is with wights of Light may safely visit the Deathlands, retrieve things for their clients, and leave quickly and safely. Elder, on the other hand, is the Tree of the Underworld and the "tube" used by shamans whose alliances remain there; they may come and go as they please by leave of the Elder-Mother.

The Elder is also sacred to Holda, the Frau Holle of German folktales who lived down the well in the Underworld. Elder is carried as a charm for her blessing, but while carrying it, one must be as the good daughter in the folktale who was willing to give aid to strangers and share food and resources with the needy. Being ungenerous and unhelpful while carrying her charm will bring down her wrath upon you.

Affinity: Earth (cooling), Stone (sedative), Mountain (relaxant), Fire (stimulant), River (moistening). Use for Storm, Fire, Earth, and Air disorders. Elder can be either heating or cooling depending on which is needed at the moment.

Point: TH 6

Plant-wight's Nature: Lady Ellhorn is a dignified crone; stern, wise, and a bit critical. She is willing to help with any sort of healing, as long as she is respected and given the kind of deference due to a wise elder, no pun intended. She has very little sense of humor, though, and does not like being made fun of. Be careful to ask before you pick any part of her leaves, flowers, or berries.

Medicinal Charm: Green Elderleaf Ointment and Elderberry Rob

To make Green Elderleaf Ointment, which is a remedy for bruises, sprains, chilblains, and wounds, make this recipe, preferably just before Beltane: 3 parts freshly gathered Elder leaves, 4 parts pork lard and 2 parts beef suet, both strained and white. Heat the leaves gently in the fat until the color is extracted, while saying the Elder charm below; then strain through a linen cloth and keep chilled.

For Elderberry Rob, which is a remedy for colds, coughs, and bronchitis, simmer 5 pounds of freshly crushed Elderberries with a pound of sugar until it is of the consistency of honey, or if you prefer honey, add it until it is the right moistness and thickness and then simmer, while saying:

> Ellen, Ellen, Lady Ellhorn,
> Eldest moon and magic born,
> Holda, heal me, Ellhorn's mistress,
> May the night give way to morn.

Two tablespoons mixed with 12 ounces of hot water, nightly, will help chest congestion and fight colds.

Elecampane

Botanical name: *Inula helenium*

Folk names: Eolone, Elfdock, Elfwort, Horseheal, Scabwort, Wild Sunflower, Marchalan, Enula, Inula campana

Anglo-Saxon Names: Eolone, Sperewyrt ("Spear Plant")

Modern German Name: Echter Alant

Modern Swedish Names: Ålandsrot, Alant, Alantkrissla, Ålandskrissla

Modern Danish Names: Alant, Ellensrod

Modern Norwegian Name: Alantrot

Deity Association: The Alfar

Height: 6-10'

Season: Perennial

History: Elecampane's Latin name is derived from a reference of Helen of Troy; supposedly it sprung up from her tears upon being kidnapped. Known to the ancient Greeks and Romans, it is included in preparations prescribed by Hippocrates.

Medicinal Uses: Elecampane root is so antibacterial that it was used as a surgical dressing in the old days. The root is used as a tonic for weakness, an aid for diabetes (it contains inulin), a treatment for stubborn phlegm from respiratory infections, and a poultice for stubbornly infected wounds that will not heal. It is a favorite domestic remedy for bronchitis, asthma, hay fever, or any upper respiratory problem; the candied root or tincture is eaten daily as an asthma prophylactic. Use it in cough syrup. The tea is a good antinauseant for nausea caused by too much phlegm in the stomach. Elecampane is a vermifuge and can flush nasty bacteria from the stomach.

Culinary Uses: Root can be cooked as a root vegetable or crystallized as a sweet. Elecampane is one of the ingredients in Absinthe.

Magical Uses: Attracts love when carried; aids in psychic powers when burned. Has long been used to see fairies, usually when breathed in an incense. Elecampane tea is said to soothe sorrow at having to leave one's home and be far away in a strange place, as Helen of Troy was taken from her home.

Shamanic Uses: This plant is beloved of the Alfar, as shown by its folk name Elfdock. It can be used as a offering to them (especially candied), and carrying it will make them both better disposed toward you, and turn away some of their lesser spells. Carve the rune Wunjo/Wyn into the root as a talisman; it is associated with Ljossalfheim, and works well with Elecampane's Latin name, which translates to "Light". However, Elecampane is too noble to take sides entirely, and will also heal people of elf-shot if it is applied quickly enough as a poultice.

Affinity: Mountain (relaxant), Fire (stimulant), Storm (bitter alterative). Use on Storm, Earth, Air, and especially Swamp.

Point: LU 5

Plant-wight's Nature:

> Elfdock is male, very much a "majordomo"-like spirit, bound to service and very competent at it. According to him, he was magically bound millennia ago by an Alf king and queen to serve people with Alfar bloodlines (both elves and humans who carry their blood) and to strengthen the Alfar as a race. He gave me two charms.

> One spell is only usable by those with Alf bloodlines. What this means is that if you suspect you may have elvish ancestry and want to be certain of it, you can gather some Elfdock and hold it in your hand while singing a certain charm which will allow you better access to your bloodlines and whatever inherent powers you have inherited from your ancestors. Be warned that this may come in the form of suddenly having the equivalent of a "recovered memory" if you happen to also be an Alf in a human body, and it can be a traumatic experience, depending on why you were reincarnated as a mortal instead of as an Alf. Elfdock will not harm you, but will not attempt to hold any information back once you've asked for it, either.

> The second service Elfdock can provide can be used by anyone. It is for the conception of a child with Alf blood and mortal blood, and it is not a spell to toy with! Be absolutely certain that you can handle the fact that once it is born you may not be allowed to keep and raise it. It may remain in Alfheim with its other parent, or it even may be stolen from you at a later age and appear to "die," if it is a mortal-bodied child. Those old tales about changelings and faeries taking children away are often based in fact, after all.

> If you really wish to do this despite the potential for trouble, plant an Elfdock in your garden (or if necessary, in a pot indoors) and sing this charm (to be given) over it, then faithfully tend the plant. Elfdock will call a potential Alf lover–an actual Alf, or possibly a mortal with elvish blood or an Alf living in a mortal form–to you within a season, and you may conceive a child together, if you're sure that's what you want and you can handle any potential magical or legal ramifications. (We will not be responsible for whatever happens as a result of this spell. Do this at your own risk!)   –Elizabeth Vongvisith

Medicinal Charm: Lung Healing

When the terrible phlegm cough has taken over your lungs and filled them with goo, Elecampane can help, but the time to act is before it happens. Dig up and wash the Elecampane root, scrubbing thoroughly, and chop into fine pieces. Fill a jar with it, and pour honey into the jar until every bit is covered in honey. You may have to keep waiting for the honey to settle and add more. When it's full, it should sit for at least two weeks before using. When you get the cough, eat the now-candied bits of Elecampane, or spoon out just the honey and put it in tea–it will be full of Elecampane now. During the period when it sits and steeps, say this charm over it:

> Eolone, Eolone, healer of the air's way,
> Elfdock, Elfwort, fare me well and clear me,
> Bring the evil from my chest,
> Let me breathe with ease and rest,
> Eolone, Eolone, healer of the air's way.

Elm

Botanical Name: *Ulmus procera*
Folk Names: Ulm, Embla, Elven, Vanishing Elm
Anglo-Saxon Name: Ulm
Old Norse Name: Embla
Old High Germanic Name: Elme
Modern German Name: Ulme
Modern Swedish Name: Alm
Modern Danish Name: Elm
Modern Norwegian Names: Almer, Almeslekta
Deity Association: Odin, Hoenir, Lodurr
Height: To 100'
Season: Perennial tree
History: While it is referred to as the English Elm, the tree is not native to England but was introduced there from continental Europe at some early point. It was considered important enough that the myth of the two surviving humans that repopulated the world are called Ask and Embla (Ash and Elm).
Medicinal Uses: Elm leaves are used in hemorrhoid ointments and a decoction is used for skin rashes. The sticky inner bark of its American cousin Slippery Elm (*Ulmus rubra*) is used to reduce mucus and phlegm, as a laxative, and in convalescent drinks.
Household Uses: All parts of the tree are used in carpentry, as Elm is a strong, hard, close-grained wood. It is water-resistant enough that it was used for boat keels and water-pipes (before the age of metal plumbing). Elm trees are good firewood, but very hard to split.
Magical Uses: Elm is supposedly beloved of the Alfar, and has been carried for charms to see them, as well as love spells.
Shamanic Uses: Like Ash, Elm is associated with the first woman—Embla—and can be used in workings to honor the ancestors. It is special to Odin, and also to Hoenir and Lodurr.
Affinity: Air (astringent), River (moistening). Elm bark balances moisture, and will dry up River or Swamp conditions or moisten Air conditions.
Point: UB 54
Plant-wight's Nature: Mother Elm came to me as a tall, stately woman in a plain brown dress. She has a farm-woman look to her, with strong arms and muscles shoulders and legs like, well, tree trunks—a woman who is not afraid to till the soil and carry water and pull up roots from a field, and yet can command a matriarch's respect. She spoke to me, strangely enough, of marriage—not love so much as choosing a partner who will work the land with you, who will respect you and toil faithfully with you, who will be a good father to a woman's children. To Elm, marriage is a working partnership rather than a romantic one; even arranged marriages, for her, are a problem only if the parties are cruel to each other or the children. I remembered that her leaves were used to love charms, but that was in a day when women wanted a husband first, for security, and a lover second if at all. She spoke also of the rune Othila, and its association with birthright and ancestry, and the sacredness of leaving a piece of good land to one's descendants.

Medicinal Charm: Against Worms of the Skin

Add 1 part of the ground inner bark of the Elm tree to 8 parts water, boil for 15 minutes, and then use as a poultice for ringworm and other afflictions of the skin by small creatures. While applying, say the following charm:

> *Thou who protected the First Mother,*
> *Thou who protected her children three,*
> *Thou who shaded my ancestors,*
> *Drive the demon worms from me.*

Fennel

Botanical Name: *Foeniculum vulgare*
Folk Names: Fenkel, Marathron
Anglo-Saxon Names: Finule, Finol
Modern German Name: Fenchel
Modern Swedish Name: Fänkål
Modern Danish Name: Fennikel
Modern Norwegian Name: Fennikel
Deity Association: Ivaldi
Height: To 6'
Season: Perennial

History: Fennel was originally native to southern Europe and the Mediterranean, but was spread by the Romans to Germany, Britain, and as far east as India. Its name still derives from the Latin *foeniculum*, meaning "a kind of hay", which was apparently not the upper-class name for it, but instead the slangy solider-camp Latin brought to the rest of Europe. Fennel quickly became so important that it was renowned as one of the Nine Sacred Herbs given by Odin to the Nine Worlds.

Medicinal Uses: Fennel soothes digestion, especially flatulence, constipation, and indigestion. Promotes milk production in lactating woman and animals. The herbalist Nicholas Culpeper relates a common use of it: its seed or leaves were boiled in Barley water and then drunk by nursing mothers to increase their milk and its quality for the infant. Used in China for food poisoning. Infusion is used for gum disease, loose teeth, laryngitis, and sore throats. Chew to relieve hunger pangs; Fennel reduces appetite and has a mild stimulant effect. The ancient Greeks referred to it as Marathron, meaning "to grow thin", as they chewed the seeds as a diet aid, and medieval people chewed the seeds to stave off hunger or help them to face unsavory food on fast days. Recently found to reduce the toxic effects of alcohol on the system. Fennel seed, bruised and boiled in water, and then added to syrup and soda water will relieve flatulence in infants (and probably everyone else as well). Fennel juice was also added to cough syrups. Fennel is a blood-cleanser and helps to repair the liver after alcohol damage; it was used as a traditional hangover herb in medieval times.

Household Uses: Use in baths or facial steams for deep cleansing, and add ground seed to homemade toothpaste for flavor. Fennel seed is sprinkled around kennels and stables (and originally homes) to drive off fleas, as it gives off ozone. Essential oil is used in muscle-toning massage. (Note: The use of Fennel oil has been observed to stimulate minor seizures in epileptics, so be careful.)

Culinary Uses: Fennel was frequently mentioned in cookery manuals of pre-Norman England. Cook in any kind of meat or fish dish, or put in salad, or add to sausage mixtures. It is traditionally used in greasy foods, to help with digestion. Chew to sweeten breath. Florence Fennel, a variety grown for its large, soft, tasty root-bulb, is traditional to many German cookery dishes. Italians eat the peeled stems in salads. Ancient Romans placed sprigs of it under loaves of bread while baking in order to scent them.

Magical Uses: Romans believed that serpents sucked the juice of the plant to improve their eyesight after shedding their skins. Greeks used it to magically lose weight and grow thin. Solomon used it as an asperger for sacred circles. Grown around the house or hung in doors and windows, it is protective. Carried, it wards off ticks and biting bugs. Burn for purification and healing mixtures. In the *Lacnunga*, Fennel is used in charms against all manner of ill-meaning wights, from elves to sorcerers, and even against insanity. It was hung, with St. John's Wort, over doorways at Midsummer to bless and protect the house.

Shamanic Uses: This is the herb of Svartalfheim and Nidavellir. Together with Sweet Cicely, it is used to protect against elf-shot, and to treat cases of that remedy. Also like Sweet Cicely, Fennel aids in the Gift of Sight, but it gives the ability to see the darknesses in life—the hidden anger and pain, the inner rot, the creeping deaths. This makes it useful in shamanic client-work when one must discern hard truths about someone's behavior, or find hidden disease or poisoning. Drink in tea or smoke it or eat the seeds (preferably seven of them). Fennel seed is also traditionally used for those who are fasting for spiritual reasons, to give them something to chew and then spit out so that ketones will not make their breath terrible.

Affinity: Earth (nourishing), Mountain (relaxant), Fire (pungent), Swamp (oily). Use on Air, Earth and Storm conditions.

Point: ST 25

Plant-wight's Nature: Master Fennel is tall, lean, and wild-haired. He is a Magician, reminding me of something between the classic mad scientist and the Magician figure of the Tarot deck—constantly running experiments, messing around with various mysterious projects. He has an alchemist's air to him, and it may be difficult to get his attention at first. When he notices you, though, his gaze is penetrating and intense, and you become a problem to be solved. He is solitary and likes it that way, so don't plant him too close to other herbs. Master Fennel is actually fairly useful when it comes to health diagnosis; he has a sharp eye for what's wrong with you, and if you have a good relationship with him, he may recommend other herbs for you to take. Master Fennel somehow manages to be friends with both the Dokkalfar and the Duergar, and he does partake somehow of the nature of both of them, although the obsessive Duergar nature is what he mostly has shown to me. that may be because I get along better with the Duergar than any of the Alfar; it may be that he would seem more elfin—and more dark—to others who have more of an affinity to the elf-people.

Medicinal Charm: Pinkeye

Make a strong decoction of 1 part honey to 2 parts water, and add equal parts Fennel seeds or weed, and Rose petals, and a pinch of salt. Use as an eyewash 4 times daily; pour it into a shot glass and hold it against your eyesocket; tip your head back quickly while keeping your eye open. Discard and use a second glassful for the other eye. Ideally, for sterility, one should make a fresh batch each time, but if this is not possible, at least make a fresh batch each day. The pinkeye should clear up in less than 48 hours. While you pour it out into the shot glass, say the following:

> *Doorguard of the dwarven delving,*
> *Weedy wizard, wave your wand,*
> *Save my sight and clear my weeping,*
> *I give my eyes into your keeping,*
> *Fail me not, Finule, Marathron.*

Feverfew

Botanical name: *Tanacetum parthenium* or *Chrysanthemum parthenium*

Folk names: Featherfew, Febrifuge Plant, Featherfoil, Flirtwort, Vetter-voo, Featherfully, Mutterkraut

Anglo-Saxon Name: Feferfugie

Modern German Name: Mutterkraut

Modern Swedish Name: Mattram

Modern Danish Name: Matrem

Modern Norwegian Name: Matrem

Deity Association: Gefjon

Height: 2'

Season: Perennial

History: Feverfew seems to have originated in southern Europe and was brought north by the Romans. According to the ancient Greeks, this plant was called Parthenium because it saved the life of a workman who fell from the roof of the Parthenon during repairs. Feverfew was one of those plants that never got much of a review from the learned doctor classes (except for Culpeper, who raved about it), but the common people used it all the time for various complaints. It became a classic low-status folk-remedy garden herb for centuries, until college-educated herbalists "discovered" it again in the mid-20th century.

Medicinal Uses: The migraine plant. Eating Feverfew, or taking a few drops of a strong tincture, every day on a prophylactic basis has been known to drastically reduce the frequency and severity of migraine attacks. It has also had such a prophylactic effect on tinnitus. Feverfew relaxes blood vessels, especially cranial ones, reduces inflammation, and is mildly sedative, and was the herb of choice for headaches during medieval times, second only to Betony. It is especially indicated in pale people who suddenly flush red before their attack, and have sluggish digestion during its duration. A weak tea is given for irregular periods and to encourage the placenta out after childbirth, and a douche relieves internal vaginal inflammation. Similarly, an enema of the tea is used for colonic inflammation. It can also be used externally, soaked in olive oil for a few days, as a poultice for skin inflammation, such as insect bites. As its name implies, it was used for fevers and chills.

Household Uses: Use dried in sachets to deter moths.

Culinary Uses: In southern Europe, Feverfew was added to dishes of bitter greens to add flavor and pungency. It never took off as a culinary plant in northern Europe, largely due to a cultural dislike of bitter food flavors (the Italians, who used it the most, are the folks who gave us broccoli rapini/raab, after all).

Magical Uses: Protection against sudden accidents. Planted around dwellings, it wards off disease.

Shamanic Uses: Opens the head energy centers, if they are constricted, allowing better energy flow. Blow smoke around the individual's head, or if they are sensitive to smoke, use an oil infusion as a massage or even compresses of hot tea.

Affinity: Storm (bitter alterative), Stone (sedative), Fire (pungent). Use for Earth and Swamp conditions.

Point: ST 8

Plant-wight's Nature: Mistress Feverfew is thin and pointy, dressed in a mass of ruffles and ribbons, with a great feathered hat. There is something very birdlike about her, but it is the sort of small bird that hops about and scolds rather than twitters sweetly. She is sharp, even a little bitchy, although I got the feeling that she could be quite flirtatious if the right person approached her (which I wasn't). Her presence does refresh and clear a room at first alighting, but it can also become irritable after a while. Flatter her and things might go better for you; this may be especially important if you're a migraine-sufferer who needs to deal with her prophylactically on a daily basis.

Medicinal Charm: Migraine Tincture

Stuff a jar full of chopped Feverfew and cover it entirely with vinegar (or grain alcohol if you must). Let it sit overnight, and the next day add more fluid if the level has sunk below the tops of the herb through absorption. Give it a good shake, and say the following charm:

> *Flirtwort, Featherfully, look upon me fair,*
> *Mutterkraut, release my pain and blear,*
> *Mother of Bulls, bring my head fine and clear.*

Repeat the shake and the charm every day for two weeks, then strain. Take a dropperful every morning, and over time Feverfew will prophylactically help your migraine. Using the charm calls on the wight, and speeds up the process.

Fir

Botanical Name: *Abies spp*
Folk Names: Various, depending on species.
Anglo-Saxon Name: Furhwudu
Old Norse Name: Fura
Old High Germanic Name: Furaha
Modern German Name: Tanne
Modern Swedish Names: Tall, Buske, Fere
Modern Danish Name: Gran
Modern Norwegian Name: Edelgraner
Deity Association: Nerthus, Jord
Height: 30-200'
Season: Perennial Tree
History: Supposedly St. Boniface made the Fir tree a symbol of Christianity after he chopped down a sacred pagan Oak and a Fir sapling grew up in its place. The Fir tree was the classic Christmas tree for hundreds of years, complete with Martin Luther's myth (and various other myths) of seeing stars in the tree branches, or seeing a glowing child speaking from a Fir tree. Before that, however, Fir species (of which there are over 50, but only about 6 are native to northern Europe) were dug up and brought into the home, along with a lot of cut evergreen boughs, as a way to welcome the woodland spirits into the home and bless it. Evergreens were a sign of life in the deadness of winter, when all other trees had lost their leaves and were slumbering.
Medicinal Uses: The liquid resin taken from bark incisions is a good gargle for sore throats, and poulticed for sinus congestion and arthritis.
Household Uses: The resin can be made into fine lacquer or distilled for turpentine, and the gum is chewed. The buds and leaves are distilled for oil in cough drops and asthma inhalations. Cones and needles are used in potpourri.
Magical Uses: Decorated sacred trees on the winter Solstice.
Shamanic Uses: Fir is the traditional Yule tree, and is sacred to the Mothers, as Yule is Modraniht. It is also one of the sacred smudging herbs for Siberian shamans, along with Juniper. It brings the blessing of the Earth with its scent, and can be used as recaning or asperger for Nerthus, Jord, or any land-wight, or the element of Earth in general.
Affinity: Fire (pungent), Air (astringent). Use for Earth, River, and Swamp conditions.
Point: ST 10
Plant-wight's Nature: Grandmother Fir is a powerful guardian. She came tall and strong, black hair tumbling down her back in many braids, cloaked in evergreen and snowy furs, holding a staff. "I protect the Mothers," she said, "for they are the hope of the tribe, and I protect hope." In her capacity of representative of that which survives the winter green, she does indeed guard hope, and she is especially protective of breeding women and children. Planting a Fir tree outside the house, or even carrying a twig, can help protect mothers and children who might be at risk for abuse. For the sake of Grandmother Fir, the disposal of any Yule tree should be undertaken with care—it should be burned, and the match set alight by the mother of the household or the oldest child, and Grandmother Fir thanked for her generosity.
Magical Charm: Afteryule

Afteryule was the month of January in the old Saxon calendar. After the New Year has started, and Twelfth Night has passed, it is time to take down the Yule tree. By this time it is likely dry and dropping its needles. If you have a place to burn it outside, take it there. If you have a place to burn it inside (like a woodstove) then it should be broken up gently and respectfully, if this is possible, into branches and trunk sections. These are then fed to the fire one at a time, saying the hearth-blessing charm below. If you are burning it outside, take some of the live coals home to the hearth and leave them to burn out inside your oven, saying the charm then.

Grandmother Fura, feathered evergreen,
Bless our hearth and all that gather
Round it, Winter Queen.

Flax

Botanical Name: *Linum usitatissimum*
Folk Names: Linseed
Anglo-Saxon Name: Linwyrt
Old Norse Name: Lina
Old High Germanic Name: Lin
Modern German Name: Lein
Modern Swedish Name: Lin
Modern Danish Name: Hør
Modern Norwegian Name: Lin
Deity Association: Frigga, Holda
Height: 3-4'
Season: Annual

History: Flax is one of the handful of plants that goes back to the Mesolithic Near East, and spread around much of the world during that time. It became the most extensively grown plant-based fiber crop in Eurasia. It is associated strongly with the feminine, and various goddesses are attributed to it. Home fiber production has nearly always been dominated by women—largely due, as Elizabeth Wayland Barber writes in *Women's Work: The First 20,000 Years: Women, Cloth and Society In Early Times*, to the fact that fiber arts work well with constant child care, being portable and easily interruptable.

The spindle, and also the plant most associated with it, became the symbols of the feminine role, and especially that of the bride and married woman. In the North, the ownership of Flax was split between Frigga, the Queen of the Gods who spins with her maidens and represents the lady of the house who supplies her family with clothing, and Holda, the Germanic goddess who is the old "spinster", the independent cloth-maker.

Flax became the female counterpart of the masculine Leek , and linen-and- Leek charms were found at archeological sites. Even though our ancestors could not have known the high estrogen content of Flax's alkaloid breakdown, Flax's feminine assignment is no accident; the Flax spirit is a very womanly creature.

Medicinal Uses: Flax seed has recently been proven to have high levels of phytoestrogens, which acts as a feminizing hormone. It should be eaten regularly by postmenopausal women, male-to-female transsexuals, and anyone else who needs natural female hormones. It also has Omega-6 oils, which are good for you, and is a deeply nourishing tonic. Flaxseed builds up muscles and tendons, moistens dry lungs, and has positive cardiovascular effects. The seeds are a natural and safe laxative for constipation;

follow them with at least 2 cups of water to make them swell in the bowel and move everything out. An infusion has been used for coughs and sore throats, flavored with honey and lemon. Soaking the seeds in water produces a thick mucilage, useful for inflammation of the mucous membranes. If you use linseed oil, try to get fresh; it deteriorates rapidly. Don't use industrial-grade (artist's) linseed oil, as it has preservatives you don't want.

Household Uses: Flax is the plant from which we get linen thread, obviously. Also, the seeds can be pressed into linseed oil for wood protection.

Magical Uses: Flax seeds are used in money spells, and placing them in your shoes will ward off poverty. Mixed with Mustard seed or Pepper, they ward against sorcery. In central Germany, children were sent into the Flax fields to dance for Holda, who would grant them growth. In Prussia, a maiden was sent into the Flax fields with food as an offering to a god named Waizganthos, and she would stand on a stool to show how tall the Flax should grow.

Shamanic Uses: Flax is sacred to both Holda and Frigga, both of whom are spinners. It can be sprinkled to call upon either of them, or to help find your way to Fensalir, Frigga's hall where the spinning and weaving is done. Also, since Lina is the female equivalent of John Barleycorn, she can be used in any ritual where a woman has to make a willing sacrifice.

Affinity: Swamp (oily), Harvest (nourishing). Use on Air conditions.

Point: SP 5

Plant-wight's Nature: Lina is almost stereotypically soft and womanly, giving and flexible, pliable in the best sense, affectionate and loving. She likes to be worked with, and to be told that she is beautiful, and indeed a field of waving Flax blooms is beautiful. (In the case of blue Flax, waterbirds flying overhead have mistaken the field for a lake and tried to land on it, much to their surprise.) If she has a fault, it is that there is not much depth to her; she loves everyone who contacts her unconditionally, but her gaze is easily turned from one person to the next and she has no loyalty, and is likely to forget you tomorrow. She is easily hurt, weeps copiously, and then quickly forgets what she was sad about. The poem I wrote below for her shows her relationship with Holda.

Magical Charm: For a Woman's Protection

Hold a handful of Flax seeds to the heart and say:

Lina, Lina, lend me (or her) your blessing,
That by your sight I (or she) be safe from harm.

Then wrap the seeds in a handwoven square of undyed linen and tie with a linen thread dyed blue. Knot the thread six times, and say,

Frigga, fair queen, keep me (or her) covered,
Cast me (or her) not into the cold;
Holda, Elder woman, wrap me (or her) whole.

The charm should be kept upon the body of she who would benefit from it, and placed under the pillow at night. This charm is especially good to give to a woman who is going away to live in the house of a man whom her loved ones do not trust, and they want her kept safe in spite of whatever may happen there.

Foxglove

Botanical name: *Digitalis purpurea*

Folk names: Cowflop, Deadmen's Bells, Dead Man's Thimbles, Digitalis, Dog's Finger, Fairy Fingers, Fairy Petticoats, Fairy Thimbles, Fairy Weed, Floppydock, Floptop, Folk's Gloves, Fox Bells, Foxes Glofa, Lion's Mouth, Lusmore, Witches' Gloves, Witches' Thimbles, Fingerhut

Anglo-Saxon Names: Foxes Glofa, Foxes Clife ("Foxes' Cleavers")

Modern German Name: Fingerhut
Modern Swedish Name: Fingerborgsblomma
Modern Danish Name: Fingerbøl
Modern Norwegian Name: Revebjelle
Deity Association: The Alfar and Dokkalfar
Height: 3'
Season: Biennial

History: Foxglove is found almost everywhere in northern Europe except for the Swiss Alps and the Jura mountains, as it dislikes high altitudes. Foxglove was originally "Folks' Glove", from the Good Folk or the Elves who love it a great deal. The mottled spots on the blossoms were said to mark where the elves had placed their fingers. When the name shifted to Foxglove, the story sprang up that the Elves had given the plant to the fox that he might wear the flowers on his feet, and thus steal about more quietly to rob chicken coops and the like.

Medicinal Uses: Heart medications are extracted from the plant, but it is poisonous and should not be used by untrained people. As well as the heart medications, digitalis injections are used as an antidote to Aconite poisoning. Atropine (Belladonna extract) is used as an antidote to digitalis overdoses. The leaves of Foxgloves were applied to a nursing mother's breasts to dry them up.

Household Uses: A fine honey plant for beekeepers. The medicinal alkaloids do not turn up in the honey.

Magical Uses: Used to see faeries. Protection of the home from evil faeries; also glamour magic. If you put the juice of Foxglove on your fingers, anything you touch with them will look glamorous and desirable.

Shamanic Uses: While all the Alfar and Fey Folk like Foxgloves, and may turn mischief aside from a house that grows them, they are especially favored by the Dokkalfar, to whom they are not poisonous as they are to us. Foxglove is loved and valued by them, and can be used as an offering or a trade item.

Affinity: Fire (stimulant). Used on cardiac Earth conditions, but too dangerous for herbalists in general.

Point: HT 8

Plant-wight's Nature: Foxglove-wight is a faery creature, sometimes female and sometimes male—a pouka, a shapechanging part-animal pointy-faced sly and slender spotted elf. For all its Brian Froud look, don't underestimate it—Foxglove has all the power of the Fey behind it, and will not work with you on anything if you don't have Fey approval and/or affinities. This can be a particular problem if you're on digitalis-derived heart medication; if this is the case, I suggest that you do a lot of Alfar propitiation. Foxglove will help if it is moved to do so, but can also turn around and trick you—remember that this plant is poisonous. Getting on the good side of Foxglove's Fey allies is fairly important in gaining any trustworthy help from Fingerhut. However, Lady Belladonna can be called in as an adversary to keep Foxglove in line if necessary—and she does not fear the Fey folk at all.

Magical Charm: Faery Folk

Carefully bruise the petals of Foxglove with your fingers, anoint your eyelids, and go forth to a wild place where faeries have been seen. Bring bread and milk and some sweet thing with you; nestle the offering in ferns or flowers and go out of sight of it. Bring a blossom of Foxglove with you in your pocket; lie down and place it under your head. If all goes well, you will soon hear their whispering and giggling. Do not trust the impulse to open your eyes. Instead, sit up carefully, keeping your eyes closed, and begin to sing. Go through a few songs to entertain them, then stay still for a moment, and then open your eyes. If they have enjoyed your offering, and the Foxglove you carry and wear makes the introduction for you, then one or more will be standing before you, waiting for you to open your eyes and see them. After that, it's all on you and how much studying you've done on how to interact with the Fey Folk and not get into deep trouble.

Gale

Botanical name: *Myrica gale*
Folk names: Sweet Gale, Bayberry, English Bog Myrtle, Dutch Myrtle, Herba Myrti Rabatini, Candleberry
Anglo-Saxon Name: Gagel
Old Norse Name: Pors
Old High Germanic Names: Gagel, Sumpf-myrta (swamp-myrta)
Modern German Name: Gagelstrauch
Modern Swedish Name: Pors
Modern Danish Name: Pors
Modern Norwegian Name: Pors
Deity Association: Laufey, Nanna
Height: 3-6'
Season: Perennial Shrub
History: Gale is a plant of Germanic origin, acknowledged to be native to the northern European lands. It is closely related to the American Bayberry shrub, which ended up with one of Gale's folk names thanks to English colonists. Its name in both modern Norwegian and old Norse, Pors, seems to go back linguistically to before the Indo-Europeans.
Medicinal Uses: Gale is an abortifacient, but its therapeutic dose is somewhat dangerous, so safer herbs should be used. Essential oil of Gale has been used to treat acne.
Household Uses: Leaves are dried to perfume linens. Catkins, boiled in water, make a waxy scum that can be skimmed off and used like beeswax. The bark, gathered in the autumn, is used to dye leather and wool yellow. A strong decoction will kill insects and vermin. Mattresses were stuffed with Gale to keep away fleas, and a sprig pushed into the hatband supposedly repelled midges.
Culinary Uses: Sometimes used as a substitute for Hops to make Gale beer. Like Hops, Gale has mild sedative action in alcohol. The berries are dried as a spice. Leaves can be steeped in soups to give flavor, but do it in a cloth bag and remove all traces of the leaves, as they taste bitter. Don't serve food flavored with Gale to pregnant women.
Magical Uses: Love and marriage spells. To this day, Gale is an ingredient in Royal Wedding bouquets in Britain.
Shamanic Uses: Candles with Gale wax in them can be lit to find loved ones who have become lost while journeying. This is especially useful for the partners of spirit-workers.
Affinity: Mountain (relaxant), Air (astringent). Use on Storm and River.
Point: ST 28
Plant-wight's Nature: Gale-wight appeared to me as a hollow-eyed woman coming up out of a swamp, bits of wet green dangling from her long hair. Her robes were soaked and draggled and blended into the water and mud, and she walked with a swaying motion, her head and whole body moving back and forth. While she was not unfriendly to me, there was a bit of Fey madness in her eyes. Unlike some abortifacient plants who simply do their jobs cleanly, Gale-wight likes to steal babies and keep their

souls until she tires of them and lets them move on. Part of her ability to drive away bugs is that she steals their souls also. Any human soul larger than an unborn fetus is too big for her to take, so you're safe, but I'd keep her away from babies and small children just in case.

Magical Charm: Shaman's Lover

It is not easy being the partner of a spirit-worker. There is always the danger that your love might get into something larger than they could handle, and come back mad, empty, possessed, dying, or dead. They often go out on long journeys and leave you behind. It can be intensely worrying. As a spell to bring them back safely to you, make a candle with Gale wax (or if you cannot get that, anoint an ordinary candle heavily with Gale essential oil) and inscribe the runes Ansuz, Gebo, and Othila on it. Light it and whisper the following charm into the flame:

> *My love has gone like a hawk in flight,*
> *May this my call carry through the night:*
> *Pors, lead my love through thick and thin*
> *And safely see love home again.*

Leave the candle to burn until it goes out naturally. You can repeat the spell with that candle until it is burnt down, as many times as you like.

Garlic

Botanical name: *Allium sativum*
Folk names: Spear Leek, Ajo, Poor Man's Treacle, Stinkroot
Anglo-Saxon Name: Garleac ("Spear-Leek")
Old Norse Name: Geir-laukr
Old High Germanic Name: Lauko
Modern German Name: Knoblauch
Modern Swedish Name: Vitlök
Modern Danish Name: Hvidløg
Modern Norwegian Name: Hvitløk
Deity Association: Thor
Height: 1-2'
Season: Biennial, occasionally perennial in hot areas
History: Grown from Egypt to the Arctic for thousands of years, pyramid builders and Roman soldiers were given a daily ration of Garlic to maintain their health. Garlic was one of the most common and popular culinary herbs in all of Europe. Its origins are so old that it is difficult to trace, but the best theory has it developed in southwest Siberia in Mesolithic times, spreading west across northern areas and south to the Baltic, and thence to southern Europe and Africa. It was widely used in ancient Sumeria, and is the first plant we have records of medicinal use for. Galen called it "villager's panacea" and in old English folks tradition it was "poor man's treacle". The immune-enhancing properties of Garlic led to its reputation as that which drives off evil spirits of all sorts.
Medicinal Uses: Eat whole Garlic cloves as a mild antibiotic in the face of any bacterial or viral infection. Garlic kills bacteria both through direct attack (its high sulfur content makes it act like a sulfa drug) and through changing the environment to make it hard on them. However, unlike antibiotics, it is selective in its killing, leaving internal flora alone. It has been used to kill intestinal parasites, to reduce cholesterol, to lower blood pressure, to prevent heartattacks, and to regulate blood sugar for diabetics. Topically, rub on acne, corns, warts, or skin infections. Drink juice for digestive disorders,

dysentery, and to remove intestinal parasites. If you use commercial Garlic pills, remember that the more "deodorized" they are, the less powerful they are. Garlic may cause digestive upset in people with liver problems, and should not be taken by people with adrenalin excess, hepatitis, pancreatitis, or extremely hot conditions in general.

Household Uses: Plant under peach, pear, or plum trees to prevent leafcurl, and make an infusion to spray for potato blight.

Culinary Uses: Use in any savory cooking, in whatever amount you prefer. As the Galloping Gourmet was said to have intoned: "If you like Garlic and your lover doesn't, get yourself another lover." Ancient and medieval northerners ate Garlic as a vegetable, using whole cloves in soups, stews, and sauces, and eating whole roasted Garlic heads straight up out of their papery packages.

Magical Uses: The ultimate protective edible plant, Garlic was carried and eaten to ward off diseases, thieves, foul weather, and any evil spirits one might run into. Islamic legend claims that it sprung up from the footsteps of Satan; apparently Muslims don't have much use for it. The Greeks offered Garlic in small stone cairns at crossroads to Hecate, and the Romans considered it sacred to Cybele. In Egypt, it was used to swear oaths on.

Shamanic Uses: Sacred to Thor, this plant protects against lightning, and is specifically a ward against the "unseelie" Dokkalfar of Svartalfheim. Wearing it while there invokes Thor's protection (make sure that He doesn't have anything against you before trying this trick) and while they may not attack you, they won't like you much either, so keep your business short.

Affinity: Fire (pungent), Swamp (oily), Harvest (nourishing). Use for Earth and Air.

Point: TH 5

Plant-wight's Nature: The younger brother of Leek, Garlic is a warrior, short, tough, skilled, and pugnacious. He can also be cheerful, but he's the sort who laughs as he kills and then tells tall tales about it later. In the heat of battle, however, he is ruthless and merciless, and will keep on destroying until he can fight no more. As a slayer of evil spirits, he has few equals, and he knows it. He carries a spear stained with the blood of evil spirits. Salute him as the powerful wight that he is, and do not underestimate him.

Medicinal Charm: Garlic's Breath

To be said over the raw clove of Garlic that you eat, or as you put it into the soup, or even when his power courses through your veins. (For those who are interested, this charm is written in the traditional "galdr-meter", which was designed for magical charms: four lines of 4 to 5 syllables apiece, with the last two lines slightly changed alliterative echoes of each other.)

> *Garlic, grant my grief*
> *Rest and right relief,*
> *Strike this sickness true,*
> *Spear this sickness through.*

Gentian

Botanical Name: *Gentiana lutea*
Folk Names: Bitter Root, Bitterwort, Yellow Gentian, Great Yellow Gentian, Centiyane, Genciana
Anglo-Saxon Names: Feldwyrt, Felwort
Modern German Name: Gelber Enzian
Modern Swedish Name: Gullgentiana
Modern Danish Name: Ensian
Modern Norwegian Name: Gulsøte
Deity Association: Vor
Height: To 3'

Season: Perennial

History: Gentian's Latin name is associated with Gentius, a medieval Illyrian king who propagated its medical use in central Europe. Gentian was used as a poison treatment throughout the Middle Ages. Its Anglo-Saxon name means "field herb," showing its common nature at that time, even though it is no longer found naturalized in Britain, having been eradicated (probably through overharvesting) by the time it was mentioned in British herbals in 1911.

Medicinal Uses: One of the most bitter herbs around, Gentian root is used as a treatment for many digestive disorders, mostly as an alterative tonic that stimulates the production of enzymes, stomach acid, and bile. It is also a liver and gallbladder tonic. However, it should not be prescribed for people with gastric ulcers. Gentian is excellent for helping the system cope in cases of exhaustion from chronic illnesses, and is sometimes combined with harsher, more purgative herbs in order to ameliorate their side effects and support the system. The tincture supposedly aids in preventing cravings for sweet foods. Gentian has also been used as a smoke in order to aid with stopping tobacco use.

Culinary Uses: The root was used in the manufacture of Gentian bitters, still used in Angostura bitters. It was also occasionally used as a flavoring for beer.

Magical Uses: Breaks hexes and curses. Used for the sorrowing and depressed, to comfort their hearts. Oaths can be sworn on Gentian root, and dedicated to Vor. Gentian is carried as a talisman in parts of Appalachia for strength and health.

Shamanic Uses: Gentian has something of an anti-magic effect, which can be very useful for people who are trying to stay in their bodies, have some mundane space, and ward off any annoying spooky stuff that is unwanted at the moment. The best way to do this is to ingest the bitter tincture. It can also help in bringing together, at least temporarily, the *lich* and the *hame*, which aids in general healing and recovery, especially from damage that is aggravated by spiritual/magical issues.

Affinity: Storm (bitter alterative), Mountain (relaxant). Use on Swamp or Storm conditions.

Point: UB 47

Plant-wight's Nature: Madame Gentian is an aristocrat. She appears as a dignified old woman garbed in a rich gown and lots of jewelry, and she likes offerings of a tiny bit of very good liquor poured out onto the ground. She has very specific ideas about medicine that may clash with modern people's ideas, so when she gives you advice, nod sagely; don't disagree with her or she'll merely leave in a huff. She's not likely to waste her time checking up on you, so you can take it or leave it later. Approach her with respect; protocol is very important to her.

Magical Charm: Gut Instincts

For those who have fallen out from their own gut instincts, who continually doubt themselves, and who are now dependent on the opinions of some healer (of any sort) to heal them, and who do not know whether it is right or not ... ask Madame Gentian. More to the point, ask her to help you to figure it out properly yourself. Make a tincture by filling a jar with chopped Gentian root and covering it with alcohol (if you are planning on enlisting her aid, it had better be good alcohol) and steeping it for one turn of the moon, or use one of the existing Gentian liqueurs such as Jagermeister. Take a dropperful of the tincture or a shot of the liqueur and say the following charm. If she decides to help you, you will get a stronger and more instinctive feeling that drowns out your internal monologue of doubt, especially in questions about your health.

> *Bitterwort, purge this drooping doubt*
> *And soak my stomach well with surety*
> *That I might know what road is best for me.*

Goldenrod

Botanical Name: *Solidago virga-aurea*
Folk Names: Blue Mountain Tea, Goldruthe, Gonea Tea, Verg D'Or
Modern German Name: Goldrute
Modern Swedish Name: Gullris
Modern Danish Name: Gyldenris
Modern Norwegian Name: Gullris
Deity Association: Sif
Height: To 3'
Season: Perennial
History: Goldenrod is native to all parts of Europe and northern and western Asia. It is a weedy plant that spreads easily and is found on heaths, cliffs, and wastelands.
Medicinal Uses: Goldenrod has a special affinity for the kidneys—not just as a diuretic, but helping the entirety of the kidneys tone up and return to health, as its actions pull blood into the kidney tissue and help the body to excrete larger proteins. It is good for people whose kidneys have been exhausted by long illness. Goldenrod's Latin name comes from the fact that it is a wound healer, solidifying tissue. It has been used for infections in the lungs, mouth, and nose, and for menstrual cramps, especially when accompanied by diarrhea. It is also used as an eyewash for conjunctivitis and a treatment for cat allergies.
Household Uses: Yields a yellow dye.
Magical Uses: Goldenrod stalks are used as divining rods to find hidden treasure. It is used in money spells and planted as a doorway protector.
Shamanic Uses: This tall golden plant is much liked by Sif, Thor's tall golden-haired wife. When carried, it brings her blessing for those going into battle, that they might not forget their skills and might prevail through clear-headedness.
Affinity: Storm (bitter alterative), Fire (pungent). Use on Earth, Swamp and Air conditions.
Point: KD 6
Plant-wight's Nature: Mistress Goldenrod is, as you'd expect, tall and blond and handsome. She is also a loud-mouthed gossipy housewife with a shrill voice, yelling after and dominating her husband and children. She loves flattery and responds well to it, but is fairly vulgar in her regular talk. Gossip with her, and give her all the dirt; she'll love it. She has a keen nose for money, both saving it and making it; unlike many plants who don't understand money, she is the sharp bargainer in the marketplace and if you have to bargain with unabashed confidence, bringing a sprig of Goldenrod along and employing her help might be useful. As a protector, she is loud, shrill, and verbally abusive to those who would harm you. She is quite willing to stick her fists on her hips and plant herself right in someone's way, cursing in their face.
Magical Charm: Golden Staff

When you feel that you have lost sight of your goal, and it happens to be the time of the year when this weed is flowering, ask Goldenrod to help you find it again. Cut four flowering stalks, and turn to each of the four directions. Name each direction as a choice, a road you might go down, a potential goal. Stand the stalks up, leaning against you, one on each of four sides. Close your eyes, raise your arms to the sky, and say: "Sif's delight, Staff of Gold, to which horizon shall I hold?" Move slightly, then a little more. Do this until all four staffs have fallen, then analyze the directions. If two or more are pointing outward in the same direction, that is your road. If all four point equally in different directions, all choices could be good and you are being allowed to choose yourself, without penalty. If all four point in towards you, there is no good choice and you must wait for circumstances to change, or simply endure to the end.

Good King Henry

Botanical Name: *Chenopodum bonus-henricus*

Folk Names: Fragrant Tiger Bones, Allgood, Poor Man's Asparagus, Lincolnshire Spinach, Tola Bona, Smearwort, Goosefoot

Modern German Names: Stolzer Heinrich, Dorf-Gänsefuß, Wilder SpinatMehlspinat

Modern Swedish Names: Lungrot, Kung Henriks Målla, Lungmålla

Modern Danish Name: Konge-Henrik

Modern Norwegian Name: Stolt-Henrik

Deity Association: The Duergar

Height: 30"

Season: Perennial

History: Good King Henry's name relates to a contrasting plant, Mercury or Bad Henry, which is similar-looking but unrelated and quite poisonous. "King Henry" comes from German myths, which refer to "Heinz" or "Heinrich" as slang terms for kobolds and other underground-dwelling spirits. It is a perennial relative of the annual Lambsquarters, also called Fat Hen (*Chenopodium album*), which has been used as a spring green for so long that it was found in the stomach of prehistoric Tollund Man. In medieval Germany, Good King Henry itself was called Fette Henne for its use in fattening poultry; it traveled from Germany to England during the Middle Ages, where it was grown in cottage gardens for centuries until most folk forgot about it; it has naturalized as a weed in many places there after escaping from the ancient kitchen gardens.

Medicinal Uses: Alterative. Eat raw or cooked as a vitamin-packed tonic for invalids. Root is used as a veterinary cough remedy for sheep. The shoots are a gentle laxative. Poultices were made of the leaves, which gave rise to its folk name Smearwort.

Culinary Uses: Use as a salad green or a cooked green. Good King Henry is rich in iron and many other vitamins and minerals. The young asparagus-like shoots can be eaten the same way as the aforementioned vegetable.

Magical Uses: General good luck charm. Used to repel faeries in some spells, to contact them in others.

Shamanic Uses: Helps with leadership charisma. Eat some before you must lead a group, and carry some of the seeds with you if possible. However, if you dishonor your followers or students, even without their knowledge, the charm will cease to work. Good King Henry also has an affinity with the Duergar of Svartalfheim, and it may be that eating it might induce them to pay attention to you ... or not; they are a private people and not much for tourists.

Affinity: River (moistening) Harvest (nourishing). Use for Air conditions, such as constipation.

Point: ST 20

Plant-wight's Nature: Good King Henry came to me first dressed as a peasant, which surprised me. Ale-mug in one hand and bowl of porridge in the other, he offered me hospitality ... and this is one of his gifts, and his geases. He grows best in your garden when your hospitality is offered up openly and wholly. "Aren't you a King?" I asked. "All Kings need to start first with feeding their people," he said, and I heard an echo of the Celtic Oak-God Dagdathe ruler who dressed as a farmer and had the overflowing cauldron with which to feed the hungry. Good King Henry is a nourisher-plant and a healer; he wants to see people's digestion working well, and their homes peaceful and open to travelers, and one of his mysteries is how those two things work together, or so he told me.

Magical Charm: King's Belly

If you are the leader of a people who need some important thing in order to survive and be happy, and you have no idea how to go about getting them this thing, call upon Good King Henry to help you. Make a pottage of the fresh plant, gently steamed; you can top it with any sauce you like. As you sit down to eat, say the following charm:

> *King Heinrich, I call you up from below,*

My people are hungry and I would feed them,
I would feed their bellies, their hearts, their souls,
King Allgood, show me the underneath road.

Eat the meal and then go and meditate while it sits in your belly; the way will be opened to you. If nothing comes immediately, wait a few days and see if the situation resolves itself or a solution appears.

Gorse

Botanical name: *Ulex europaeus*
Folk names: Furze, Fyrs, Gorst, Goss, Prickly Broom, Ruffet, Whin, Honeybottles, Hoth
Anglo-Saxon Name: Gorst, Fyrs
Old Norse Names: Hvingras, Hvene
Old High Germanic Name: Gerst
Modern German Names: Europäischer Stechginster, Gaspeldorn, Spindeldorn
Modern Swedish Name: Ärttörne
Modern Danish Name: Tornblad
Modern Norwegian Name: Gulltorn
Deity Association: Surt, Logi, fire-etins, Beyla
Height: 3-6'
Season: Perennial Shrub
History: Gorse is native to nearly the entirety of western Europe, from Scotland to Portugal. It was grown deliberately as a hedge-plant, keeping livestock from wandering. The Celts considered Gorse to be one of the sacred grove plants for its ability to attract bees to its flowers and make sweet honey, and called it Onn. Its two Anglo-Saxon names mean "wasteland" and "fierce". Its name "Gorse" comes from a Germanic variant for Barley, because of its spines. Its name "Furze" comes from the Greek name for Wheat, while its British name "Whin" is from the Norse name.
Medicinal Uses: Gorse seeds are a powerful purgative.
Household Uses: Burned, Gorse makes excellent alkali ashes for lye and soap, or the ashes can be left to dress a field for fertility. Gorse bushes were routinely burned every three years for this purpose. Ground up, it makes a fine ruminant fodder.
Magical Uses: Used as a general-purpose protection spell when planted in hedges. Flowering Gorse was put in bridal bouquets to keep romance burning. It is associated with the spring equinox.
Shamanic Uses: Gorse is what is referred to as a "fire-climax" plant, meaning that it is designed to burn to the root during forest fires and regrow; its seeds are even adapted to germinate after a slight scorching with fire. Its fire-affinity, as well as its strong sense of guardianship, make it an excellent protective plant to guard a sacred area, as well as a guide and guardian through Muspellheim. It also has a strong affinity with bees—it is a yellow-flowered stinging plant that the yellow stinging insects love—and thus is loved by Frey's beekeeper Beyla, although she treats it more like a nasty dog that will lay down lovingly for her.
Affinity: Air (astringent). Not to be used without someone knowledgeable, which we are not at this time.
Point: ST2
Plant-wight's Nature: Gorse is a biter, even more than Nettles. Where Nettles can be trained as soldiers in a mass, Gorse is the border guard, the barking dog, the hypervigilant one who is ready to snarl and jump at anything. He tends to dislike and distrust warriors and responds much more docilely to domestically-oriented women. If a family wishes him to adopt them and guard their home, it is the mother who should go forth and make the connection, if she is such a woman; if not, a girl-child of

peaceable temperament will do. Admiring his golden flowers in summer appeals to his vanity and helps him to like you a little better.

Magical Charm: Blessing a Gorse Hedge

When your Gorse plants are three years of age, you can go out at midnight and then "hire" them to be your border guards and protect your home from all evils physical and nonphysical, with this charm:

> *Fiercest Furze, Golden Gorse,*
> *Guard my gates with bark and bite,*
> *Be as my bear, O Honey-bottle,*
> *My bees that swarm and set affright*
> *All that would harm this home, this night.*

Ground Ivy

Botanical Name: *Glechoma hederacea*

Folk Names: Alehoof, Catsfoot, Gill-Over-The-Ground, Haymaids, Hedgemaids, Lizzy-Run-Up-The-Hedge, Robin-Run-In-The-Hedge, Tunhoof, Hederich

Anglo-Saxon Name: Eorðifig ("Earth Ivy")

Modern German Names: Echte Gundelrebe, Efeu-Gundermann, Gewöhnlicher Gundermann, Gundelrebe, Gundermann

Modern Swedish Name: Jordreva

Modern Danish Name: Korsknap

Modern Norwegian Name: Vårkorsknapp

Deity Association: Aegir

Height: 6'

Season: Perennial

History: Ground Ivy is a common weed everywhere in Europe, taking over hedges and waste places and stripped fields. It was a common herb for flavoring ales in the days before Hops became popular. Its medieval country name, Gill, came from a pun on the similarity between Old French words "brewing" and "maiden"; it will still respond to the name "Gillie" today.

Medicinal Uses: Ground Ivy has a strong affinity for the ear, and especially the inner and middle ear. It treats ear infections and any head infections that began in the ear. Snorting the juice up one's nose will treat sinus infections. Ground Ivy thins the blood and thus regulates the heartbeat, and helps the gastrointestinal tract. It is a tonic, blood cleanser, diuretic and expectorant, used for UTIs and colds. It has been known to help in cases of lead poisoning, casting lead out of the body, and may well work for other heavy metals as well. It has also been used to treat cancer.

Household Uses: Used as a flavoring in brewing.

Culinary Uses: Young leaves are eaten in salads and brewed into aromatic "gill" tea.

Magical Uses: Ground Ivy is used as a hex-breaker, and to discover who planted the hex. It is also used as a surrogate substance for a large body of water in magical practice. Wearing a wreath of Ground Ivy on the head is said to make one immune to glamour of any kind, and allow one to see faeries, sorcerers, and other various folk of power.

Shamanic Uses: One of the plants that Aegir the brewer likes, Ground Ivy can be used to flavor sacred ales. A patch of Ground Ivy can be used to link to a body of water in pathwalking practices.

Affinity: Storm (bitter alterative), Mountain (relaxant), Air (astringent), Earth (cooling). Use on Swamp and Earth conditions.

Point: KD 4

Plant-wight's Nature: Ground Ivy has the temperament of an overgrown hyperactive six-year-old—one part Calvin, one part Dennis the Menace. Enthusiastic, bouncing, and somewhat sly, he will take over any area as fast as he can, the second your back is turned, and laugh at you. If you start working with him medicinally/magically, and you are growing this very invasive herb on your property, be warned—he may expect the price for his involvement be that you let him grow anywhere he likes, and this may have to be negotiated carefully.

Medicinal Charm: Gill Tea

Infuse an ounce of chopped Ground Ivy in a pint of boiling water, sweeten to taste, and drink a cupful a day to maintain kidney health and treat chronic bronchial problems, or to treat ear-aches or any of the other suggestions above. As it boils, say this charm:

> Gillie, gillie, Earth Ivy, Sea-On-Land,
> Haymaid, Hedgemaid, keep me hale,
> Well of Waters never fail, ale to my hand.

Hawthorn

Botanical name: *Crataegus oxacantha*

Folk names: Bread And Cheese Tree, Gaxels, Hagthorn, Halves, Haw, Huath, Ladies' Meat, May Tree, Mayblossom, Quickthorn

Anglo-Saxon Name: Hægþorn ("Hedge-thorn"), Þefeþorn ("Bushy Thorn")

Old Norse Name: Hagþorn

Old High Germanic Name: Hagendorn

Modern German Name: Zweigriffeliger Weißdorn

Modern Swedish Name: Hagtorn

Modern Danish Name: Tjørn

Modern Norwegian Name: Hagtorn

Deity Association: Thor

Height: 15-30'

Season: Perennial; small shrub-tree

History: The Hawthorn, or May-Tree, has been a classic hedge-tree all over Europe for millennia. It was used especially in England and Germany to keep in roving livestock, as its two-inch brutal thorns were the ancient equivalent of barbed wire. The Celts associated it with the love-goddess. The top wreath of the classic pyramidal triple-ring Maypole wreath is traditionally made of Hawthorn.

Medicinal Uses: An important cardiac herb, Hawthorn berries improve cardiac circulation, dilating the blood vessels and improving the pump action, which helps both high and low blood pressure, as well as angina. Hawthorn works well with Yarrow for high blood pressure. It also lowers bad cholesterol and causes more efficient patching of blood vessels. In general, it works on the heart muscle itself, calming cardiac arrhythmias and making the heart more efficient. It has been used in autoimmune disease, gently calming the immune system, and as an antihistamine in sinus infections. The berries, when cooked with meat, help digest fats.

Household Uses: Hawthorn-blossom liqueur can be made by steeping the spring blossoms in brandy.

Magical Uses: Protects against lightning and the dead. Hawthorn is used in love charms, especially where there is pain or unrequited love involved, and also to maintain chastity or fidelity. Traditional Maypoles had three rings on the top, and the highest and smallest was made of Hawthorn. Some writings will tell you to climb to the top of a Hawthorn tree to gather its wood; these folks have clearly never grown Hawthorns. They don't grow very tall—more like a large shrub—and to attempt to climb even the tallest would be to incur grave injury from the one-to-two-inch spikes all over it, if you didn't knock the whole thing over. Hawthorn is one of the traditional British "hedgerow" plants.

For soothing the pain of your denied passions, make a simple tea of crushed fresh haws (or dried ones, if you can obtain no other) and sip it while asking Hawthorn's aid in redirecting the energy of your thwarted passion to a more appropriate place. Do this as often as you need to, then when you have achieved your goal, go out and make an offering of wine or honey to the nearest Hawthorn. If you cannot find one, pour out your offering onto the earth while invoking a blessing and gratitude to the Hawthorn spirit.

Shamanic Uses: Supposedly Thor created the Hawthorn with a single bolt of lightning. It is one of the nine woods used in funeral pyres for the cremation of warriors. The Alfar love Hawthorn, and it is a good propitiatory plant for them as well. Its thorns can be broken off and stabbed through something that you wish to harm or stop, or a symbol of your foe. If you are unsure of the whether such an action is ethical, ask for Thor's blessing and protection on your action. If he does not seem inclined to give it to you, perhaps you shouldn't do it.

Affinity: Earth (cooling). Use for Fire conditions.

Point: HT 6

Plant-wight's Nature:

Hawthorn is a gender-ambivalent tree in that it will present itself to you as the gender you have the easiest time relating to and/or the gender of your primary sexual preference. Aside from that, Hawthorn is, for all its extremes in fruit and thorns, a straightforward and approachable spirit. It is particularly fond of those with Alf bloodlines and is one of the trees sacred to both the Ljossalfar and the Svartalfar. However, Hawthorn is willing to work with anybody regardless of blood, provided you evince enough respect for its power and are suitably grateful for whatever aid it offers you.

Hawthorn's magic centers around passion—not solely in the romantic sense, but also as concerns raw, unbridled desire and longing. This emotion can be for a god, a place, a thing, a talent or gift, anything in your life for which you have strong emotions that run deep. In what seems to be a reversal of appropriate symbolism, it is the long, wicked thorns of the Hawthorn tree that have to do with the expression of one's passions, while the attractive red haws (berries) are for the assuaging of the suffering that comes from passions that are denied.
                                                                                -Elizabeth Vongvisith

Magical Charm: Passion And Thorns

To strengthen your heart's passions, take as many thorns from the Hawthorn as you have loves you wish to honor and express. Make a small red clay or wax heart about 3 to 4 inches in diameter. Before it hardens, sing this charm and plunge each thorn into the heart one by one at the appropriate line:

> *Soul of the tree*
> *Tree of the fruit*
> *Fruit of the fire*
> *Fire of the blood*
> *Blood of the heart*
> *Heart of the soul*
> *Soul's longings revealed:*
> *One for [name]*
> *Two for [name]*
> *Three for [name] etc.*
                                                                                -Elizabeth Vongvisith

Heather

Botanical Name: *Calluna vulgaris*
Folk Names: Ling, Scots Heather, Ura
Anglo-Saxon Name: Hæð
Old Norse Name: Lyng
Modern German Names: Besenheide, Heidekraut
Modern Swedish Name: Ljung

Modern Danish Name: Hedelyng
Modern Norwegian Name: Røsslyng
Deity Association: Gna
Height: 2'
Season: Perennial
History: There are more than a thousand varieties of Heather, and they are found around the entire northern hemisphere, but are especially associated with the British Isles. White Heather is believed to be lucky, while Pink or Purple Heather is supposedly the spilt blood of the Picts.
Medicinal Uses: General tonic, treatment for UTIs and kidney problems. A bath made with the flowering tops of Heather relieves rheumatic pain.
Household Uses: Flower tips yield a green dye. Used as thatch and fodder. Bark contains tannin and is brewed into tea. Heather has been used for thatching, making baskets and brooms, and flavoring ale. Flowering tips yield a yellow dye; leaves and stems a dark gold dye. Heather was also used by the northern ancestors for thatch, bedding, fuel, floor mats, ale flavoring, pegs and nails from the roots, baskets, brooms, and feed and bedding for livestock.
Magical Uses: Carried as protection against rape and other violent crimes. When burned with ferns, it brings rain. For a good sleep in the face of terrible insomnia, make a bed of freshly cut Heather and lie on it. A bath of Heather is said to maintain youth and beauty, and Heather tea will supposedly prolong life and possibly bring immortality.
Shamanic Uses: Heather is a plant of the wind, and is much loved by Gna, Frigga's messenger who rides the winds. Scatter Heather to the winds and call out your message, and entreat Gna to carry it to its destination.
Affinity: Mountain (relaxant), Stone (sedative), Air (astringent), Storm (general detoxifier), Fire (pungent). Use for Cold Earth, Swamp, Storm.
Point: KD 10
Plant-wight's Nature: Sister Heather is another dancer, but unlike Cherry she is feral and dances alone in the wild places, flowers in her long tangled hair. She appeared to me as an adolescent girl, dark-skinned and dark-haired, dressed in ragged skins; I wondered if she still held the spirit of the long-lost Picts. Unlike some greenwights who are happy to adapt to modern civilization—Grandfather Plantain, for instance, doesn't care a whit if the roads are traveled by cars, horse-drawn wagons, or bare and dusty feet—Sister Heather fears modern technology and prefers the age of thatched huts and open hearthfires. She is more likely to be comfortable with humans who approach her in archaic dress and can speak about old ways of life. Heather, unlike many greenwights, can fly on the winds in any area where she is naturalized.

Magical Charm: Wind Calling

There is no spoken charm for this; Sister Heather encouraged me to simply pick her, scatter her, and sing to the four directions on a still day—not even words, just random singing notes. You might choose to *galdr* the rune Ansuz. Then you wait. The wind will start blowing from a particular direction, and that's the wind-wight that is interested in you. Make friends; ask Sister Heather to introduce you, and make an offering. You can repeat this twice more, to see if two other winds might come. Be warned, though: no one ever gets an alliance with all four winds. They won't allow it. It would be too much power. It is said that shamans of old abused that privilege, and now it has been withdrawn and only three winds will ever speak to any one person. Sister Heather knows the story, although she won't tell it to you.

Herb Bennet

Botanical name: *Geum urbanum*

Folk names: Avens, Ram's Foot, Gold Star, Wild Rye, Wood Avens, Way Bennet, Goldy Earth Star, City Avens, Pesleporis, Harefoot, Minarta, Clove Root

Anglo-Saxon Name: Benedicte

Modern German Names: Echte Nelkenwurz, Benediktenkraut, Stadt-Nelkenwurz

Modern Swedish Names: Nejlikrot, Nejlikkummer

Modern Danish Name: Febernellikerod

Modern Norwegian Name: Kratthumleblomst

Deity Association: Bragi

Height: 2'

Season: Perennial

History: We don't know what the original Anglo-Saxon name for this plant might have been, as its Latin name took over and became popular. It was associated with St. Benedict, and was sometimes used as a motif for church carvings in the 13th century. Unlike other plants with Latin names which have come north from southern Europe, Herb Bennet is solidly native as a weed all over Europe and central Asia, as far north as Finland and Norway. In America today, the name "Avens" is usually applied to its ornamental cousin *Geum coccineus*, and few know about Herb Bennet, which is a shame.

Medicinal Uses: In the Middle Ages, a cordial against the plague was made by boiling the roots in wine. Today, an infusion is used to treat diarrhea, dysentery, fever and chills, and excess phlegm. The powdered root is sometimes mixed with Arnica in the making of bruise salve. Both leaves and root are an astringent, and can be gargled for sore throats, halitosis, and mouth ulcers. While the leaves are safe, the root can cause stomach problems and nausea if overdosed internally.

Household Uses: Used to keep moths away from clothing.

Culinary Uses: Rhizome is used to flavor beer, wine, and liqueurs, and sometimes in soups or stews. Leaves can be added to salads and soups. Traditional "Augsburg Ale" owed its clove-like flavor to Herb Bennet.

Magical Uses: General good luck herb. In the past it was worn as a charm to ward off evil spirits.

Shamanic Uses: Herb Bennet can be used, with Bragi's permission, to give you welcome in strange places. Bragi himself is one of the few Gods who is welcome anywhere he goes, takes no part in politics, and all hearths are open to him. Carrying Herb Bennet can help your welcome into a possible hostile place, as long as you follow Bragi's path when visiting dangerous places—be urbane, courteous, entertaining, impossible to provoke, and never take sides with anyone about anything. If you get defensive, the spell will break and people will start scowling at you.

Affinity: Air (astringent), Fire (pungent). Use for River and Earth conditions.

Point: TH 4

Plant-wight's Nature: Herb Bennet is a rotund, bald, cheerful and patient wight. Usually dressed in crinkled green robes, he is a bit shy and unassuming at first, but then is much more outgoing once he knows you, although he does spend a good deal of time smiling and nodding silently at you. He is not simple, however: just not a talker. He reminds me of a pleasant old monk, bustling about, answering people's questions with homilies. "I'm a blessing herb, you know," he says. "Not just for places, but for people too. Sprinkle leaves on people to bless them. It's a small blessing, but a good one."

Medicinal Charm: Plague Cordial

I don't exactly mean the Black Plague. I mean the sort of small plagues that run through households ... you know, you call them up, and every single person is groaning and coughing, and they say, "Don't come over ... we all have the plague." This is a good cordial for a household full of adults who can all drink alcohol, are all sick and miserable, and are settling in for an overnight plague-siege with tea, tissues, and trips to the toilet. Take a gallon of decent wine (not the sort that comes in a box) and heat it with 6 ounces Herb Bennet, 1 ounce of Agrimony, and 2 ounces of some kind of Mint. Heat for about half an hour at a good simmer, and then strain out the plant matter. Cut it with a half gallon of fruit juice—grape, pomegranate, blueberry, or any other non-citrus juice, add some Cinnamon and Nutmeg, and reheat until quite warm but still drinkable. Then give everyone a cupful and break out the old movies. Dose per person: 1 cup at first, another 2 hours later, and then 1 cup every 6 hours until the pot is demolished. It can be drunk warm or cold but is better warm. As you stir the pot, say this blessing:

> *Benedicta banish baneful spirits from the body,*
> *Ram's Foot right fever, Pesleporis slay plague,*
> *We beseech thee, Avens, for victory over ague.*

Holly

Botanical Name: *Ilex aquifolium*
Folk Names: Hulver Bush, Holm, Hulm, Holme Chase, Holy Tree, Christ's Thorn
Anglo-Saxon Name: Holen
Old Norse Name: Bein-vitr ("Bone-tree")
Old High Germanic Name: Hulis
Modern German Names: Stechpalme, Stechlaub
Modern Swedish Name: Järnek
Modern Danish Name: Kristtorn
Modern Norwegian Name: Kristtorn
Deity Association: Tyr, Thor, Holda
Height: 30'
Season: Perennial Tree
History: Holly was the tree of Saturn to the Romans, which created much of its association with the Yule season. Northern Europeans did revere Holly as one of the sacred evergreens—the trees who stayed green in the snowy season and thus were brought into the house—but they also honored the Holly in the summer, which almost no one does today. The Celts named the lunar month of Tinne (around July) after the Holly, as this was its season of flowering. The Holly King mythically triumphed over the Oak King at the summer Solstice, showing the transition from the Oak month (Duir) to the Holly month (Tinne), and he ruled during the waning part of the solar year. For the Celts, the Holly was the tree of the sacred warrior, as the Oak was the sacred king.

Holly trees were considered to be able to ward off evil, and were often planted near houses for this reason. In Scandinavia, Holly was Thor's, as the crooked lines of its leaves resembled lightning, and the trees were said to ward it off. In Germany, Holly was Holda's, in her guise as Frau Holle, the Winter Hag whose tree bears only in the snows. With its poisonous berries, Holly was the "dark side" of Frau Holle—the summer-fruiting Elder being her "light side". Holly trees have two sexes, and both are needed for fruiting; old Germanic myths claimed that if the Yule wreaths were made from the female Holly tree, the wife would rule the house for the year, and the husband if it were made from male Hollies.

Medicinal Uses: Holly is an emetic, used to induce vomiting in an emergency. However, as it is somewhat toxic, it should only be used by a trained herbalist who understands the dosage.

Household Uses: Holly wood has been used for turned ware and fancy inlaying. The twigs are given to cattle as fodder. The berries, while poisonous to humans, are favored by many birds and a Holly bush in the yard will encourage birds to your window.

Magical Uses: Protective tree when planted around the home. Holly water is sprinkled on infants to protect them. Nine Holly leaves tied up in a pillow with nine knots and slept on will help you to control your dreams. Holly leaves brought inside for the winter are a pledge to the local earth elementals to care for them.

Shamanic Uses: Holly is a weapon-tree in its own way. It was said that throwing twigs of Holly at attacking animals would cause them to lie down or run away, and so it is with Holly if you bring it to journeys in Otherworlds. Its flowers have the strange quality of making the rivers of Otherworlds temporarily freeze over, if you use the charm below.

Affinity: Earth (cooling), Air (astringent). Do not use without more information from trained professionals.

Point: ST 12

Plant-wight's Nature:

> Holly is a warrior's tree. I first encountered the spirit of this plant after a very rough period of ordeal with the God that owns me (Odin). I was at a point of deep despair and struggling to make sense of what had occurred and the sacrifice Odin had asked of me. Holly's spirit came to me offering to become an ally—on the condition that I mark myself with its ogham symbol and, should I ever own property, plant a Holly tree on my land. Visually, the spirit was very androgynous (in fact, I could not assign it a gender had I wanted to try), lean, slender, dressed in olive and deep forest greens...not drab at all but very matte, very much of a color that would blend with the flora and fauna of a place. The spirit's 'skin' appeared olive complexioned and it had a cap of short, black hair. The features were sharp-pointed, the eyes a glittering blue. It seemed lithe and fine boned but wiry strong.

> Magically, Holly is associated with warriors' craft and with the power of blood, specifically with the type of bond and oath that can be created through magical use of one's blood. It will not substitute for blood necessarily but added to spells and workings that demand blood as part of their binding force, it can dramatically (and dangerously) increase that bond. It is the warrior in service to a higher calling or power. There is a very strong cosmic groove here of the warrior in service to a sacred king. Holly is part and parcel of that archetypal "groove". Much of its power stems from that place. The spirit has a slightly glittering quality that I associate with the wildest of the Sidhe spirits, but for all of that it is down to earth and very pragmatic. It's extremely no nonsense and there is a momentum, a barely contained energy about it. It has work to do.

> Holly is, as noted above, strongly connected to both warriors and weapons. This spirit is very aware of obligations, caste, and one's place in the web of duty, loyalties, powers, and particularly the obligations in which a person maneuvers, navigates and exists. It is defined by these things in some very essential way. This spirit is very duty oriented and can be called upon to aid one in fulfilling one's sworn duties in the face of difficulties. But keep in mind, this particular spirit is exquisitely aware of hierarchies. Archetypally, the sacred warrior sacrifices herself for the sacred king. This pattern is embedded deeply in this spirit's nature. This is not a ronin, an unbound, unfettered, rogue warrior. This is a warrior bound deeply in service, and there is a great deal of pride in that service and in doing it rightly. In fact, I would not suggest calling on this particular spirit if you are the type of person who is sloppy about keeping his or her obligations and sworn word. My impression of Holly is that it would have only contempt for such a person. Also, once an obligation is entered into with this spirit, it isn't likely to forget about that tie.

> There is a sacred reciprocity between Holly and Oak, as Oak represents the sacred king and the attributes of sovereignty. Holly has some strong capacity to serve as a diplomat and may be willing to serve as a conduit and negotiator between two conflicting Powers. Given its warrior energy, magically Holly has a great deal of power to clear away blockages and obstacles (particularly spiritual obstacles).

> Holly can teach you what is worth fighting for, how to navigate the threads of conflict, and how to govern one's unruly passions and tongue. This spirit has a firm grip on wyrd, and knows exactly when it is

right and proper to sacrifice oneself and when doing so would be hubris and stupidity. When it comes down to it, Holly can also be called upon to augment one's power, particularly if one must make a territorial display of force. Holly understands the accoutrements of the warrior and how they are best and rightly used."   -Galina Krasskova

Magical Charm: Warrior's Will

To protect a warrior of any kind, be it that they are going into battle or must take on some tricky diplomatic mission, one can make this charm. Since it takes something like a year to make, it might be best to make it ahead and have it on hand. In the spring, pick three Holly leaves, dry them, and wrap them in a piece of red cloth. In the summer, pick three Holly blossoms and dry them, and add them in. In the autumn, scrape off a bit of bark, dry it, and add it to the cloth. In the winter, take three berries and dry them, and add them as well. Then add a tiny, sharp piece of iron and tie the whole thing up with white thread. Say the following charm, before giving it to the warrior of your choice:

> *Bone-Tree guard thee flesh and bone,*
> *Tyr thy tongue and hand shall bind*
> *To honor, truth, and skill at war,*
> *In four seasons, in four directions,*
> *In the four quarters of the world,*
> *Bone-Tree bring thee safely home*

Hops

Botanical Name: *Humulus lupulus*
Folk Names: Beer Flower, Hopbine
Anglo-Saxon Name: Hymele
Old High Germanic Name: Hopfo
Modern German Name: Hopfen
Modern Swedish Name: Humle
Modern Danish Name: Humle
Modern Norwegian Name: Humle
Deity Association: Frey
Height: To 20'
Season: Perennial
History: Hops is native to southern Europe and was spread to northern areas at some point in ancient times. It was naturalized in England by the time of the Anglo-Saxon herbals, and used widely in Germany as a beer-bitter at that time, although the English preferred to use other ale-flavors for several more centuries.
Medicinal Uses: Infuse as a mild sedative tea and bath soak. Hops is a muscle relaxant and urges good sleep. Female flowers contain estrogen and are used in tincture for menopause; it is also used on men for cases of inflammation of the sexual/urinary tracts and prostate problems. Hops, and beer containing Hops, should be avoided during depression, as it can make it worse.
Household Uses: Dried ripe female flowers preserve, clear, and flavor beer. Boil the leaves for a brown dye.
Culinary Uses: Male flowers can be parboiled and tossed into salads.
Magical Uses: Sleep spells, when sewn up in a pillow. Sprigs of the plant were hung on hearths for luck.
Shamanic Uses: Another of Frey's sacred plants, Hops are slept on to increase fertility and sexual energy. If your libido is flagging, you can propitiate Frey for help with an offering of hop blossoms. Ironically, the estrogen content of Hops has been known to impair the female menstrual cycle and lower male

libido ... why, then, is it associated with the rampant fertility and sexual energy of Frey? Besides the fact that it is used in beer, that is. It seems to be one of Frey's mysteries ... linked to the fact that some of Frey's worshippers were "unmanly men", and that he appreciates people of varying sexual preferences and places on the gender continuum. For Frey, the human hormone system is a tool to work with, and desire can be expressed in many different ways, including channeling it into nonphysical pursuits.

Affinity: Mountain (relaxant), Stone (sedative), Storm (bitter alterative). Use on Storm and (as a bitter tonic) Swamp conditions.

Point: LI 8

Plant-wight's Nature: Hops is a dream-plant—androgynous, smiling, twining. Hops-wight can be called on for dreaming, but not the sort that come true—more the sort of fantasies that make life worth living. Hops-wight is very useful for writers, artists, and others who make a living off of narrating dreams and fantasies, as long as they're the highly motivated type who won't get sunk in Hops-wight's sweet embrace. (There's a reason this plant is put in alcohol, beyond even the issue of flavor.) Hops-wight tends to appear in a high place, reaching down to you, and is always in a mellow mood; they can be more male or more female, often depending on the sex of the plant you have in front of you (Hops is a dual-gendered plant). If you ask Hops-wight to make a dream come true, you'll get an answer of "Of course! You should have that come to you." Then nothing will happen, because Hops-wight's idea of bringing that to you is to increase the intensity of the fantasy. This is not a wight for concrete manifestations ... but they are great for peaceful sleeping with beautiful dreams.

Magical Charm: Hops Sleep Pillow

Make a small flat pillow stuffed with dried Hop blossoms, and embroider the following words on it, to lay on in times of insomnia:

> *Light lay heavy head*
> *Ears hear no tired tread,*
> *Sound sleep, dream deep.*

Horehound

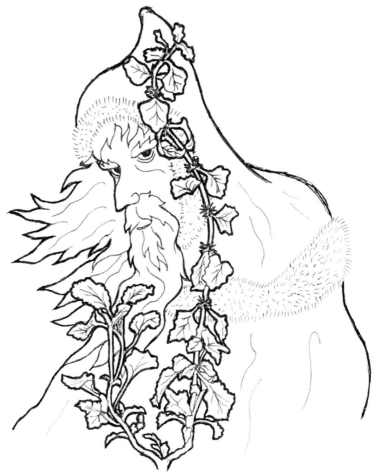

Botanical Name: *Marrubium vulgare* (White Horehound), *Ballota nigra* (Black Horehound)

Folk Names: Marubie, Bulls' Blood, Eye of the Star, Haran, Har Hune, Llwyd Y Cun, Marob, Seed of Horus, Soldier's Tea

Anglo-Saxon Name: Haranhune

Modern German Name: Gemeiner Andorn

Modern Swedish Namess: Kransborre, Andorn

Modern Danish Name: Hunderod

Modern Norwegian Names: Borremynte (white), Hunderot (black).

Deity Association: Odin

Height: 18"

Season: Perennial

History: Horehound originated in

Mediterranean Europe and northern Africa, where the Egyptians considered it sacred to Horus and one of their greatest healing herbs. It was probably introduced to the Germanic peoples during the Roman occupation of Germany, brought to England by the Saxon invasion and to Scandinavia even later. It was naturalized in England by the time of the Anglo-Saxon herbals.

Medicinal Uses: The classic cough herb, White Horehound is usually put into cough drops or syrup. An infusion relaxes muscles and helps expel mucus, and is good for asthma and bronchitisIt destroys worms, is a liver tonic, and a mild laxative. Externally, the tea is used as a wash for eczema. Both Horehounds are very mild sedatives which can help soothe rapid heartbeat. A hot infusion of Black Horehound helps to break fevers and is used to treat malaria when quinine is ineffective; Black Horehound is good for diseases that include fever and chills, diarrhea, nausea, cramps, belching, and/or coughing blood.

Household Uses: Infuse in fresh milk and set in a dish as a fly killer. Infuse in water and spray fruit trees for cankerworm. The woolly leaves were once used to clean milk-pails, in order to keep away milk-spoiling faeries. The dried flower can be floated on oil as a candle wick, especially good for seidhr-workings that involve Odin.

Magical Uses: Healing potions, and strengthening the mental powers and memory. Used in sacred fasting to cleanse the body, and in spells to maintain focus and clarity. Horehound can also be used to clear an area of old magic, and to repel any spell not of the person holding the Horehound.

Shamanic Uses: White Horehound is beloved of Odin; supposedly when its leaves are mixed with those of the Ash tree, they emit healing vibrations together and can be burned to heal people or left as potpourri in a sickroom. Horehound links us to the power of Huginn and Muninn, Odin's ravens who symbolize Thought and Memory. Carry it or breathe its smoke or drink it in tea to invoke their aid to strengthen your mind. (Despite its name, it has nothing to do with hounds; the name comes from the Old English *haranhune*, possibly meaning downy plant.)

Affinity: Storm (bitter alterative), Fire (pungent), Air (astringent). Use on Swamp, Earth, and River conditions.

Point: ST 14 (white), PC 3 (black)

Plant-wight's Nature: Grandfather Horehound is like a frost-thurse—sweeping silver beard and hair, moustaches long enough to blow in the wind, grim grey eyes that fix on you. His voice is a hoarse wind, and like frost-thurses, he does command the winds to a small extent, although this is not knowledge he will share with you. As a plant wind-wight, he has power over the respiratory system, especially the throat which is the tunnel of the wind. The best time to speak to him is when the wind is blowing, and you are actually standing in it, which can be fun if you've got a cold.

Medicinal Charm: Horehound Cough Drops

Make 3 cups of a very strong tea of the following herbs:

3 parts White Horehound

1 part Black Horehound

2 parts Mint

2 parts Thyme

1 part Lemon Balm

Heat on the stove and slowly stir in 3 pounds of brown sugar. Keep heating it until it reaches 300 degrees, which is the hard-crack candy stage. Then turn it out on a greased board and stretch it out like taffy, snipping it into drop-size bits with scissors, as quickly as possible. Let it set on a tray, sprinkle with powdered sugar to keep them from sticking together (or wrap them all separately in bits of wax paper), and store in a jar. Don't let the jar get warm; I did once and discovered that I now had one giant cough drop that I had to chip out bit by bit. Here is the charm to say while stirring the pot:

Bull's Blood, Star's Eye, stay the cough,
Woden, wheel the wind of breath
To freely flow with Soldier's Joy.

Horseradish

Botanical name: *Armoracia rusticana*
Folk names: Red Cole, Mountain Radish, Great Raifort
Anglo-Saxon Names: Hrædic, Ontre, Antre
Old High Germanic Name: Ratih
Modern German Names: Meerrettich, Kren, Bauernsenf
Modern Swedish Name: Pepparrot
Modern Danish Name: Peberrod
Modern Norwegian Name: Pepperrot
Deity Association: Surt, Farbauti
Height: 3'
Season: Perennial

History: Horseradish seems to have originated in eastern Europe, through Russia and Poland to Finland, and thus come to Germany, Denmark, and the rest of Scandinavia, where it was not only a medicinal plant but a popular condiment as well. It seems to have passed into Britain during the Middle Ages, but it was not recognized for its culinary value for many centuries, even after it had naturalized by the 16th century. The English knew of the German custom of Horseradish sauce, but claimed that it was too strong for their sensitive British bellies; it did, however, eventually make it into their cooking as well. The French also learned of Horseradish, both medicinally and culinarily, from their northern neighbors.

Medicinal Uses: Grated Horseradish root can be taken in a syrup for bronchitis and coughs, for hoarseness, and for chronic coughs after a flu has been beaten but the symptoms linger, or used as a mild antibiotic for colds, or poulticed and applied to arthritic joints, or on the chest like a Mustard plaster. Horseradish glycerite has been used to help children with whooping cough. It is a strong diuretic, and was given to children as a safe vermifuge. It is best in cold, depressed conditions.

Household Uses: Leaves yield a yellow dye. Grow near other plants for insect repellent. Root infusion can be sprayed on Apple trees against brown rot. Horseradish soaked in milk is used as a cosmetic to clear the skin.

Culinary Uses: Young leaves can be added to salads. The freshly grated root can be made into Horseradish sauce for real German cookery, or added to cream sauces. It is a strong aid to digestion, especially of greasy foods.

Magical Uses: Grated Horseradish root is sprinkled around homes for protection.

Shamanic Uses: This plant is highly valued by Surt and the fire-etins of Muspellheim, and can be used to propitiate them. While you carry it, they are unlikely to attack you, especially if you share some. Carve the rune Cweorth into it to make an offering of it.

Affinity: Fire (pungent). Use on Earth and Swamp.

Point: LI 20

Plant-wight's Nature: Horseradish-wight has brick-colored red skin that looks rough and shingled to the touch, close-set eyes, and a great mouth Filled with crooked teeth. He seems all muscled arms and legs and very little torso, like a great hairless red troll. He gives off a great deal of heat that you can feel radiating from him, and likes to punch things. He is good-natured if you don't mind foul and scatological jokes, often about people's digestion. He has been known to turn into large ugly red animal-shapes as well as his somewhat humanoid form. Sometimes he just looks like an enormous radish root with his eyes and mouth.

Medicinal Charm: Clearing the Sky

To get rid of the last of that winter cough, grind Horseradish fine (wearing a gas mask if you need to) and mix it with a bit of oil, and smear it on a thin cloth covering your chest (or a layer of plastic wrap, which is even better) and relax. As you lay there, say the following charm:

Hraedic, raid my rainy sky
Of horrid clouds and hideous birds
That wheel in hordes and bate my breath,
Great Raifort, frighten them away.

Houseleek

Botanical Name: *Sempervivum tectorum*
Folk Names: Hen and Chicks, Thor's Beard, Sengren, Donnerbart, Welcome-Home-Husband-Though-Never-So-Drunk (I particularly like that one, and I sometimes wonder if it was Sif who made that up!)
Anglo-Saxon Names: Sinfulle ("Always-Abundant"), Singrene ("Always-Green")
Modern German Name: Echte Hauswurz
Modern Swedish Name: Taklök
Modern Danish Name: Husløg
Modern Norwegian Name: Takløk
Deity Association: Thor
Height: 4"
Season: Perennial
History: Houseleek is native to central and southern Europe; it moved to the northern part of the continent in preliterate times and came to England in the medieval period. Charlemagne declared that all householders grow the plant on their roofs to prevent lightning-strike.
Medicinal Uses: Rather like a weak version of aloe vera, its petals can be cut open and the salve smeared on burns.
Magical Uses: Protects a house from lightning, especially when placed on the roof in a pot. Brings good luck. Sacred to Thor in his aspect as Hurler of Lightning. The juice of Houseleek, mixed with crushed Nettles and rubbed on the hand, is said to attract fish when you put your hand in the water.
Shamanic Uses: Affinity to the rune Sowelu/Sigil. Carve a Sigil rune on a leaf of Houseleek for protection and victory.
Affinity: Earth (cooling), Air (astringent). Use on Fire and River.
Point: LI 15
Plant-wight's Nature: Houseleek is mysterious and strange. She grows leaves, and her babies, in a spiral pattern, and indeed if one wishes to speak with her it is best to draw a spiral on one's self or trace it in the dirt before you speak. She sits in the earth like a plump lump, skirts spread out in a spiral pattern, looking up at you with a face full of wrinkles and bright black birdlike eyes. She speaks in riddles, too, and sometimes what seems like complete nonsense, including odd clucks and chirps.
Medicinal Charm: After Lightning Strikes
  While Houseleek can be used like aloe on burns, it has a special relationship with burns caused by electricity. Cut open a leaf and smear the goo onto the electric burn, and say the following charm:
  Soothe the skin where lightning lit,
  Fell the fire with Singrene's spit.

Hyssop

Botanical name: *Hyssopus officinalis*
Folk names: Issopo Celestino, Azob
Anglo-Saxon Name: Ysope
Modern German Name: Ysop
Modern Swedish Name: Isop
Modern Danish Name: Isop
Modern Norwegian Name: Isop
Deity Association: Gerda
Height: 3'
Season: Perennial

History: Hyssop's European name comes from the Greek *azob*, meaning holy herb, as it was used in sacred aspergers and to wash down temples. An herb named Hyssop is mentioned in the Bible, but scholars generally agree that it is not *Hyssopus officinalis*, but another plant entirely, as it is not native to those parts of the Middle East. The Greeks, on the other hand, described Hyssop clearly; several of the Greek physicians recommended it highly. Its origin seems to be Mediterranean, coming north to the upper parts of Europe via Roman trade with the British. It is established in England as a deliberately grown medicinal herb by the time of the Anglo-Saxon herbals, although it may never have really naturalized in colder climates.

Medicinal Uses: An excellent expectorant and cold treatment, the flowering tops of Hyssop are used in cough teas, cough syrups, cough drops (especially combined with Horehound), plasters and chest rubs, and for asthma treatments. The tea is also a powerful vermifuge and aids in digestion. It is used for long-term fevers that make people stupid and slow; its action is penetrating and clearing, acting on catarrh and heat-hardened mucus in deep respiratory infections. Another of its long-term uses is in salve for rheumatoid arthritis which can also be used on cuts and bruises to quicken healing. A leaf poultice was applied to fresh wounds in order to head off tetanus. The German abbess Hildegard of Bingen recommended chicken soup made with Hyssop as a curative for coughs and depression. The leaves contain an antiseptic, antiviral oil that is, however, mildly poisonous when distilled out and concentrated, unlike the entirely safe concentration in the unadulterated flowers and leaves. It is used to treat cold sores, bruises, and scarring, increase alertness, and is a gentle nerve tonic for stress, but the oil should only be used by a qualified herbalist who can get the dose right. Some people have reported that Hyssop oil aids in reducing the progression of HIV. Pregnant women should not ingest any form of Hyssop, as it has emmenagogue effects and is sometimes used in abortifacient mixtures.

Household Uses: Excellent bee plant. Formerly used as a strewing herb in medieval times, it is added to potpourri and laundry rinses. The essential oil is used in perfumes, and is an insecticide. A companion plant for cabbages—luring away the cabbage moths—Hyssop should not be grown next to radishes, as they are enemies.

Culinary Uses: The leaves are an ingredient in the liqueur Chartreuse. At one time they were added to meat as a flavoring, as they aid in the digestion of fats, but Hyssop is rarely used culinarily today.

Magical Uses: Purification of any space or object, or in baths for personal purification. Can be used as a wash for sacred/magical clothing and objects.

Shamanic Uses: Hyssop baths are a good thing for cleansing one's self after coming back from any kind of journeying where you might have picked up something nasty on your astral body. Add a strong cup of tea to the bath, or at least stand in the shower and pour it over yourself, and make sure that you drink some of it as well. If you have picked up anything, expect Hyssop to present as an expectorant and make you start coughing things up. Coughing during a Hyssop purification should be a sign to stop and check yourself over, or be checked over, for psychic filth that needs to come out.

Affinity: Fire (stimulant), Storm(bitter alterative). Use on Earth and Swamp conditions.

Point: ST 40

Plant-wight's Nature: Mistress Hyssop appears to me as one of the Wisewoman plant-wights, but unlike witchy Mugwort, she is more the herb-wife in her tidy cottage, flowers blooming about the place and a cat curled up on the mat. Hyssop is a Teacher, and she knows a great deal about healing, although she is not much consulted these days. I was surprised to find that she not only knows all about how to use her plant, she knows a good deal about other plants as well, as if her sharp eyes and ears note everyone else's business. "That one over there, he's going to be trouble if you take him as an ally. Be careful. And move him out of that bed next year." She is sharp and precise, with a tongue that I expect could be tightly sarcastic if she didn't like you—there is definitely something of the schoolmarm about her—but she will generally teach you what she knows, because she feels that it is her Duty, whether she likes you or not. I grow blue-flowered Hyssop, and she always appears to me dressed in a neat, modest blue gown and cap. She does like cats, for some reason.

Medicinal Charm: Hyssop Tea

Infuse a quarter of an ounce of dried Hyssop flowers, or a half ounce of fresh flowering tops, in a pint of boiling water for ten minutes. Add honey to taste and drink. Before you ingest it, say this charm:

> Hail Hyssop, Holy Herb,
> Cleanse the wind that I breathe,
> Cleanse the road that I walk,
> Cleanse the rivers within me,
> Cleanse lich and hame together,
> Bind me together as one.

Iceland Moss

Botanical name: *Cetraria islandica*

Folk names: Bread Moss, Consumption Moss, Eryngo-Leaved Liverwort, Fever Moss, Iceland Lichen, Lung Moss, Swine Moss

Old Norse Name: Mosa

Modern German Name: Isländisches Moos

Modern Swedish Names: Islandslav, Brömosse, Renhorn

Modern Danish Name: Islandmos

Modern Norwegian Name: Islandslav

Deity Association: Hyndla

Height: 4"

Season: Perennial Lichen

History: Icelandic Moss is not actually a moss, but a lichen. It grown in the mountainous regions of all parts of northern Europe—Scotland, Ireland, Norway, etc.—but is especially characteristic of the lava-hills of Iceland.

Medicinal Uses: Iceland Moss was popularly used to fight tuberculosis, as it contains mucilage and is an expectorant, soothes nausea, and is a mild antibiotic. It has been used in tincture form to fight chest colds for many centuries, and is used in teas to nourish sickly individuals during their recovery, or elderly people. Its constituents form a soothing layer over mucous membranes of the mouth and throat. Some compounds in Icelandic Moss have been found in laboratory studies to inhibit HIV progression. Not recommended for people with gastrointestinal ulcers. There have recently been some problems with supplies of Icelandic Moss, as it concentrates lead from gasoline in the air, so if you live in the right climate you might want to try growing it yourself.

Household Uses: Yields a brown dye. Used to tan hides.

Culinary Uses: Used as an emergency food in desolate circumstances. Icelandic Moss contains a large amount of lichen-starch, which can be dried and used for neutral thickeners in cooking. During times of famine, *Cetraria islandica* was soaked in lye to neutralize the lichen acids, powdered and added to bread to make the flour go further. The hardened jelly of that lichen was used as a thickener for jellies, jams, and other desserts.

Magical Uses: Survival in very cold weather.

Shamanic Uses: Icelandic Moss may be a good travel charm, especially when crossing water. It is also useful for traveling in very cold places. Take it with you to Niflheim. The various cold-weather mosses are much liked by Hyndla, goddess of bloodlines and genealogy, and make a good offering to her.

Affinity: Storm (bitter alterative), River (moistening). Use on Swamp and Air conditions.

Point: UB 43

Plant-wight's Nature: Many of the Lichens tend to appear in animal forms to me for some reason, and Icelandic Moss was no exception ... it appeared as a great snowy owl, swooping through the air and landing in a nearby Fir tree. It communicated to me that part of its gift of survival in cold weather was not just about consuming the lichen itself, but that the lichen-wight could lead you to other sources of nourishment ... if you weren't too picky about what it was.

Medicinal Charm: Lichen's Life

Infuse 1 ounce of dried Icelandic Moss in a pint of boiling water. If you want to decrease its bitterness, you can discard the water and reboil it in another change of water, but this may decrease its antibiotic effects. This can be drunk once a day for any of the above problems, saying, "Tell the trees, Bark-Clinger, that I am well, Winter-Singer, and let no lasting chill linger."

Ivy

Botanical name: *Hedera helix*

Folk names: English Ivy, Bindweed, Lovestone

Anglo-Saxon Names: Ifig, Yfig

Modern German Name: Efeu

Modern Swedish Name: Murgröna

Modern Danish Names: Efeu, Vedbend

Modern Norwegian Names: Eføy, Bergflette

Deity Association: Jormundgand

Height: Up to 100'

Season: Perennial Vine

History: Ivy is native to every part of Europe from Norway to Iran. The Celts named the month of Gort after the Ivy, which twines to the sky and has been associated with reaching for the heavens, and with feminine energy (if one assumes that femininity equals passivity and needing to be supported). As it came right after the month dedicated to the grapevine, it was said to be "the enemy of the vine" and often used against intoxication. The ancient Greeks associated Ivy with Dionysos and his Maenads—in Greece it was most definitely a friend to the grapevine—and thus it became a symbol of gaiety. The Romans considered it a symbol of fidelity and used it in wedding wreaths and bouquets, where it is used to this day. To them, it was the herb of Saturnalia, because it was the home of the gold-crested wren, the bird associated with Saturn.

Medicinal Uses: Specific. Ivy is poisonous to humans, although it has been used in the past for dysentery, to soothe neuralgia, sciatica, and rheumatic pain, in a tincture for whooping cough and toothache, and as a poultice for sunburn. Only trained herbalists should mess with using it internally, but externally it can be used as a poultice, or in liniment (traditionally mixed with Rose water or Rose oil) to rub on the temples for headache.

Household Uses: Used as an overdye to darken black silk, or darken hair.

Magical Uses: Carried against natural disasters, and put in fidelity charms. Wreaths of Ivy were bound around the brow in Greece in order to prevent intoxication while drinking, and it was also added to alcohol for that purpose.

Shamanic Uses: Binding spells. This is a plant sacred to Jormundgand in its capacity as knotter and binder, and pieces of Ivy can be used on one's self or another for any kind of spell for behavioral change. Just tie the strands in a knot while calling upon the Great Snake to bind something unwanted. It won't get rid of it, just prevent it from occurring.

Affinity: Storm (antispasmodic), Fire(pungent), Air (astringent). Use for Earth or Swamp conditions.

Point: LU 2

Plant-wight's Nature: Ivy-wight is sometimes female and sometimes male, but always s/he holds out twining arms to embrace you. "Let me hold you. Let me surround you." Ivy-wight can play the helpless child—"Please, I need someone to support me!" and then refuse to let go if you're foolish enough to give in. Ivy-wight smiles slyly when you're not looking, then winsomely and charmingly when you are, and keeps trying to slip graceful arms about you. It's an effort to keep removing them, keep fending Ivy off. Then Ivy turns to a different face—"No one will love you like I can. Let me be your lover. I'll never leave you." (This is not recommended, for a variety of reasons. I've seen tree-women entirely dragged down by the Ivy-men that entwine and smother them.) However, Ivy is very old and very sacred, and should be treated with respect, even as you are setting good boundaries.

Magical Charm: Resisting Desire

Sometimes it is necessary to resist the desire of the loins for a time. Perhaps one is being monogamous and finding it difficult; perhaps one is in close daily contact with a much-desired person who would not welcome one's attentions or any knowledge thereof; perhaps one is dealing with sexual problems and needs a time of celibacy, but just can't seem to get it together. Traditionally, while Ivy was a plant of excess dedicated to Gods of wine and revelry, it was also propitiated as a remedy for drunkenness and inappropriate desire; castrated gallae (priest/esses of Attis and Cybele) had Ivy tattoos. What can give, can take. To do this, take three long ropes of Ivy and stand naked under the moonlight. Wind the Ivy about your hips and between your legs; it should be tight enough to press roughly and uncomfortably against your genitalia. Knot the vines three times, look up at the moon, and say the following charm:

> *Like the Serpent I am bound,*
> *Like a gateway I am wound,*
> *I am a stone wall held up by twining Ivy.*

Then carefully pull the Ivy garment down and step out of it without undoing any knots. Hang it up to dry, and when it is dry wrap it in black cloth and place it under the bed. When you are ready to loose your desire again, bury it in the Earth, lie on the burial place, and ask the Earth to give you back your body's free urges again.

Medicinal Charm: Removing Corns

Soak a few Ivy leaves in lemon juice for three hours, pat gently dry, and bandage them over the corn that needs removing. Leave for three hours and repeat daily until the corn drops off. While you wear it, say the following charm:

> *By that which binds,*
> *My feet are set free.*
> *By that which sheds its skin,*
> *My feet slough their foe.*

Juniper

Botanical name: *Juniperus communis* or *Juniperus sabina*
Folk names: Enebro, Lady Geneva, Gin Berry, *Ginepro*, Gemeiner Wacholder, Genevrier
Anglo-Saxon Name: Safine
Old Norse Name: Einir
Modern German Name:
  Gemeiner Wacholder
Modern Swedish Name:
  En, Ene, Järnbuske
Modern Danish Name: Ene
Modern Norwegian Name: Einer
Deity Association: Austri, Vestri, Sudri, Nordri
Height: To 30'
Season: Perennial Shrub/Tree
History: Juniper is native to northern Europe, northern and southwest Asia, and parts of North America. It varies greatly in its size and form depending on its habitat. Its trunk, in areas where it grew tall, was used as a sacred wood for temple pillars, and its branches were used for strewing and burned in the streets against plague. Juniper was said to be good against the "king's malady", an unspecified complaint that has come down through the ages applied to different things. Its berries take three years to ripen and turn blue, and this was considered a sign of its great age and wisdom.

Medicinal Uses: Juniper's ripe berries are good for UTIs and digestive problems (especially flatulence), and they clear acids from the system, which is useful in arthritis. Juniper is a uterine stimulant, so the tincture can be used for stalled labor. Pregnant women should not ingest it, though. The oil is used for an external liniment for arthritis and coughs (often mixed with Thyme oil); if you don't have the oil, a poultice will do also. The oil was mixed with lard by old-time veterinarians to apply to exposed wounds on animals, and keeps flies off the wounds. Juniper can stimulate and protect the immune system, and chewing the berries is recommended for people while in contact with the sick or when visiting swampy tropical countries. The leaves can also be smoked for relief of a head cold, or burned to disinfect a room.

Culinary Uses: Ripe berries are used to flavor spirits, especially gin, and also in game marinades and stuffings.

Magical Uses: An all-around purifying, exorcising, and protective herb. Used to keep disease at bay when burned. The berries can be ground and sprinkled for this purpose as well, if smoke would be a problem.

Shamanic Uses: Juniper is the sacred smudging herb of the Siberian shamans, used in much the same way as Mugwort, and for the same reasons. It can be substituted for Mugwort in any shamanic ritual. It was also one of the earliest-known incense plants in ancient Greece. It seems to have a strong affinity for the Guardians of the Four Directions, who tend to appear as Duergar to Northern Tradition folk, but have other forms as well. If you make friends with them, they can help keep you from getting lost while journeying or pathwalking, as they always know where every place in the Nine Worlds is. They are also fine protectors of those whom they value. Burn some to ask for their aid.

Affinity: Fire (stimulant and irritant), Storm (bitter alterative), Air (astringent). Use for Earth, Swamp, and River conditions.

Point: CV 5

Plant-wight's Nature: Grandfather Juniper came to me as a Siberian shaman, in a robe covered in rattling charms. His blue-grey hair hangs down in several braids, each tipped with bells or bones. He speaks in a sing-song voice, his old weathered face severe, but his eyes may twinkle at you in occasional humor. Getting him to help is not easy—he may well test you in order to find out your level of attainment, on a scale that you may not understand, and if you fail out he will simply start singing and ignoring you. It is always possible to come back and try again later, though, and he may even send you a vision of what you have to do next in order to get further down the "path" to his satisfaction. If he agrees to work with you, he will want a great deal of formal ceremony every time he is used, or he will consider you disrespectful.

Medicinal Charm: Gin Berry

Put fifteen crushed berries in a pint and a half of water, bring to a boil, and infuse for ten to fifteen minutes. Strain and drink. Alternatively, put two ounces of the berries into a pint and a half of white wine and macerate, then put it in a jar and shake it daily for two weeks, then strain. Drink one wineglassful per day for any of the above problems. While drinking either concoction, say the following charm:

> Grandfather of snow and ice
> Whose name is written in the hoofbeats of reindeer,
> Whose ashes are scattered across the sky,
> Grant me good healing, Grandfather Enebro.

Kelp

Botanical Name: *Fucus vesiculosus*
Folk Names: Bladderwrack, Sea Wrack, Kelp-ware, Tang, Blacktang, Cutweed
Angle-Saxon Name: Sæwær
Old Norse Names: Döngul, Dang (seaweed in general), Söl, Sölin (Dulse)
Modern German Name: Seetang
Middle High German Name: Blasentang
Modern Swedish Name: Blåstång
Modern Danish Name: Kelp, Tang
Modern Norwegian Name: Blæretang

Deity Association: Ran and her nine daughters, the Undines

Height: To 3'

Season: Perennial

History: Kelp, or Bladderwrack, is found along all the shores of the northern Atlantic Ocean and the Mediterranean, and is probably one of the earliest human foods. While we specifically mention *Fucus vesiculosus* here, the ancestors used a variety of seaweeds with similar properties, calling them all "seaweed". They appear frequently in old herbals, but there is no differentiation between them, except that the Norse had a special term for Dulse (or Sweet Wrack, *Laminaria saccharina*, was another popular seaweed with the ancients). If you are drying seaweed for your own use, take only the living seaweed that is still growing in the ocean; it begins to rot as soon as it is washed up onto the shore and won't dry properly. Spread it out carefully under hot sun or in a low oven to dry it.

Medicinal Uses: Kelp and other seaweeds were traditionally used in goiter or other thyroid problems. Herbalists disagree today on whether that's still useful; some say it's great, others say that modern thyroid problems aren't caused by lack of iodine like in the old days, and Kelp won't work. Kelp charcoal, sea-pod ointment, and the weed itself was used to heal sores and ulcers. It helps nausea and morning sickness during pregnancy, cleanses the lymphatic system, helps the prostate, is moisturizing to skin, is nutritive and probably the best mineral supplement you can get, and has some antiviral capabilities. Eating seaweed helps make people thinner, as it stimulates the thyroid gland. People with overactive thyroid should avoid it.

Household Uses: Kelp is collected for livestock fodder (it's as good as a mineral salt lick for them), a mineral-rich manure, fuel for smoking bacon and cheese, and the ashes are used to cover cheese for aging. It was once burned for glassmaking, and alcohol was extracted from it. Hung in the home, it makes a good barometer, as the pods will inflate or shrivel with the moisture in the air.

Culinary Uses: Kelp is edible and the dried powder can be used as a salty flavoring. Dulse is often eaten as a snack food. Seaweeds were burned to get sea salt for cooking.

Magical Uses: Seaweed was kept in the house in bags to ensure friendships and the safety of friends, one for each friend. Hung in a high place in the home, it protects against fires. Swinging it around your head at the beach will bring the wind; it was often taken on board ships for this reason.

Shamanic Uses: There are many kinds of seaweed, and each one is under the care of one of the Nine Undines, while Kelp proper is Ran's, although the Nine like it too. For communicating with them while inland, eating a bit of powdered Kelp may help you hear them, and tossing some in a bowl of water may invoke their sea-powers for scrying. Kelp was also known as "Loki's Fishing Lines", because it so easily breaks, and because he is credited with spinning the first fishnet.

Affinity: River (moistening), Harvest (nourishing). Use on Air conditions.

Point: SI 17

Plant-Wight's Nature: The Kelp-woman is a sea elemental, rising out of the water with pupilless greeny-blue eyes and a long mane of seaweed hair floating around her. Seaweed floats from her fingers as well. She speaks in a singing voice with hardly any consonants, and she knows a great deal about the sea's healing magic. She likes to touch and stroke people (endure her touch if you want her help, even though it is slimy) and on occasion, has been known, mermaid-like, to try to drag them down to her. Usually, though, she will be better behaved.

Magical Charm: Sea Travel

If you are traveling over water, you may want the blessing of Ran and her daughters. Fill a bag with dried Kelp, eat a little of it, and then just sing their names: "Ran, Ran, Ran; Kolga, Duva, Blodughadda; Hronn, Hevring, Bylgja; Bara, Unn, Himinglava; Ran, Ran, Ran." Carry the bag with you, and eat a little if the weather gets bad over the ocean. This goes for plane flights too.

Lady's Bedstraw

Botanical Name: *Galium verum*

Folk Names: Yellow Bedstraw, Bedstraw, Maid's Hair, Petty Mugget, Cheese Renning, Cheese Rennet, Vegetable Rennet

Modern German Name: Echtes Labkraut

Modern Swedish Name: Gulmåra

Modern Danish Name: Snerre

Modern Norwegian Name: Gulmaure

Deity Association: Gerda

Height: 10-40"

Season: Perennial

History: Lady's Bedstraw is native to Europe and western Asia, and is also found all over North America. Its English name referred to it as a mattress-stuffing for "delicate" ladies who wished a softer bed than ordinary hay-straw. During the Middle Ages, it became Our Lady's Bedstraw and was dedicated to Mary; the legend said that she used either Yellow Bedstraw or its cousin, Cleavers, as her bedding. This legend came from the general use of these two herbs as magical bedding for safe childbirth, and this practice supposedly originated, according to some authors, with the fact that deer will bed down in Cleavers or Yellow Bedstraw when giving birth in order to disguise their scent. Bedstraw's ability to curdle milk gives it the Greek name of Galium, from *gala* "milk". It was formerly much employed by herbalists for hysteria and epilepsy.

Medicinal Uses: Like its cousin Cleavers, Lady's Bedstraw is a good urinary tract cleansing herb, and is used in formulas for UTIs and kidney stones. It is also a mild laxative. Lady's Bedstraw tea has been drunk by pregnant women to prevent miscarriage, and to build up muscles for labor.

Household Uses: Lady's Bedstraw's most common usage was to curdle milk; thus its various "rennet" names. It is used by heating the milk and then soaking a bunch of the fresh weed in it; it can be combined with Nettle for an even stronger curdling action. The roots, ground and boiled, yield a red-orange dye, and the stems and leaves yield a yellow dye which was used on everything from cloth to hair to cheeses. It can still be used to stuff mattresses—try stuffing a pillow with the dried plant.

Magical Uses: Good dreams, when placed in the mattress.

Shamanic Uses: Gerda, the goddess of the walled garden, and one of the goddesses of herbs in general, has a great love for all the members of the Galium family—Cleavers, Lady's Bedstraw, and Sweet Woodruff.

Affinity: Earth (cooling), River (moistening). Use for Air and Fire.

Point: SP 11

Plant-wight's Nature: Mistress Bedstraw appears to me as a dark-haired young girl, just a few years past puberty, small and neat and sitting modestly in the garden, usually doing embroidery of some kind. She is the patroness of child-brides, girls sent to be married in their early teens, and she protects them and aids them in the intimidating work of managing a household. There aren't many child-brides these days, which seems to make her wistful, but she is still partial to young women.

Magical Charm: Birthing Bedding

Dry a handful of Lady's Bedstraw while the pregnant woman in question is still in the last stages of her pregnancy, and say over it the following charm:

> *Sweet and light thy labor be,*
> *Not one drop shed that's needed not,*
> *Bairn and dam delivered safe*
> *In Lady Bedstraw's blithe embrace.*

Then place it under the pillow or mattress of the woman when she is in labor, and all shall be well. This works especially well for very young first-time mothers (e.g. ones under the age of 20).

Lady's Mantle

Botanical Name: *Alchemilla vulgaris*
Folk Names: Bear's Foot, Leontopodium, Lion's Foot, Nine Hooks, Stellaria, Pied-de-Leon, Frauenmantle
Anglo-Saxon Name: Leonfot ("Lion-foot")
Modern German Name: Frauenmantel
Modern Swedish Name: Daggkåpa
Modern Danish Name: Damekappe
Modern Norwegian Name: Marikåpe
Deity Association: Frigga, Mengloth
Height: 2'
Season: Perennial

History: Lady's Mantle is very much a native plant of northern Europe, found beyond the Arctic circle and on the tops of the highest mountains. It was spread to other areas of Europe and the world during the early Middle Ages; ironically its botanical name is from the folk name given it by the Arabs, "alchemy". It has the ability to make water bead up on its leaves, due to some subtle chemical process, and as such it dries and strengthens wet organs and membranes.

Medicinal Uses: Lady's Mantle is both a specific for uterus problems and a short-term alterative (no more than 6 months) in order to get the uterus ready for pregnancy. Tea is drunk to contract the uterus after childbirth, and menopausal symptoms. It is also taken for gastroenteritis or diarrhea, or bloody stools. An ointment, vaginal suppository (use cocoa butter) or douche of the leaf infusion reduces vaginal itching; a wash of Lady's Mantle is the classic remedy for vaginitis discharge. Post-pregnancy, the tea helps the milk supply during lactation; post-lactation, poultices applied to the breasts shrink and tighten them. Practitioners vary as to whether it is safe for pregnant women; most suggest that those with any history of miscarriage should avoid it. The tea has been used to treat PMS and other female hormonal upsets, including delayed menarche in girls.

Lady's Mantle has also been used as a wound-healer, a trait which has been eclipsed by its "woman's herb" reputation. Use it as a mouth rinse after tooth extraction, or for mouth ulcers or laryngitis, or as a poultice or wash for any wound which has trouble healing. It is good for perforated eardrums—actually, for any perforated membrane; it was said to be able to restore the hymen itself. It has been used not only in uterine prolapse but for hernias of all kinds.

Household Uses: Boil for a green wool dye. Leaves increase milk production in dairy animals.

Culinary Uses: The sharp young leaves are used in Swiss tea blends and are sometimes added to salads.

Magical Uses: Used for charm bags for safe pregnancies and childbirth. The dew collected off of her leaves is said to add power to magic potions. The Arabian alchemists appreciated this herb so much for its ability to add power to a spell that they named it after their own art. It is an excellent protective herb for women who are nurturing sorts and are being taken advantage of or abused.

Shamanic Uses: This plant is well liked by Frigga in her role as matron of birthingand families. Use it with the rune Berkana/Beorc for safe pregnancy, birthing, and protection of babies and small children. Some folklore also claims it as one of Freya's herbs, although those sources may be conflating Freya with Frigga (a disrespectful but all too common problem) and the Vanadis should probably be asked directly whether it is also hers. It is also liked by Mengloth, the Jotun healing goddess who specializes in women's complaints.

Affinity: Air (astringent), Storm (bitter alterative), Earth (cooling). Use for River (especially), Swamp and Fire conditions.

Point: CV 4

Plant-wight's Nature: Mistress Leonfot is a large, round matron with a great pregnant belly and several chins. She tends to squat a lot, with short fat arms and legs buried in her voluminous ruffled green dress. She is very proud of her ruffles. She clucks and calls everyone "chick" or "dear", she bustles about after children, shooing them into her embrace and then tucking them in their beds. There is something like a fat housecat in her demeanor. She has reams of motherly advice to give to women, especially pregnant or nursing mothers. "You know, dear, you really ought to..." She seems uniformly cheerful and nurturing, but what you don't see is that she has a temper. It isn't easy to trigger, but when mothers are mistreated, she becomes dark red in the face and begins to growl. She might be a good wight to call on when a mother is in a situation of domestic abuse; if nothing else, she could give the woman more of a backbone.

Medicinal Charm: Womb Blessing

For any woman's complaint regarding the uterus or hormonal cycle, this charm will bless the womb and the female waters with Mistress Leonfot's gentle touch. It may be said over tea (one pint of boiling water poured over a cup of the fresh or dried plant) or tincture (cover the plant with alcohol and shake the jar daily); give one cup of tea or three drops of tincture per day for at least one turn of the moon, but not more than six moons worth. Say the following charm as you prepare the potion:

> Frauenmantle, lay your cloak
> Over the womb; may woman's strength
> Well be wrought; Lioness and She-Bear
> Follow in footsteps of the moon's white mare.

Lambsquarters

Botanical name: *Chenopodium album*
Folk names: Fat Hen, Frost Blite, Mutton Tops, Dirtweed, Dirty Dick, Midden Myles, Baconweed, White Goosefoot
Modern German Name: Weißer Gänsefuß
Modern Swedish Names: Svinmålla, Mjölmålla, Vitmålla
Modern Danish Name: Svinukrudt
Modern Norwegian Name: Meldestokk
Deity Association: Nerthus
Height: To 2'
Season: Annual
History: Lambsquarters—the name by which it is most generally known in America—is one of those plants that is usually considered a pernicious weed, and one horrifies modern gardeners by eating it as you pull it out of their petunias. Never mind that it is so ancient that it has been found in graves,

Paleolithic middens, and the stomachs of prehistoric corpses. It may be one of the oldest surviving tonic greens of our ancestors, and is found all over the northern hemisphere.

Medicinal Uses: Alterative. Eat raw or cooked as a vitamin-packed tonic for invalids.

Household Uses: Roots yield a mild soap. Used to fatten livestock, especially poultry.

Culinary Uses: Salad green, when young, or you can just eat the leaves as you pull it out of the garden, as this plant quickly becomes an invasive weed. Seeds can be ground into a nutritious flour and made into gruel.

Magical Uses: Survival spells in the wilderness.

Shamanic Uses: This innocuous plant, like Plantain, has been around since Neolithic times. Its seeds were found in the stomach of the preserved Iron Age Tollund Man. It can be used to call on the ancestors. To do so, you do have to eat it, raw, cooked, or dried. Lambsquarters seems to be one of the Ancestral Mothers, like the grains and legumes, but she is a very old one and has since become somewhat wild and detached. She can still be called on as an Ancestral Mother, however, and she will respond as one.

Affinity: Harvest (nourishing), Mountain (relaxant), Storm (bitter alterative). Use for Air and Swamp conditions.

Point: SP 7

Plant-wight's Nature: Lambsquarters came to me as a broad, squat woman with a weathered face and brown hair in many thick plaits. She was tattooed with petroglyphs and had the large teeth of some ancient animal thrust through her ears. She wore garments made of skin and knotted, netlike fiber, and squatted back on her heels while speaking to me. Her voice was low and humming, and she continually looked about—perhaps as if for danger, perhaps for food. She is a creature of the era of hunting, gathering, and herding—she understands livestock, but not much more about agriculture than small plantings that one returns to in a yearly rotation. She does understand nourishment, though, and will poke at your ribs and tell you what you need to eat. Her advice may or may not be available, or may even be extinct, but it's probably worth listening to.

Magical Charm: Nourishment

Many people do not properly absorb all the nutrients from their food. For a variety of reasons—stress, for example, or disease, or the side effects of harsh medications—much of it goes through them. To help your body absorb more from the food you are eating, you need a supply of fresh Lambsquarters and the following charm.

Lambsquarters, being a hardy weed, can be grown indoors in the winter or the city easily so long as there is light and soil—in fact, it will grow ridiculously in fertile potting soil. One caveat: Don't even bother using this spell if your diet consists mostly of non-nutritious food—white flour, white sugar, processed soy products, chemicals, high-fructose corn syrup, etc. You don't want to be absorbing more of that. This is for people who are eating food that is entirely made of actual food, and still resembles it. We won't go into it further—people's diets and preferences are their own—but if the ingredients were cooked up in a lab, forgo this spell.

Before each meal, pluck and eat a leaf of Lambsquarters, saying:

Hale and hearty my meal shall make me,
Goosefoot give me green health,
Fat Hen fill me fair and fine.

Lavender

Botanical Name: *Lavandula spp.*

Folk names: Elf Leaf, Nard, Nardus, Spike

Anglo-Saxon Name: None; AS herbalists called it "stecas" after *Lavandula stoechas*

Modern German Name: Lavendel

Modern Swedish Name: Lavendel

Modern Danish Name: Lavendel

Modern Norwegian Name: Lavendel

Deity Association: The Alfar

Height: To 3'

Season: Perennial

History: Lavender began in the mountains of the western Mediterranean, but spread all over the world with Roman trade. Its Roman ancestry can be seen in the fact that everyone to the north and east simply used its Latin name, which comes from the Latin *lavare* meaning to wash, because the folk of the Mediterranean put it in their wash water and bath water for fragrance and therapeutic properties, or its Greek name Nard (from Naarda, a Syrian trade city). The plant was a favorite strewing herb, dropped on the floor of sickrooms. Its antiseptic properties were well-known in ancient times. It reached Germany and Gaul during the Roman conquest, but did not come to England until the Saxon period and was not common there until the Middle Ages.

Medicinal Uses: A tea made of the flowers of Lavender treats anxiety, headaches, flatulence, nausea, dizziness, and halitosis. As a hot fomentation, it is laid on stiff, painful joints. It is rolled into herbal cigarettes along with Uva Ursi and Wild Ginger as part of smoking mixtures to aid in quitting tobacco. The essential oil is an antiseptic that kills many common bacteria, is mildly sedative and mildly painkilling, and is used in massage for tension headaches. It is also a powerful antidote to some snake venoms. It can be applied to insect bites and first-degree or healing burns, compressed on infected wounds, gargled in water for sore throats, added to baths as a relaxant for insomnia and depression, and rubbed on the temples for headaches. Pregnant women should avoid large doses, as it can be a mild uterine stimulant. In general, Lavender is the essential oil of choice for the stressed-out human.

Household Uses: Dried flowers are used in potpourri and sachets; flower water is a skin toner useful for speeding cell renewal and is an antiseptic for acne; essential oil is added to soaps, lotions, and just plain perfume. Fresh flower sprigs are fly repellent. Lavender "bottles", or bunches of flowering stems wrapped in ribbons and allowed to dry, are placed among linens to deter moths. Excellent bee herb, as Lavender honey is much sought after. The tincture added to shampoo strengthens hair and prevents hair loss from wear and tear. The oil kills lice on animals and people, and in a strong salve is used to embalm corpses.

Culinary Uses: The flowers flavor jams, vinegar, sweets, cream, and are crystallized for decoration.

Magical Uses: Love spells and sleep magic. Lavender pairs well with Mugwort in recels. It was traditionally burned in the birthing room for purification, and incorporated into food and wreaths for weddings. Some lore claims that it intensifies sexual desire, some that it calms it. It may be a matter of whether becoming serene and calm makes a given person more ready for sex, or less likely to bother with it.

Shamanic Uses: Lavender is much loved by the Alfar. When dealing with them, wear Lavender and use it to "project" an air of goodness and pleasantry. Rudolf Steiner claimed that Lavender helps conditions where the astral body "clings too tightly" to the physical body, creating tension, paralysis, and nerve-wasting. While I've never seen a *hame* that clung too tightly to a *lich*—usually it's the other way around—perhaps this can happen when someone has a strong *lich/hame* connection (usually a good thing) but is so stressed that their astral body is affecting their physical body; literally thinking themselves sick. The sort of person who could do this could probably also think themselves well, with the right guidance. Perhaps Lavender is a good guide for this.

Affinity: Earth (cooling), Mountain (relaxant), Fire (stimulant). Lavender first warms and opens the capillaries, paradoxiacally bringing on a cooling effect. Use on Storm and Fire.

Point: TH 23

Plant-wight's Nature: Lavender-wight is tall, pale, slender, and androgynous, with a graceful swaying motion and long thin fingers that often brush your cheek. Lavender can appear as either male or female, in which case address this greenwight as Mistress Lavender or Master Lavender, or as something in between (but the latter usually only happens for those humans who are also in-between). Lavender-wight is most concerned with the air and the winds, and works well with wind-wights. Lavender gets on well with the Alfar, but is not necessarily an Alfar plant—Lavender has no allegiance and will smile prettily on anyone who admires the scent and flowers of this lovely plant. In a way, Lavender is quite "airy"—not concerned with deep things, preferring everything to be harmonious and beautiful, etc. Lavender-wight is quite capable of performing a non-confrontation spell on people that are found to be too belligerent for this languid spirit.

Magical Charm: Peace Bringer

When the cares of the world are too much for you, and you feel like you're going to scream, rub Lavender oil into your temples and around your ears, and lie down. Whisper the following charm, and Lavender will give you good dreams.

> *Lovely Lavender, lover of the breeze,*
> *Spikenard send me sights of dream's delight,*
> *Garden-dancer give me scented ease.*

Leek

Botanical Name: *Allium porrum*
Folk Names: St. Davy's Herb, Spear-Onion
Anglo-Saxon Names: Leac, Cropleac, Bradeleac ("Broadleek")
Old Norse Name: Laukr
Old High Germanic Name: Laukaz
Modern German Names: Porree, Küchenlauch
Modern Swedish Name: Lök
Modern Danish Name: Porre
Modern Norwegian Name: Purreløk
Deity Association: Thor
Height: 2'
Season: Biennial
History: The word "leac" in Anglo-Saxon meant any layered vegetable, or more specifically a member of the allium family. The allium that seems to have the oldest history in northern Europe is the vegetable

that we still call "Leek"; to us it may be an obscure soup veggie in the back of the garden, but to the Germanic peoples it was a sacred plant of the highest order. It symbolized the male principle, being long and stavelike, and it was paired with Flax ("lina") as the female principle. The spear and the spindle were symbols of male and female, and Flax was spun while Leeks were spear-shaped. Both alliums and Flax have preservative qualities, and they were used together to preserve amulets made of flesh—for example, in the Icelandic *Flatyiarbok* story, a farm wife preserves a horse's penis by wrapping it with Leeks and other herbs in order to make a cult object (likely for male fertility).

Medicinal Uses: All alliums contain iron and vitamins and raise the immune system to one extent or another. Check the medicinal indications for Onion; they are basically the same medicinally, although somewhat different magically.

Culinary Uses: Cooking. Lots of it, especially if it's traditional Northern food. Leek soup is traditional all over northern Europe.

Magical Uses: Leeks are carried as protective amulets in battle, and are planted around the house to drive away evil. They are protective for men in general, and a man who puts bits of Leek into ale drunk out of a vessel inscribed with the Nauthiz rune will never be deceived by a woman.

Shamanic Uses: Sacred to Thor, along with all the other allium family, these can be offered as tribute or cooked and eaten to ask his blessing. Along with Garlic, you can feed them to people whose bodies need a thorough cleansing, of the lightning-bolt variety. These are also powerful protective plants for any kind of safety charm; call on Thor's aid when you empower it.

Affinity: Fire (stimulant), River (moistening), Harvest (nourishing), Mountain (relaxant). Use on Earth conditions.

Point: LU 4

Plant-wight's Nature: The Leek-wight is very masculine, stoic, but with an inner fire. This is not the young, hot-headed warrior; this is the older, seasoned, controlled fighter who is nonetheless eager for the fight. Leek-wight is focused, goal-oriented, and protective, and it is no wonder that this was a good protective plant for possibly hotheaded men. Leek-wight also seems able to calm down excess drinking, if it gets in the way of effectively doing what is necessary.

Magical Charm: For a Man's Protection

Chop a Leek finely and spread out in a warm, dry place to dry thoroughly in the air—do not bake in the oven! You can sprinkle the dried Leek into food (but it should not be cooked unless it is immediately eaten; it needs to go from dry form to cooked to eaten in less than half an hour) or place it in a pouch to be carried, or just have the recipient eat a handful straight up. Before cooking, eating, or carrying it, hold it in your hand and say this charm;

> *Laukaz, laukr, leac,*
> *Let thy wisdom guard my (his) wits,*
> *Let thy guidance lead my (his) way,*
> *Thy might may Thor thee guarantee,*
> *Thy hand and help give forth to me.*

Lemon Balm

Botanical Name: *Melissa officinalis*

Folk Names: Melissa, Bee's Delight, Balm, Sweet Balm

Anglo-Saxon Names: May have been referred to as Medewort (confused with Meadowsweet, a native plant) but by the time we have clear mention of it, it is being referred to simply as Balm.

Modern German Name: Zitronenmelisse

Modern Swedish Names: Citronmeliss, Hjärtansfröjd, Honungsblomma, Melissört, Modergräs

Modern Danish Name: Citron-Melisse

Modern Norwegian Name: Sitronmelisse

Deity Association: Frey

Height: To 4'

Season: Perennial

History: Lemon Balm is a native of southern Europe, where it was much valued as a honey-plant by the Greeks and Romans for over 2000 years. It was introduced later to northern Europe, perhaps by the Roman occupation, and became popular in Germany. It did not become naturalized in Britain until after the era of the Anglo-Saxon herbals.

Medicinal Uses: Lemon Balm tea is a cooling sedative, used for insomnia, depression, anxiety, and panic attacks; it calms tensions and is good in herbal cold treatment combinations. It helps to break fevers and reduces heart palpitations. Poultice is good on insect bites and painful swellings; the essential oils are antiseptic. Essential oil is also an antidepressant. Lemon Balm is used to cool the body in cases of hyperthyroid or hyperadrenalism. It is also an excellent herb to put in nasty-tasting medicinal combinations, to make them a little more palatable. In medieval times, it was a sovereign remedy for impotence.

Household Uses: Good to plant around beehives. Infuse as a facial steam and a wash for greasy hair.

Culinary Uses: Makes a truly wonderful tea. Leaf can be chopped into salads, sauces, fruit salads, jellies, and wine cups.

Magical Uses: Drunk in tea, it gives longevity and banishes melancholy.

Shamanic Uses: Frey is said to greatly enjoy Lemon Balm, and it can be baked into goodies, brewed into mead, or floated in ale as an offering to him. It can be used to call him, or to find which world he is in—he alternates between Asgard (where he is technically a hostage), Alfheim (where he has a hall), and Vanaheim (his home).

Affinity: Earth (cooling), Stone (sedative). Use for Fire conditions.

Point: LU 3

Plant-wight's Nature: Dealing with the Balm-wight is like standing in a sunbeam. Lemon Balm carries the energy of a cool, breezy, wet summer morning just as the sun comes blazing over the horizon and bathing everything in light, and almost instinctively you lift your arms to the sky and bask in the beauty of it. Androgynous and serenely brilliant, this wight is a specialist in temporarily lifting the spirits. However, Balm-wight is ephemeral, and can only promise short-term joy. Take its gift for the passing sunbeam that it is, and don't ask more of it.

Medicinal Charm: Light In The Darkness

When things are grey and depressing and glum, and the spirits need a lift, make a tea of 4 ounces of dried or two ounces of fresh Lemon Balm steeped in a pint of boiling water. Drink it warm or cool, saying this charm:

> *I wait for the light*
> *Though in darkness I lay,*
> *Golden God, give me*
> *The summer-steed's hay,*
> *Balm be my guide*
> *To a brighter day.*

Lichens

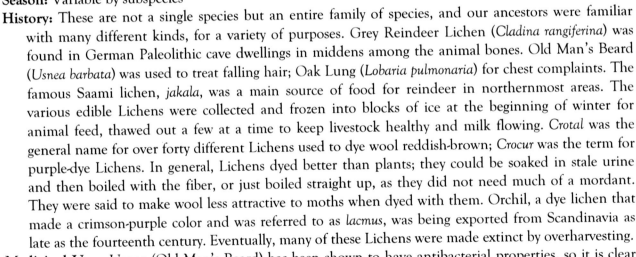

Botanical name: *Usnea barbata* (Old Man's Beard), *Cladina rangiferina* (Grey Reindeer Lichen), *Lobaria pulmonaria* (Oak Lung), and other *spp.*

Folk names: Crotal, Crocur, Lacmus, Litr-mus, Old Man's Beard, Oak Lung, Grey Reindeer Lichen, Wolf-Lichen, and other more specific names

Modern German Name: Flechten

Modern Swedish Name: Lichenes

Modern Danish Name: Lav, Renlav (*Cladina*)

Modern Norwegian Names: Lav, Strylav (*Usnea*), Reinlav (*Cladina*), Neverlav (*Lobaria*)

Deity Association: Frost-etins

Height: Variable; usually under 3"

Season: Variable by subspecies

History: These are not a single species but an entire family of species, and our ancestors were familiar with many different kinds, for a variety of purposes. Grey Reindeer Lichen (*Cladina rangiferina*) was found in German Paleolithic cave dwellings in middens among the animal bones. Old Man's Beard (*Usnea barbata*) was used to treat falling hair; Oak Lung (*Lobaria pulmonaria*) for chest complaints. The famous Saami lichen, *jakala*, was a main source of food for reindeer in northernmost areas. The various edible Lichens were collected and frozen into blocks of ice at the beginning of winter for animal feed, thawed out a few at a time to keep livestock healthy and milk flowing. *Crotal* was the general name for over forty different Lichens used to dye wool reddish-brown; *Crocur* was the term for purple-dye Lichens. In general, Lichens dyed better than plants; they could be soaked in stale urine and then boiled with the fiber, or just boiled straight up, as they did not need much of a mordant. They were said to make wool less attractive to moths when dyed with them. Orchil, a dye lichen that made a crimson-purple color and was referred to as *lacmus*, was being exported from Scandinavia as late as the fourteenth century. Eventually, many of these Lichens were made extinct by overharvesting.

Medicinal Uses: Usnea (Old Man's Beard) has been shown to have antibacterial properties, so it is clear why it was used to pack wounds. It was used in Finland for cuts, athlete's foot, viral warts, and skin eruptions. It is a gentle but strong immune tonic, especially good for strep and staph infections, and respiratory or urinary infections. It is damaged by heating as tea, and doesn't like the acidity of vinegar, so it is best as a cold alcohol or glycerine tincture.

Household Uses: In ancient times there were many different kinds of Lichens in Scandinavia, especially in glacial areas, that were valuable dye plants. Unfortunately, they were overharvested some centuries ago and have mostly become extinct. Their Mediterranean relatives—the Litmus Lichens—are used to this day in the production of litmus paper. (*Litmus* itself is from the old Norse word *litr-mus*, meaning color-moss.) Wolf-Lichen (*Letharia vulpinaa*) was used as a poison, cooked with reindeer blood and inserted between the muscle and bone of a reindeer carcass and left to poison wolves; Yellow Thallus (*Vulpicina Juniperina*) was similarly used. Oak Lung was used as a substitute for Hops to flavor beer.

Culinary Uses: While Lichens could be a survival food for humans and animals, they don't have much of a taste, nor much nutrition for us. The exception in cookery was Iceland Moss, which has its own entry.

Magical Uses: Old Man's Beard was used as a magical wound-healer, especially if it was found growing on the skulls of the Dead. It was even rubbed on the weapon that caused the wound, as a sympathetic way to heal the wound itself. Grey Reindeer Lichen was placed between storm windows and permanent windows, both as an insulation and as a magical protection, in Sweden. Lichens growing on shoreline rocks could be secreted in a boat as a curse to crash it, as it was believed that "what came from the rocks would return to them."

Shamanic Uses: Lichens are a way to bond strongly with the land-wights and the small spirits of the land. Lichens are both humble and mysterious. To continually ingest the edible Lichens of a particular place is to slowly make yourself one with that place, until you cannot be parted from it.

Affinity: Lichens in general are neutral with regard to Hot or Cold, are nutritive (Harvest) and bitter (Storm). Use on Air and Swamp.

Plant-wight's Nature: The Lichens are all different, of course; for some reason most of them tend to appear to me as animals rather than as humanoid forms. The reindeer Lichens do appear as reindeer; Usnea appears as a shaggy grizzly bear, and Oak Lung as a seagull. Others simply appear as vague pale shapes without form, speaking mostly in images rather than words. They are somewhat more removed than the plant greenwights, and don't have the trick or the affinity for shaping themselves as more familiar to us. Or perhaps they just don't want to.

Medicinal Charm: Wound Powder

Before you bandage a newly cleaned wound, sprinkle powdered Usnea on it, saying: "Old Man of the white beard, fasten flesh and keep fair, if it be the will of Wyrd." The wound will stay cleaner and heal quicker.

Lily of the Valley

Botanical Name: *Convallaria majalis*
Folk Names: Mayflower, May Lily, Jacob's Ladder, Ladder to Heaven, Convallily
Anglo-Saxon Name: Glofwyrt ("Glove Plant")
Modern German Names: Maiglöckchen, Maiblume
Modern Swedish Name: Liljekonvalje
Modern Danish Name: Liljekonval
Modern Norwegian Names: Liljekonvall
Deity Association: Freya
Height: 6"
Season: Perennial
History: Native to meadows in Eurasia. Used as a poison gas element in World War I, an odd homage to Freya in her Valkyrie form.
Medicinal Uses: Like the Foxglove, this flower was used for sluggish heartbeats, but it is now considered too toxic to use except in a careful fluid extract. The distilled flower water of this very poisonous plant is used by experienced herbalists to make a face wash called aqua aurea, which whitens the skin.
Household Uses: Essential oil used in perfumes, but is very difficult to extract.
Magical Uses: Used to improve the memory. This flower was said to be the spilled blood of St. Leonard, another dragonslayer. The Greeks associated it with Apollo and used it to gain his favor.

Shamanic Uses: Supposedly the Lily of the Valley was created when the goddess Freya first came to Asgard as a hostage. After the lush flora of Vanaheim, she found the bleak winters and lack of spring flowers to be depressing, and when she wept her tears fell to the earth and created the Mayflower. These little flowers are strongly tied to land-wights, and it is considered unlucky to transplant them. If you have a good relationship with your own land-wight, carry some in a pouch to keep the bond strong while traveling.

Affinity: Mountain (relaxant), Stone (sedative), Air (astringent). Use on Fire conditions.

Point: HT 9

Plant-wight's Nature:

> Mistress Convalilly is disdainful and catty, and will turn on you without warning. She's very much an aristocrat, but the idea of noblesse oblige is foreign to her. However, she may take a liking to you for reasons of her own. She is very unpredictable. That being said, she has a perverse love of bringing people down from their high horses. She has two powers she will share with those she deems worthy. One is to forcibly strip away glamour, no matter how powerful or multi-layered. The other is to reveal liars. Mistress Convalilly is not very popular with the Alfar, particularly the "high court" sort, who deem it impolite to the highest degree to poke around at other people's glamours, and will not look upon you kindly for doing so, either. If you already have the ability to see beneath or through glamour, Mistress Convalilly will refuse to talk to you. Also, if she does not like you, the anti-glamour spell will not work no matter how many times you sing it.   -Elizabeth Vongvisith

Magical Charm: Anti-Glamour

> The way you accomplish this most safely is by taking some of Lily of the Valley and casting her into a basin of pure water. Flowers are best, but the leaves will do in a pinch. Sing the following charm and then sprinkle the water around where the person is likely to walk or stand. Barring that, wet your fingers and try to (secretly) touch some part of his or her clothing. Do not ingest either the water or the plant parts! Any glamour that the person is wearing will vanish long enough for you to see what's really underneath, and you will also know if the person is lying or has stretched the truth.

> Sweet singing, bells ringing,
> Fair clear air all around,
> And the leaves turning, falsehoods burning,
> Glamour slipping, falling to ground.
> Come and see beyond the lies,
> Come and see through lily's eyes,
> Come and see and be made wise.

> The catch to this is that once the spell is enabled, there is no way to prevent the other person from knowing that you have either seen through their glamour or revealed their falsehood. —Elizabeth Vongvisith

Linden

Botanical Name: *Tilia europaea*
Folk Names: Lime Tree, Linn-Flower
Anglo-Saxon Name: Lind ("soft, pliable")
Old Norse Name: Lind
Old High Germanic Name: Linta
Modern German Name: Lindenbaum
Modern Swedish Names: Lind, Skogslind, Sommarlind
Modern Danish Name: Lind
Modern Norwegian Name: Parklind
Deity Association: Freya

Height: To 130'

Season: Perennial tree

History: Linden trees, native throughout northern Europe but especially the British Isles, were famed not only for their medicinal tea leaves, but for their wood which was said to make good shields (perhaps bringing Freya's blessing and the notice of the Valkyries).

Medicinal Uses: Linden-flower tea is a digestive and calming tonic. As a sedative, it is used for insomnia, treating hyperactive children, and formerly for epilepsy. Used prophylactically, it breaks fevers, heals and relaxes blood vessels and prevents arteriosclerosis. A tea of wilted flowers can sometimes produce mild intoxication. Linden-wood charcoal is used for dysentery.

Household Uses: Flowers are used to flavor sweets and liqueurs, and the blossoms are used in soothing skin salves. The wood is suitable for small, intricate carvings, and makes the best artist's charcoal. The tree bark has been used for mats, rope, and baskets. The world's most valued honey is made from Linden blossoms. Useful as cattle fodder. The sap can be boiled down for sugar.

Magical Uses: The branches are used protectively to ward a house the flowers are used in love spells, and the bark is used to prevent drunkenness. It is a tree of immortality, and can be used in spells of this nature. The Greeks saw Linden as a female tree, and various mortal women end up changed into Lindens in their stories, so one was supposed to make sure that the Linden whose flowers you were picking wasn't a transformed mortal woman who might curse your line.

Shamanic Uses: Sacred to Freya in her capacity as Love-Goddess, the tree can be used as an anchor to visit her hall.

Affinity: Earth (cooling), Stone (sedative), River (moistening). Use for Fire and Air.

Point: HT 3

Plant-wight's Nature: Linden is a graceful, slender dancer whose silvery-gold leaves and delicate flowers cascade down in a trembling mass through her ankle-length hair. Tiny-breasted, narrow-hipped, and long-fingered, she is attenuated but inhumanly graceful in her movements. Linden is closely allied to the air and the winds; she knows all the winds by name and can aid you in introductions ... although she'll also warn you of the old truism, that no one can have all four winds as allies as that would be too much power and they wouldn't stand for it. She loves to have bells and other high-pitched dangles hung in her branches; she came to me with bells on her ankles and jingling necklaces. She is a healer in her own right, and can switch from ethereal to soothing in a moment, especially for tense and headachy types.

Medicinal Charm: Linden's Light

When you are troubled by nerves and cannot get your thoughts to stop circling about, pour a pint of hot water over an ounce of Linden leaves; steep, strain, and drink. As you sip, recite this charm:

> *Light as leaves my thoughts are thrown,*
> *Nestling softly on the ground,*
> *Linden, light me like a leaf*
> *In silvery spirals ever down.*

Lovage

Botanical Name: *Levisticum officinale*

Folk Names: Love Herb, Lubestico, Sea Parsley:

Anglo-Saxon Name: Lufestice ("Love Stitch")

Modern German Names: Liebstöckel, Maggikraut, Maggi-Pfeffer, Echtes Liebstöckel

Modern Swedish Name: Libbsticka

Modern Danish Name: Løvstikke

Modern Norwegian Name: Løpstikke

Deity Association: Lofn
Height: 7'
Season: Perennial
History: Lovage is native to the Mediterranean area, where it was important in Greek and Roman cookery. It was introduced to the Germanic peoples during the Roman occupation, and spread to England via the Saxon conquest, or possibly even later.
Medicinal Uses: Lovage calms an upset stomach, aids digestion, reduces water retention and deodorizes people. The root is an expectorant for cough syrups, and is mildly sedative and anticonvulsant. Lovage contains a lot of salt, and is used for kidney problems where minerals and water need to be reabsorbed. Like its cousin Celery, it is good for gout. Lovage infusions are contraindicated for pregnant women or people with active inflamed UTIs.
Household Uses: Steep in brandy for a settling digestive, or distill for perfume.
Culinary Uses: Chop into soups and stews. Grate the root into salads, or powder as a condiment. Sprinkle seeds into bread and rice.
Magical Uses: Love potions. love spells—wear the seeds in a bag around the neck to attract the perfect mate. Laid in shoes to revive weary travelers.
Shamanic Uses: One of the herbs found in the Oseberg burial, Lovage is much liked by Lofn, the handmaiden of Frigga who aids warring lovers in reconciliation. It can be used in a soup or tea to help arguing, angry partners in mediation and processing their problems. To call on Lofn while making an offering of Lovage can be a last-ditch effort before a divorce. When doing divination about relationship problems, a stalk of Lovage can be brushed over the area of the reading before laying stones or cards, or powdered dried Lovage sprinkled on it.
Affinity: River (moistening), Harvest (nourishing), Fire (slightly pungent), Storm (slightly bitter). Use in Air, Earth, and Swamp conditions.
Point: ST 23
Plant-wight's Nature: Lovage is so often used in love magic that one almost expects the Lovage-wight to be a passionate, suave romantic. Instead, I was surprised to find that Brother Lovage is rather like a shy, awkward, unsophisticated young man. One gets the image of the tall, gawky country youth who comes to his beloved clutching the slightly bedraggled bunch of wildflowers and trips over himself handing them to her, but when he says, "I'll love you forever," with a big naive grin, you know that he is speaking the absolute truth and that he will mean it until the end of time. When he says, "You're beautiful," you know that you could have a giant wen on the end of your nose and you are still the most beautiful thing in the world to him. There will be few passionate scenes, but he would die rather than hurt you. Sincerity, not sophistication, is the energy of this wight. Even though Lovage is an ancient plant, there is still a quality of green youth to his nature.

Medicinal Charm: Stomach Seeds

When a child is having trouble with erratic digestion, have them eat as many seeds of the Lovage plant as they can manage, perhaps mixed into some easy food like yogurt or Applesauce, and say the following charm:

> *Lovage, let the rivers run*
> *Smooth and slow and churn thee none,*
> *May all aching be undone.*

Lupine

Botanical name: *Lupinus albus* and other *Lupinus spp.*
Folk names: Elehtre, Wolf Plant, Many-Leaved Lupine, Lupin, Wolfbohne
Anglo-Saxon Names: Elehtre, Eolectrin

Modern German Name: Vielblättrige Lupine
Modern Swedish Name: Vitlupin
Modern Danish Name: Lupin
Modern Norwegian Name: Lupiner
Deity Association: Angrboda
Height: 5'
Season: Perennial
History: Lupines may originally hail from Egypt or the Mediterranean, but they came north with trade or the natural spreading of seeds. They were known in northern continental Europe by the time of writing, and are known to the Anglo-Saxon herbals, although their Anglo-Saxon name was still a Mediterranean one, from the Greek *electra*. The seeds were used by Roman actors in plays to represent money, which inspired the phrase *nummus lupinus*, or an insignificant amount of cash.
Medicinal Uses: Powdered seeds are poulticed for oily skin, scabs, and blemishes. They are also eaten to absorb toxins, as that is one of their finest properties. As they absorb radiation well, they are planted around radioactive accident sites such as Chernobyl.
Household Uses: Good green manure crop. Companion planting with vegetables deters rabbits. Seeds are excellent livestock fodder.
Culinary Uses: Seeds can be ground into an emergency flour.
Magical Uses: Protection.
Shamanic Uses: Lupine, or Wolf Plant, as the name suggests, is a Jotunheim plant that is especially bound to the magically-radioactive werewolf-inhabited Iron Wood area of Jotunheim. There is even a possibility that it came from that world to this one. It can also be used to absorb psychic and magical "radiation" as well as physical gamma rays, and as such is good for cleaning up serious psychic "messes". Powder the leaves, root, and especially the seeds for this task.
Affinity: Harvest (nourishing). Use on Air conditions.
Point: SP 17
Plant-wight's Nature: Lupine plants don't look like wolves. You can circle them around, and still see no wolflike aspects. They're tall and lovely and have interesting-looking seed pods. However, when you try to connect with the plant-wight, suddenly a pair of yellow eyes raises to yours, and you get the full force of the Wolf Plant's gaze. They are called Lupines for a reason. The seed-pods, especially, are furred and Master Wolf-Plant likes to have them stroked, though not too much—he'll control whether and how much he's touched. Lupine is hard to get to know and trust, unless you have Iron Wood blood, in which case you're a brother or sister immediately. People with Iron Wood bloodlines can carry Lupine seeds as protection charms.
Magical Charm: Pack Order

This is a risky spell, and should only be used for situations with the following: You are in authority over a group of people, lawfully by their own agreement. You have been a fair and worthy leader, and they would agree on this point. Someone is challenging your leadership, on no grounds other than believing that they should have it. While your people are not disenchanted with you, they are enchanted by this challenger and there is an actual—not merely a perceived—danger that you could lose your position due to enthusiasm. If these are all true, take the furred seeds of Lupine and scatter them underfoot about the room where you are next to meet your challenger in public, before your people. Hide them in the corners. Carry a pocketful on you. As you scatter, say, "Wolfebohne will it, Hag help me, they will show throat." When the confrontation comes, the spirit of the Wolf Plant will help you to face down and intimidate your opponent, and hopefully save your position.

Madder

Botanical Name: *Rubia tinctorum*
Folk Names: Rose Madder, Dyer's Madder
Anglo-Saxon Names: Mædere, Wrætt, Wrætte
Old Norse Name: Mathra
Old High Germanic Name: Matara
Modern German Names: Färber-Krapp, Echte Färberröte
Modern Swedish Name: Krapp
Modern Danish Name: Krap
Modern Norwegian Name: Krapp
Deity Association: Holda
Height: To 3'
Season: Perennial
History: Madder is native to northern Europe, and has been used as a dye plant for thousands of years. The excavation of the Viking settlement at York shows extensive use of Madder as part of the dyeing industry there.
Medicinal Uses: Madder root is a blood purifier and helps move toxins out of stagnant blood. It is a diuretic that helps break down and prevent kidney stones; however, the expelled urine will be red. Don't be frightened; it's not blood, just the Madder's dye. Madder root is cooling, and cools off areas of inflammation; it is a good poultice for bruises and hot hemorrhoids. It has supposedly been used to treat hemolytic anemia from the spleen destroying too many red blood cells.
Household Uses: Root yields red, pink, and brown dyes. This dye is so powerful that it can turn one's bones red when taken internally for a long time.
Magical Uses: Marked on young women for coming-of-age ceremonies.
Shamanic Uses: As Woad is Odin's, and Weld is Frigga's, so Holda seems to have claimed Madder. Using the plant to dye things, especially household items, can bring her blessing and can be used as a propitiation.
Affinity: Storm (bitter alterative), Fire (stimulant), Earth (cooling). Use on Swamp.
Point: UB 67
Plant-wight's Nature: Mistress Madder is a bustling housewife, appearing to me as tiny and fat and round, almost gnomelike. Her long shapeless dress drags on the floor, and she chatters constantly as her busy, dexterous hands work from one project to another. She is the sort who would have a full stillroom, make all her own clothes and her children's as well, and always have something tasty going on the fire. Her hair is pinkish-red, as is her clothing. She is quite friendly and will talk to anyone for a short time, but doesn't stick around if she has things to do and you are wasting her time.

Magical Charm: Home Thread

If your household is disorganized, filthy, cluttered, and disharmonious—and you are the one responsible for keeping it otherwise—then ask for the help of Holda and Mistress Madder to aid you. Dig up the roots of Madder at the right time—books on dyeing can help you with the particulars; check the resources at the back—and dye a skein of handspun woolen thread with them. You could also use handspun Flax, which is more Holda's fiber, but Flax is harder for the beginner to get to take dye, so it's more the choice of experienced fiber arts people. While it soaks, recite the following charm:

> *Bring hamingja to my hearth,*
> *Bring hamingja to my home.*
> *Clean and clear of clutter see it,*
> *Hands that help lay order be it,*

Madder's mark, make rose my work,
Frau Holda hark, help me not shirk.

When the skein is dry and is some shade of pink to red, hang it in the center of the home. When you need reminders to do something, snip off bits and tie them around your finger. Burn bits of it to get the energy to clean and organize. Tie pieces around your wrist while you work, to stay on task.

Mallow

Botanical name: *Malva sylvestris*
Folk names: Cheeses, Cheeseweed, Blue Mallow, Common Mallow
Anglo-Saxon Name: Geormenlaef
Modern German Name: Wilde Malve, Große Käsepappel, Roßpappel
Modern Swedish Name: Rödmalva
Modern Danish Name: Katost
Modern Norwegian Name: Apotekerkattost
Deity Association: Eir
Height: To 2'
Season: Perennial
History: The common Mallow seems to have reached northern Europe before its more powerful cousin, Marshmallow; it is unknown whether or not it was native before Roman occupation. In the Mediterranean, it is one of the oldest recorded plants, planted on graves so that the dead might feed on them. During the Middle Ages, it symbolized home, hearth, and pastoral living.
Medicinal Uses: Leaves, roots, and flowers soothe mucous membranes, reduce inflammation, are given for bronchitis and gastrointestinal irritations, and can be added to soothing skin ointments and cough syrups.
Culinary Uses: Flowers are used in salads. The leaves and young shoots contain vitamins A, B, and C, and were boiled for a vegetable. The "cheeses", or tiny pumpkin-shaped fruits, are also edible.
Magical Uses: Mallow was used in spells to return lost loves. It symbolizes domestic contentment. Ointment made from Mallow and lard, smeared on the body, casts out demons and protects against evil magic.
Shamanic Uses: Like all of Eir's plants, Mallow can help you to speak with her, if you rub leaves or flowers on yourself or ingest the plant.
Affinity: River (moistening), Air (astringent). Mallow balances fluids and works on both Air and River conditions.
Point: CV 16
Plant-wight's Nature: Mallow-wight reminds one of a very quiet, self-enclosed child. Androgynous in the way of a child who has not yet begun to understand why gender matters anyway, Mallow-wight's attention is difficult to get at first; its quietness is not so much about shyness as about self-absorption, like the child who is playing wonderful imaginative games alone under a tree, and completely ignores the call for lunch and even dinner. When you do get Mallow-wight's attention, make your contact quick and sincere; don't bore this spirit's wandering attention.
Magical Charm: Ancestor Hearth

Dry a quantity of Mallow leaves and "cheeses", and place them on your ancestor harrow, saying the following charm:

I feast and feed my honored Dead,
I give their graves the Mallow's healings,
So hallow here my hearth and home,
And living luck in all my dealings.

Maple

Botanical Name: *Acer spp.*
Folk Names: Old Mapley, Sugar Tree
Anglo-Saxon Names: Mapul, Hlyn
Old Norse Name: Möpurr
Old High Germanic Name: Maplo
Modern German Name: Ahorn
Modern Swedish Name: Skogslönn
Modern Danish Name: Ahorn
Modern Norwegian Name: Lønneslekten
Deity Association: Hlin
Height: To 100'
Season: Perennial tree
History: Several forms of Maple tree are native to northern Europe; the famous Sugar Maple, however, is an American tree
Household Uses: Any Maple tree can be tapped for syrup, although most will only produce a little watered-down amount. Sugar Maples have the most, followed by Norway Maples. Maplewood is a wonderful wood to use for carving because of its fine grain.
Culinary Uses: Maple syrup and sugar are wonderful natural sweeteners.
Magical Uses: Love spells. A child passed through the branches of a Maple tree will have a long life, although he may outlive all his loved ones.
Shamanic Uses: One of the names for the Maple tree in Old Anglo-Saxon was Hlyn, and this is one of the handmaidens of Frigga. Hlin is the Goddess of Mourning, and Maple sugar or syrup can be used in potions to get beyond mourning for someone, reminding them that life is still sweet. Also, as Maple is one of the craftsman's woods and the rune Yr is sometimes given to craftspeople to aid their skill, a Maple talisman can be carved with this rune.
Affinity: Harvest (nourishing), Mountain (relaxant), Air (astringent). Use on Air and Storm conditions.
Point: KD 17
Plant-wight's Nature: Mother Maple is sensuous and strong. She appears as a bright-haired woman with sweet-scented golden skin, square-framed, firm and muscled. There is a "pioneer wife" quality to her—the feel of a woman who could bear ten children, milk ten cows a day, work a 20-acre field, and still be smiling and joyous at the end of the day. I commented to her that she seemed very different from Hlin, the Goddess of Mourning, and she replied, "That's why She works with me." While not one of the official Ancestral Mothers per se, she does have a strong affinity for feeding and aiding humans and will gladly reach out to any who call her.
Magical Charm: Dark Sweetness

Procure some very dark Maple syrup—not the clear golden stuff that they call Grade A and sell in stores, but the really dark concentrated stuff. You may have to resort to a Maple sugar farm during sugaring season. Say this charm over the bottle:

When all is dark, when will declines,
When I cannot catch a glimpse of joy,
Dark Mother Hlin, remind me still
That there is sweetness left in life.

When all you can see are the negative parts of life, take a taste of Mother Maple's charmed syrup. Then sit down and make a list of good things that you are grateful for, and they will come.

Marshmallow

Botanical Name: *Althaea officinalis*

Folk Names: Althea, Mallards, Hock Herb, Schloss Tea, Mauls, Mortification Root

Anglo-Saxon Name: Merscmealuwe

Modern German Names: Echter Eibisch, Samtpappel

Modern Swedish Names: Läkemalva, Altearot, Apoteksaltea

Modern Danish Name: Lægestokrose

Modern Norwegian Name: Legestokkrose

Deity Association: Eir

Height: To 6'

Season: Perennial

History: Marshmallow is native to southern Europe; it is unclear whether its introduction to northern Europe starts with Charlemagne's mandate that certain herbs be grown on his estates, or whether it had spread somewhat before this. It was naturalized in the marshes of England by the time of the Anglo-Saxon herbals. Its botanical name comes from its association with a minor Greek garden goddess of healing herbs, Althea.

Medicinal Uses: Marshmallow is the most mucilaginous herb in the Western pharmacopoeia, and its big job is to soften tissue, and give relief to anything that is hard, or dry, or inflamed, or raw. The flowers are infused and then made into an expectorant cough syrup; the leaf tea is used for bronchial and urinary infections. It is especially good for softening hard-packed mucus. The root is poulticed for wounds, burns, boils, skin ulcers, cystic tissue, and inflamed organs. It is made into a tea for treating inflammation of any mucous membrane, from the esophagus to the bladder. The liquid from the steeped root is spread on sunburns. Ointment for skin wounds can be made from Marshmallow powder, lanolin, and beeswax in a 2:1:7 ratio.

Today, Marshmallow is also used to help the lungs of smokers, or (ideally) people who have just quit smoking and need their lungs nourished. It is also used to help cancer patients tolerate chemotherapy better; the suggested dosage is 2 liters of Marshmallow tea per day to reduce nausea and other nasty side effects. It can be taken for relief of some symptoms of colitis, and to soften the kidneys and gallbladder enough to more easily pass stones. It has been known to soften hardened arteries, and in some cases lower blood pressure.

Having said all this about how it can be made into tea, there is the fact that Marshmallow doesn't extract well in any medium. Water is better than alcohol or vinegar, but still only mediocre. The best way to take Marshmallow internally for a long period of treatment is to take the ground root in capsules. In the old days, they cut up the root and soaked it in egg white and sugar, making "comfits" that could be eaten daily, because taking it straight is better than any extract. These sweets later evolved into the confection that is referred to as a "Marshmallow" today, made with all the ingredients except for the plushy root.

Household Uses: Used in cosmetics for weather-damaged skin. The liquid from the steeped root is used as a moisturizing facial cream.

Culinary Uses: All parts of the plant are edible, especially the seed "cheeses" The roots were boiled and then fried, the nutty seeds and flowers added to salads, and the leaves eaten as a vegetable.

Magical Uses: Spells for lost loves, healing spells, and casting out of demons. Marshmallow was used as an aphrodisiac for sexual potency, and has been incorporated into magical lubricant for this purpose. It was also a funeral herb.

Shamanic Uses: Much loved by Eir, the Healer among Frigga's handmaidens, Marshmallow can be made into a healing salve and spread on an astral wound while invoking her aid. A talisman can be made of the dried root carved with the runes of her name–Eihwaz Raido.

Affinity: River (moistening). Use on Fire and Air together.

Point: CV 17

Plant-wight's Nature: Grandmother Marshmallow is tall and graceful, much like her plant. She smiles often, and seems honestly glad to see people, although it may just be her exceptionally gracious attitude. Her hair and gown are of a rosy hue, and indeed she is gifted in that quality that the Norse called *litr*, or "blooming hue". *Litr* is vitality, joy in life, and it is often predicated upon physical health. Grandmother Marshmallow is one of the great healer plants; her touch is sweet-scented and brings blooming health to whatever place she touches, if only for a moment. If there is dry, hot, crackling, she soothes it.

Medicinal Charm: Healing Comfits

To make the original Marshmallow comfits–a very pleasant way to take one's medicine–use this recipe. It makes a lot, and you'll probably be baking all day, and get an awful lot of them, but it will be worth it. To keep them for the long term, freeze them in sealed plastic bags.

½ lb. (8 oz.) powdered Marshmallow root

5-lb. bag white organic raw white sugar

¼ lb. gum:arabic

2 quarts water

2 tablespoons vanilla

¼ cup Orange flower essence (optional but really nice)

8 egg whites, whipped

Beat the sugar into the egg whites, slowly, a little at a time. Mix the vanilla and Orange flower essence into the water, and beat that slowly into the egg whites. Finally, whip in the Marshmallow powder a little at a time, and then the gum:arabic. You will have a light, fluffy batter that resembles meringues. Drop it onto trays spoonful by careful spoonful, and then bake them like you would meringues: check the oven frequently, and when they are solid and only very lightly browned, pull them out. While you are whipping the batter, say this charm over it:

> *Eir's caring flower who bears so fair a blossom,*
> *Althaea, healer, soothe what can be soothed.*

Meadowsweet

Botanical Name: *Filipendula ulmaria or Spiraea ulmaria*

Folk Names: Queen of the Meadow, Bride of the Meadow, Bridewort, Lady of the Meadow, Dolloff, Meadwort

Anglo-Saxon Name: Medewyrt

Modern German Names:
Echtes Mädesüß, Wiesen-Spierstrauch, Wiesen-Spierstaude

Modern Swedish Names:
Älggräs, Älgört, Mjödört

Modern Danish Name: Mjødurt

Modern Norwegian Name: Mjødurt

Deity Association: Sif

Height: To 6'

Season: Perennial

History: Meadowsweet is native to the British Isles and to parts of southern Europe; we do not know whether it was grown in Germany or Scandinavia before the migration era. It was considered the best strewing herb of all during medieval times. It was one of the three herbs that was used to create the Celtic flower-golem Blodeuwedd, and is generally associated with maiden goddesses and brides.

Medicinal Uses: The flowering plant tops of Meadowsweet have natural aspirin in a form more gentle on the stomach than commercial aspirin; drink in tea to relieve fevers and pain. Unlike aspirin, which is harsh on the stomach, Meadowsweet has a true affinity for the stomach, and soothes all its pains and ills. The tea is excellent in treating diarrhea, especially in children. Use for gastric ulceration, nausea, vomiting, and stomach flu. Meadowsweet is good for building the gastrointestinal tract back up after long periods of fasting due to illness, starvation, or anorexia. It treats rheumatic joints, especially when upset by cold. Avoid Meadowsweet if there is a salicylate sensitivity.

Household Uses: Flowers yield a yellow dye, leaf and stem a blue dye, and the root a black dye. The dried flowers are used to scent linen.

Culinary Uses: Flowers give an almond flavor to mead, wine, jam, and stewed fruit.

Magical Uses: Used in love spells, and spells to keep the home peaceful. Used in divination, and for garlands at Lammas. Used to protect young women. Breathing oil of Meadowsweet nightly is said to make a woman more attractive to her lover.

Shamanic Uses: This lovely herb is much beloved of Thor's lovely wife Sif. Use it to make offerings to her, or gain her favor.

Affinity: Storm (bitter alterative), Air (astringent), Earth (cooling). Use for Swamp, River, or Fire conditions.

Point: UB 21

Plant-wight's Nature: Mistress Bridewort does appear as a bride, very tall and very lovely, draped in pale colors and wreathed in flowers. She is a romantic, somewhat dramatic, although more dignified about it than Mistress Bramble and more apt to swoon for effect than cry hysterically. She has had many husbands—other plant-wights, I got the feeling—some of whom she left, and some of whom left her (Grandfather Waybread was one of the latter, she told me, and this is preserved in song), and some of whom were human men. Be warned, if you are male and unmarried, she may propose to you. (As I'm extremely married and she knew this, I was unable to get more out of her regarding what that entails.)

Medicinal Charm: Stomach Storms

When there is pain and nausea in the stomach and it is rejecting food, pour a pint of boiling water over an ounce of the leaves and flowering tops of Meadowsweet. Let steep, strain, and drink, saying the following charm during the steeping:

> *Bridewort, bide my belly,*
> *Meadow's Queen, quell swells and aches,*
> *Sif-Friend, soothe the searing,*
> *Calm the seas of Dragon's Lake.*

Milk Thistle

Botanical Name: *Silybum Marianum*
Folk Names: St. Mary's Thistle, Marian Thistle, Pig Leaves, Vehedistel (Venus Thistle)
Anglo-Saxon Name: Đistel
Old Norse Name: Þistill
Old High Germanic Name: Distel
Modern German Name: Mariendistel
Modern Swedish Name: Mariatistel
Modern Danish Name: Marietidsel
Modern Norwegian Name: Mariatistel
Deity Association: Sigyn
Height: To 6'
Season: Annual
History: Native to Europe (especially southern Russia and the Mediterranean), central Asia, and north Africa, Milk Thistle has been used as a folk remedy for thousands of years. Mentioned by Theophrastus and Pliny the Elder, and later Hildegard of Bingen, it has been known to "carry off bile for the entirety of its written history. It is probably the best-researched and best-tested herb in modern pharmacology.
Medicinal Uses: Milk Thistle is excellent for nourishing the liver, spleen, and gallbladder; Milk Thistle seeds stimulate the flow of bile and encourage the expulsion of stones. It is indicated for use for anyone whose liver is in danger—those taking necessary but liver-stressing drugs, anyone with hepatitis, chemotherapy patients, and moderate to heavy drinkers. It is a potent antioxidant. It has been known to expel phlegm in cases of catarrh and pleurisy. As its name suggests, it encourages the flow of milk in nursing mothers. All parts of Milk Thistle have been tested in large doses and found to have no toxicity. The concentration of useful bioflavonoids is highest in the seed coats, although they are also present to some extent in the leaves and root. They are not, however, easily soluble in water, so tea is not necessarily the best method of absorbing Milk Thistle. Oddly enough, it works well in capsules, and very well as a glycerite tincture. Don't tincture it with alcohol—there's no point in putting a liver tonic in a liver-stressing medium.
Household Uses: Used as a fodder crop for pigs. Seeds are a favorite food of goldfinches.
Culinary Uses: Young leaves can be eaten in salads, although you have to cut all the thorns off by hand. The young spring shoots, cut close to the root with part of the stalk on, were made into a boiled salad. Roots are eaten like salsify. The heads can be boiled and eaten like artichokes. The seeds have been roasted as a coffee substitute.
Magical Uses: The root, hung around the neck, was said to repel serpents. The white lines on the leaves of Milk Thistle were associated with the milk of many maternal goddesses, including Mary during the Christian era, and as such were protective for everyone, but especially pregnant or nursing mothers and small children.

Shamanic Uses: Sacred to Sigyn, the second wife of Loki who is a goddess of nurturing and loyalty, Milk Thistle can be used to gently cleanse those who are silted up with resentments and pain. It is the least harsh of purifiers, and a promoter of necessary tears. It is especially good for those who have been in mourning for a long time.

Affinity: Swamp (oily), Storm (bitter alterative), Air (astringent), Harvest (nourishing). Use on Air and Swamp conditions.

Point: GB 24

Plant-Wight's Nature: Mother Milk Thistle is the gentlest of healers. Her soft hands gently pull away all the old poisons that you have salted away inside you, and wash you clean. She bears thorns, but they are merely her protection so that folk do not take advantage of her. If you truly in need, she will respond to that need. Every time I've needed to work with her, I first go out and take a thorny bit of leaf and put it in my mouth to chew—and I've never felt a single prick, unlike when I clumsily stumble into the plant. She is completely capable of being harmless when she chooses. She appears to me as a motherly woman robed in white-patterned green robes, much like the "milk splash" on her leaves, with only her face and hands showing. Others have seen her with cow or she-goat imagery, or bare-breasted and nursing a child.

Medicinal Charm: Liver Cleanse

For the best liver-remedy ever, make this combination either in a glycerite tincture or by combining dried and powdered herb into capsules. Use three parts Milk Thistle, one part Burdock, one part Yellow Dock, and one part Dandelion. As you pour in the glycerine or fill the capsules, and as you take the remedy, say the following charm:

Mother Milk Thistle, clean and cleanse
That which lets me live and mend;
Clate, Docce, Puffball lend
Your aid to Mother Thistle's ends.

Mints

Botanical Name: *Mentha spp.*

Folk Names: Various, depending on variety.

Anglo-Saxon Name: Minte

Old Norse Name: Mintr

Old High Germanic Name: Minza

Modern German Name: Minze

Modern Swedish Name: Mynta

Modern Danish Name: Mynte

Modern Norwegian Name: Mynter

Deity Association: Fulla

Height: 2-24"

Season: Perennial

History: All the above names for Mint come from the Latin *mentha*, because this herb originated in southern Europe and was spread to the Germanic people by the Roman occupation. Most of the Mint varieties found today have been developed since the 17th century. The original naturalized Mint is unlikely to have survived. The Anglo-Saxon herbals identify Garden Mint (*tunminte*) which is likely to be, or to be close to, common Spearmint (*Mentha spicata*); Water-Mint (*Mentha aquatica*) which is available in various subforms today; and Cornmint, which may be either Applemint (*Mentha suaveolens*) or what is referred to as Japanese Mint (*Mentha arvensis*) today. Medieval German writings on monastery gardens mention several species of Mint. The famous Peppermint was developed in the Renaissance. However, any Mint will do for the purposes involved.

Medicinal Uses: Mint tea is excellent for digestive upsets, especially in babies and children; Mint is harmless and gentle for them, and is excellent for any kind of gas. Good for any bronchial problem as well, in tea or essential on a sugar cube. Poulticed leaves can be rubbed into aching heads,, muscles, and joints, and even onto stomachs when they are too upset to take food. Mint is a gentle stimulant and antidepressant, almost as good as caffeine in some cases, but without the side effects or addictions. It has been used throughout history for hysteria and emotional shock. Spearmint and Peppermint oils are mildly anesthetic, and are good for inhaling for lung clearing. Peppermint has additional antiseptic qualities, combats internal parasites, fights viruses, aids in the healing of skin conditions and the formation of white blood cells, and induces sweating during fevers. Unique among Mints, it tastes cold but acts warm and stimulating, and as such is a remedy for mixed fever and chills. Menthol in any concentrated form kills infestations of mite species, in bees, birds, and people. Breastfeeding mothers should be careful using Peppermint, as it can dry up milk.

Household Uses: Use in potpourri and baths.

Culinary Uses: A great tea, or candy syrup. Used in certain meat sauces.

Magical Uses: Money spells, spells for success, healing spells. Rub on the head to relieve headaches. Mint was said by the Greeks to be a transformed maiden who was fleeing a lustful Hades, and as such was associated with funerals and the Underworld.

Shamanic Uses: All the Mints are loved by Fulla, younger sister of Frigga and goddess of abundance—where Mints grow, they are almost always in abundance, and the Earth has given us many species of their refreshing green glory. It can be used as an offering to her, for financial or other abundance. Mint flushes the atmosphere of a room or other place, and is an important purification herb. While it can be burned, it is best as an asperger; the water-sprinkling spreads its scent better than burning. It is especially good for asperging a person who is panicking, angry, frustrated, or having trouble containing some "hot" emotion, as it is very cooling and soothing. It is a good purification bath for anyone ill with bronchial problems.

Affinity: Fire (stimulant, Earth (cooling). Use on Fire or Earth conditions; Mint will know whether to warm or cool.

Point: CV 14

Plant-wight's Nature: *I am congested, and tired, and feel out of sorts. I go out to my garden and pick a few leaves of Chocolate Mint; laying in the grass, I chew on them. Almost instantly I am suffused by its power, like a cool green wave washing through me from mouth to lungs. I breathe green, and my lungs are immediately opened, taking in green air. I call to her, and she comes—a green woman like a water nymph, rising from the green waters of a deep lake or a river that winds beneath overhanging trees, her long wet hair still festooned with weeds. She smiles at me, kneels dripping by my side, places her cold wet hand on my forehead and then my neck, abating my fever. She is beautiful, and I love her unreservedly for that moment, and she returns that love like a reflection in the water. The tall grass I am laying in becomes rushes; I am laying in the waters of a river, of a lake, and the water closes over me. Lady Mint bathes me in coolness, and I am refreshed yet again.*

Mint is the Florence Nightingale of the Green World. She gives of herself unreservedly; there is almost no one from whom she withholds her healing touch. Most greenwights find it more difficult to act on or communicate with a body the further they are from green plant matter—extract, or even synthetic—but not Lady Mint. Her powers are so strong that she is one of the very few plant-wights who is easily able to act not only through your cup of Mint tea, but through your jar of Vicks or your bottle of liquid Peppermint soap, or even a candy cane. She is abundant in all things—they call Mint invasive, but she calls that giving to the utmost. Her green gowns may be many and varied—the rough everyday tunic of Spearmint, the crisp healer's robe of Peppermint, the wafting gown of Applemint, the ruffled Calamint—but she is unmistakable in any guise.

There is something about fresh water in the Mint-wight, even when she is growing in a field or garden far away from anything bigger than a puddle. She brings the essence of lakes and rivers wherever she goes, cooling heat and cleansing filth, blessing your breath with her green kiss. I admit that she has been one of my favorite plant spirits since I was very young, and she still holds my love, even when she is so familiar that I forget her—touching her just for a moment through the commercial cough drop in my mouth, and even then she cools and heals without asking any price except your appreciation and momentary love.

Medicinal Charm: Liquid Green

To be said over a cup of Mint tea, or any other concoction with menthol in it; Lady Mint doesn't care and will give you the benefit of her fine nursing no matter what.

Pure as peace the river runs,
Green as glass the glinting sun,
Sister Mint may soothe my pains,
Green her gift, her mighty rains.

Mistletoe

Botanical Name: *Viscum album*
Folk Names: Misseltoe, All-Heal, Birdlime, Devil's Fuge, Donnerbesen, Golden Bough, Holy Wood, Lignum Sanctae Crucis, Thunderbesom, Herbe de la Croix, Mystyldene
Anglo-Saxon Name: Misteltan
Old Norse Names: Mistelteinn, Hróðr-baðmr, Hróðr-barmr ("Famous branch")
Old High Germanic Name: Mistil
Modern German Name: Mistel
Modern Swedish Name: Mistel
Modern Danish Name: Mistelten
Modern Norwegian Name: Misteltein
Deity Association: Loki, Baldur, Odin, Thor, Frigga, Freya
Height: Tiny parasitical plant, under 6"
Season: Perennial

History: Mistletoe is an evergreen parasitic plant that grows on a number of species of deciduous trees. Despite the mythology, it is actually fairly rarely found on Oak trees, being most common on old Apple trees and also found on Linden, Ash, and Hawthorns. It is native to the temperate parts of Europe, although it does not survive well in very cold climates. Other varieties of Mistletoe are found everywhere from Africa to Australia. The Celtic Druidic groves always had at least one Mistletoe-Oak , to be harvested during important times with great ceremony. Their belief was that to let it touch the ground would bring bad luck to the country. It is associated with the thrush, which is a great disseminator of its berries. A Mistletoe tincture or infusion must be made with the green, freshly gathered plant—dried, it loses all its potency. This probably explains the fancy ritual for gathering it among various European peoples. It also acquires the taste of the tree that it parasites on, which was why it was cultivated on Oaks—the taste was apparently better, and the magical powers more potent.

Medicinal Uses: Mistletoe is a narcotic and nervine, and requires very careful handling. It is used as an emergency nervine, to sedate someone who is gone completely hysterical. It is also useful for cases of sudden emergency high blood pressure, and heart problems where there is hypertrophy of the heart with valvular insufficiency. It has been used for severe epilepsy and convulsions. Since it is somewhat poisonous, we recommend that it be used only under the aegis of a trained herbalist who has experience with this plant.

Magical Uses: Besides being used as a love-spell for kissing under at Yule, Mistletoe has been used as a ward against lightning, fire, disease, and misfortune of any kind. It seems to be an all-purpose warding plant, used against bogeys and demons too multitudinous to mention. The wood has been used to fashion magic wands and ritual knife handles. However, it is also the plant that Loki used to slay Baldur, and so it is also a plant of mourning. It has been associated with a whole slew of Norse gods; not just Loki and Baldur, but Odin, Thor, Frigga and Freya. In some parts of Scandinavia, it must be shot out of a tree, not harvested by hand.

Shamanic Uses: Mistletoe is a tiny but powerful plant that contains all the power of holy sacrifice. It has been associated with sacrificial religions of both the Germanic peoples and the Celts, and it is used when any kind of a great and holy and perhaps painful sacrifice must be made. Loki used it as the weapon to slay Baldur, the sacred king. It can be used to add power to any working, but it must be accompanied by a sacrifice. The rune Ing is useful with Mistletoe. The power locked into this tiny, insignificant plant is amazing; use it carefully and only after much thought and prayer.

Affinity: Mountain (relaxant), Stone (sedative). Use on Storm and Fire cardiac/circulatory conditions.

Point: GB 44

Plant-wight's Nature:

> Mistletoe was white, gold, and metallic. He wasn't entirely keen on giving me a charm, believing that sacrifice was necessary to gain his attention, not just the recitation of a charm. I explained that only people serious about working with him were likely to use the charm in the first place; he agreed with this, saying that he would explain his true charm to them anyway. So this is just a way of getting his attention. Like Loki, Mistletoe will speak to who he wants to speak to and appear when he wants to appear.
>
> Speaking of Loki, Mistletoe is unhappy with his subordinate position relative to the God. The way we talk about Loki and Mistletoe make it sound like the plant is just a tool, but in fact he is a vital, intelligent being in his own right. He is deeply concerned with the dynamic of sacrifice, especially blood sacrifice. Mistletoe balances and communicates between worlds via the medium of sacrifice. He is also exacting, hating sloppy and half-assed approaches to such a solemn, precise art. I got the impression Mistletoe doesn't like speaking with many people, but might be willing to teach those who are very serious about learning the mysteries of sacrifice. Mistletoe won't tolerate being crossed, either. He made sure that I understood how serious he was about getting payment from me for his assistance–it would be disastrous to anger a plant who happens to be a parasite."
>
>   -Silence Maestas

Magical Charm: Mistletoe Charm

> The charm is partly his words, partly mine; I had to add my own finesse to it because his "key" was very abstract and he was reluctant to be too specific; even so, he personally approved the words I used and had very particular ideas in mind about what the charm would say and do. It doesn't rhyme like most of the plant charms I've come across do, but this is what he gave me to work with; there's some music that the words can be set to and I'm sure Mistletoe will work on this with whoever he chooses to teach. Before he agreed to work with me on this, I had to give him something. I promised to write about him (my standard bargaining chip when dealing with plant spirits; they seem to appreciate it); he accepted this, but there will definitely need to be some follow-up sacrifice as well–probably my blood. I'd say that anyone wanting to deal with Mistletoe have blood or something very personal ready to offer to him. Makes me wonder what Loki gave to earn Mistletoe's cooperation . . ."

> Lofty and brazen, spread on a branch
> Between earth and heaven the golden spear lives.
> Catch if you may in most sacred sport
> The game the Gods play–I take life and give.
>   -Silence Maestas

Motherwort

Botanical name: *Leonurus cardiaca*

Folk names: Lion's Tail, Heartwort, Agripaume, Echtes Herzgespann, Echtes Lövenschwanz, Løvehale, Herbe battudo

Anglo-Saxon Name: Modorwyrt (Originally another name for Mugwort, later applied to this plant.)

Modern German Name: Echter Löwenschwanz

Modern Swedish Name: Hjärtstilla

Modern Danish Name: Almindelig Hjertespand

Modern Norwegian Name: Løvehale

Deity Association: Mengloth

Height: to 6'

Season: Perennial

History: One form or another of the *Leonurus* species is native to the northern areas of every continent. Motherwort probably originated in Central Europe, and is found in Europe and North America, although it may not have originally been native to the British Isles and may have been brought there. It has a long history of being the herb to give to new mothers, usually in a tea. The entire plant is useful for medicinal purposes.

Medicinal Uses: Motherwort tones the heart, regulates blood pressure and too-rapid heartbeat, and reduces muscle spasms. It is mildly sedative and anti-depressive, and reduces cholesterol levels. Motherwort reduces bleeding during birthing, contracts the uterus after birth, helps to expel stubborn placentas, is used for post-partum depression, treats menstrual irregularities, and calms the symptoms of menopause. Do not give to pregnant women, as it hastens birth. Motherwort is useful for hyperthyroidism, especially with cardiac symptoms. As a tea, it's effective but not very tasty, so it was often brewed into a fruit conserve or made into a syrup. The infusion can also be used as a douche for vaginal infections. Be advised that it may be habit-forming (not physically, but psychologically) if used regularly as an antidepressant

Magical Uses: Hung over the bed of a laboring woman, dried Motherwort brings a quicker and easier birth. In the Middle Ages, it was considered to be powerful against all sorts of "wykked sperytis". Has been used as a magical tonic to build confidence, purpose, and a sense of joy in one's work.

Shamanic Uses: A sprig of Motherwort will aid you in getting up Lyfjaberg Mountain to see Mengloth, if you are female. Showing it to Mengloth's door-guard will convince him that you are serious and in need of healing.

Affinity: Mountain (relaxant), Stone (sedative), Earth (coolant), Fire (not through stimulant means, but through special bitter combination that drains heat from the upper body to the lower), Air (drying through those same). Use on any Storm, cardiac Fire, uterine Earth/Air conditions.

Point: HT 5

Plant-wight's Nature: Little Mother, as she is called, is a bustling maternal sort, as her name suggests. She is the sort who will listen to your troubles, give you a cup of tea and a pat on the head and an apronful of sympathy, again and again. "That's all right, dear," she says, and yet if you continue to do foolish things, her tongue can become as tart as the thorns on her seed-stalks. Generally, though, she is kindly and sympathetic, and loves mothers and children. Little Mother is a good nurse and midwife, and can be called upon to help in difficult births. She shows herself to me as large and buxom, with a lap suitable for cuddling two or three children at once. Her fingers, long and curling and spindly, are the only thing at odds with her rounded appearance.

Medicinal Charm: Heart-Healer

For heart irregularities—especially after heart attacks or angina—infuse an ounce of Motherwort in a pint of boiling water and drink daily, saying the following charm:

Heart-healer, Seat of Love,

May the tides of the four seas
Beat strong in rhythm against the shore.

Medicinal Charm: Little Mother

For a woman who has given birth and is dreary and depressed, whose endorphin levels have not risen and whose hormones may be in an uproar, who is sleep-deprived (although the best cure for the latter might be a babysitter and a tall glass of Chamomile tea) and who is generally filled with grey clouds, make a tincture of 3 parts Motherwort, I part Sage, and one part Borage. Take a dropperful twice a day, saying the following:

> *Little Mother, may dark clouds lift from my days.*
> *Sage being serenity, Borage bring courage.*

Mugwort

Botanical Name: *Artemisia vulgaris*
Folk Names: Felon Weed, Sailor's Tobacco, Artemis Herb, Muggons, Naughty Man, Old Man, Old Uncle Henry, Cingulum Sancti Johannes, Una
Anglo-Saxon Name: Mugwyrt (from AS *moughte-wort* or "moth-plant")
Modern German Name: Gemeiner Beifuß
Modern Swedish Name: Gråbo
Modern Danish Name: Gråbynke
Modern Norwegian Name: Burot
Deity Association: Likely the Norns, if any.
World Association: Midgard
Height: 8'
Season: Perennial
History: The Artemisia species are native to every continent; Mugwort is the European version thereof. Also on every continent, Artemisia species are found to be burned to clear negative energies away. This has been a frustrating thing for ethnobotanists, who don't understand why people on different sides of the planet somehow independently figured out the same superstitious and mythical use for the same plant species. We, of course, know better. Mugwort is very old, and has been used magically for a very long time. It has no active hallucinogenic parts, unlike Wormwood (whose alkaloid thujone isn't useful while burning anyway; it must be ingested), but it doesn't need them to do the trick of creating a sacred space and enhancing one's psychic powers. It's always been the best plant for the job. And, of course, it is the first plant listed in the thousand-year-old power song of my ancestors, *Song of the Nine Sacred Herbs*. In this charm, Mugwort is referred to as Una, the Oldest Herb.
Medicinal uses: Mugwort is very much a woman's herb, as it promotes secretion of the pituitary sex hormones and balances the female hormonal system, especially when there are pathological amounts of androgens. It is indicated for artistic, lunar people who are having trouble focusing and being

articulate as it helps associative memory and brings together the hemispheres of the brain. It helps those who live in dreamworlds to come into the physical world with the rest of us, and helps those whose imagination holds them hostage to escape it.

Mugwort's leaf tea is diuretic and induces sweating. Regulates erratic menstruation, brings on delayed periods, expels afterbirth, helps with menopausal symptoms. Promotes appetite and bile production, and is a stimulant for stagnant livers and sluggish digestion. Tonic for nerves; mild sedative. Used for bronchitis, colds, colic, kidneyailments, fevers. Bath additive for rheumatism and tired legs. Juice relieves itching of Poison Oak. Disinfectant and antiseptic, and used as the classic herb for moxibustion in Oriental medicine. Avoid when pregnant; it can bring on labor; conversely, Mugwort is used in abortifacient recipes.

Household uses: Powder for a moth repellent. Lay branches between Onion and carrot rows to deter them. Given to animals to worm them; useful as livestock fodder for any animals (but don't give it to pregnant ones). Mugwort fluff (made the same way as moxa—rubbing the leave through a sieve until only cottony fibers remain) was used as tinder.

Culinary uses: Leaves were once added to goose stuffings, and are put in rice cakes in Asia. Used as a substitute for China tea in times of poverty.

Magical Uses: In the Middle Ages, Mugwort was connected with St. John the Baptist, who was said to have worn a belt of the herb during his time in the wilderness. St. John's Herb, as the plant became known, had the power to drive out demons, and sprays of the herbs were worn around the head on St. John's Eve as a protection against possession by evil forces.

In China, bunches of Mugwort were hung in the home during the Dragon Festival to keep away evil spirits. The Ainus of Japan burn bunches to exorcise spirits of disease, who are thought to hate the odor. It was planted along roadsides by the Romans, who put sprigs in their shoes to prevent aching feet on long journeys, and carried to ward against wild beasts, poison, and stroke. Mugwort prevents elves and other evil things from entering houses, and is said to cure madness and aid in astral projection. A pillow stuffed with Mugwort and slept upon will produce prophetic dreams.

Mugwort is burned during scrying rituals, and a Mugwort-and-honey infusion is drunk before divination. The infusion is also used to wash crystal balls and magic mirrors, and Mugwort leaves are placed around the base of the ball, or beneath it, to aid in psychic workings. Pick just before sunrise on the waxing moon, preferably from a plant that leans north.

Shamanic Uses: This is the plant of Midgard, burned at the start of a ritual. One starts and ends with Mugwort, as one starts and ends with Midgard. Its shamanic purpose is purification. We tend to think of purification, in these days of advanced medical antisepsis, as being sterile. To us, "pure" has come to mean "without life". When we use something whose basic power is purification, we expect, on some level, for it to clean everything and leave it a blank slate.

However, that's not what magical purification actually does. Perhaps a better term for it would be "sanctification." Purifying magics create that aura of sacred space, which is so clear when you're in it but so elusive to describe. In order to create that energy, they do push out other sorts of energy, including the busy, well-worn, "messy" energy of the everyday. After the purification energy fades, the other stuff may drift back, or it might not, so it can have a cleaning effect in some cases.

Mugwort is the herb that is most often burned as *recels*, the Old English word for incense; pronounced *ray-kels*. The act of burning it is referred to as *recaning*, which can be pronounced various ways, but the most graceful seems to be *reek-en-ing*; the verb *recan* is cognate to our work "reek." Celtic-tradition people use the term *saining*. It's an alternative to the Native American-derived term "smudging", and it can be bound in lashed bundles and burned in the same way as White Sagebrush. It also has a clearing effect on the mind, and a heightening of the extra senses, so it is a good thing to start any working that is going to involve an altered or trance state at some point.

Some spirit-workers have a stronger reaction to Mugwort than others. A few report that just having it by the bed can cause vivid journeying dreams; some can go into trance immediately just by smelling it. It may depend on how much the plant-wight likes you, or considers you her sort of person.

Affinity: Fire (stimulant), Mountain (relaxant). Use for Earth and Storm.

Point: SP 8

Plant-wight's Nature: Grandmother Mugwort is witchy, spooky, and incredibly powerful. Most report Mugwort as feminine, if ancient and mysterious. She is very lunar, but she is not the shining maiden new moon or the swollen full moon, she is the mysteries of the dark moon, the witchy crone with the wild mane of silver hair and the long, pointy fingers. Her voice is rough and cracking and she cackles. She opens her arms and silvery magic pours forth in a cloud, and she can fill a space like no other plant I know, even beating out Juniper and American Sage. She loves to work with psychic folk and lays very few rules; her attitude seems to be more one of, "Knock yourself out! If you get screwed up, it's your own fault and you'll learn, now won't you?" After which she cackles at you further. To her, your safety is not her problem ... which can be good and bad.

Botanically speaking, Mugwort and Wormwood are very similar, considered "sibling" plants and both of the Artemisia genus; they are sometimes confused for each other. Chemically, Mugwort lacks the thujone content of Wormwood, so the psychoactive properties haven't been conclusively proved by science. However, Mugwort's spiritual potency is such that people are affected when it is an ingredient in incense, steeped in wine, or just by having it around them (hence its reputation as an herb to aid in dreamwork). Where Wormwood possesses a masculine spirit, Grandmother Mugwort is feminine and full of classic Crone energy. She is wily and will lead you in circles before giving you a clear answer; she can be a bit of a tease, appearing ornery one moment and crafty the next. Her secrets are given up only at her discretion, though she is not generally picky about who gets to use her plant children. She is of the opinion that we learn best by seeing for ourselves just how big a mess we get into, and she generally won't interfere when

people seek to add her power to something they are doing. Having her direct permission to use her powers seems a bit more rare, and is a special thing.

Mugwort has a variety of magical uses, including aiding in dreamwork, divination, protection, and the creation of magical tools. She also adds a layer of refinement to some workings, particularly those relating to cleansing and banishing since she has a scrubbing effect that clears out all kinds of energetic and astral clutter without the muscle that other herbs, like Rue, have. Simply put, she doesn't need the muscle to get the job done with a great deal less fuss. I have used fresh sprays of Mugwort as miniature flail to cleanse the body's energy field; the slap of the leaves and twigs had a very pronounced effect.

"Grandmother Mugwort has always appeared as an elderly woman all hunched over and wrapped in a shawl. She has long grasping fingers and hands that are fast and clever; she herself is quite fast, though she may cultivate the illusion of being little more than a feeble old woman. Meeting her, that illusion is quickly banished; Grandmother is quick, intelligent, insightful, and very, very wise". —Silence Maestas

Magical Charm: Recels

The best magical charm for Mugwort is to use it in recels, for recaning an area before spiritual working, or to clean out the vibes of what's been going on there. I've never asked for a charm from Grandmother Mugwort, as one was already provided in the *Song of the Nine Sacred Herbs* (see chapter on that charm). I use the first verse of that charm—the Mugwort verse—when binding the stalks together into fat recaning sticks and hanging them to dry, and again when blessing them. I use the last verse regularly, as it wards the directions during the actual recaning; it's my usual purification charm that I do before divination, journeying, ritual, or anything else of that sort. Be warned that some spirit-workers don't have a good relationship with Mugwort for some reason, and can use Agrimony or Juniper instead.

Mullein

Botanical Name: *Verbascum thapsus*

Folk Names: Aaron's Rod, Blanket Leaf, Candlewick Plant, Graveyard Dust, Clot, Doffle, Feltwort, Flannel Plant, Flannel Leaf, Hag's Taper, Hedge-Taper, Jupiter's Staff, Lady's Foxglove, Old Man's Fennel, Peter's Staff, Shepherd's Club, Torches, Velvetback, Velvet Plant, Cow Lungwort, Our Lady's Flannel, Adam's Flannel, Rag Paper, Bullock's Lungwort, Beggar's Stalk, Cuddy's Lungs, Hare's Beard, Clown's Lungwort, Wild Ice Leaf, Moleyn, Agleaf

Anglo-Saxon Name: Molin

Modern German Name: Kleinblütige Königskerze

Modern Swedish Name: Kungsljus

Modern Danish Name: Kongelys

Modern Norwegian Name: Filtkongslys

Deity Association: Loki

Height: To 6'

Season: Biennial

History: Native to all parts of Europe, central Asia, and northern Africa, Mullein has been helping people breathe for thousands of years. The down on the leaves and stem makes excellent tinder when dried, from whence came its name "Candlewick Plant". It was also dipped in tallow and used as a rough candle by country people, and later these Mullein candles became the traditional lighting for outdoor occult rituals. The term "Hag's Taper" supposedly harks back to this time when witches used them for their rites, although the actual etymology of the word seems to come from the Anglo-Saxon term meaning "Hedge-Taper", referring to Mullein's tendency to stick up out of hedges. For whatever reason, Mullein seems to have more folk names than any other herb. It is also a capricious plant, disliking transplanting but seeding itself randomly and springing up wherever it likes, often in unauthorized places.

Medicinal Uses: Mullein is a classic respiratory herb; drink in tea to clear lungs of mucus and stop coughing, or make a strong infusion into a syrup. It is especially good for chronic long-term coughs. Mullein is a very mild sedative, and can help with sleeping when bronchial complaints keep you up. The fresh flowers, steeped for 21 days in olive oil in the sun, are a topical bactericide and help with ear-aches and eczema inflammation. Herbal smoke mixtures containing Mullein are smoked for dry, raspy coughs caused by too much smoking of less benign substances. Mullein leaves have long been employed as emergency bandages when wounded in the wild, both for their antiseptic properties and their softness. Mullein seals up leaking organs and joints; Matthew Wood has used it to set ribs and believes that it can set difficult bones and seal up leaking spinal discs.

Household Uses: Leaves can be placed in shoes when soles become thin. Leaf down makes good tinder for starting fires, and a Mullein stalk is the best horizontal tinder for a fire-bow. Leaves can be used to wrap meat for preservation. Flowers can be used in facial cream to soften skin, and their honey scent is used to flavor liqueurs. The crushed seed capsules are dropped into small ponds to stun fish.

Magical Uses: Guards against nightmares when placed under the pillow, keeps wild animals away while traveling, keeps colds away, banishes demons, and is used as a substitute for graveyard dust. Mullein prevents against being enchanted by enemies, as Odysseus found when he used it against Circe. Mullein was dipped in wax and used as a candle, or dipped in oil and used as a lampwick, for medieval magical rites as a general herb of protection. It is a substitute for fire energy where real fire can't be used (although if Mullein manifests strongly enough, it might bring real fire).

Shamanic Uses: This plant seems to have been claimed by Loki. (Look at how many interesting names it has—what a Loki thing! It's also telling that one of its names is Hag's Taper, when his first wife is the Hag of the Iron Wood and she certainly loves his taper, as it were.) Dry it and light it up like a torch to invoke him, and perhaps he will come. Or maybe he won't. At any rate, he will take notice, and appreciate an offering. It can also be used with the rune Os to give skill in speechifying, something that Loki has in abundance when he wants to use it. It can also be used with Nauthiz, the fire-bow rune, and Cweorth the fire-twirl, and of course Kenaz. The leaf smoke has been used by many cultures the world over to awaken the unconscious.

Affinity: River (moistening). Use for Air conditions.

Point: KD27

Plant-wight's Nature: Lady Mullein leaped forth like a flaming spear when I contacted her. She danced around me in a circle, laughing, sparks flying from her fingers. Her hair was in a single thick golden braid which stuck straight up, against gravity, like the golden-flowered taper of her plant. "I am friend of the first flame," she told me, and I recalled her relationship to the firebow. When she stopped moving, suddenly her flame went out and she was wreathed in witchy smoke, which solidified around her into an old-gold-velvet dress. "Breathe me," she said. "I'll open you up inside, just let me in. See what I can do." Lady Mullein is a Hedgewitch-herb like Mugwort, but younger and more energetic. She understands a myriad of old spells and could probably be an enervating teacher if you can keep up with her. She likes dancing—dance with a Mullein stalk in her honor. If you can manage it, dance with it dipped in oil and set on fire.

Medicinal Charm: Breathing Tea

Pick a flowering stalk of Mullein, and blow into each yellow flower, as if blowing on a flame to heighten it. Once you've "activated" it in this way, use it fresh or hang it up to dry. It can be used for any fire-spell, or for the following medicinal tea to use when the wet cold has overtaken your lungs. Pour a quart of boiling water over a handful of crushed Mullein leaves, let steep for half an hour, and then strain and drink. As you take it into you, say the following charm:

> *Hare's Beard, Hag's Taper, hail to you, bright lady,*
> *Feltwort, Flannel Leaf, Flamehair's favorite,*

Candlewick, Cuddy's Lungs, clean me out clear through,
Bullock's Lungwort, Blanket Leaf, I breathe in you,
Velvetback, Graveyard Dust, you breathe in me true.

Mustard

Botanical Name: *Brassica juncea* (Brown Mustard), *Brassica nigra* (Black Mustard), *and Brassica hirta* (White Mustard)

Folk Names: Hotseed, Sinapis, Mostarde, Moutarde, Mustus Ardens

Anglo-Saxon Name: Senep

Old High Germanic Name: Senfe

Modern German Name: Senf

Modern Swedish Name: Senap

Modern Danish Name: Sennep

Modern Norwegian Name: Sennep

Deity Association: Tyr

Height: To 6'

Season: Annual

History: Mustard usage all over Europe goes back to prehistoric times. Every ancient continental European culture used it frequently in dishes, more so than we do today. It was brought to the British Isles by the Saxon invasion. Some accounts confuse the true Mustards with wild field Mustard, or charlock, which was used for the same purposes.

Medicinal Uses: A poultice of the powder, laid on the chest, relieves congestion, especially for pneumonia. The same plasters can be used on rheumatism and neuralgia. Mustard also relieves aching joints and is good in a footbath for chilblains and increasing circulation. It can be used for numbness of the limbs, and is generally good for people who are old, Cold, gloomy, and numb. Do not leave Mustard on the skin for too long; anything past a pleasant burning is too much. Internally, Mustard is good for indigestion, stomach cramps, and flatulence; make sure to swallow the seeds whole.

Household Uses: Mustard is a good deodorizer, antiseptic, and sterilizing agent.

Culinary Uses: Make Mustard sauce by mixing water with ground or powdered seed in the following proportions: 3 parts Brown Mustard, 2 parts White Mustard, 1 part Black Mustard. Add just enough to make it smooth. If you can't get all three kinds, it's all right.

Magical Uses: Throwing the seed into the air can supposedly help you fly, and sprinkling it over your doorstep will keep out unwanted visitors. Sprinkling it in a place with enemies will cause confusion to them, and cause them to make poor decisions. Carrying it in your pocket when arrested or when going to court will cause confusion there too, and one can supposedly get away.

Shamanic Uses: One of the herbs found in the Oseberg burial, Mustard is much liked by Tyr, and can be used in conjunction with his rune Teiwaz/Tyr. You can make a Tyr rune on the ground out of Mustard seeds, or eat a few while invoking the rune.

Affinity: Fire (stimulant). Use for Earth conditions.

Point: SP 21

Plant-wight's Nature: The Mustardseed spirit is a fierce little plant. His energy is solar, fiery, warriorlike, and extremely masculine. There is something iron-like about the "astral smell" of Mustard; one gets visions of smithing, hammer on anvil, perhaps the banging out of swords and other weapons. Sun as warrior, rather than sun as beneficent warmer. He is a fighter, and will fling himself against your cold, moist problems if you let him, but he can be harsh and go with a scorched-earth policy, so be careful.

Medicinal Charm: Mustard Plaster

To make a Mustard plaster, finely grind 1/3 cup of Mustard seed, preferably White Mustard. Add a tablespoon of olive oil and stir (or put it in a blender), then keep drizzling in little bits of olive oil until it's a thick liquid. Pour into a pan and heat until very warm but not boiling hot, just enough to melt the beeswax that you're grating in (use a fine grater). Periodically test for hardness by dripping some on a cold spoon and letting it cool; if it hardens right up like wax, it's enough. Then spread it on a clean linen or cotton cloth with a spoon, in an oval of about 8" by 10", and let it dry. It can be stored in a cool place for a couple of years. When there is congestion in the chest, take it out and warm it, and place it Mustard-side down onto the chest. It will begin to heat up and redden the skin; leave it for 15 minutes until the area is warmed and stimulated. This brings blood to the area for healing. While using it, say the following charm:

> *Hail Hot One, harsh as noontime heat,*
> *Senep, Sun-Savior, seek and sear*
> *The moisture moldering my labored lungs*
> *Burn them bright, clean them clear.*

Nettles

Botanical name: *Urtica dioica*

Folk names: Nessel, Noedl (Needle), Ortiga ancha

Anglo-Saxon Names: Stiðe (Harsh, Stiff), Netele (Needle)

Old Norse Name: Netla

Old High Germanic Name: Nessel. All stem from the Indo-European word *net* or *ne*, meaning to sew. It is generally assumed that Nettle's name stems both from its needlelike pricking and the fact that it is a fiber crop, a double-entendre that was not lost on the ancestors.

Modern German Name: Grosse Brennessel

Modern Swedish Name: Brännässla

Modern Danish Name: Nælde

Modern Norwegian Name: Brennesler

Deity Association: Surt

Height: 3-5'

Season: Perennial

History: Stinging Nettle is native to all of Europe; Nettle-fiber has been found in Danish Bronze Age graves. Its smaller cousin the Lesser Nettle (*Urtica urens*) is more common in Eastern Europe, and its southern cousin Roman Nettle (*Urtica pilulifera*) was grown in the Mediterranean area. Nettles were used by the Roman Legions in Britain, who would rub their joints with the leaves to keep their blood flowing in the cold, damp weather. All have similar value and uses, but *Urtica dioica* grows the tallest.

Medicinal Uses: A Scots proverb goes "If they wad drink Nettles in March and eat Muggins (Mugwort) in May, sae many braw maidens wadna gang to clay." Nettles is one of the great polyvalent multipurpose weeds in the herbalist's roster. While it is admittedly a royal pain to gather, it's worth it. Nettles will grow on the nastiest part of your land, with no care and little bother, and will come back year after year. They can be harvested twice a year; more than that will kill them off eventually. Nettles' stinging property comes from the formic acid—the same stuff in an ant bite—on its tiny needlelike hairs, which causes a histamine reaction. Drying or cooking will neutralize it fine, though. In general, Nettles bring warmth and dryness to a concoction, and combine surprisingly well with many other herbs.

Nettle-plants are one of the few herbs sometimes juiced and drunk, but you have to be careful that none of the stingers get into the juice, so a really good green-plant juicer should be used, or the juice is then cooked—in which case you might as well just make a strong green decoction of the plant. The decoction promotes circulation, mildly lowers blood sugar, cleanses the system, and repulses general dampness and inflammation. It is a mild diuretic; it tones the kidneys, clears uric acid from the system, and is used for arthritis and lupus. Nettles seem to have the ability to turn waste materials into protein—as evidenced by their ability to produce an amazingly high-protein plant out of waste places. As such, it can regenerate the function of organs, and thus is used for impotence (giving the testes a boost) and low thyroid function. Nettle tea stops bleeding; for a nosebleed, dip a cotton ball in Nettle tea and place it in the nostril. Similarly, Nettles can dry up internal hemorrhaging.

The juice does all this plus provide a protein-and-vitamin-rich tonic (often given for anemiadiabetes, or scurvy), and is used to treat skin conditions such as eczema (especially on the hands); nursing mothers can take it to keep their milk flowing, and post-nursing mothers can use a poultice to dry them up. Mixed with honey and water, it can be drunk for asthma; the dried leaves can also be smoked for this ailment. Taken prophylactically, it helps keep pollen allergies low. The juice is an antidote to the sting of the needles. Alternatively, the juice of Yellow Dock—which often grows near Nettles—will take away the sting.

Fresh Nettles are used to promote circulation in frostbitten skin. Until recently, "urtication", or flogging rheumatic joints with Nettle plants in order to increase circulation, was sometimes done. This practice is still used for regrowing skin nerves after spinal injuries. It can also be used in compresses used on sore joints and tendonitis. Nettle poultices are a superb burn remedy, even for deep burns, and speed healing.

Household Uses: The whole plant yields a greenish-yellow dye, and can be retted and prepared like Flax; this is called "Nessel-Garn" in Germany, which is also made into rope and paper. While it is more difficult to gather, Nesselgarn is finer than Hemp, a good substitute for linen, and almost as good as cotton; mixed 25% with cotton, it makes excellent clothing. It is said to make better plush velveteen than cotton. The astringent young leaves are used in facial steams, bath mixtures, and hair preparations. The silica in the root of the Nettle plant is a traditional remedy for falling hair and dandruff. Nettles are very nutritious as a livestock feed; they can be cut and dried like hay twice a year, and won't sting once dried. Chickens lay more eggs and milking animals give more milk on a diet supplemented by Nettle hay.

Culinary Uses: Nettles can be cooked and eaten as a pot herb, like Mustard greens or spinach. Once they are cooked, there is no sting left to them. It is said that the best French cooks knew a dozen different things to do with a Nettle-top. In many places in Europe, Nettles were forced under glass jugs for spring vegetables. For a spring tonic, cook and eat the top third of Nettle plants that are under 8" tall; they are high in iron and vitamins. Don't eat fall plants, as the formic acid is more concentrated in them and they are gritty and don't taste as good. Gather them to dry for medicinal uses.

For Nettle Beer: In a large pot combine 2 gallons of cold water, 5 cups of washed, young Nettle leaves, 2 cups each of Dandelion leaves and Cleavers, and 2 ounces of bruised Ginger root. You can also add Horehound and/or Meadowsweet if you have any. Boil gently for 40 minutes, then strain and stir in 1 ½ cups of brown sugar. When cooled to lukewarm temperature, toast a slice of bread and spread with one cube of fresh yeast. Float the bread yeast side up on the top of the mixture, cover and allow to ferment for 24 hours. At the end of this time, open and remove the residue from the top of the beer. Add 1 tablespoon of cream of tartar and bottle as you would an ale.

For Nettle Pudding: Combine several handfuls of Nettle-tops with a head of broccoli, one large chopped Leek or Onion, and a small chopped cabbage. Add a quarer-pound of rice, tie the whole thing up in a muslin bag, and boil in salted water until everything is cooked. Serve with melted butter.

Magical Uses: Associated with Surt, Nettles send curses back to their owner. Sprinkled around the house, it keeps evil away; thrown onto a fire, it averts danger; held in the hand, it keeps away ghosts. It is considered a "carnivorous" herb, and is used in purification baths and burned for exorcisms. Two surviving charms for curing Nettle wounds with Yellow Dock juice are to be said as thus: First, "Nettle in, Dock out; Dock rub Nettle out!" The second one goes, "Out Nettle, in Dock; Dock shall have a new smock; Nettle shall get naught but rock."

Shamanic Uses: This is the herb of Muspellheim, the burning land, and its power is aggressive defense. About a year before I discovered the *Lacnunga* and the Nine Herbs, a great stand of Nettles grew up by my door. A few people got brushed by them, and complained; I was told that I should cut them all down, that they were a hazard. Others shrugged and said that they had walked right by them and were never bothered.

I went out with clippers, ready to hack them down, but I couldn't seem to do it. Something stayed my hand, giving me a strong feeling that I shouldn't touch them, so I gave up and went back inside. After a while I began to notice that the people who got "attacked" by the Nettles were folks who later gave me trouble, or turned out only to want to use my resources and give back as little as possible. My old friends were never touched by them, nor were the members of my household.

Nettle is an aggressive defender, in the sense that it will not only absorb any harmful magic that is thrown at you or the space, it will strike back if you let it. Due to its difficult nature, it's nearly impossible to handle fresh in ritual, but dried or cooked Nettle will lose its sting—physically, anyway. Nettles keeps its rabid-guard-dog energy when burned, or sprinkled dry around an area. You can drink it in tea in preparation for any kind of guardian duty. Sometimes Nettle's aggressive defensiveness will slip over into offensiveness, so it's not a bad herb to use before any duty where you're going to be armed and going into danger.

Because of its association with Muspellheim, Nettle likes being burned, but throwing it into a fire may make the fire burn longer and hotter, perhaps dangerously so. Take care that you have plenty of water around before infusing your little campfire with the power of the Fire World. On the other hand, it can be a symbolic substitute for fire in a place where you aren't allowed to actually light a flame.

Affinity: Fire (stimulant), Harvest (nourishing), Storm (bitter alterative). Use for Earth, Air, and Swamp.

Point: ST 36

Plant-wight's Nature: Nettle-wight is exactly what you'd expect—fiery, prickly, and eager to attack and defend. It is a warrior plant, and likes to have something to attack, especially something wet and cold. Nettle is tireless, faithful, and enthusiastic, but if you do not give him a job, he will run amuck and overdo things. Make sure you set good boundaries with this one; he respects a good commanding officer, but will run roughshod over anyone who is weak or indecisive.

Medicinal Charm: Nettle Tea

To be used for any of the above problems: Put 2 ounces of dried Nettles into a quart of boiling water, infuse for ten minutes, and then strain. Sing over the boiling tea the following charm:

> *Border-guard of the burning land,*
> *Nettle nourish, Stithe stand,*
> *Drive out dampness by the fire-lord's hand.*

Oak

Botanical Name: *Quercus robur*

Folk Names: Duir, Jove's Nuts, Iron Wood

Anglo-Saxon Name: Ac

Old Norse Names: Eikar, Eik, in Iceland where there were no Oaks it became a reference to a tree in general.

Old High Germanic Name: Eih

Modern German Name: Eiche
Modern Swedish Name: Ek
Modern Danish Name: Eg
Modern Norwegian Names: Eiketrær, Sommereik
Deity Association: Thor, Angrboda
Height: To 130'
Season: Large perennial tree

History: The ragged bark of the Oak tree gives it a peculiar trait when struck by lightning: instead of conducting the electricity into the ground, it blows apart into many flaming pieces. These were valued by Paleolithic ancestors as a source of fire, gifted from the Gods, and so the Oak was associated with lightning and the gods of the sky, most notably Thor, but also Zeus and the Lithuanian Perkunas. It was one of the two most sacred trees of the Indo-Europeans, the other being Ash—and the two most popular Norse gods, Thor and Odin, are associated with the Oak and Ash respectively. The Oak also became the sacred tree of the British Druids. According to some Siberian tribes, the World Tree was an Oak rather than an Ash. In Finland, the great Oak World Tree was planted by the three Fates and grew tall enough to block out the light, and had to be cut down by an Underworld spirit with a golden hatchet, thus creating the world from its trunk (reminiscent of Ymir) and the stars from its scattered acorns.

Medicinal Uses: The most useful medicinal varieties are the English Oak (*Quercus robur*) and the American White Oak (*Quercus alba*). Oak is highly astringent, high in tannins. A mild decoction of the bark can be drunk for diarrhea and bloody stools, gargled for sore throats, applied as a compress for burns, added to ointments for hemorrhoids, and sniffed powdered for nosebleeds. The tannin-rich inner bark tones the intestines, and cleanses rot anywhere it goes, it has been used as a wash for gangrenous sores, a gargle for the early stages of tonsillitis that can prevent suppuration, and a rinse for tooth rot that has been said to reverse gingivitis. Soaking in an Oak bark bath will treat hemorrhoids and varicose veins, as it tones the blood vessels.

The acorns, broken up and soaked in alcohol to make a tincture, treat conditions where the spleen (and possibly liver) is enlarged, and there is a great deal of edema and/or ascites involved, and a general sagging of the veins and sluggishness of the lymphatic system. It has been used to help people whose spleen has been removed and who are suffering the lymphatic-dysfunction consequences, or who have had any lymph nodes removed with the same result. (The tincture, or sometimes the flower essence, is sometimes combined with regular soaks in a bath of the inner Oak bark.) This "Spirit of Oak" has also been used to treat alcoholism; it was found that it worked even better for its various uses if it was distilled, taking out much of the tannins. Spirit of Oak is especially good when the drinking is small-scale and chronic rather than large-scale, and motivated by loneliness or disappointment with life. It is said to be especially good for strong-willed people who have been broken down by a long battle with illness or Life.

Household Uses: Bark extract used for facial astringent on dark skin only. Strong tea of Oak bark used for vegetable tanning of leather, although it will dye the leather dark brown. The same strong infusion will make a highly permanent dark purple-brown dye, which needs no mordant. Oak galls have been ground for a remarkably permanent ink. Acorns can be ground as a coffee substitute or made into flour, but they must be peeled and soaked for a few hours in a couple of changes of water to leach out most of the tannin. They are also an excellent feed for pigs.

Magical Uses: Oak twigs and acorns are hung up in windows to keep away evil and lightning. Oak wood, in a stave, lends strength. Acorns are used for any magics involving good beginnings. Oak ink is useful for signing contracts before the Gods, as it lends an energy of strength, permanence, and commitment. An equal-armed cross of Oak, tied with red thread, is a good-luck charm to be hung in the home. It was considered bad luck to gather from an Oak who hosted Mistletoe. In Russia, sacred Oaks were set with boar tusks protruding from them. The Greeks associated it with Zeus, and the rustling of its leaves were said to be Zeus prophesying. Oak is the tree of the sacred King, and anyone in such a sacred leadership position would do well to have a talisman of Oak.

Shamanic Uses: Oak is claimed by various different Norse deities. The most common is Thor, but it is also claimed by the giantess Angrboda, the wife of Loki, and Hag (or Hagia, Wise Woman) of the Iron Wood. The term "iron wood" was used to refer to the rot-resistant Oak, and it can be used as a talisman to get to that place. It is the tree of the rune Ac.

Affinity: Air (astringent), almost archetypally. Use on River and Swamp.

Point: LI 10

Plant-wight's Nature: Anyone who has touched an Oak tree understands its nature—strong, sturdy, enduring, patient, strongly protective. Oak expects you to keep your promises, so don't work with it in a flighty manner. Oak has a hidden temper; it is not all phlegmatic. Remember that this tree is associated with fire and lightning. It is a warrior's tree, and knows how to fight to defend those in its care. Oak is good at being the "lightning rod" and enduring the heat so that others may be safe.

Magical Charm: Oakleaf Wreath for Strength

Make a wreath of leafy Oak twigs, at a time when they are green and flexible, on a day when you know that a thunderstorm is coming. Oak leaves are fairly thick and tough, so they will tend to last quite a while before crumbling. If there are acorns on the twigs, even better. The wreath should be sized to fit on your head. Hang it in a high place in your house, and wait until the thunderstorm comes. Then go outside with it and hold it up to the sky, saying the following charm:

> *Hail to the storm-lord and his hammer blows,*
> *Hail to the ancient Hag who knows,*
> *Hail to the strength of Eikar that grows.*
> *Thunder my might,*
> *Lightning my sight,*
> *Ac be my thews and I shall do right.*

Stand until the thunder has answered you three times, and then take the wreath in and let it dry in a warm place. When you have need of strength, put it on your head and go outside to be under the sky. If possible, stand with your back to an Oak at this time, and strength shall pour into you.

Medicinal Charm: Spirit of the Mighty Oak

If you are up to the task of home distilling, soak a pound of broken-up acorns in enough brandy or whisky to cover them. After a month, strain and put the Oak-drink in a pot on the stove. Find a bowl just big enough to fit into the pot, floating on the Oak-drink with very little space around it. Then find a big metal bowl larger than the top of the pot, and place it on top like a lid, open side up. Fill it with ice. (You'll need a lot of ice for this trick; it may be best to do it in winter when there's plenty of snow on the ground, if you live in a snowy area.) Bring the Oak-drink to a boil and continually change out the melted water for fresh ice or snow as it melts. Don't let steam escape. The idea is to keep the pot hot and the bowl cold. The steam rises from the Oak-drink, hits the cold bowl, congeals, and falls into the dish. After several hours of this, you'll have a floating bowl of Spirit of Oak. Throw out the dregs and bottle carefully. As you have tended the pot, this is the charm to keep saying:

> *Eikar, Eikar, Lightning's Tree,*
> *Ac, Ac, healer be,*
> *Spirit mend, deliver me.*

Oats

Botanical Name: *Avena sativa*
Folk Names: Groats
Anglo-Saxon Name: Æte
Old Norse Name: Hafrar
Old High Germanic Name: Habaro
Modern German Name: Hafer
Modern Swedish Name: Havre
Modern Danish Name: Havre
Modern Norwegian Name: Havre
Deity Association: Frey
Height: 3'
Season: Annual
History: Oats were the last of the major European grains to be domesticated, around 3000 B.C., and this shows in the constant referral to "wild oats" in folkloric sayings. There are still more wild versions of Oat bouncing about in Europe than, say, Wheat. The Saxons made a differentiation between "Æte" and "selfæte", the latter being the self-sowing wild versions. Greeks and Romans considered Oats to be fit for nothing but animal fodder, while northern Europeans embraced it due to its ability to grow in cold, wet conditions. The other objection to Oats was that Oat flour went rancid faster than other grains. This is true, and happens because Oats have a large amount of (largely healthy polyunsaturated) fats in them. Keeping them cold helped, another reason why they did better as a northern crop. Oat flour has little gluten and a lot of fiber, and as such doesn't make big fluffy bread like Wheat; this meant that during medieval times Oats were remanded to duty as peasant food (and, as always, animal fodder) and became lower-class until they were boosted to Health Food status in the 1800s.
Medicinal uses: Alterative. For this, the whole plant is used, and especially the Oatstraw. Infusions or fluid extracts are taken for insomnia, depression, and anxiety. It aids in cases of thyroid and estrogen deficiency, and for recurrent or persistent colds. Oat bran lowers cholesterol levels. Oatmeal makes a soothing poultice for shingles and sores. It is a nerve tonic, slowly regenerating nerves over time, good for people who have recurrent shingles or other nerve-damaging issues such as repeated surgeries.
Household Uses: Powdered Oats are good in soap ... or, if you're broke, *as* a soap. It is good for skin, especially sensitive skin, and also useful as a skin powder.
Culinary Uses: Oat bread, Oatmeal, cookies, and anything else you can think of to do with a whole grain. Yum.
Magical Uses: Use in money and prosperity spells, and as a medium to feed blessed food to livestock. Oatcakes are baked as sacred breakfast on Celtic high holidays such as Beltane, and eaten in the mornings as a prosperity spell.
Shamanic Uses: Like all the Ancestral Grains, Oats is a good friend to Frey and can be given as an offering. Oats also has a strong connection to livestock, and as such the rune Ehwaz, the Horse. Supposedly, if you come across a horse in other realms who isn't exactly a horse, you can sprinkle Oats on the ground in the shape of an Ehwaz. If the "horse" eats them, they will be bound to act like a real horse and carry you where you will ... for a little while. It's unclear how long this will last, and you'd better be off their back and gone before it wears off.
Affinity: Harvest (nourishing), Swamp (oily). Use on Air, especially nervous Air.
Point: GB 12
Plant-Wight's Nature: Father Oat is one of the four Ancestral Fathers dealt with in this book. He comes to me as short and round and cheery, talking in abrupt bursts like sudden rainstorms on a field. He is

rarely still, but tends to bounce slightly as he talks or waits. Like Master Clover, he has a great love for domestic animals. Father Oat will slap you on the back and make small talk about the quality of the soil in your garden; he may look like a round little buffoon, but do not underestimate him. His presence is vital and enlivening, bringing energy to the very air and making you want to get out and move. He is a good one to talk to with your morning Oatmeal on days when you lack vitality.

Medicinal Charm: Cholesterol Cleansing

Make bread with the following recipe:

2 cups Wheat flour

1 cup Oat flour

½ cup Oat bran

½ cup rolled Oats, divided in half

4 tablespoons olive oil

¼ cup honey, for Frey

1 cup water

1 teaspoon salt

1 ½ tablespoons yeast

Combine ingredients and make bread according to your usual methods. As you knead, say the following charm:

> *Clear and clean the many rivers,*
> *Father Habern, sweep away*
> *All the trash of life and living*
> *That I shall add more living days.*

Let dough rise, punch down, and then let rise again. Before baking, cut a bind rune of Uruz and Laguz into the top of the loaf. Bake at whatever temperature works best for your oven, and eat.

Onion

Botanical Name: *Allium cepa*

Folk Names: Oingnum, Onyoun, Unyoun, Yn-leac

Anglo-Saxon Name: Hwit Leac ("White Leek")

Old High Germanic Name: Unyo

Modern German Name: Zweibel

Modern Swedish Names: **Matlök,** Gullök, Potatislök, Rödlök, Syltlök

Modern Danish Name: Løg

Modern Norwegian Names: Matløk, Kepaløk

Deity Association: Thor

Height: 12"

Season: Biennial

History: The Onion was grown by Greek and Roman farmers in ancient times, and introduced to the Teutonic peoples by Roman soldiers and merchants during the Empire's occupation, which is why its earliest Germanic name is derived from the Latin "unio". It quickly became an essential vegetable, spreading to Scandinavia and brought by the Saxons to Britain.

Medicinal Uses: All alliums contain iron and vitamins, and raise the immune system to one extent or another. A juice of Onion is good for colds and coughs, if you can stand it. It has an affinity for the lungs; chopped and roasted Onion is placed on the chest to liquefy and bring up impacted mucus, and as an expectorant. Eaten raw, they help catarrh, clear the sinuses, and help the eyes to stop watering (once they're done with you, that is). Onions are also a mild nervine; eaten before bedtime they help with calming sleep.

Culinary Uses: Onion was a staple food of northern Europe, valued not only for its taste but for its slight antiseptic qualities, which kept food cooked with it from spoiling a little longer than otherwise. If you're cooking traditional Northern food, you'll use a lot of Onions.

Magical Uses: Onions have long been sliced and rubbed on the body to heal warts, disease and infections, thus transferring the sickness into the Onion, which is thrown away. They have also been stuck with pins and used as protective charms. Chains of Onions hung in the home are said to absorb illnesses of visitors so that you don't get them, and can be specifically enchanted to this effect. Supposedly if the string of Onions starts to go bad, they've picked something up, and you should bury them and start another one. Onions are also used in spells for loneliness, when someone feels left out and friendless; one eats the raw Onion while concentrating on the feeling, and then by the time its flavor has left your mouth, you'll feel better and things will start to turn around.

Shamanic Uses: Sacred to Thor, along with all the other allium family, these can be offered as tribute or cooked and eaten to ask his blessing. Along with Garlic, you can feed them to people whose bodies need a thorough cleansing, of the lightning-bolt variety. These are also powerful protective plants for any kind of safety charm; call of Thor's aid when you empower it.

Affinity: Fire (stimulant), River (moistening), Harvest (nourishing), Mountain (relaxant). Use on Earth conditions.

Point: LU 11

Plant-wight's Nature: Onion-wight is like a huge, fat troll-figure with a deep-rolling laugh and breath to stun anyone in range. His mouth is enormous and takes up half his face. He likes people (especially women, to whom he will make lewd comments), although his sense of humor is fairly coarse and he may play practical jokes for fun. If he decides that he likes you, he will defend you—probably by playing practical jokes on your enemies and fouling their plans in embarrassing ways. In order to cleanse and heal you, he hits you with his fist. That's just the kind of guy he is, so roll with the punches.

Magical Charm: Protection Soup

The best way to ask for Onion's protection is to eat him. Cook a soup that is very heavy on the Onion (you may add anything else, so long as it doesn't overpower him), and don't brush your teeth for a day afterwards—you're proud to smell like him, right? Before you eat the soup (and make sure that you finish all of it, or you'll offend him), say the following charm:

> *Unyo, Unyo, save my head from blows,*
> *Blow me safe with your heavy breath,*
> *That heartily frightens fears and foes.*

Parsley

Botanical Name: *Petroselinum crispum*
Folk Names: Devil's Oatmeal, Percely, Persil, Petersilie
Anglo-Saxon Name: Petorsilie
Modern German Name: Petersilie
Modern Swedish Name: Persilja
Modern Danish Name: Persille

Modern Norwegian Name: Persille
Deity Association: Odin
Height: 12-18"
Season: Biennial

History: Native to the Mediterranean area, Parsley was considered a death-god herb by the Greeks and Romans, who strewed it over corpses and placed Parsley wreaths on tombs. It was introduced to the Germanic peoples by the Roman occupation of Germany, and came to England and Scandinavia even later; the northern names of this plant are derived from the Latin name, which meant "rock celery". Parsley was associated with Hermes in his guise as Psychopomp of the Underworld, and as such the association was transferred to Woden.

Medicinal Uses: Parsley is one of the best herbs for the kidneys and bladder; as a diuretic it is used for edema. All parts of the plant aid in reducing free radicals, and lower histamine levels. Parsley relieves rheumatism, tones the kidneys, aids digestion, and helps to tone uterine muscles after birth. It acts on hormones, helping to regularize a woman's cycle; it also nourishes the thyroid and adrenal glands, and treats oozings from venereal diseases. It is a vitamin-packed tonic that reduces fatigue over time, and it is eaten as an appetizer for a reason—it prepares the digestive system to better process food.

Household Uses: Parsley freshens breath when eaten. Grown near Roses, it aids their health and scent. Infusions are used as a hair tonic and conditioner.

Culinary Uses: Chop into salads or cook into any savory dish. Parsley is incredibly versatile. Its variant, Hamburg Parsley, has been bred for a parsnip-flavored root, which is a double crop from one plant, excellent for thrifty gardeners.

Magical Uses: Talking to the Dead, and protection from them. It was said that the reason Parsley takes so long to sprout is that it must go to Hel and back seven times first. The Greeks claimed that Parsley sprang from the blood of slain heroes, and fed it to chariot horses to keep them swift. It is said to heal fish when thrown into the water.

Shamanic Uses: This herb is special to Odin in his role as leader of dead souls; he is sometimes shown riding on a Wild Hunt with his Valhalla dead, and supposedly if they come upon you, you can divert them by offering them Parsley. Wearing it may allow them to miss you entirely. If you want to speak to the Volva of the Mound, the old spirit that spoke to Odin, offer her Parsley. Don't, however, try to convince her that you are Odin. You can also use Parsley as an asperger to banish ghosts.

Affinity: River (moistening), Swamp (oily), Storm (bitter alterative), Fire (pungent). Use on Air, Earth, and Swamp conditions.

Point: UB 20

Plant-wight's Nature: Parsley is a grinning green imp with a froglike body and an impossibly wide mouth full of teeth. While at first glance it seems harmless and gnomelike—and most people will only see that side of its nature—I saw it sitting on a tombstone, among graves. Still cheerful, but happily existing in a place of death. Parsley-wight is at home with ghosts, although he likes to leap at them, a tiny screeching creature, and scare them off for the fun of it. They aren't so fond of him, in general, which is why he makes a good guardian for those who need to live near graveyards. He likes people, and is generally helpful, but thinks nothing of handing you a dead thing he's collected, assuming you'll find it just as fascinating as he does. He's not a trickster so much as simply playful, and doesn't understand why people flinch at his hobbies.

Medicinal Charm: Parsley Dysentery Tea

When one has drunk from the wrong well, and the dread Dysentery strikes, drink Parsley Tea to keep one's strength up. This concoction was used by soldiers of World War I when dysentery struck the trenches. Simmer one part Parsley in 6 parts water. To make it even more potent, you can add an equal part of Cinquefoil. You can strain, or even add broth to it and eat it as is. Many cupfuls can be drunk, until the bowels firm up. As you take it into you, say the following charm: "All-Father's Friend, Herjan's Helper, Sleipnir's Supper, stop the flow."

Pellitory of the Wall

Botanical Name: *Parietaria officinalis*

Folk Names: Lichwort, Hammerwort

Anglo-Saxon Names: Dolhrune ("Wound Whisperer"), Homorwyrt ("Rock-herb")

Modern German Name: Aufrechtes Glaskraut

Modern Swedish Name: Väggört

Modern Danish Name: Springknap

Modern Norwegian Name: Blidnesle

Deity Association: Eir

Height: To 2'

Season: Perennial

History: Pellitory is a native weed of middle-to-southern Europe, from the British Isles south to the Mediterranean. It's "wall" appendage is to differentiate it from the Pellitory from Algeria, a different sort of plant altogether.

Medicinal Uses: Pellitory stimulates the kidneys and bladder, and helps to expel stones. It is a powerful diuretic, good for excessive water retention. Pellitory is also used in gout to clear acids from the system, and for bronchial infections and asthma.

Magical Uses: Pellitory, like Cinquefoil, is a magical "activator", making other charms and spells stronger with its presence. It is used modernly to quiet a spinning mind.

Shamanic Uses: As its name "Wound-whisperer" implies, Pellitory is used as a diagnosis herb. Running a bit of it over the affected area may give insight as to what is wrong; a twig of it can also be used as a divining rod in the herb garden when you are looking for the right plant to use for the job.

Affinity: River (moistening), Earth (cooling). Use on Fire conditions.

Point: UB 39

Plant-wight's Nature: Master Pellitory appeared as a quiet, mysterious white-haired man wreathed in vines, appearing out of a rock wall. He whispered something that I couldn't quite make out, and beckoned me closer. When I came closer, he chuckled and vanished back into the wall. Hopefully I will be able to tell more about him some time the future, but it's an example of how some greenwights take patience and will only be met on their terms.

Medicinal Charm: Stones in the Wall

When there are stones in the kidney and bladder, make a strong infusion of Pellitory tea, one ounce of fresh or dried plant matter to one pint of water. Drink a cup three times a day for at least a week, saying as you drink:

> Strike these stones, hard Homoruyrt,
> Pellitory ease my pain,
> And let the river flow like rain.

Pennyroyal

Botanical Name: *Mentha pulegium*

Folk Names: Pollaie, Lurk-In-The-Ditch, Organ Broth, Organ Tea, Piliolerian, Pudding Grass, Run-By-The-Ground, Squaw Mint

Anglo-Saxon Name: Pollegie

Modern German Names: Polei-Minze, Frauen-Minze

Modern Swedish Name: Polejmynta

Modern Danish Name: Polejmynte

Modern Norwegian Name: Poleimynta

Deity Association: Syn

Height: 10"

Season: Perennial

History: Pennyroyal is native to northern Europe. A member of the Mint family, it is the only Mint that is very mildly poisonous. At one time it was used to stuff pork puddings; now it is no longer used for culinary purposes due to its strong scent. Its name comes from the Old French *pullio real*, or "Royal Thyme".

Medicinal Uses: Pennyroyal is an abortifacient, causing uterine contractions; don't give to pregnant women. Pennyroyal steeped in vinegar makes excellent smelling salts. Used for stomach cramps and gaseous indigestion. It encourages sweating and is used to break fevers. Since Pennyroyal is mildly poisonous, it should not be used on children, and care should be taken with dosage.

Household Uses: Strewn in cupboards and beds, it deters ants and fleas. Pennyroyal oil wards off flies and midges, but don't ingest it.

Magical Uses: When carried, it aids business dealings in honesty and fairness. Given to quarreling friends or lovers or business partners, it helps them to achieve peace. It supposedly brings immortality under the right circumstances (which we aren't sure of). It is associated with pearls and can be used to consecrate them in ritual jewelry.

Shamanic Uses: Pennyroyal is beloved of Syn, Frigga's handmaiden who oversees the fair binding of contracts and the fair giving of one's word. Sprinkle Pennyroyal on your surface cloth before doing divination on contracts of any kind. Carry it as a charm when negotiating anything, for love or money or other value.

Affinity: Mountain (relaxant), Earth (cooling), Fire (stimulant). Like the other Mints, Pennyroyal first warms and then cools. Use on Storm and Fire conditions.

Point: SP 4

Plant-wight's Nature: Mistress Pennyroyal is like a dotty old maiden aunt in many ways. Mint's older—and plainer—sister, she is both prim and eccentric, strict and erratic—or perhaps she believes that she is prim and strict while coming across to humans as mostly eccentric and erratic. When she is on her game, she can be a great healer, the sort of maiden aunt who doses you with just the right potion for your bellyache. When she's distracted—which is not uncommon—she bustles about while rattling on various impossible-to-follow trivia and makes up a potion with the wrong ingredients, one that will make you worse instead of better. If you are patient and can keep redirecting her, you can get her to focus on healing properly—but don't offend her by implying that she is less than competent, or you'll receive the edge of her tongue, as well as being made ill.

Medicinal Charm: Fever-Breaker

Make a tea of a half-ounce each of Pennyroyal and Yarrow in an ounce of boiling water, and quietly ask Grandmother Yarrow to exert her quiet control on Mistress Pennyroyal and keep her properly focused. Drink the tea—no more than once a day—in order to break a fever and induce sweating, while saying the following charm:

> Polly, Penny, Piliolerian, break the burning of my brow.
> Yarroway, Milfoil, Devil-Nettle, heal my head of the heat.

Periwinkle

Botanical Name: *Vinca major* (Greater Periwinkle) and *Vinca minor* (Lesser Periwinkle)
Folk Names: Vinca Pervinca, Sorcerer's Violet, Blue Buttons, Centocchio, Hundred-Eyes, Devil's Eye, Joy-On-The-Ground
Anglo-Saxon Name: Parwynke
Modern German Name: Kleines Immergrün
Modern Swedish Name: Stor Vintergröna
Modern Danish Name: Singrøn
Modern Norwegian Name: Gravmyrt
Deity Association: Odin
Height: 12"
Season: Perennial
History: Periwinkle is native to all of Europe, where it has long been a low, attractive ground cover—and long been associated with magicians and sorcerers. The Greater and Lesser Periwinkle are similar but slightly different in usage.
Medicinal Uses: The leaves of both Periwinkles are tonic and astringent, reducing internal and excess menstrual bleeding. They are given for ulcers, sore throats, and to reduce blood pressure. In a salve, they treat hemorrhoids, nosebleeds, and small wounds; while they tend to dry up excretions when used fresh, after being dried and reconstituted in small amounts, they relax the guts and help constipation. Lesser Periwinkle increases blood flow to the brain, and is used for cardiovascular disorders. Greater Periwinkle is a lymphatic tonic and cleanses the body.
Magical Uses: Vinca flowers of either variety are supposedly to be gathered only on the first, ninth, eleventh, or thirteenth night of the lunar month. They are then dried and carried for protection against nearly anything. They are also put into love spells, sprinkled under the bed to increase the passion of a couple, and gazed upon to restore lost memories. (The latter use is especially good if you're dealing with faeries, who can cause memory loss.) It was planted on the graves of dead children, and placed in their graves with them, to protect their spirits.
Shamanic Uses: One of the best plants to carry if you're dealing with the folk of Alfheim, or their cousins in Svartalfheim, and fear being enchanted in some way. Said to have been carried by Odin when he went to study with the Dark Elves, for protection.
Affinity: Mountain (relaxant), Air (astringent). Use on Storm and River.
Points: KD 8 (greater), SI 17 (lesser)
Plant-wight's Nature:

> Periwinkle is very old and sleepy and somewhat grumpy, though he can be persuaded to speak to you if you're patient and respectful, and give him enough time to wake up after you've caught his attention. His power is that of dreams—specifically, climbing the World Tree in your dreams. The catch is that you

can only ascend and return to the worlds in the Tree that are above the one you live in—so for mortals, that means Jotunheim, Vanaheim, Ljossalfheim and, if you have permission, Asgard. I asked Periwinkle if there was another plant that allowed one to descend to the worlds below one's own, and he admitted there was, but would not tell me which one.   -Elizabeth Vongvisith

Magical Charm: Traveling the World Tree

In order to use the charm, you must take a leaf of Periwinkle and place it under your tongue, then say the following charm once, twice, three or four times, depending on which world you wish to visit in your dreams. For example, if you want to dream of Vanaheim, you would say the charm twice, since Vanaheim is two worlds above Midgard on the World Tree. For Jotunheim, say the charm once; for Ljossalfheim, three times, and for Asgard, four times. Then take the leaf out of your mouth and place it under your pillow before you go to sleep. The charm is as follows, and is chanted rather than sung:

Up and down the Tree,
Upward climbing,
Upward pausing,
Upward seeing.
Up and then down again,
Downward looking,
Downward descending,
Downward home.

Note that this is not exactly the same thing as hamfara (astral travel) or pathwalking—you may not have any control over what you see and do while visiting each realm. You should probably also have a good reason for wanting to go; simple curiosity might not get you in trouble, but then again it might, and Periwinkle will take you there regardless of whether or not you're expected or can anticipate a warm welcome. However, this is a useful charm for those who cannot do hamfara or pathwalk, but need to visit one of the other Worlds for one reason or another.   -Elizabeth Vongvisith

Magical Charm: Sorcerer's Protection

Traditionally, sorcerers were said to gather Periwinkle when they were "clean of any uncleanliness", meaning (we assume) healthy and bathed; on the first, ninth, eleventh, or thirteenth night of the lunar month, while saying the following charm:

I pray thee, vinca pervinca, thee that art to be had for thy many useful qualities, that thou come to me glad blossoming with thy mainfulness, that thou outfit me so that I be shielded and prosperous and undamaged by poisons and water.

The plant is then carried for protection in any form. It is particularly good at driving off faeries. You can also hang it around your doorsand windows in order to keep your home safe.

Pimpernel

Botanical Name: *Anagallis arvensis*
Folk Names: Scarlet Pimpernel, Poor Man's Weatherglass, Shepherd's Barometer, Shepherd's Clock, Adder's Eyes, Bird's Eye, Red Chickweed, Herb of Mary, Luib na Muc, Greater Pimpernel
Anglo-Saxon Names: Pipeneale, Nædderege ("Adder's Eyes")
Modern German: Pimpernel
Modern Swedish Name: Pimpinell
Modern Danish Name: Arve
Modern Norwegian Name: Nonsblom
Deity Association: Freya
Height: 3-5"
Season: Annual

History: The Red Pimpernel is an ancient common weed in all the temperate zones of Europe. Its flowers open and close with passing pressure systems, so it was used to predict weather. Used in cosmetics since ancient times, it was associated with goddesses of love and beauty. The rarer blue variety (*Anagallis caerulea*) was thought to be the female version of the flower, to the more masculine common red variety.

Medicinal Uses: Pimpernel infusion is used in mild fevers to bring on sweating; for high fevers due to plague or series pestilence, use the decoction, as hot as can be drunk. It drives out toxins through the skin, and also draws them out of wounds and bites when applied topically. It is best used fresh, or in a cold-water or alcohol tincture. It closes and heals wounds and helps old sores. Its other main use is as an antidepressant; it calms rages and disperses melancholy, and has been used on epilepsy. It is especially good for the depression that comes with liver troubles, low-grade anger, or long-term exhaustion. Pimpernel is mildly toxic if not prepared correctly or if used in large amounts, so be careful with dosage. It loses some virtues when dried, so either use it fresh or make it fresh into a preparation. (Love goddesses like fresh flowers.)

Household Uses: A wash of the flowers has been used since prehistory to lighten and soften the complexion, and the tea is drunk for this as well.

Magical Uses: The red flowers are carried for protection from illness and accident, and to see through the lies of others. Bladed weapons were rubbed with its juice for power, probably due to its vulnerary nature. Its power is supposedly so great that when dropped into running water it was said to float against the current.

Shamanic Uses: This is not one of the plants traditionally associated with Freya, but when I asked, She told me authoritatively that it was Hers. Freya and her brother Frey are both light-bringers and joy-bringers, although the nature of their light and joy is subtly different. The Pimpernel is Freya's joy-plant; its ground-hugging nature and relationship with the sky reflects Freya's earth-goddess Vanic nature that reaches upward to connect with the Aesir sky-nature. (For Frey's antidepressant plant, see Lemon Balm.) The charm below was the one She gave me.

Affinity: Mountain (relaxant), Stone (sedative), Earth (cooling). Use on Fire conditions.

Point: SI 5

Plant-Wight's Nature: Tiny Master Pimpernel laughs continually. He is bright and fiery, a spot of color in darkness, and nothing darkens his indomitable nature. Adventurous and nonjudgmental, he is an "opener of the heart", giving laughter and joy to the depressed and surly. No one can look on his countenance without smiling.

Magical Charm: Freya's Joy

When it seems as though there is no reason to smile or laugh ever again, and creases of melancholy are having their way with your countenance, take a double handful of flowering Pimpernel aerial parts, bruise them thoroughly in a mortar, and steep them in cold water in bright sunlight for the length of a long summer day. Take a tablespoon of the strained water three times a day, saying:

> *Lovely Lady of the Spring,*
> *Vanadis this day I sing,*
> *Love's own flower, laughter bring.*

Plantain

Botanical name: *Plantago major*

Folk names: Waybread, St. Patrick's Dock, Snakeweed, Snakebite, Rat's Tail, White Man's Footprint, Dead Man's Footprint, Slan-Lus, Ripple Grass

Anglo-Saxon Name: Wegbrade

Modern German Name: Großer Wegerich

Modern Swedish Names: Groblad, Gårdsgroblad
Modern Danish Name: Vejbred
Modern Norwegian Name: Groblad
World Association: Helheim
Height: Under 12"
Season: Perennial

History: Native to all parts of Europe, the humble Plantain was so valued as a cure-all that it was claimed by medieval herbalists to help everything from rabies to snakebite. Pliny claimed that boiling it in a pot with dead body parts would cause them to rejoin and reanimate. When it was brought to America, Native Americans began to call it "White Man's Footprint" as it got loose and became naturalized, which is an interesting twist on its other name, Dead Man's Footprint. Its name Snakeweed refers not just to its ability to draw out snake venom, but also the snakelike shape of the seed head.

Medicinal Uses: Plantain is a very important herbal "drawer", meaning that its main job is to draw out infection. It is used in an ointment, or an external wash, or in an emergency just packing on the chewed leaf, to draw out splinters, foreign objects, insect venom, and even snake venom. For the latter two, the poultice or wash must be done fairly immediately. While it may not get everything out, it can make the difference between living to get to the hospital or not. Plantain draws infection out from all wounds, removing pus and closing the flesh. It is especially good for infections in the teeth and gums, even when abcesses spread to other parts of the head. It is good for dirty wounds when you may not be able to get ground-in dirt out of the flesh, and will treat the nastiest, most horrible oozing infections. Externally, it is used in ointment or wash for wounds, burns, hemorrhoids, sores, boils, inflammations, conjunctivitis, ringworm infestations, Nettle stings, thrush, chicken pox, and shingles. It is also used internally to help the urinary tract, kidneys, and bladder; Plantain heals gastrointestinal ulcers and is used to get out deep-seated bronchial infection. It will repair lungs damaged by breathing in harmful materials, removing the particles and expelling them. Expect to cough up a lot of pus. The seeds are edible and can be ground into flour; their mucilage is high in fiber and lowers cholesterol. It is a confirmed antimicrobial; stimulates healing processes. It has been used to help stop smoking, as it makes tobacco smoke taste bad, and cleanse the lungs out afterwards. Plantain's cousin, Psyllium, absorbs 25 times its weight in water and is used as a laxative.

Household Uses: Seeds are used as bird and poultry feed.

Culinary Uses: Seeds were ground for flour by hungry travelers; thus its name Waybread.

Magical Uses: Bind with red wool to the head to cure headaches. Like Mugwort, place in shoes to cure weariness on long trips. Hang it in your car to prevent evil from entering. Carrying the root protects from snakebite.

Shamanic Uses: This is the plant of Helheim, the land of the Dead. Its shamanic uses are many and varied and rather subtle. First, it can create a certain amount of invisibility for a short period of time. Notice how the weedy Plantain manages to make itself so inconspicuous? That's a power that you can harness, especially if you are journeying or pathwalking. Second, it can be used in recels to speak to the ancestors, or to find your way to the Helvegr. Its name "waybread" echoes this usage—waybread will help you find the way. If you actually manage to get yourself astrally wounded, Plantain is the plant to resort to. In some cases, it can even save you from astral death, if your body is still healthy. Its regenerative gift of bringing flesh back to life doesn't work on the physical plane, but I have good reason to suspect that it works on other planes. Since I've not ever been astrally killed by enemies, I've never been in a position to experiment. Those who find the need to implement it should let me know how it goes.

Affinity: Earth (cooling), Air (astringentRiver (moistening), Harvest (nourishing). Use for Fire, Air, River, and Earth conditions. Plantain can be either drying or moistening depending on the needs of the situation.

Point: KD 15

Plant-wight's Nature:

Grandfather Waybread is an ol' travelin' man. Lean and weathered, with a wide, knowing grin beneath his tattered moustache, clothes full of holes and leathery bare feet, he knows every byway and roadside from Chicago to Paris to Philadelphia or to Helheim. He is a whistling gypsy with rings in his ears and a scarf knotted around his neck, a singing friar on eternal pilgrimage, a wandering old hobo camping in your woodshed. He has a special relationship with the rune Raido, and can be called upon to help when you're lost, as long as you're walking—he doesn't really understand vehicles much, and navigates you by the weeds on the roadside. While he seems like a happy-go-lucky sort, don't underestimate his intelligence—this is one of the Nine Sacred Herbs, and Grandfather Waybread is the one who knows *where* everything is. If there's a *where* in existence, he's been there, and can give you advice. He watches the heroes go on their adventures, and shakes his head after them, knowing what they've forgotten to bring or look out for that will be their downfall. If he really likes them, after they've fallen he may do the regeneration trick. He is a powerful ally for journeyers, as his powers extend through all nine worlds and our own. (Note: Although I met Grandfather Waybread as male, I got the feeling that he used to appear more as female—his rhyme calls him *wyrta modor*—but he prefers appearing as male now, for some unknown reason.)

Medicinal Charm: Plantain Salve

Gather about a pound of fresh Plantain leaves and put them through the food processor until they're a paste—not an easy thing, as Plantain is full of stringy fibers which may need to be fished out. Once you have green paste, blend with a cup of olive oil. Then heat it gently on the stove and slowly grate in beeswax, using a fine grater. You know you've put in enough when you can dip in a spoon, let it cool, and the stuff firms up and becomes salve-like but not candle-hard. Keep it refrigerated unless you're traveling with it, and when you rub it on, you can either sing or recite the Waybread verse of the Nine Herbs Song, or say the charm below. Grandfather Waybread will help to regenerate the flesh quicker.

Snakeweed, slay the serpent's bite,

Ripple Grass, rip the grief from my flesh,
Waybread, bear the invader away.

Purslane

Botanical name: *Portulaca oleracea*
Folk names: Garden Purslane, Golden Purslane, Pigweed, Hogweed, Verdolaga, Pusley
Anglo-Saxon Name: Porclaca
Modern German Names: Portulak, Gemüse-Portulak, Postelein
Modern Swedish Name: Potulak
Modern Danish Name: Portulak
Modern Norwegian Name: Portulakk
Deity Association: Bragi
Height: under 12"
Season: Annual
History: Originated in the Mediterranean, but spread like the weed that it is all over Europe, Asia, and North American. We don't know when it reached the North, but it is mentioned in the Anglo-Saxon herbals. Medieval monks cultivated it as a vegetable.
Medicinal Uses: Purslane is a good tonic and alterative, especially for the digestive system. The leaves make a soothing, cooling poultice for skin diseases. They are also rich in Vitamin C and iron, and contain more Omega-3 acids than any other vegetable.
Culinary Uses: Purslane is an excellent salad herb. I know that there are a lot of plants in here where we say "You can use it in salads," but really, that just means that they're edible and nutritive but you might have to be desperate to do it. Purslane, on the other hand, is totally worth growing as a salad herb all to itself. It is a fleshy succulent with a lemony zing to it, and given the chance it will spread and self-sow and come back next year. The seeds are dried and added to flour, and the leaves can be cooked up like spinach in soups and stews.
Magical Uses: Laid under the pillow, Purslane is a nightmare-repeller. Growing it in a pot on the windowsill will help those who are afraid of the dark. It is given to soldiers to keep them safe in battle. It was worn as an amulet to repel evil and heal.
Shamanic Uses: Purslane is a good food for replenishing one's self after severe magical work. Bringing a spring of the fresh stuff when you're doing *utiseta*, for a quick snack afterwards to get you on your feet, is a good idea. When I asked the Gods about Purslane, it was Bragi the skald who spoke up, surprisingly. He told me that the leaves could be used as edible Os-runes, to give you temporary eloquence. The spell for that is below.
Affinity: River (moistening), Swamp (oily), Harvest (nourishing), Earth (cooling). Use for Fire and Air conditions.
Point: GB 15
Plant-wight's Nature: Purslane is fat, lazy, opportunistic, and sly. There's something very froglike about his shape. He is usually good-natured, being as he's usually napping and only wakes up enough to open one eye and give you a lazy smile. Somehow, however, when you're not looking, he'll manage to take over half your garden, and then give you that lazy "Who, me?" smile again. Getting him to work at anything is difficult, but if you're on good terms with him he'll usually give you an extra zing of nutrients and energy when you eat his plant. However, the cost will be allowing it to spread pretty much at will. If you do weed it out, eat what you weed—that way you won't be offending him; you're harvesting and ingesting, not merely removing.
Magical Charm: Eloquence

When you have to speak in public and you're afraid that your own eloquence will not be up to par, beg some of Bragi. Pluck five leaves of Purslane (since it doesn't dry well, if you want to do this spell in the cold weather I suggest freezing them and eating them right out of the freezer) and scratch an Os-rune on each of them. Eat them one at a time, saying the following charm and eating one leaf after each line:

> *Skald-Lord, sincerely I beseech thee*
> *To wish me words of golden weight;*
> *Porclaca, carry Bragi's blessing*
> *Past my tongue and may it linger*
> *That I might speak like Asgard's singer.*

Raspberry

Botanical name: *Rubus idaeus*
Folk names: Bramble, Framboise, Hindebar, Braamboss, Raspbis, Bramble of Mount Ida
Anglo-Saxon Name: Hinbrer, Hindberge
Old Norse Name: Klungr (Bramble)
Old High Germanic Name: Bramal
Modern German Name: Wald-Himbeere
Modern Swedish Name: Hallon
Modern Danish Name: Hindbær
Modern Norwegian Name: Bringbær
Deity Association: Nerthus
Height: 5'
Season: 3-year perennial
History: Raspberry, Blackberry, and other brambles are found all over Europe and Asia in temperate zones. They have been an important wild food for a long time.
Medicinal Uses: Raspberry leaf is one of the best uterine tonics, safe—and recommended—for most women to use during pregnancy. A uterine alterative, Raspberry can decrease menstrual pain over time if there are no other serious factors. Leaf tea treats diarrhea and is a tonic for prostate problems. The leaves of Blackberry, its cousin, are a blood purifier as well. Raspberry vinegar-syrup helps to dissolve tooth tartar, and is used for sore throats and coughs. The berry juice is drunk for UTIs, as it is astringent.
Household Uses: The berries yield an impermanent red dye.
Culinary Uses: Just eat them any way you like.
Magical Uses: Raspberry canes were hung in the windows and doors of homes after a death in the family, in order to keep a wandering ghost from re-entering the home. The leaves were carried by pregnant women to assure an easy birth.
Shamanic Uses: If the Bramble-wight allows it, you can use Bramble canes as a barrier when sleeping outside, to keep away noncorporeal invaders.
Affinity: Air (astringent), Earth (cooling). Use for River, Swamp, and Fire conditions.
Point: CV 7

Plant-wight's Nature: Mistress Bramble is a highly emotional and passionate lady. She has the sort of personality that will fling itself on you and smother you with kisses one moment, and then fly into a rage at some slight and slap you. She is both the delicious ruby fruit and the vicious thorns, and expects you to love her anyway. She adores children and loves pregnant women; they seem round and ripe to her. Women are often drawn to tell her how they are mistreated, and she will rage and weep with them. Her relationship with men is more stereotypically like the volatile, emotional female who flirts and reviles them by turns. Third-gender spirit-workers tend to trigger neither of her sharply gender-divided reactions, and she tends to be rather distant and neutral to them. Her colors are deep crimsons and purples, and it is advised to wear them when working with her, in order to please her.

Medicinal Charm: Bramble Tea

A pregnant woman should make a tea of 2 ounces of dried Raspberry leaf, with a pint of boiling water poured over it and left to steep. As it is drunk, the following charm is recited:

> *Mistress Bramble build me better*
> *That this babe I bear may flourish,*
> *That my body may birth as sweetly*
> *As your sweet fruit, with ne'er a thorn.*

This should be repeated daily until the babe is born.

Rosemary

Botanical name: *Rosmarinus officinalis*
Folk names: Compass Weed, Dew Of The Sea, Guardrobe, Incensier, Libanotis, Polar Plant, Sea Dew, Rose Of The Sea
Anglo-Saxon Name: Bothen
Modern German Name: Rosmarin
Modern Swedish Name: Rosmarin
Modern Danish Name: Rosmarin
Modern Norwegian Name: Rosmarin
Deity Association: Njord
Height: 6' in warm climates, 3' in cold ones where it must be potted
Season: Tender Perennial
History: Rosemary's name comes from the Latin *Rosa marina*, or "Rose of the Sea", as the plant's natural habitat is on cliffs overlooking the ocean. During times of plague, it was carried in pouches and the handles of walking sticks to be sniffed when traveling through plague-ridden areas.
Medicinal Uses: Rosemary is a warm, stimulating herb that helps with oxidation throughout the body. It burns the metabolism cleaner and thus helps with weight loss; it helps burn up excessive blood sugar and thus is good for diabetics. Rosemary was burned in sick-chambers to purify the air. Rosemary

stimulates blood circulation, and eases pain in arthritic joints by increasing blood supply where applied. The oil is rubbed into the chest for heart edema. Rosemary tea makes an antiseptic gargle and mouthwash, and is added to potions for colds, chills, and coughs. It is a superlative migraine remedy, especially for migraines that come on after great tension. Rub the oil on the forehead, drink the tea, or even wrap the boughs around the head as the ancients did. Rosemary tea is also drunk to aid memory and mental retention, as well as to relieve mental stress. It is contraindicated for those with high blood pressure.

Household Uses: Fresh boughs placed in a room will cool the air. Boiling a handful of Rosemary in water yields an antiseptic cleaning solution. An infusion makes a good hair rinse for dandruff, especially for dark hair.

Culinary Uses: Hundreds of them. Rosemary is a natural preservative for meat, and meat dishes that have a strong Rosemary content may be sat out on the counter overnight without going bad—one of the reasons that Rosemary was loved in medieval times. It is used to flavor shellfish, pork, lamb, sauces, and any other savory thing. It is rather strong and has the tendency to overwhelm other flavors, especially when used fresh. The antiseptic, antioxidant leaves aid digestion of fats and grease. Rosemary stems make a flavorful barbecue skewer, and the leaves can be candied as a garnish.

Magical Uses: Rosemary under the pillow drives away nightmares, protects the sleeper from harm when laid under the bed, and keeps away thieves when hung from the porch. A chaplet of Rosemary aids the memory and preserves youthfulness. It is carried into battle for protection (especially against PTSD) and put into wedding wreaths for good memories. Healing poppets are stuffed with Rosemary, and binding a bag of it to your right arm is said to clear away depression. As a herb of remembrance, it is placed in and on graves, and given out at funerals. In some areas, Rosemary is said to grow well only in gardens where the mistress is master, so she might be a good herb for a dominant woman to carry.

Shamanic Uses: Rosemary is a very powerful recaning herb, as powerful in its own way as Mugwort and Juniper, and one of the oldest incenses. It will cleanse and purify an area, with the added benefit that it can also stimulate memories when one walks into the cleansed area, including ancestral memories. It is also used to remove memories—it can be placed on an area of the body that was attacked or assaulted, and asked to remove the memory of the wounding. Rosemary and Juniper are often burned together in sickrooms, and healers once washed their hands in a Rosemary infusion before beginning their healing work.

Rosemary is much loved by Njord, the god of ships and sailing; as "Rose Of The Sea", she grew on ocean cliffs and looked out over those departing or returning. The loved ones who waited for them on land would tell their sad tales of longing for faraway sailors to Rosemary, and she thus became the Keeper of Memories. While she started out as a southern herb and came late to the north, it was the sailors who were the first to go to foreign places and bring back new goods and customs, so it is appropriate that Rosemary looks to Njord. As can be inferred by the Anglo-Saxon song "The Seafarer", the shamanic journey was sometimes cast in a metaphor of traveling on the ocean by northerners. Thus Rosemary can be burned in preparation for faring forth, with the imagery of a ship sailing over the unknown waters as one's mental construct, and asking for Njord's blessing and safe return.

Affinity: Fire (stimulant), Swamp (oily), Air (astringent). Use for Earth and Air.

Point: GB 9

Plant-wight's Nature: Mistress Rosemary has the air of a salt sea breeze about her wherever she goes. Even speaking to her inland in a sheltered garden, there's the whiff of salt. Indeed, salt is one of her sacred affinities, and you can make her offerings of sea salt when she's not near the seashore (not so much that it poisons the soil in your garden; just a touch); this affinity is part of what gives her such marvelous preservative ability. She appears to me as a dark-haired girl with large dark eyes and a wild mane of hair blown in the sea wind, who likes to perch on rocky cliffs and watch the ships go by. She is a good traveling protector for those who must cross water, and is generally friendly and willing to help in a household.

Medicinal Charm: Head Healer

When the terrible headaches strike, take Rosemary inside and out. Make a hot cup of water and steep a tea ball full or Rosemary leaves in it, and drink. Then take Rosemary oil and lie down, and massage it on your head. Even if only the front of the head hurts, make sure to massage it into the area on the side of the head, above and behind the ear, as well; Rosemary's point is there. As you rub, breathe deeply and imagine that the essence of the tea you've drunk is moving upward into your head, to come just to the other side of the skin from where you've rubbed in oil, Rosemary to Rosemary, and is soothing the headache away from both sides. As you relax, whisper this charm:

> *Rose of the Sea, in a sea of pain I float,*
> *Compass Weed, see me safe to home.*

Magical Charm: Unremembering

As Rosemary rules remembrance, so she can take memories away. This is not the same as repressing them; when they are repressed, you still have them with you, hot and heavy in the depths of your mind where they lay in wait to attack. Taking memories away means making them misty and faded, like old movies; you can grasp at them all you want but they simply float away like mists. Some memories need to be removed, especially ones of physical trauma—and in those cases, where they need to be removed from is the body, which can hold onto trauma longer than the mind. To remove the stain of an assault on the body, first rub Rosemary oil onto the area of the client's body that was struck. (Yes, in the case of rapes, this does mean the genitals.) Then dip a sprig of Rosemary in clean water, sprinkle it lightly on them, and lay the sprig on that area. Sing this charm to Rosemary, and she may agree to take those body memories away.

> *Incensior, I call you from the salt winds of the sea,*
> *A black gift once was given, and the salt spray fell like rain,*
> *We beg you, Libanotis, take back this memory of pain,*
> *Cleanse this ancient shadow, blow this body clear and free.*

Rosemary tells me that this ritual should not be done without due preparation—perhaps a lot of mental work, perhaps physical cleansing over a period of days by other herbs, perhaps other sorts of cleansings. Give her as few obstacles to work with as possible. The practitioner should be prepared for an emotional reaction, and a support system should be standing by. Make sure to check in on the client frequently over the next couple of weeks.

Roseroot

Botanical name: *Rhodiola rosea*
Folk names: Rose Sedum, Midsummer Men, Golden Root
Modern German Name: Rosenwurz
Modern Swedish Name: Rosenrot
Modern Danish Name: Rosenrod
Modern Norwegian Name: Rosenrot
Deity Association: Kari the North Wind, and various Saami deities
Height: 6-12"
Season: Perennial
History: Roseroot has a long history in the Arctic and subarctic areas of Eurasia, where it was eaten frequently to combat the physical stress of living in such harsh conditions. In Siberia, it was given as a wedding gift to newlyweds to ensure many sturdy children.
Medicinal Uses: Roseroot is an adaptogen, helping the body to adapt to stress and run more efficiently. In Siberia, where they call it Golden Root, it is infused to treat coughs and ease pain. It does cause mild euphoria and a hangover the next morning if you take too much. Roseroot is said to increase libido and fertility for both men and women.
Household Uses: Root was made into a tonic called "poor man's Rosewater" for perfume.
Culinary Uses: The leaves were eaten by the Saami for salads
Magical Uses: This is one of the sacred plants of the Saami and the Siberians, as it will grow on tundra conditions and stay green and succulent in terrible weather, and the root does smell faintly of Roses.
Shamanic Uses: Carried as a carved talisman or eaten, Roseroot gives stamina in the face of physical endurance. This is good both for clients and for the shaman, especially for rigorous journeying or all-night rituals or climbing mountains or whatever other ridiculous effort the spirits put you through.
Affinity: Harvest (nourishing), Storm (bitter alterative), Fire (stimulant). Use for Swamp and Air conditions.
Point: GB 38
Plant-wight's Nature: Roseroot appeared to me as a twirling spirit dressed in layers of clothing—coats and skirts, and gender was indistinguishable. It carried a staff with which it tapped me, and then it hunkered down and squatted on the ground. Its face was dark-skinned and impassive inside the frame of a fur hood. There was power reverberating off of it, but I felt that a much longer period of alliance was necessary before it would speak much to me. I get the feeling that Roseroot is unhappy with its current spate of popularity and would rather go back to being barely known.
Magical Charm: Midsummer Men

  This is the charm that Roseroot indicated that it wanted written here, all its other celebrated aspects notwithstanding. For three days leading up to the Summer Solstice, a couple who wish to conceive should eat Roseroot—and the wight gave me the image of actually eating the root straight, not in any preparation—and then go out on Solstice Morning and dance in a circle together as the Sun comes up, singing "Midsummer Men makes us merry, my love." Then they should make love on the grass and a child will be granted to them. Possibly multiple children.

Rowan

Botanical Name: *Sorbus acuparia*
Folk Names: Delight of the Eye, Luis, Quickbane, Quicken, Quickbeam, Ran Tree, Mountain Ash, Royne-Tree, Roden-Quicken, Sorb-Apple, Thor's Helper, Whitty, Wicken-Tree, Wiggin, Wiggy, Witchen, Wiky, Wild Ash

Anglo-Saxon Names: Cuicbeam, Reynir, Reyni-runnr
Old Norse Names: Raun, Reynir
Old High Germanic Name: Raudnia
Modern German Names: Eberesche, Vogelbeere
Modern Swedish Name: Rönn
Modern Danish Name: Røn
Modern Norwegian Name: Rogn
Deity Association: Odin, Thor
Height: To 30'
Season: Perennial tree

History: The Rowan is native to all parts of subarctic Europe and has been one of the sacred European trees for millenia. The Celts consider it the tree of Brigid, the goddess of fire and smithcraft and healing and poetry, and Rowan is Luis, the second Celtic tree-month. Rowan twigs tied with orange-red thread were hung as a common charm across medieval Europe to repel evil spirits and bring blessings.

Medicinal Uses: Alterative and occasional specific. Berries are high in Vitamin C and are eaten as a tonic to prevent scurvy. (Throw away the seeds, as they contain hydrocyanic acid.) The bark and leaves are used as a gargle for thrush. A decoction of the bark has been given as a douche for vaginal fungal infections.

Culinary Uses: The berries, which are rich in Vitamin C, can be made into a tart jelly. They were also dried and powdered into a flour by German peasants, and brewed into a strong ale in both Germany and Wales. In the last century, Russian and Siberian horticulturalists have bred cold-hardy fruit trees by crossing Rowans with pear and Cherry trees, selecting especially for high vitamin content and ice-hardiness. These have recently come on to the market and are a good investment for cold-climate farmers and homesteaders.

Magical Uses: Wands of the wood increase psychic powers and are used for divining. The tree is protective, and the classic anti-demon spell consists of Rowan berries tied with red thread, while an equal-armed cross of the twigs tied with the same red thread wards off evil magic. A Rowan staff keeps nighttime predators at bay, and is good for travelers in general. It is used for invoking spirit teachers, and banishing spirits you don't want around. Magic wands were often carved from Rowan.

Shamanic Uses: Rowan seems to have a predilection for the rune Raido, and can be used not only for travel, but in a talisman for Raido's "higher" purpose, which is finding one's own path in life. While it is also associated with Thor, it is also well-liked by Odin, as it is symbolic of the time of his life when he went wandering in the world for nine years to gain wisdom. A Rowan staff or Rowan amulet is a good companion for one who wishes to go that road, giving up everything in their life and starting out on the journey of discovery, which may be a hard ordeal. Odin ended up, among other things, trading an eye to Mimir for the two birds Huginn and Muninn, and hanging sacrificed on the World Tree to gain the knowledge of the runes. Rowan can be a helper in the human version of those hard times, keeping one's will focused on one's path even when it is painful.

Affinity: Air (astringent), Earth (cooling), Harvest (nourishing). Use for Fire, River and Swamp.
Point: TH 9

Plant-wight's Nature: The Rowan tree spirit is surprisingly feminine, for all that it is associated with two Germanic male deities. Her energy is clear, strong, and hardy, with a firm but delicate touch, and strangely "virginal", in the sense of being comfortable with solitude and self-enclosedness. One gets the vision of a slender, athletic, self-sufficient woman with red hair. She is not so much a spirit of healing as a spirit of general health and self-maintenance, of preventative medicine. The Rowan nature is strong enough that even crosses of Rowan and other fruit trees have a spirit closer to Rowan than to their other tree-parent.

Magical Charm: Traditional Rowan

This is the way that the age-old charm goes: Wrap a Rowan twig, or several of them, together with red thread, and say: "Rowan Tree and red thread, send the faeries to their speed." Other versions have "witches" or "evil" or any manner of two-syllable nasty wights that you might wish to ward off. Traditionally it was either carried or hung over the doorway as a protective charm.

Rue

Botanical name: *Ruta graveolens*

Folk names: Hreow, Herb O'Grace, Bashoush, Rewe, Clubgrass

Anglo-Saxon Name: Rude

Modern German Name: Wein-Raute, Garten-Raute

Modern Swedish Name: Vinruta

Modern Danish Name: Rude

Modern Norwegian Name: Vinrute

Deity Association: Hel

Height: 2'

Season: Perennial

History: Originally a sacred Mediterranean and Middle Eastern herb, Rue made its way north with early Germanic trade. Rue was an important medicinal ingredient in both the legendary "cooking:vinegar:of the Four Thieves" and the Roman *mithridate*, or all-purpose poison antidote.

Medicinal Uses: Bitter Rue cleans out the blood supply, and has been used as a cancer treatment to remove stagnant blood where cancers like to spread. It is famous as an abortifacient and brings on delayed menstruation. The tincture is rubbed on arthritic joints, especially the sort that get worse in cold weather. Antispasmodic; it treats high blood . pressure and colic. Tincture is rubbed on skin to strengthen capillaries. Do not give to children or pregnant women. Rue may give some people contact dermatitis.

Household Uses: Moth repellent and insecticide. Used in herbal smoking mixtures.

Culinary Uses: The seed has been infused with Lovage and Mint as a marinade for partridge, or with damson plums and wine for a meat sauce. It tastes bitter, but a little bit supposedly gives an interesting muskiness to cream cheese, egg, and fish dishes.

Magical Uses: The ultimate hexbreaker, Rue was worn to ward off poisons, plagues, bad luck, illness, evil spirits, werewolves and vampires, and all manner of things. Wrapped up with a bit of bread, salt, and hair from everyone in the household, it is a family protection spell. Rue was also used in bunches during a spiritual "session" when a medium will be in trance and very open psychically, the Rue plants will hopefully protect her. Supposedly Rue grows best when stolen. It is the inspiration for the suit of clubs in the ordinary card deck.

Shamanic Uses: Rue is one of Hel's herbs, and can be used as an asperger (dip it in water and sprinkle with it) to sanctify a place to her, and to beg her to leave your life for a little longer. It can be used as an offering to her, or as a divining rod to the Helvegr.

Affinity: Storm (bitter alterative), Fire (warming), Air (astringent). Use on Swamp, Earth, and River conditions.

Point: LI 4

Plant-wight's Nature: When I first went to speak to Grandmother Rue, I bit off a tiny piece of leaf ... and promptly regretted it. I'd forgotten how bitter Rue is. I went to spit it out, and there she was, right in my face, saying, "Oh, no you don't! Yes, it's bitter; so is life! Swallow that down!" So I did. Grandmother Rue is a stooped old woman leaning on a cane, grey-haired and grey-clad, beady black eyes glaring at me. Part of her mystery is that she is a witness to the Universal Sorrow, the grief of all the worlds. She understands bitterness and loss, but in a different way than Mother Dill, whose compassion is for personal grief. Grandmother Rue has a wider view than that; she sees the fullness of all that goes wrong in Creation. She demanded that I weep a few tears in exchange for her time and attention, an offering to the Universal Sorrow. "You wanted to know what I'm about; well, here it is!" So I allowed myself to carefully touch the cloud of archetypal mourning behind her, until I could squeeze out a couple of tears. She humphed and said that at least it was something, and hobbled away.

Magical Charm: Hex Breaker

I asked Grandmother Rue for a spell or charm, and she told me that all one has to do in order to break hexes with her power is to dip a bunch of Rue twigs in water, asperge vigorously in all directions while uttering "Ha!" and that is enough. Fancy rhymes? Not for her. Go with the "Ha!" I'd trust her on that one.

Rye

Botanical Name: *Secale spp.*
Folk Names: Swale
Anglo-Saxon Name: Ryge
Old Norse Name: Rúg
Old High Germanic Name: Rocko
Modern German Name: Roggen
Modern Swedish Name: Råg
Modern Danish Name: Rug
Modern Norwegian Name: Rug
Deity Association: Frey
Height: 3'
Season: Annual
History: The principal staple cereal grain of northern Europe, Rye could be grown where the climate was too cold and damp and short-summered for Wheat. It makes a hard, nutritious dark bread, and seems to have been used by the Germanic peoples from the very beginning, possibly their first grain.

Medicinal Uses: Carrier of ergot, poisonous fungus used as a painkiller (under herbalist supervision only).

Household Uses: Ryestraw, braided and soaked and stitched into shape, makes the best straw hats.

Culinary Uses: One of the hardiest cold-weather grains in existence.

Magical Uses: Used in spells of fidelity.

Shamanic Uses: Rye, like Wheat, is sacred to Frey. However, it recalls Frey's courtship of Gerda, and his willingness to do anything for her love. As such, this hardiest and most weather-proof of grains is used in magic to keep couples faithful, and to rekindle love during hard times. Sprinkle it for weddings where couples differ in their faith, race, age, or have to love across some other divide. Better yet, serve it at the reception.

Affinity: Harvest (nourishing). Use on Air conditions.

Point: UB 5

Plant-wight's Nature: Father Rye is one of the four Ancestral Fathers dealt with in this book. He comes across as leaner and darker than the other three, with a weathered, wrinkled face that looks as if he has gotten up with the dawn and followed the plow in every sort of bad weather for a thousand years ... which he has. His lean arms are corded with muscle, and his short-cropped hair tops a jutting chin and eyes which squint at the sky, appraising the wind and moisture. He is silent and hardworking, the archetypal laconic farmer who speaks in one or two words at a time, and can give the gift of enduring hard labor, day after day.

Magical Charm: Endurance Bread

Make Rye bread with the following recipe, one of the traditional Finnish ones:

2 cups Rye flour

1 cup Wheat flour

2 tablespoons honey, for Frey

1 ¼ cups potato water or beet water (the latter will redden it, unless you use yellow beets or mangels)

1 tablespoon butter

2 teaspoons salt

2 ½ tablespoons yeast

Mix ingredients and make the bread in the way that you are used to making bread. While kneading, say, "Ancestral Father, build my bones, thy body my bread, thy altar my belly, my body thy memory forever." Let rise, punch down, and rise again. Before baking, cut a bind rune of Uruz and Ac into the top of the loaf. Bake, and eat for endurance and resilience in the face of difficulty.

Sage

Botanical name: *Salvia officinalis*

Folk names: Salvia salvatrix, Sawge, Garden Sage

Anglo-Saxon Name: Salfie

Modern German Name: Echter Salbei

Modern Swedish Names: Salvia, Luktebia

Modern Danish Name: Salvie

Modern Norwegian Name: Salvie

Deity Association: Vor

Height: 32"

Season: Perennial

History: Sage was a sacred ritual herb of the Romans, and came north to Germany and central Europe with their troops. Sage's name comes from the Latin *salvere*, meaning to be in good health. Roman tradition had it that one should never use iron tools in the harvesting or preparation of Sage, which makes some sense as apparently Sage's alkaloids react badly with iron salts. There are a number of different varieties of Sage, and although we are concentrating mostly on common garden Sage here, we should also consider its useful cousin Clary Sage (*Salvia sclarea*) as well. Sage was said to alleviate grief just by looking at it or smelling it, and for this reason some areas of Europe planted Sage in graveyards.

Medicinal Uses: Sage is antiseptic, antifungal, and contains a small amount of estrogen. Sage aids digestion (especially fats, which is why it's stuffed in meat), combats chronic diarrhea, is a blood tonic, reduces sweating, soothes coughs and colds, helps the body to stave off bacteria and viruses, and has hormone precursors that may be used to treat menopause. Hormonally, Sage is drying for premenopausal women and moistening for postmenopausal women. Sage balances fluids—if you're dried out it will nourish your tissues; if you're losing fluids it will check that, if you're bloated it will open the pathways. Generally, hot Sage tea releases fluids while cold Sage tea dries them up, which is why it is good for stopping lactation.

The dried leaves are smoked for asthma, and tea or capsules are used regularly to treat chronic asthma. Sage has a special affinity with the mouth and throat, and is especially good for sore throats, mouth ulcers, and tonsillitis. It dries up excessive saliva and has been used in conjuction with medications that create that problem. It is also of use to treat blood clots and blood that has stagnated in the veins, making the tissue purple, blue, or black; Sage safely dissolves them without releasing clots into the bloodstream to wreak havoc. It is also used as a blood thinner. Sage reduces sexual desire to a greater or lesser extent, so be wary of that side effect.

While Sage is safe as a culinary herb, it is really more of a specific than an alterative, and it's not wise to take it daily for a long period of time. Its effects on the nervous system are definite, but debated. Some say that it sedates, some that it stimulates. It may well have a different effect on different people, and must be used with that in mind. Considering the nature of the Sage spirit, I have to wonder if perhaps it has the mental effect that Sage-man thinks you ought to have, whoever you are. Pregnant women can have small doses, but not large ones. Sage dries up milk, so it shouldn't be taken by lactating women unless they are weaning their babes.

Clary ("clear eye") Sage infusion is famous as an eyewash (but don't ever put it in alcohol, it doesn't do well there). Its essential oil is good for stress and fatigue, but may be an anaphrodisiac that lowers desire.

Household Uses: Good bee plant. Use in facial steams, cleansing lotions, mouthwashes, and as a rinse to darken grey hair. Rub on the teeth to whiten them. Sachet the dried leaves in your linens to discourage moths. Boil on the stove to disinfect a room, or use Sage smoke to deodorize animal and cooking smells. Add Clary Sage to brewing beer to strengthen its effect. Various Sages are added to wines by the French.

Culinary Uses: Scatter the flowers on salads. The leaves can be used in stuffings, sauces, cheeses, vinegars, and butters. Sage is very good when paired with strong-flavored or fatty meats and cheeses, but doesn't play well culinarily with other herbs; he is strong enough to want the stage to himself. Wrap curing cheeses in Sage leaves. In Germany, a popular and delicious Sage dish is *Mausen*—batter-frying large Sage leaves stem and all, making a little "mouse" shape.

Magical Uses: Sage is the plant of longevity, and its most common use is in potions or charms to this end. It also brings wisdom, as its name implies, and a small horn filled with Sage was carried to repel the evil eye. Toads were rumored to love Sage plants. For a wish spell, write your wish on a Sage leaf and put it under your pillow; however, if the wish is not granted within three nights, you must give up and bury the Sage leaf, or bad luck will result.

Shamanic Uses: Eating Sage for nine nights in a row was said to be a good cleansing; I would go one step further and say that it is a good pre-journeying cleansing, when you have that much notice. Sage is also much loved by Asvid, the giant runemaster, and can be brought to him as an offering if you wish to be taught by him. It can also be used as a recaning herb to cleanse and sanctify a space, although the garden Sage that we deal with here is a different variety from that which the Native Americans are partial to as a smudge, and its energy is different.

Affinity: Fire (pungent), Swamp (oily), Air (astringent). Use on Earth, River, and Air.

Point: GV 11

Plant-wight's Nature: Grandfather Sage is so old and wizened that he was practically a thin stick hidden under a mountain of white hair and beard. He reminded me of one of those anchorites on the tops of mountains who has meditated for over a century, but when you ask him for advice, it's terribly sensible and prosaic. When he moved, he was nimble and quick, fluid in his movements like a t'ai ch'i master. He is another of the "doctor plants" who can look at you and diagnose what's wrong. He is less of a sorcerer and more of a holy hermit, however; his wisdoms are more abut the sacred and the cosmic, in spite of his practical advice, than of the occult or the wizardous. Grandfather Sage is choosy about who he will take for allies; he may turn down a spirit-worker in favor of a housewife with no apparent reason, and there seems to be no way to stack your chances. He squints at you, reads something in you, and decides, and that's that.

Medicinal Charm: Against Asthma

When the asthma is acting up, pour a pint of boiling water over an ounce of Sage leaves, let steep, strain, and drink. Repeat this three times a day for nine days. As it steeps, say this charm over the tea:

> *Wisdom's Herb, in my hall of winds,*
> *All is shrunken and shut; open me up*
> *As the storm blows open the shuttered room,*
> *Let my breath flow deep and free.*

Magical Charm: Longevity

If there is someone that you would have live long and hale, make a Sage tea by the above recipe and give to them. As it steeps, whisper into its fumes:

> *Salvia, Salvia, salvation is thine*
> *It is given to thee to choose,*
> *And I beg thee cast thy lot, O seer,*
> *In favor of one whom I value dear*
> *In the wager of who will win long years*
> *And who is bound to lose.*

Shepherd's Purse

Botanical Name: *Capsella bursis-pastoris*
Folk Names: Shepherd's Bag, Shepherd's Scrip, Shepherd's Sprout, Lady's Purse, Witches' Pouches, Rattle Pouches, Case-Weed, Pickpocket, Pick-Purse, Blindweed, Sanguinary, Mother's Heart, Clappedepouch, St. James' Wort, Pepper-And-Salt
Anglo-Saxon Name: Thyaspis
Modern German Name: Hirtentäschel
Modern Swedish Name: Lomme
Modern Danish Name: Hyrdetaske
Modern Norwegian Name: Gjetertaske
Deity Association: Mengloth
Height: 18"
Season: Annual
History: Shepherd's Purse is a long-time native of Europe, but like the weedy plant it is, it has spread all over the world.
Medicinal Uses: Tincture of Shepherd's Purse will stop internal bleeding, including uterine bleeding after childbirth or during excess menses. It is especially good for poor uterine muscle tone, fibroids, or other unspecified rampant menorrhagia. It will also dry up bloody diarrhea and bloody urine—if the latter is due to kidney problems, Shepherd's Purse can clear out sand and small stones and promote urination. The tincture or fluid extract will stanch wounds; put a little on a swab for nosebleeds. The herb produces a short-term drop in blood pressure. It has been used as a quinine substitute for malaria. Don't let pregnant women ingest it, as it may contract the uterus and begin labor.
Magical Uses: Charm for pregnant women to carry for a safe birth.
Shamanic Uses: Shepherd's Purse is much liked by Mengloth, the Jotun healing goddess on Lyfjaberg Mountain in Jotunheim. It can be used as a dowsing-rod to find your way to her heavily-guarded castle. This plant is good in charm bags for healthy pregnancy, especially where there is a question as to the mother's survival.
Affinity: Air (non-astringent astringent; works through its Fire function), Fire (stimulant). Use on River and Swamp conditions.
Point: KD 7
Plant-wight's Nature: Shepherd's Purse is a pinched, dry little stick of a plant and its spirit reflects this. Shepherd's Purse always feels a bit shriveled and withdrawn, prim and critical, with a dry wit as its only saving grace. He does not expect to be liked, and is a bit taken aback by effusiveness, preferring to keep people at arm's length. One must never forget, however, that this unassuming little plant is the best stauncher of internal hemorrhage in the herbal pharmacopoeia. I sometimes see Shepherd's Purse as a sort of fussy, precise surgeon, sealing up wounds. Remember to thank him, although he doesn't expect thanks.

Medicinal Charm: Blood Tincture

Shepherd's Purse loses its potency when dried, so all preparations should be made from fresh material. This means that fresh-herb tincture is your best bet. Make up a tincture of Shepherd's Purse by filling a jar with the fresh chopped herb and then pouring grain alcohol or vinegar over it. Let it steep for two months, ideally on an altar to Mengloth the healing goddess. Strain and rebottle, and use for any kind of hemorrhage, be it too heavy a menstrual flow or too much blood after a birth. Use half a shot-glass's worth, while saying the following charm:

Shepherd's Scrip and Sanguinary,

Mengloth's Man, Mother's Heart,
Stanch the flow and stop the flooding,
Keep the blood within the body.

Snapdragon and Toadflax

Botanical name: *Antirrhinum majus* (Snapdragon), *Linaria vulgaris* (Toadflax)
Folk names: Calf's Snout, Dog's Head (Snapdragon); Butter-And-Eggs, Eggs-And-Collops, Devil's Head, Fluellin, Buttered Haycocks, Patterns-And-Clogs, Dragon's Bushes, Pedlar's Basket (Toadflax)
Anglo-Saxon Name: Hundesheafod ("Dog's Head")
Modern German Names: Garten-Löwenmäulchen, Großes Löwenmäulchen
Modern Swedish Names: Lejongap (Snapdragon), Gulsporre, Flugblomster (Toadflax)
Modern Danish Names: Løvemund (Snapdragon), Torskemund (Toadflax)
Modern Norwegian Names: Løvemunn (Snapdragon), Torskemunn (Toadflax)
Deity Association: Mordgud, Garm
Height: to 3', depending on variety
Season: Perennial, annual in cold places
History: Snapdragon originated in the Mediterranean area, from southern France to Turkey and Syria. However, as anyone who has grown this flower in profusion knows, it self-seeds itself, and Snapdragon seems to have slowly worked its way north throughout ancient and early medieval times until it was naturalized in Britain and Germany. As a common decorative Roman garden plant (sacred to the Hounds of Hades), it is thought to also have been brought north during the Empire's conquest by transplanted Roman matrons whose northern villa gardens it then escaped. It may have been further north before the medieval "mini ice age", but it only reached Scandinavia as a medieval garden plant, grown as an annual.

Snapdragon's wild cousin Toadflax (also called *Linaria vulgaris*, Butter-And-Eggs, Eggs-And-Collops, Devil's Head, Fluellin, Buttered Haycocks, Patterns-And-Clogs, Dragon's Bushes, Pedlar's Basket, and a number of other weird names) has the same medicinal properties, only stronger for being uncultivated for longer.
Medicinal Uses: Both Snapdragon and Toadflax are astringent and diuretic, and bitter. Use Toadflax as a liver and gallbladder purgative, but only for a few days at a time. Made into a cooling ointment, the flowers are used for hemorrhoids. Remember that these herbs taste *nasty*, and take proper precautions for internal usage.
Household Uses: The seeds were pressed for a substitute for olive oil in Russia.
Magical Uses: Wearing a Snapdragon secreted on your body prevents anyone from deceiving you. It repels evil and negative influences. Placing a case of Snapdragons in front of a mirror will return curses to their sender. Toadflax, also, was used to repel evil magic.
Shamanic Uses: This flower will bear you safely down the Helvegr to Mordgud's Tower, and making an offering of it to her may sweeten her attitude toward you, although (like Heimdal) she is unbribeable and you can't sweet-talk your way past her. She may, however, help you in some way with your quest, depending on why you're there. Snapdragon is also associated with Garm, although a better choice of offering for that huge dog would be meat. I got the feeling that Toadflax is also associated with other, lesser known guardians of the Helheim gates, but could not get better information on the matter.
Affinity: Storm (bitter alterative), Air (astringent), Earth (cooling). Use on Swamp.
Points: UB 51 (Snapdragon) UB 22 (ToadFlax)
Plant-wight's Nature: These two—Snapdragon and Toadflax, apparently great cronies, appeared to me like a pair of comic characters in a medieval play—the sort that get into great scrapes together, and then have to get out of them much to the laughter of the crowd. Snapdragon was larger and somewhat

doglike, with bright red hair and a quick temper; he carried a club and sniffed the air constantly with wide staring eyes. Toadflax was short, squat, and waddling, with a shock of bright yellow hair and a sly, cunning grin—and a pouch of darts with which to shoot innocent passersby. It's not that these two can't be helpful, but one gets the idea that you would pay for that help by becoming the butt of one of their jokes at a future date.

Magical Charm: Guardian's Blessing

If someone you know is about to descend willingly into the underworld—however you conceive of what that means—you can send with a Snapdragon, if they are in season, and beg Mordgud's blessing on it. Pick the flower and press it in a book until it dries, and give it to them to carry, saying: "May Mordgud keep thee; may Hound's Head watch over thee, may the Gate-Guardian get thee through."

Medicinal Charm: Liver Yellow

For a cleansing of the liver, pour a pint of boiling water over the chopped aerial parts of ToadFlax. Steep, strain, and drink quickly—it will taste very bitter, and you might want to have a second drink there as a chaser to cover each swallow. As you drink, say this silly charm which will please ToadFlax

> *Fluellen fair my liver scrub,*
> *O Eggs-And-Collops, yellow clean away,*
> *O Dragonbush, O Pedlar's Clogs,*
> *The Well of Plenty purify*
> *For I am a fool, and so say I.*

Soapwort

Botanical name: *Saponaria officinalis*
Folk names: Bouncing Bet
Anglo-Saxon Name: Biscupwyrt ("Bishop Plant")
Modern German Name: Gemeines Seifenkraut
Modern Swedish Name: Såpagräs
Modern Danish Name: Sæbeurt
Modern Norwegian Name: Såpeurtå
Deity Association: Holda
Height: 1-2'
Season: Perennial
History: Soapwort is native to northern Europe, although it did not reach Britain until it was spread from Germany by monastery culture. Ancient Romans used it to wash both people and (especially) wool.
Medicinal Uses: The aerial parts of the plant can be decocted and used as a wash for eczema, acne, boils, and Poison Ivy. The root is poisonous and should not be taken internally, which is why it shouldn't be grown on the banks of fishponds—if there's enough of it, it will literally poison the fish. If it is specially treated, it can be used as a diuretic, expectorant, and laxative, and to stimulate gallbladder , but it needs to be specially prepared for internal use.
Household Uses: To get the soap solution, boil the entire plant in untreated water for 30 minutes and strain. It will miraculously revive old, faded fabrics, and is good for delicate cloth and delicate skin. It has been used as a water softener. The flowers are used in potpourri, and retain their scent for some time. Some old brewers put Soapwort into their beer to create a "head" on it, although this seems like a shifty sort of thing to me.
Magical Uses: Put into magical floorwashes and cleaning solutions for more magical cleansing "kick".
Shamanic Uses: : Cleansing magically charged garments
Affinity: Fire (irritant), Storm (bitter alterative). Not to be used medicinally without special preparation, but would be used on Swamp conditions.

Point: GB 30

Plant-wight's Nature: Mistress Soapwort is a merry maiden, plump and bright-eyed with a head full of rather alarming black curls. She is friendly but rather scattered, and often forgets your presence in the middle of an interaction, and is off to do something else while you say, "Wait-" to no avail. Housecleaning will get her attention for a short while, but little else will. She likes offerings of tiny fabric scraps, bright and soft, especially silks and the like.

Magical Charm: Housecleaning

When the home is feeling dull and less than fresh in its energies, take down all the curtains, wall hangings, cushion covers, anything that is fabric and can be laundered, and wash them all in a huge batch of Soapwort soap, singing "Hail Holda, bless and blow open my windows and doors! Let all filth fade, let the wind weave whole!" Wash the walls, the floor, anything that seems to need it. Frau Holde will help bring vitality back into your home.

Sorrel

Botanical Name: *Rumex acetosa* (Cultivated Sorrel) *or Rumex acetosella* (Sheep Sorrel)

Folk Names: Little Vinegar Leaf

Anglo-Saxon Name: Ampre

Old Norse Name: Akr-Súra ("Field Sorrel")

Old High Germanic Name: Amfer

Modern German Name: Ampfer

Modern Swedish Name: Ängssyra

Modern Danish Name: Syre

Modern Norwegian Names: Syrer, Engsyrer (acetosa), Småsyre (acetosella)

Deity Association: Snotra

Height: To 2'

Season: Perennial

History: Indigenous to all of Europe, Sorrel is a lemony-tasting weed that was a staple in Germanic cooking; "Sauerampfer" soup is still popular in Germany. Cultivated Sorrel (*Rumex acetosa*) is larger and milder than wild Sheep Sorrel (*Rumex acetosella*); the two have slightly different medicinal uses.

Medicinal Uses: The leaves reduce fevers and are a mild diuretic. Cultivated Sorrel is better for this one. A poultice of either treats acne and infected wounds. Where Sheep Sorrel shines is as a poultice to remove skin cancers, from benign tumors to, in some cases, malignant ones. It is taken both internally and externally in those cases, and has been taken internally as a general cancer treatment. Since there is a high level of oxalic acid in Sorrel, do not take it for more than 3 weeks without taking a week off.

Household Uses: The leaf juice will bleach rust, mold, and ink stains from linen, wicker, and silver. Sorrel roots lifted in early winter boiled with yarn mordanted with alum gives an olive yellow; adding ammonia (urine) gives a range of colors from brownish-orange to brick red. Used as an after-mordant for Woad to increase the fastness of the blue dye. It is a mordant for black dye, and the leaves picked in summer produce a blue-green dye.

Culinary Uses: Eaten widely in salads and as a cooked green, but cook in one change of water to reduce bitterness and they will taste like spinach. The ground seeds were once made into flour or gruel. This is a classic soup and salad herb for those who want to try period cooking.

Magical Uses: Eaten or carried to make the day's labor go quicker.

Shamanic Uses: The "little vinegar leaf" is much liked by Snotra, handmaiden of hard labors. In ancient times, the four sacred preservation foods—salt, honey, wine, and vinegar—all gained symbolic meanings, and vinegar's was hard work. Carry and eat Sorrel as a way to invoke Snotra to provide motivation and persistence at hard but necessary tasks.

Affinity: Air (astringent), Earth (cooling), Harvest (nourishing). Use on River and Fire conditions.

Point: SI 4

Plant-wight's Nature: Mistress Sorrel is very old, not quite as old as Lambsquarters, but still quite ancient. She appears as a hunched old woman bundled in rough woven cloth who goes about muttering to herself. Her speech appears to be mostly nonsense, but she is not mad. She knows what you're saying, and if you listen closely and are patient, she will acknowledge you somewhere in the stream of muttering. Don't become impatient with her. She is a good forage guide in the woods and fields, if you are willing to put up with her oddities.

Magical Charm: Sauerampfer

> To build up one's strength for hard physical labor, make soup from the following ingredients:
>
> 1 ½ quarts strongly-herbed vegetable broth or meat broth
>
> 1 lb Sorrel
>
> 4 tablespoons sour cream
>
> 2 tablespoons butter
>
> 2 tablespoons flour
>
> While stirring the ingredients, sing softly, "Snotra's Sourweed, send me strength," and then eat it daily for four days.

Southernwood

Botanical name: *Artemisia abrotanum*

Folk names: Southern Wormwood, Old Man, Old Woman, Lad's Love, Boy's Love, Maid's Ruin, Appleringie, Garderobe

Anglo-Saxon Name: Suþernewudu

Modern German Name: Eberraute

Modern Swedish Name: Åbrodd

Modern Danish Name: Ambra

Modern Norwegian Name: Abrodd

Deity Association: Lofn

Height: To 3'

Season: Perennial

History: Southernwood was an import from southern Europe during the early medieval period. The Anglo-Saxon herbals mention it as grown in England by their time. It was placed in churches to help people stay awake during services.

Medicinal Uses: Southernwood is a mild wormer, gentler than Wormwood. It is an emmenagogue and abortifacient, a stimulant tonic, and a bit of a nervine. Prisoners were given bunches of Southernwood and Rue in order to ward off jailhouse fever. The leaves in a poultice draw out splinters. The seeds were pressed for an oil that was rubbed on the back for pain and sciatica. It was used to treat diseases of the spleen, and gangrene. Southernwood should not be given to pregnant women.

Household Uses: Plant near cabbages and fruit trees to deter moths, and near henhouses to deter lice. Boys once made an ointment from Southernwood to help their beards grow. Its name "Garderobe", like several other plants who bore that appendage, referred to its use as a moth repellent. It is also a flea repellent, scattered on beds and floors to get rid of the small creatures. The branches have been used to make a yellow dye, and the oil was used in perfumes.

Culinary Uses: The leaves have a bitter lemony taste; the French and Italians used them to flavor cakes and aromatic vinegars.

Magical Uses: Southernwood is classically burned for love and lust spells (the two often blend together, it seems) and as a general protection, especially for threatened lovers. It was said to give sexual potency to men and make girls swoon; thus its names Lad's Love and Maid's Ruin.

Shamanic Uses: Used to beg Lofn to intercede on the part of troubled lovers.

Affinity: Fire (stimulant), Storm (bitter alterative). Use on Earth and Swamp conditions.

Point: UB 61

Plant-wight's Nature: Southernwood is the wayward daughter of Mugwort, or so she introduced herself to me. Round and lush, with a dreamy, distracted look in her pale blue eyes and a great cloud of silvery hair, she speaks at length of her various lovers over the centuries, both green and red (plant and flesh, I took that to mean). Her fickleness seems to be more about a short attention span than any great passion; she drifts in and out of love, always on the move to another pretty face. Like all the Artemisias, she is lunar in nature and tied to the moon's cycles, but she is more the changeable Moon Maiden than her dark-moon mother. Becoming lovers with her, even for a short while (and that is all that it will be) brings great luck, but it must be spontaneous and sincere, not planned, or she will know and avoid you.

Magical Charm: Troubled Lovers

To get Lofn's attention during romantic trials, take dried Southernwood and sprinkle it around the bedroom where the lovers last cohabited, saying:

> Lofn's love, I ask your leave
> To tell your mistress merry where
> Our troubles lie; O tell her true
> And nigh ask aid of her and you
> That we might mend this net of cares.

If you cannot get to that bedroom, write a letter detailing what is wrong, wrap it around some dried branches of Southernwood, and burn it while reciting the above charm. One word to the wise: The charm works better if both lovers each write their own letter and wrap them together without looking at what each other says, and burn them. If Lofn decides to help you, the solution will appear, if you have eyes to see it.

Speedwell

Botanical name: *Veronica spicata*
Folk names: Veronica
Anglo-Saxon Name: Hleomoc
Modern German Name: Ähriger Ehrenpreis
Modern Swedish Name: Ärenpris
Modern Danish Name: Ærenpris
Modern Norwegian Name: Aksveronika
Deity Association: Sjofn
Height: 12–18"
Season: Perennial

History: Speedwell is native to most of Europe, and was once an important medicinal herb, although it has mostly been forgotten now. Its common named reflected its medicinal uses, and its more formal name associated it with the Catholic mysteries of St. Veronica.

Medicinal Uses: Speedwell is used as a cough-and-cold herb, breaking up hardened mucus and treating asthma. It is rubbed on itchy skin conditions, arthritic joints, and gout for pain relief. It stimulates the kidneys and breaks up stones. Speedwell helps to replace the mucosal layer of the stomach, and as such is useful in treating gastric ulcers. As it is a mild sedative, it should be administered in the evening, before bedtime.

Magical Uses: Magically, Speedwell is a student's herb, and can help to retain knowledge when carried in a pouch on the person.

Shamanic Uses: Speedwell's energy is quick and brisk, and can help with stamina and moving quickly out of one area and into another—or out of one world and into another, if you are journeying between worlds. Other spirits are better at the actual transition; Speedwell just gives extra deftness. Speedwell can also be used to facilitate communication between people who care about each other greatly, but are having trouble reaching an understanding. Invoking Sjofn's blessing on the herb can help; ask for her help before burning it as an incense in the home.

Affinity: Storm (bitter alterative), Air (astringent), Stone (sedative). Use on Swamp and River.

Point: UB 42

Plant-wight's Nature: Master Speedwell is small and thin, with sharp dark blue eyes. His hair is, oddly enough, the same color. His gaze is intelligent and very sharp; like Fennel, he is a Magician—although not as old or powerful—but he does not reveal the nature of his magics easily. He is a messenger, and one of his gifts is getting information out of other greenwights, so if you have an alliance with him, he might help you with the plant-spirits that won't speak to you. (There are always some. No one is liked by every plant-spirit any more than they are liked by every human.) Master Speedwell can also carry on an interesting conversation about many things occult; he excels in listening and retaining knowledge. One wonders how many gardens he lay in, listening through windows as people carried on their strange activities.

Magical Charm: Student's Head

If you are worried about retaining a large amount of information given out very fast, carry a bag of Speedwell to school and sniff it often during class, and it will help the information stay in your head. When you tie up the bag, say this charm: "Blue of sky and blue of eye; wisdom in to stay."

Spruce

Botanical name: *Picea abies* or *Picea obovata*
Folk names: Snowgreen, Hunter's Tree
Modern German Names: Gemeine Fichte, Rottanne
Modern Swedish Name: Blågran
Modern Danish Name: Gran
Modern Norwegian Names: Gran, Granstre
Deity Association: Ullr, Skadi
Height: 20-60'
Season: Perennial Tree
History: Spruce is found on most continents, but is common in the cold coniferous forests of northern Europe. The English name comes from an old word for Prussia. Spruces are used as "nurse trees" for the reforestation of less hardy trees, showing their strongly protective nature.
Medicinal Uses: Spruce needle tea is high in vitamin C and is a scurvy preventative in snow-ridden environments.
Household Uses: Spruce wood is light and used for various light construction.
Culinary Uses: Needle tips can be used to brew Spruce beer and Spruce tip syrup.
Magical Uses: Strewing Spruce branches about is said to be able to raise storms.
Shamanic Uses: Spruce tea can be used as a magical tonic during *utiseta* to make communication with the ancestors more clear.
Affinity: Mountain (relaxant), Stone (sedative), Fire (stimulant). Use on Storm.

Point: LI 12

Plant-wight's Nature: Grandfather Spruce, the husband of Grandmother Fir, is a hoary old warrior. Much like his wife, he came tall and strong in spite of his age, cloaked in dark green and snowy furs, and carrying a spear. His beard was long and grey, as was his hair, and his moustache bristled. To him, he explained, was given the task of guarding and fighting for the elders of the tribe—the old men and women who might be forgotten when all the young people leaped in with their strength and made rash decisions. Grandfather Spruce is a link to the hard-won wisdom of thousands of generations of elders who lived and died in cold northern forests under his watchful eye. His twigs protect the elders from abuse when they can no longer care for themselves, and he is interested in giving them good and painless deaths.

Magical Charm: To Protect a Beloved Elder

Take ten twigs of Spruce, still bearing their needles, and bind them together with red thread for life and vitality, making them into the shape of a human being. Then swaddle the figure in strips of white cloth, and then red cloth to completely cover the white cloth. As you wrap, say, "Sacred Hunter and Winter's Queen, Grandfather Evergreen, bless and keep them sharp and keen." Let the beloved elder keep it in their home until their deaths; at that time, remove the red wrappings and bury it with them, or at the same time as their funeral, to keep them safe into the next world.

Strawberry

Botanical Name: *Fragaria vesca*

Folk Names: Erdbeer

Anglo-Saxon Name: Streawberge

Modern German Name: Wald-Erdbeere

Modern Swedish Name: Smultron

Modern Danish Name: Jordbær

Modern Norwegian Name: Jordbær

Deity Association: Freya

Height: 10'

Season: Perennial

History: The earliest form of Strawberry is the wild mountain variety, growing in all high northern places, but likely originally native to the Alps. As it was cultivated and bred for larger fruit, it was spread across the continent, but even by the Middle Ages it was still mostly a fruit of northern Europe, just as olives were a southern fruit.

Medicinal Uses: Strawberry is cooling and moistening, and very good for hot dry conditions. Wild Strawberry leaves are a uterine tonic, and good for pregnant women. The leaves are infused for anemia, diarrhea, dysentery, and gastrointestinal problems. They cool an overacid stomach, and treat gut cramps from allergic reactions. In fact, they are an excellent allergy treatment, helping the liver to break down foreign proteins. They are also a good gargle for tooth plaque prevention. The fruit is an iron supplement, a liver tonic, a good food for hot sick stomachs, and cools fevers. It has been used to treat blood sugar problems, mold allergies, to rebuild health in convalescence, and to treat nervousness and melancholy.

Household Uses: The fruit can be rubbed on teeth to reduce tartar and stains; leave the juice on for 10 minutes and then rinse with salt or baking soda. Strawberry juice will whiten skin as a face pack.

Culinary Uses: Jam, pie, or just plain eating. The Saami people of Lapland make a Yule pudding with Strawberries, blueberries, and reindeer milk.

Magical Uses: Love spells, luck spells, and pregnancy spells. Strawberries are loved by the faeries, and in Germany they hung a basket of Strawberries between the horns of cows so that the wights might bless the cows with abundant milk.

Shamanic Uses: Sacred to Freya, they can be used to find her when she goes home to Vanaheim periodically. They make a good community offering eaten in honor of Freya.

Affinity: Earth (cooling), Harvest (nourishing), River (moistening), Air (slightly astringent). Use for Fire conditions.

Point: SP 9

Plant-wight's Nature: The Strawberry-wight's spirit is neither masculine nor feminine, or perhaps it is both. What it is, is eternally youthful, perhaps in that stage where children are not conscious yet of gender, or perhaps an androgynous eternal youth. It is cheerful, playful, occasionally shy, and loves children and babies. It can be fickle and prickly when mistreated or taken for granted. It likes to be sung to, but the song should be upbeat.

Magical Charm: Strawberry Luck

This is especially good when sung over a pregnant belly, to give luck to the unborn child. Rub the juice of the Strawberry fruit, or if it is not in season rub the fresh or dried leaf, onto the belly. Say the following charm:

> *Strawberry, earthberry, find my fortune,*
> *Fickle and fey, fair Freya's fruit,*
> *Earthberry, Strawberry, strew my way with*
> *Luck laid out like little lovers*
> *On the ley lines of my life.*

St. John's Wort

Botanical Name: *Hypericum perforatum*

Folk Names: Goatweed, Scare-Devil, Fuga Daemonum, Herba John, Sol Terrestis

Anglo-Saxon Name: Corion

Modern German Names:
Echtes Johanniskraut,
Tüpfel-Hartheu

Modern Swedish Names: Johannesört, Mannablod, Johannesblöda, Randpirk

Modern Danish Name: Johannesurte

Modern Norwegian Names:
Prikkperikum, Johannesurt

Deity Association: Baldur

Height: To 3'

Season: Perennial

History: St. John's Wort is native to Europe and western Asia. It has been associated with holiness and the repelling of evil spirits in almost every culture that has used it. Its botanical name means "Over An Apparition" in Greek, for this reason. It is also associated with the faeries and Little People, both the alien Fey and the local spirits:earth-.

Medicinal Uses: St. John's Wort is first and foremost a healer of wounds and nerves. It is used, both internally and externally, on any infected wound, and on any wound that might get infected. It is especially good for staving off blood poisoning or tetanus on rusty-nail-type wounds; if the injury is doused with St. John's Wort, it will likely not ever develop tetanus. Some advanced cases have been cured with it, but the further it goes, the harder it is to help. It is used for localized stabbing nerve pain, including back pain and sciatica. It is a very important pain reliever after surgery, which is basically a careful injury. The tea is drunk for colds and the red infused oil is rubbed on the chest for coughs, the skin for wounds and sunburn, and joints for inflammation. It is good for long-term chronic-pain illnesses such as fibromyalgia, although be warned that its detoxifying effect may begin as a temporary rash that needs to be waited out. Some herbalists have reported good luck using St. John's Wort to treat the effects of active HIV.

Both the tea and the tincture are used for anxiety, nervous tension, and depression, especially depressionstemming from long-term nervous tension. Like Betony, St. John's Wort acts on the solar plexus, harmonizing the digestive system and teaching people to better recognize their instincts. It has been used for hallucinations with some success, or perhaps it simply taught people to better recognize what is a hallucination. Some people experience contact dermatitis or heart palpitations as an allergic reaction to this plant, so be careful. St. John's Wort can also make your skin more sensitive to sunlight after taking it internally. It's as if you have a bit of sun within you already, so more might be too much.

Household Uses: Plant gives four different colors of dye, depending on part and mordant.

Magical Uses: Associated with Baldur and the Sun, St. John's Wort is carried by soldiers for victory, and is used in spells to ward off depression and insanity. It wards off demons, necromancers, and evil spirits. Burning it in your fireplace or woodstove during a thunderstorm was said to ward off lightning. Bunches of flowering St. John's Wort were suspended over pagan icons in order to sanctify the space; in general, the plant seems to have been employed as a sort of all-purpose herbal exorcist. It is highly protective and has strong solar energy. St. John's Wort is associated with the summer Solstice (St. John's Day), and is supposed to be gathered naked on that night. Where I live, it doesn't bloom until July, unfortunately.

Shamanic Uses: No, you can't use it to find Baldur, as he is guarded safely in parts of Helheim that few people can get to. This plant seems to have an affinity for the rune Sowelu/Sigil; carry a pouch of it in a yellow bag embroidered with that rune for the kind of burnt-mind craziness that comes from too much worldwalking. If you don't get a reaction from it, eating it can help that feeling as well, especially if you trace the rune over it before ingestion. It is also good for getting on the good side of the Alfar if you have to deal with them; it's not an Alfar or Alfheim herb specifically, but they have great respect for Lord Baldursbrow. Some shamans have used it in spells to bind the aid of the local small spirits: earth-wights, or even the Alfar or Fey, into healing someone. This, however, requires a close alliance with all the wights involved.

Affinity: Fire (stimulant), Swamp (oily), Harvest (nourishing), Mountain (non-acrid relaxant). Use on Air, Earth, and Storm conditions.

Point: KD 25

Plant-wight's Nature: Lord Baldursbrow is tall and golden and angelic, with eyes that can turn from warm and inviting to sharp and glittering. He moves and speaks with pleasant gravity, and has a politician's graciousness, making one feel welcomed and attended. Most of the time, this is what you'll see—his warm golden side, which is usually willing to help, although he will expect some kind of fairly immediate payment. He considers himself nobility, and though he will grant boons, he expects to be treated as befits his rank. It is possible to anger him through discourtesy and ingratitude, and then the warmth turns cold and he will strike at you, so be careful. While he can grant some measure of relief from depression, he can also cause problems if he dislikes the way that he is treated.

Medicinal Charm: Sol Terrestris

This is the name of St. John's Wort that most reflects its nature as one of the Sun-On-Earth plants. Rather than charming a recipe for a specific complaint, Lord Baldursbrow wanted me to make his tincture as an All-Healer, bringing solar warmth and healing to anything he could, inside and out. So be it, then. Gather the flowering aerial parts of this golden plant in late summer, chop, fill a jar, and cover with alcohol. While I prefer vinegar tinctures in general, St. John's Wort wanted to be in alcohol, and who am I to argue? It may well be because this tincture is applied as often outside as inside, and often both at once in the case of wounds or skin issues, and alcohol carries alkaloids more cleanly through the skin. At any rate, shake the tincture daily, saying the charm below:

Sol Terrestris, I open my arms to thy light,
I open my skin, my flesh, every river and well
That runs within me. I take in thy healing might,
O Corion, greater thy power than time can tell.

After a month of this, strain and decant the tincture. It can be used for any of the above-mentioned problems; if the problem is a wound, use it both internally and externally. If the body you are using it on has not dealt with St. John's Wort before, start small with no more than 3 drops daily and work up to 10 slowly if there are no side effects or allergic reactions.

Magical Charm: Driving Out Evil

This spell is for when someone feels tormented by evil spirits. They could be real, or not; really, it doesn't matter because the truth is that St. John's Wort has been known to drive away the imaginary ones as well. It is that powerful a spirit. The spell is threefold: Each day at noon for three days, burn some St. John's Wort as an incense, drink a cup of St. John's tea, and sprinkle the dried leaves under your bed, in that order. As you do each step, recite the charm below. In three days, what can be banished will have been.

Baldursbrow, banish all banes,
Scare-Devil, sweep demons away,
Fuga Daemonum, may they fly before you,
As shadows they fly from each
green-gilded ray.

Sweet Cicely

Botanical name: *Myrrhis odorata*
Folk names: British Myrrh, Garden Myrrh, Sweet Fern, Sweet Chervil, British Chervil, Great Chervil, Smooth Cicely, Sweet Bracken, Sweet-Cus, Sweet Humlock, Cow Chervil
Anglo-Saxon Name: Fille
Modern German Name: Süßdolde
Modern Swedish Name: Spansk Körvel
Modern Danish Name: Spansk Kørvel
Modern Norwegian Name: Spansk Kjørvel
World Association: Ljossalfheim, the Alfar
Height: 2-4'
Season: Perennial
History: Sweet Cicely is native to all parts of subarctic Europe and western Asia, and has been cultivated there as long as anyone can

remember. Its botanical name refers to its sweet smell. It was known as "British Chervil"; as the traditional Chervil (*Anthriscus cerefolium*) was begun in the Levant, bred in Italy, and moved north slowly through the centuries, until it became widespread in France during the Middle Ages. However, the hardier perennial Sweet Cicely was the favorite in more northerly climes for some time, until French cooking overcame Saxon/German traditions in England with the Norman conquest, and Sweet Cicely was relegated to a mere brewing herb. (In Germany, the recipes containing Sweet Cicely remained more popular for a much longer time.) The name "Spanish Chervil" was applied to it in Scandinavia, even though it had been imported from England and Germany, presumably to give it more exotic appeal. While the exact identities of the Nine Sacred Herbs are debated a good deal by scholars, when I found that classic cookery Chervil didn't respond to the charm as it ought to, I looked around and found Sweet Cicely's older name, and found that this delicate, lacy plant did indeed work, solidifying its identity.

Medicinal Uses: Infusion used for flatulence, coughs, and general stomach upsets. Sweet Cicely's action is very gentle, so it can be used on children with little problem. Roots have antiseptic action and were used to cure the bites of mad dogs and snakes. Steeped in wine, they were a remedy for consumption. Eat as a general tonic—Sweet Cicely was said to be an especially good tonic for girls between the ages of 15 and 18.

Household Uses: The seeds make an aromatic furniture polish, and are used to flavor Chartreuse liqueur. It is very attractive to bees.

Culinary Uses: The entire plant is edible. John Gerard, garden keeper to Queen Elizabeth, reports its leaves and roots were commonly eaten in salads in his day. The fresh leaves can be used as a sweetener for diabetics, and can be cooked with tart-tasting fruits (such as Crabapple). The seeds can be cooked into cakes and biscuits. The boiled roots were given as a tonic to elders who had become weak, dull, and afraid of life.

Magical Uses: It is said that this plant "comforts the heart and increases a lust for life." The essential oil is said to be an aphrodisiac.

Shamanic Uses: This is the herb of Alfheim, used to honor the Alfar and the Fey races. It is a pair with Fennel—*"felamihtigu twa"*, the mighty two, and they are most often used in conjunction. Tea of Sweet Cicely and Fennel protects against elf-shot; tea to drink or salve rubbed on the afflicted area treats mild cases of it. Sweet Cicely also aids in the Gift of Sight, in this case the ability to see beauty beneath ugliness, power beneath simplicity, and possibility beneath limitation. It is a useful plant when faced with clients who are living in a swamp of negativity, and you have to find them some hope. Drink in tea or smoke it or eat the seeds (preferably six of them).

Affinity: Fire (stimulant), Harvest (nourishing). Use on Earth conditions.

Point: GB 7

Plant-wight's Nature:

> Lord Fille's personality and energy are much like that of a male Alf—somewhat effeminate and passive at first, but sharp as a deadly blade if pushed too far. There is also a song used by the Alfar to return home from any point in the Nine Worlds with his help, but Lord Fille will not reveal it to outsiders, exiles or mortals wishing to play tourist. He is remarkably stubborn about it. Persuasion, pleading and threats will not work, but there are other ways to get into Ljossalfheim if need be.   —Elizabeth Vongvisith

Magical Charm: Going Home

> Sweet Cicely is one of the Nine Sacred Herbs and is bound to the land of Ljossalfheim. His primary gift is that of finding one's way home, and while this is mostly aimed at Alfar who wish to return to their native land, this magic can be used by anyone who may be lost within the Nine Worlds while journeying, or by those who are lost in the physical world, and wish to return home.
>
> The charm works thusly: you may use water, fire, air or earth to cast the charm, but you must have a small handful of Sweet Cicely (dried or fresh leaves will work, but it's best to use seeds) to use. For water, cast the plant bits onto the surface of a basin of water, noting any symbols that form. For fire, burn Sweet

Cicely and pay attention to which way the smoke blows. For air, cast it into the air around you and note the direction in which the leaves or seeds fall or are blown away. For earth, go to a bare patch of ground and cast the Sweet Cicely over your shoulder onto it, then look at the pattern of the bits for a hint as to which direction to travel to get home. Again, you may do this while pathwalking or when actually lost in the physical realm. For guidance before the start of any journey, take some Sweet Cicely and chew it before bedtime, then go to sleep and look to your dreams for advice.
                                                                            -Elizabeth Vongvisith

Sweet Flag Iris

Botanical name: *Acorus calamus*
Folk names: Nithoweard, Sweet Sedge, Sweet Root, Sweet
    Rush, Sweet Cane, Myrtle Grass, Myrtle Sedge
Anglo-Saxon Name: Beowyrt ("Bee Plant")
Modern German Name: Kalmus
Modern Swedish Names: Kalmus, Kalmarerot, Kalmerot,
    Kallmansrot, Kalmusrot
Modern Danish Name: Kalmusrod
Modern Norwegian Names: Kalmusrot
Deity Association: Sigyn
Height: To 5'
Season: Perennial
History: When Sweet Flag Iris came to northern Europe is
    not clear. It was known and grown by the ancient Greeks, and was popular in western Asia, and is
    mentioned in the Anglo-Saxon herbals. Some sources, however, claim that it was introduced from
    Asia in the fifteenth century, which would conflict with its presence in the herbals. At any rate, it has
    been naturalized in continental Europe at least since the medieval period.
Medicinal Uses: The only Iris in Europe that is not entirely poisonous, the root of Sweet Flag is
    supposedly a mild hallucinogen and stimulant, but people who have used it have not found it to be
    hallucinogenic yet; perhaps this is a matter of appealing to the greenwight? At any rate, the root is an
    appetite stimulant used for anorexics and people who are on medications with unwanted appetite-
    suppressant side effects. Sweet Flag helps stomachaches, is a gargle for sore throats, and has been given
    to babies (tied up in a bit of cloth to prevent swallowing) for teething. The essential oil is added to
    stomach teas, but use sparingly and infrequently. It is better used in baths for convalescents.
Household Uses: Leaf buds and inner stems are used in salads and were a popular strewing herb for their
    scent. Root is used to flavor alcohol and can be candied; it is used as a fixative in potpourri and was
    once dried and ground for homemade toothpaste. the powdered root deters ants and sterilizes rice
    weevils when stored in the grain.
Culinary Uses: The root has been candied, and the leaf buds can be added to salads. Powdered, the root
    can be used like Cinnamon or Nutmeg. The leaves have been used to flavor creams with a vanilla
    tinge.
Magical Uses: Taken on riverboats to prevent sinking by mischievous water faeries. It is said to have been
    used in large amounts as an entheogen for the initiations of boys, but this seems dubious.
Shamanic Uses: This plant seems to be special to Sigyn, the second wife of Loki. To work with her, carry
    a talisman of the root carved with her name in runes. One of her gifts is that of marital loyalty in the
    face of hard times and social disapproval.
Affinity: Fire (stimulant), Stone (sedative), Storm (bitter alterative). Use for Earth, Fire or Swamp
    conditions.

Point: UB 49

Plant-wight's Nature: Mistress Calamus is quiet, and stillness seems to be one of her gifts. She can stay in one place, motionless, her eyes averted onto something else (usually the surface of water) for a very long time. Sitting with her is very meditative, and one finds oneself also staring at water and lost in the light dappling off of its surface. "Everything you need to find is in the water," she finally whispered to me, and then was gone. The message didn't seem personal; rather it summed up her world view. Rather than being green, she seems to reflect the colors of the waters where she grows.

Medicinal Charm: Appetite

When you are having trouble facing down food, and it has gone on for a while, make up a tincture of Calamus root with any decent alcohol. Let it sit for one turn of the moon, shaking it every day and saying the charm below. Then strain, decant, and take a few drops of it in the morning, repeating the charm.

> *Lady Beowyrt, like the bee to the flower*
> *I shall be drawn to the goodness of food*
> *And let myself need it, O Nithoweard,*
> *And care, O Calamus, for the body's nourishment.*

Sweet Woodruff

Botanical Name: *Galium odoratum*

Folk Names: Herb Walter, Master of the Woods, Wood Rovelle, Wuderove

Anglo-Saxon Name: Wuduhrofe

Modern German Name: Waldmeister

Modern Swedish Name: Myskmadra

Modern Danish Name: Skovmærke

Modern Norwegian Name: Myske

Deity Association: Walburga, Gerda

Height: 6"

Season: Perennial

History: Woodruff is native to continental Europe, where it was plentiful in the thick forests of Germany. It was apparently spread to the British Isles by the Saxon invasion.

Medicinal Uses: Sweet Woodruff is a mild nervine, used for neuralgia, panic, and insomnia. It increases milk flow in nursing mothers. However, its best use is as a bloodthinner, used to treat phlebitis, varicose veins, and problems with hepatic blood supply. It is not recommended for people who are already on blood thinners.

Household Uses: Woodruff is a potpourri herb; when dried it smells of vanilla.

Culinary Uses: Traditionally put into May wine, the new wine served at Walpurgisnacht, for flavor.

Magical Uses: Used in pouches for protection and valor in battle. Wards the Beltane circle and protects the revellers.

Shamanic Uses: Sacred to Walburga, the goddess of Walpurgisnacht who may well actually be Ostara, the spring-bringer. Can be used to escape pursuers, as Walburga is pursued through the woods each year by hounds. If you carry it, you can use her trick of standing in a triangle carved into a stump-top, and your pursuers will pass you by.

Affinity: Sweet Woodruff is one of the few herbs that has an equal balance of hot, Cold, wet and dry, meaning that it partakes equally of all four elements but has a personal affinity with none. Use with any appropriate formula.

Point: CV 13

Plant-wight's Nature: Sweet Woodruff is a wood-nymph, slender and silent. She rarely speaks, occasionally dances, and frequently makes wild leaps like a deer. She seems to communicate through motion rather than words, and is very shy. She dislikes the sun, and hides herself in the shadows. Difficult to talk with; if she smiles at you, that's likely all the answer you're going to get.

Magical Charm: Maibowle

To make May wine: Pick a good handful of Sweet Woodruff, hold it to your heart, and say:

> *Run, Lady of Spring, run through the wood;*
> *Let the winter not catch you,*
> *Let the winter not see you,*
> *Let the winter fly to the far side of the world.*

Marinate a handful of freshly dried Woodruff in the juice of one lemon and half a bottle of Rhine wine for four hours; then add 6 tablespoons of sugar and another bottle and a half of the wine. Just before serving, add a bottle of seltzer for sparkle, and/or a bit of brandy for a stronger drink. All who drink the Maibowle will gain luck to outrun any bad fortune pursing them in the months to come, but they must not sit idle if they wish the charm to work.

Tansy

Botanical Name: *Tanacetum vulgare*
Folk Names: Athanasia, Buttons
Anglo-Saxon Name: Helde
Modern German Name: Rainfarn
Modern Swedish Names: Renfana, Batram
Modern Danish Name: Rejnfan
Modern Norwegian Name: Reinfann
Deity Association: Walburga
Height: To 4'
Season: Perennial
History: Tansy is native to nearly all of Europe, spread hardily on fields and wastelands.
Medicinal Uses: The tea is a traditional abortifacient. It is used to expel worms in children and adults, but there are less harsh remedies. The oil is used to stimulate healing on bruises and torn tendons. Not to be used by pregnant women, obviously. Tansy has been known to bring on a delayed menstruation in very sensitive women just by handling the leaves and flowers.
Household Uses: Sprinkle for ant repellent. Hang to repel flies. Boil flowers for a yellow dye. Mix into compost heap for potassium content. Use in astringent baths and facial steams. Before refrigeration, meat was wrapped in Tansy to preserve it.
Culinary Uses: Tansy was used in a small amount in Tansy pudding, below.
Magical Uses: As Tansy has strong preservative and antiseptic qualities, dead bodies were often treated with strong Tansy tea in hot weather to preserve them for the funeral. Thus it is said to bring immortality. It is also associated with women's mysteries, perhaps harking back to the day when abortions had to be done in secret by the local witch-wife.
Shamanic Uses: The early young leaves are used sparingly in a Walpurgisnacht pudding called "Tansy", which is special to Walburga/Ostara. Eat it on her eve to lend her your power to avoid the yearly hunt, and she will thank you.

Affinity: Storm (bitter alterative), Mountain (relaxant), Fire (pungent). Use for the actions listed above.

Point: ST 29

Plant-wight's Nature: Mistress Tansy is an odd one. She appears to me as a peasant woman, tall and large-boned and somehow crookedly made—rolling eyes a little unevenly set in her broad face, wide-spaced peglike teeth in a friendly grin, large hands and feet in oversized shoes. and a bit of a shambling walk. Her speech is slurred and it is sometimes difficult to understand her, and her gaze sometimes wanders, but she is not stupid. In her own strange way, she knows what to do, and is usually affable and helpful ... although sometimes there is a mad glint in the back of her crooked eyes and an extra twist to her gap-toothed grin, and it's wise not to trust her then. She is most often called upon to aid in abortifacient potions, and while it sounds grotesque, if she lends her aid she really likes to have some of the blood returned to a Tansy patch for her to eat.

Magical Charm: Funeral Potion

For those who want to care for their own dead, and bury the body themselves in hallowed ground (or give it a funeral pyre) rather than leaving it to the harsh chemical depredations of the funeral industry which leave bodies unable to naturally rot, there is the problem of preserving the body for the few days it takes to get a funeral underway. To do this, first get some ice—dry ice is preferable—and pack that around the torso to retard internal bacteria and layer it under the body. It should be changed out as it melts. Then make a very strong decoction of Tansy tea. Boil as many flowers as you can find for an hour in water, and then strain and boil the tea down still further into a dark potion. (Do not let pregnant women touch this, or be part of this potion-making process.) Add 10 drops of Rosemary oil and 10 drops and Thyme oil for every pint of water. If the body of your loved one needs color, you can add a bit of red ochre, or sandalwood, or safflower. Paint the body with a thin wash of the tea, including gently and respectfully moving it into open orifices like the nose and ears. Wait an hour and then paint on another thin layer. For the funeral, remove the ice and lay out the Tansy-preserved body. While making the potion, chant this charm:

> Death, we give you your due,
> Yet Athanasia golden shall give us
> Time out of time to bid goodbye.

Teasel

Botanical Name: *Dipsacus fullonum* (Fuller's Teasel) or *Dipsacus sylvestris* (Wild Teasel)

Folk Names: Brushes-And-Combs, Barber's Brush, Card Thistle, Church Broom, Venus's Basin

Anglo-Saxon Name: Tæsel

Old High Germanic Name: Zeisala

Modern German Name: Wilde Karde

Modern Swedish Name: Kardvädd, Kardtistel

Modern Danish Name: Kartebolle

Modern Norwegian Name: Kardeborre

Deity Association: Holda

Height: To 6'

Season: Biennial

History: The Teasel is a weedy plant native to northern Europe, often found in hedgerows and waste places. The original Wild Teasel (*Dipsacus sylvestris*) was bred into the Fuller's Teasel (*Dipsacus fullonum*), a sturdier version grown to brush woolen cloth and raise the nap into a soft fuzziness. For centuries it was a symbol of the weaver's trade. Both versions are used medicinally in the same way.

Medicinal Uses: Teasel is good for rebuilding bones, joints and muscles when taken internally, especially for arthritis. It is especially indicated in autoimmune dysfunction of the joints such as in rheumatoid arthritis and lupus, and is used to treat the side effects of Lyme disease. Some people claim that it completely cures their Lyme disease. Teasel goes deeply into the immune system and can calm it down. It also rearranges and heals torn muscles and reduces adhesions and scarring, taken—unlike most such herbs—internally rather than externally. It gently tonifies the kidneys and releases water. One caveat is that when used to rework things during or after severe disease or dysfunction, Teasel can cause pain, fever, and a temporary worsening of symptoms during the first week, after which things clear up and go away entirely. One not uncommon "crisis point" side effect is for Teasel to funnel the toxins out through the genitals, causing temporary genital rashes. Hold on and don't let it get to you; it will pass.

Household Uses: Used in fulling cloth, where it is even better than modern wire.

Magical Uses: In Romany lore, the rainwater collected in the leaf joints of Teasels cures wrinkles and dark circles under the eyes.

Shamanic Uses: Special to Holda, who is one of the patrons of spinning and cloth-making. She also becomes angry at those who are lazy and do not keep their houses clean, and planting Teasels around the house will stay her wrath. They are also good to wave to banish small spirits that are plaguing your home; keep a bouquet of dried Teasels in the kitchen to keep it free of mischievous sprites that hide your things. Matthew Wood says that Teasel has an affinity with deer, so one could perhaps assume that Teasel could talk to marauding deer around your property and persuade them to keep away from your garden, if a hedge of Teasels were planted.

Affinity: Storm (bitter alterative). Use on Swamp conditions.

Point: GB 39

Plant-wight's Nature: Mistress Teasel is tall, plain and prickly. She has a "schoolmarm" or "old maid" feel to her—the prim-faced, critical teacher that everyone disliked. In point of fact, when you first make her acquaintance, she will probably start criticizing you, because that's her way. If you stay courteous and cheerful, she may decide that you aren't so horrendous after all, and deign to keep at least a few of her criticisms to herself. Flattery can help if it's at least somewhat sincere. However negative she may seem, Mistress Teasel's criticisms are actually usually pretty accurate, and they aren't personal—she's that way with everyone, and doesn't dislike you any more than most. If you can stand to hear yourself so described, it's worth it to let her pick apart your habits, your values, and your current projects. Her points will be objective, if not compassionate, and it's a useful perspective for the thick-skinned. If she doesn't bring it up, you can be sure that it's fairly flawless, anyway. When she works on the body, it's not always gentle—she tugs and yanks things into place, and while you're better off in the end, the process can feel painful while it's happening.

Medicinal Charm: Joint Vinegar

Teasel, for me anyway (like Nettles), really wanted to be tinctured in vinegar rather than alcohol, and not just because of Mistress Teasel's character. I expect that this may mean that it has some mineral effects that we don't know about. Anyhow, pack a jar with chopped Teasel leaves picked before the big jointed stems go up, and cover with Apple cider vinegar. Shake daily, saying the following charm, then strain and take 5 drops per day until all effects have ceased.

> *Stitch me sound and weave me well,*
> *Every bone and joint a spell*
> *Of wholeness, moving muscle's might,*
> *Teasel turn me round and right.*

Thistle

Botanical Name: *Onopordium acanthium*
Folk Names: Thrissill, Ass-wind, Cotton Thistle, Scotch Thistle
Anglo-Saxon Name: Distel

Old Norse Name: þistill
Old High Germanic Name: Distil
Modern German Name: Eselsdistel
Modern Swedish Name: Ulltistel
Modern Danish Name: Tidsel
Modern Norwegian Name: Eseltistel
Deity Association: Thor, Thrym and other frost-thurses
Height: To 10'
Season: Biennial
History: The official symbol of Scotland, and the totem of the Order of the Thistle which ordained Scottish knighthoods, Thistles are a pervasive weed common to all of Europe. In England, evil wizards were said to carry staves made of the tallest Thistles.
Medicinal Uses: Juice is said to relieve skin infections; root is said to diminish mucous discharges.
Household Uses: Thistle seeds produce an oil for cooking and lamps. Thistledown has been used to stuff pillows and quilts, and would be excellent for a magical protective pillow or quilt for children. Thistles make a good fodder for goats, who don't seem to mind the thorns. The alum-mordanted plant yields a yellow-green dye.
Culinary Uses: The large disk can be cooked like an artichoke; remove the petals and tough outer bracts and steam until tender. The stems can be blanched and eaten like asparagus.
Magical Uses: Often used as a curse plant, Thistle can also be used for protection. It is sacred to Thor, and can be used to invoke his wrath when those he watches over have been wronged. It is associated with the rune Thorn. Modernly, it is used for spells of endurance and healing for animals.
Shamanic Uses: Thistles have also been used by those who work with the Jotnar to do any magic regarding frost-thurses; it seems to have an affinity for their energy, especially the floating Thistledown. Spinning thread with Thistledown (and some other fiber, such as silk or very fine wool, to hold it) is good for thread-magic involving frost-thurses.
Affinity: Air (astringent). Use on River conditions.
Point: GV 25
Plant-wight's Nature: As you might expect, Thistles in general are prickly plants, and not just physically. Although they have a sense of humor (their botanical name means "donkey-farts", which they know and think is hilarious), it's often a mean one—they laugh at you while you're swearing and rubbing your stuck places. They are fiercely defensive and stubborn, with an attitude of "Try and take me!" For some reason, though, if you come for their fluff, splitting open their pods and letting it fly, they will be much more pliant and cooperative; perhaps because they know you are helping to spread their tribe. It takes a while to get Thistlewight to trust you in any way, but once you are their friend, they will be very protective of you in a rough, coarse way.

Magical Charm: Children's Protection

To give a child Thor's protection—especially good for children who are being physically bullied by their peers—make a small pillow and stuff it with Thistledown, and place it under their pillow. As you make the last stitch, say the following charm:

> *Jord's youth, you were young once*
> *As my child is; cheer and keep him*
> *Safe as steel against haters' harm.*
> *Let neither blow nor battering befall,*
> *But lend him luck and let him walk unscathed*
> *Through path as soft as Thistledown*
> *And free of thorns and fear.*

Thyme

Botanical Name: *Thymus vulgaris* or *Thymus serpyllum*
Folk Names: Thumus, Garden Thyme, Mother-of-Thyme, Serpolet
Anglo-Saxon Name: Organe, as they confused it with Marjoram and Oregano
Modern German Name: Thymian
Modern Swedish Name: Timjan
Modern Danish Name: Timian
Modern Norwegian Name: Timian
Deity Association: Frigga
Height: 6-18"
Season: Perennial
History: Thyme is a Mediterranean herb, long known to Greeks and Romans, but a latecomer to northern Europe. It may have been introduced to the rest of the continent with Charlemagne's herbal edicts. Some of the Anglo-Saxon herbals seem to refer to it, but not know it that well.
Medicinal Uses: Thyme was once used for diseases such as anthrax, typhoid, and whooping cough. Tincture is antiseptic and preservative; dead bodies were anointed with Thyme oil to keep them fresh for the funeral. Tea is good for hangovers and colds, and added to cough drops and syrups. A mild immune stimulant and strong expectorant, Thyme is good for loosening thick phlegm. It was an old standby treatment for whooping cough. The tea is also used for cold stomach flus with diarrhea. The essential oil is antibacterial and antifungal, and can be used topically as a chest rub or on infected wounds. Wild Thyme, or Mother-of-Thyme, is also a mild sedative as well as a good cold herb.
Household Uses: Plant around beehives, and decoct for a household disinfectant.
Culinary Uses: Thyme is one of the most useful of culinary herbs; it enhances almost any savory dish and combines well with almost any other herb. It is also one of the antiseptic-preservative herbs used to marinate and sauce meat, so that it would keep from spoiling immediately in times with no refrigeration.
Magical Uses: Purification and healing spells. Thyme is also protective, and medieval knights made use of it in their heraldic devices. It is used in funeral rites and protection from the Dead. It is used to commune with the garden devas, the small earth elementals who might hang out in your garden. Its antiseptic abilities were so strong that folk said it could be laid in bunches next to a pitcher of milk and prevent the milk from souring. Thyme also has strong affinities to dreaming; drinking Thyme tea is said to help with disturbed dreaming and bring the unconscious issues to the conscious mind.
Shamanic Uses: Thyme is beloved of Frigga, and offerings can be made to her of its leaves and blossoms. To honor her, one might plant a Thyme clock with different Thymes for the hours of the day. You can also plant Thyme in the shape of the rune Berkana/Beorc, her rune. Thyme is also good to drink or burn in order to stave off nightmares that may be caused by outside influences, especially for children.
Affinity: Fire (stimulant), Mountain (relaxant). Thyme is hot and versatile. Use on Earth, Storm, Air, or Swamp conditions.
Point: UB 13
Plant-wight's Nature: Thyme-wight, above all else, likes things clean and neat. He is in many ways like one of the archetypes of the classic domestic servant—fastidious and a little fussy, paying attention to detail, taking pride in good service, knowing his place and being content with it, having no ambition to do more than run a clean, neat place. He is a small, tidy plant and has no wish to be larger; he is happy to have people walk on him. He is disturbed by filth and untidyness; if you are doing a charm to work with Thyme-wight, the best thing you can do is to clean the area thoroughly first, including all

the pots, cups, and other implements you intend to use. He will respond more happily to being used in a freshly cleaned place.

Medicinal Charm: Clearing Out Clutter

When the yellow goo is having its way with your head and chest, call upon Thyme-wight to clean out the mess. Pour a pint of boiling water over an ounce of fresh-bruised or dried Thyme, add a tablespoon of honey and a tablespoon of linseed or olive oil for demulcency, and let steep. Drink a half-cup three times a day as needed, saying the following charm:

> *Time indeed that this invasion*
> *Shall trouble me and mine no more,*
> *Thyme for taking guests unwanted*
> *And their troubles out the door.*

Tormentil

Botanical Name: *Potentilla erecta* (formerly *Potentilla Tormentilla*)

Folk Names: Thormantle, Septfoil, Biscuits, Earthbank, Ewe Daisy, Flesh And Blood, Shepherd's Knot, Shepherd's Knappety, English Sarsaparilla

Anglo-Saxon Name: Seofenleafe ("Seven-Leaf")

Modern German Name: Blutwurz

Modern Swedish Names: Blodrot, Blodstilla, Fårarot, Solöjda

Modern Danish Name: Tormentil

Modern Norwegian Name: Tepperot

Deity Association: Thor

Height: 6-12"

Season: Perennial

History: A native weed of European wastelands, Tormentil's name comes from the Latin word for torment, referring to what it relieved. However, medieval Germans and Saxons heard it as "Thor-mantle", and it became one of his sacred plants.

Medicinal Uses: Specific. Highly astringent, high in tannins. Tormentil root decoction is a very safe but quite strong astringent, is used to reduce bowel inflammation and internal bleeding associated with diarrhea, and generally aids in bowel nourishment. The fluid extract is an excellent styptic for wounds. Recently, the rhizome has been found to stimulate the immune system. It has been used to stop asthmatic attacks.

Household Uses: As good as Oak bark for tanning, although Tormentil rhizomes are rarer and harder to find in quantity than Oak bark. The Saami people of Lapland use the red juice of the root, boiled down and thickened, as a red leather dye. It has been used in the Faroes islands for pig fodder.

Magical Uses: Used to invoke Thor's protection and for male sexual potency. Those who work with spirit-possession drink the tea to prevent against unwanted spirit invasions. The root is hung up in the home to keep away evil. Septfoil is a close relative of Cinquefoil—his rougher, less sophisticated brother—and has some of the same magical properties of Cinquefoil in magically clearing up issues of boundaries, lawsuits, and hierarchical relations; bring a leaf to the workplace to resolve problems.

Shamanic Uses: Root carved with runes of Thor's name can be used to take one to his hall Bilskrudnir, but only if one has prior permission to be in Asgard.

Affinity: Air (astringent), Earth (cooling), River (moistening). Use for Swamp, River, and Fire conditions.

Point: SP 1

Plant-wight's Nature: Tormentil appeared to me as broad, squat, dark-skinned, and muscular, a somewhat troll-like male figure with a deep guffaw. He speaks bluntly and punctuates his words with the occasional poke. He calls himself a "Binder", and demonstrated that by tying a firm knot in a skein of red thread which he seemed to yank out of nowhere with one muscled arm; I could only assume that this refers to his styptic tendencies. He seemed quite willing to be helpful, but also seemed to be a spirit who valued brute force over subtlety, so keep that in mind when using him in situations of delicate health.

Medicinal Charm: Bloody Flux

That's what they used to call it when there was blood in the diarrhea. Tormentil will stop it; simmer the aerial parts in water for half an hour, strain, and drink. Wait about 6 hours to see if it stops before taking another dose. The dose can be repeated every 6 hours for seven doses, but if it's going into the second day you may want to take other steps. Recite this charm over the tea as it simmers, or as you drink it:

> *Thor's Mantle fall over me, turn the torment,*
> *Septfoil, Seven-Leaf, seven times I say,*
> *Flesh and Blood be bound, flux fall away.*

Valerian

Botanical name: *Valeriana officinalis*

Folk names: Amantilla, Bloody Butcher, Capon's Tail, Cat's Valerian, Garden Heliotrope, St. George's Herb, Sete Wale, Vandal Root, Wayland's Wort, All-Heal, Setwall, Setewale,

Anglo-Saxon Name: Lost; the Latin version Ualeriane took over.

Modern German Names: Echter Baldrian, Katzenkraut

Modern Swedish Names: Vändelröt, Bösne, Vändelört, Vänört

Modern Danish Name: Baldrian

Modern Norwegian Name: Legevendelrot

Deity Association: Wayland

Height: To 6'

Season: Perennial

History: Valerian is native all over Europe and northern Asia; its name comes from the Latin verb "to be in health". Its smell either draws or repels people—it's has been described as a cross between stinky feet and cow manure—but once it was considered so fragrant that it was used in perfume and scented linens. (Perhaps, next to medieval unwashed bodies, musky Valerian was an improvement.) The Greeks called it Phu, as in "phew!" referring again to its smell. It has long been known to have a weird effect on cats and mice, who become intoxicated by it—the Pied Piper was said to have used it to make rats follow him.

Medicinal Uses: Valerian is a classic sedative for insomnia. The pharmaceutical Valium is the artificial analog of the traditional tranquilizer Valerian, which is the herbalist's second line of defense for relaxing someone and getting them to sleep, if the problem is too strong for Chamomile. It is especially good for people suffering from nervous overstress. It was used for epilepsy in ancient Roman times, and actually has a good effect on that disorder, as it is relaxing and antispasmodic, and good as a muscle relaxant.

Household Uses: Boosts growth of nearby plants. The composted leaves are rich in minerals.

Magical Uses: Protection, usually hung above doors and windows. Valerian has been used as a sacred asperger. It was referred to as one of the "witches' herbs" during the Middle Ages.

Shamanic Uses: This is traditionally referred to as "Wayland's Wort", and can be used to call on the power of Wayland/Volund the Ghost Smith. In olden times, when a horse had thrown a shoe and the owner didn't have the money to replace it, they would take it to a particular hill where the ghost of Wayland the Smith had his smithy, and leave the horse overnight with three coins; it would be shod the next morning. While most of us don't need this service, it might be a good thing to carry some Valerian root in your car and ask Wayland to help out with emergency mechanical problems.

Affinity: Mountain (relaxant). Use for Storm conditions.

Point: UB 15

Plant-wight's Nature: Grandfather Valerian comes to me as a tall, cloaked figure, more of a Wiseman than a warrior. His voice is low and gravelly, his touch is soothing, and he has a tendency to stroke your head in a way that makes your eyelids automatically droop. He tends to think that all belligerence and interpersonal problems could be cured if people would just calm down and relax, and that everything will be better after a good sleep. He reminds people that whatever may be wrong with them, sleep deprivation will make it worse. Even listening to him talk will sometimes put you out.

Medicinal Charm: Sleep in Desperation

When the demons in your head will not shut up during the day, and you fear that you will face hours of agonized worry when night comes, start early. Soak an ounce of finely chopped Valerian root in 12 ounces of cold water for 12 hours. If the scent and flavor revolts you, add Mint and/or Lemon Balm. Chamomile, of course, plays well with Valerian. Strain and drink one cup per hour, starting an hour before bedtime. As you drink, say the following charm:

> *Wayland's Wort, see well I weary*
> *Of words and wiles and sleepless ways,*
> *Sing me now to dream unwaking,*
> *Show the way to rest unbreaking,*
> *Let my eyes sink beneath your gaze.*

Vervain

Botanical Name: *Verbena officinalis*

Folk Names: Brittanica, Verbena, Enchanter's Plant, Holy Wort, Herba Sacra, Hiera Botane, Herb of Enchantment, Juno's Tears, Ironwort, Pigeon Grass, Pigeonwood, Simpler's Joy

Anglo-Saxon Name: Berbane

Modern German Name: Eisenkraut

Modern Swedish Name: Järnört

Modern Danish Name: Jernurt

Modern Norwegian Name: Jernurt

Deity Association: The Norns

Height: To 2'

Season: Perennial

History: Although many herbs were introduced into the British Isles by the Romans, Vervain is one that went the other way. Its common name comes from the Celtic *ferfaen*, meaning "repelling stones", for its gallstone-removing qualities. Its Latin name, meaning "beneficent green", was a term for sacred altar-plants in general, and its other Latin name, *hiera botane*, meant "sacred plant". In Welsh, it is *Ilysiaur Hudol*, or "enchanting herb".

Medicinal Uses: Vervain is made into an infusion as a sedative for nervous exhaustion, insomnia, depression, and the kind of stress peculiar to stubborn overachievers, especially when it shows up as stomach pains and painfully knotted muscles. It was once given for epilepsy. Vervain has an affinity for the neck muscles, and treats neck tics and spasms. It is a liver detoxifier, and is used to treat urinary tract infections and pass gallstones. The tincture encourages milk flow, stimulates uterine contractions during labor and menstruation, and is used for conditions dealing with excess uric acid, such as gout. Vervain has some hormonal effects, and is good for PMS with obsessive feelings and menopausal hot flashes. Poultice is used for eczema and sores. Ointment helps neuralgia, and mouthwash is used for mouth ulcers and soft gums.

Household Uses: Infusion is used as a hair tonic, usually mixed with Rosemary.

Magical Uses: An all-purpose powerful herb for protection, exorcism of spirits, vision-work, healing, peacefulness, and (should you want it) vows of chastity. Vervain was used for dream magic, and the Druids made their holy water with it. It is associated with opals, agates, and also bards and skalds, as it aids their performance. As such, it could be associated with the rune Os. Swordsmiths quenched their blades in Vervain water in order to strengthen the iron, so Vervain is a good blessing for blacksmiths and weapons-makers, and could be rubbed onto weapons to prevent breaking.

Shamanic Uses: Vervain is sacred to the Norns, and can be used to draw you to the Well of Wyrd. Brushed or sprinkled across a divination area, it helps in seeing more clearly the individual's wyrd. A second rune to use with it might be Peorth.

Affinity: Mountain (relaxant), Storm (bitter alterative). Use on Storm, and Air or Swamp as Vervain's bitters help the body absorb nourishment.

Point: GV 8

Plant-wight's Nature: She appeared to me first as Lady Vervain, tall and clad in midnight blue, dark hair to her shoulders, craggy rather than beautiful. Her dark eyes were penetrating under thick brows. Partway through the interview, she suddenly became Lord Vervain—not much different in looks, just a touch more masculinized, and with the same lean form and long bony fingers. Vervain is a Magician herb, and his sharp gaze looks through you and judges your motivations keenly. Like the other Magician herbs, he knows the magic of other plants as well as his own, and can explain the ones who you can't connect with, although he is secretive and keeps his own counsel. Meeting him once will not be enough for him to share any secrets—or much in the way of aid—with you; you will have to work with him more regularly than that.

Medicinal Charm: Birth And After

When a pregnant woman is near to her time, she should make up strong infusion of Vervain, enough for many cups. As it is not good-tasting, she may flavor it also with Mint or Lemon Balm, or other fragrant herbs, and sweeten it with honey. It should be made to taste good cold. As it is brewing, she should say the following charm:

> *Berbane, Brittanica, may my birthing be easy,*
> *Pigeon Grass, pluck the babe from my belly,*
> *Simpler's Joy, simple and sure my labor shall be,*
> *By all the ancestors, by the Norns' weighty will.*

A cupful should be frozen into ice and chipped into small pieces, and those kept in a bag in the freezer. When she gives birth, as the laboring belly will often not hold food or drink, chips of the Vervain ice should be given to her throughout. The room in which she labors should be kept warm, for Vervain cools bodies down. Then, after birth, she should drink a cupful every night before sleeping, both to calm her and to increase her milk flow for the inevitable wee-hour feeding.

Magical Charm: Well of Wyrd

This is a divination spell, to be done before casting runes or any other form of seeing, where you must look at the destiny of some person other than yourself. Make a bundle of Vervain stalks, dip them in well water, and asperge the area where you will be sitting, saying, "Herb of Enchantment, I chant thy names. Berbane, Ferfaena, Herba Sacra, Hiera Botane, I would see into the Well of Urda, I would will that Wyrd appear here." Then sit down and meditate for a while on the Urdabrunnr; if you can do *utiseta* to fare forth, all the better. Keep the Vervain in your lap as you go. When you come back, cast your runes forth and the way should be clear.

Viola

Botanical Name: *Viola tricolor* (Heartsease) and *Viola odorata* (Sweet Violet)

Folk Names: Banewort, Banwort, Bonewort, Bird's Eye, Garden Violet, Heart's Ease, Horse Violet, Johnny Jumper, Johnny Jump-Up, Kiss-Me-Over-The-Garden-Gate, Little Stepmother, Love Idol, Love-In-Idleness, Loving Idol, Meet-Me-In-The-Entry, Pensee, Thoughtflower, Tittle-My-Fancy

Anglo-Saxon Name: Banwyrt ("Bone Plant") for *Viola tricolor*; *odorata* unknown

Modern German Name: Acker-Stiefmütterchen

Modern Swedish Names: Styvmorsviol, Blålock, Käringtand, Natt och Dag, Sanct Ola tuppar, Skatblomma, Skatblomster, Skatros, Solblomma, Svalblomster, Tjäleblommor, Vildpensé (*Viola tricolor*); **Doftviol**, Luktviol (*Viola odorata*)

Modern Danish Names: Stedmoderblomst (*Viola tricolor*), Viol (*Viola odorata*)

Modern Norwegian Names: Stemorsblomst, Natt Og Dag (Viola tricolor), Marsfiol (Viola odorata)

Deity Association: Nanna

Height: 6"

Season: Perennial

History: The two Violets—Sweet Violet and Viola/Heartsease (often known today as Johnny-Jump-Up) have similar medicinal properties and were used throughout ancient Europe for a host of problems. The ancient Celts steeped them in goat's milk to increase female beauty, and the ancient Athenians used them as a potion against anger.

Medicinal Uses: The aerial parts are used for a wide range of skin disorders, from diaper rash to varicose ulcers, in a cream or poultice. An infusion is a good mouthwash for throat infections and wash for skin issues; a syrup made from the infusion is a good cough expectorant. Viola is a gentle laxative, safe for children in weak form; it tonifies and strengthens the blood vessels and is good for capillary fragility, especially in the retinas, and for people who bruise easily. It is also a gentle immune-stimulant, and contains salicylic acid in small amounts. Avoid high doses, as Viola contains saponins which can cause nausea when overdosed. Sweet Violet has been prescribed for breast and lung cancer, especially after surgery to prevent reoccurring. The famous Syrup of Violets is used for all these things.

Household Uses: A purple food dye is made from the petals of both flowers. They are also popular in potpourri.

Culinary Uses: Edible flower; candy and use in salads.

Magical Uses: These are traditional love-magic flowers; for love spells, carry Violas, or eat them, or plant them in the shape of a heart, or bury sea sand in the flower bed to bring back a sailor lover.

Shamanic Uses: Heartsease seems to be much loved by Nanna, Baldur's wife who followed him into death. It can be used as an offering to her.

Affinity: River (moistening), Earth (cooling). Use for Air conditions, Fire if there is also Air, and, surprisingly, Swamp, especially for lymphatics.

Points: TH 1 (Viola), SI 3 (Sweet Violet)

Plant-wight's Nature: Violet is indeed small and modest, as her Victorian associations would say, but there is a silent stubbornness to her that shows she is a survivor. She will come up between cracks, and even if you pull her out she'll quietly come back again next year. There is no arguing with her; giving her an order would result in a submissively lowered head, and then as soon as your back is turned she would unobtrusively do what she wanted anyway. Her sister Viola is cheerier and more outgoing, but conversely more sensitive and easily hurt; she cries loud tears while Violet simply waits patiently and gets her way. Viola desperately wants to be noticed and get attention; if you grow her in the garden, make sure to compliment her while she's in bloom ... every time that you pass by. Violet, of course, needs your approval not at all.

Medicinal Charm: Syrup of Violets

This takes a whole lot of flowers, so it is best done with access to them all at once. Pick the flowers of either Sweet Violet or the purplest of Violas, and pull off the petals. Pour boiling water over them, just enough to wet down and cover the flowers. Let steep, strain, and add sugar in twice the amount that you have liquid. As you stir it in, say the following charm:

> *Heartsease, hie thee to my hand,*
> *Violet, delicate maid of the land,*
> *Give me your blessings wherever I stand.*

When it has all dissolved, let it cool and keep refrigerated. Dosage is one spoonful daily until progress has been noted and then tapered off.

Viper's Bugloss

Botanical name: *Echium vulgare*

Folk names: Harespeckle, Blueweed, Blue Devil, Blue Thistle

Anglo-Saxon Names: Haranspical ("Hare Speckle"), Atterlothe ("Poison Hater")

Modern Swedish Name: Blåeld

Modern Danish Name: Slangehoved

Modern Norwegian Name: Ormehode

World Association: Jotunheim

Height: 40"

Season: Biennial

History: Viper's Bugloss is native to Europe from Scandinavia to Spain and eastwards to Asia Minor. It has since naturalized in North America. Its botanical name comes from the Greek words "viper" for the red spots on the stem, the

snake-head shape of the seeds, and the black snakelike root; and "ox's tongue" for the shape and roughness of the leaves. The Anglo-Saxons seem to have called this plant Harespeckle for its grey spots, but the herbalists also called it by the Greek name *ecios* and stressed its snakelike appearance and its supposed use for treatment of poisonous snakebite and any other poison.

As I describe in the chapter on the Nine Sacred Herbs, I went looking for the identity of the mysterious Atterlothe in an entirely different way than most people; I first lined up all the possibilities and asked the runes if Atterlothe was among them; getting a positive response, I asked which one it was, and the runes told me that it was Viper's Bugloss. Then I sat down with the different plants and called them by that name, and Viper's Bugloss responded. That's the difference between a historical herbalist and a shaman—when it comes down to it, there's nothing like going to the source. So this is Atterlothe, the "poison-hater", and one of the Nine Sacred Herbs.

Medicinal Uses: The tea breaks fevers, is a diuretic and expectorant, and is used for pain from inflammations. Once used for snakebite, although this seems to be more a magical than a medicinal cure. Seeds were decocted and mixed in wine "to comfort the heart and drive away melancholy"; i.e. as an antidepressant. Today, herbalists use the juice as a soothing emollient for sensitive skin, and in a poultice for treating boils. The leaf infusion is a general tonic and alterative, as well as a diuretic.

Household Uses: Add flowers to salads, or make into a cordial, or crystallize them. The root yields a red dye, but it requires a great quantity.

Magical Uses: Keeps away snakes. *Culpeper's Complete Herbal* describes Viper's Bugloss as follows: "It is a most gallant herb of the Sun; it is a pity it is not more in use than it is. It is an especial remedy against the biting of the Viper, and all other venomous beasts, or serpents; as also against poison, or poisonous herbs. Discorides and others say, That whosoever shall take of the herb or root before they be bitten, they shall not be hurt by the poison of any serpent."

Shamanic Uses: This is the plant of Jotunheim, the land of giants and trolls. It is a land of great mountains, great storms, great beasts, and great hunters, and this is the herb that hunts down sickness. To use, charge the plant with a spell of seek-and-destroy. I find that this is best done with a song (you don't have to be a great singer or carry a tune, Atterlothe doesn't care) which describes to the plant the nature of the prey, why this prey is its natural enemy and deserves to die, and gives it praise and thanks for its great hunting ability. Then you eat the herb, whole or in tea, and let it do its work.

Affinity: River (moistening), Earth (cooling). Use on Fire conditions.

Point: GV 15

Plant-wight's Nature: Viper's Bugloss is a hunter. He is tall and vigilant, and often appears as some sort of Jotun in animal skins and feathers and body paint. His head is held high and moves in short jerks, like a hunting bird or animal, constantly watching what is going on around him. His eyes miss nothing. He doesn't talk much, and pays little attention to humans in general, but he is usually quite willing to go on a seek-and-destroy mission. He is skilled at the art of utter focus, and is a good ally and teacher for medical herbalists who need to track down a difficult diagnosis.

Medicinal Charm: Tracking Inflammation

The best sung charm for this herb is, of course, the Atterlothe verse from the Nine Sacred Herbs charm. However, for those who can't handle the Anglo-Saxon, here is a modern English charm instead. Make a tea of the flowering tops of Viper's Bugloss—about 2 ounces of fresh herb or 4 of dried herb to a pint of boiling water—and as it steeps, say this charm over it:

> *Serpent who slays serpents, seek out my ills,*
> *Hare who outruns hares, swiftly may I heal,*
> *Hunter of the Mountain Land, track this painful heat,*
> *Seek the swelling and the ache, lay it dead at my feet.*

Then drink the tea, and it will seek out and bring down any inflammation you may have, from headache to fever, but as it is an expectorant it may also force you to cough out your illness, so be warned.

Watercress

Botanical Name: *Nasturtium officinale*
Folk Names: Scurvy Grass
Anglo-Saxon Name: Stune, Cyrse
Old High Germanic Name: Krasjon
Modern German Name: Echte Brunnenkresse
Modern Swedish Names: Källfräne, Källkrasse, Vattenkrasse
Modern Danish Name: Brøndkarse
Modern Norwegian Name: Brønnkarse
World Association: Niflheim
Height: To 2'
Season: Perennial
History: Watercress is found all over Europe and northern Asia, in streams of running water, swamps, springs, and other consistently wet places. It has been a traditional gathered food herb for millennia.
Medicinal Uses: Rich in Vitamin C and iron, Watercress is an excellent tonic, used for cases of scurvy and as an appetite stimulant. Watercress has a strong affinity for the lungs, warming up chilled bronchials in catarrh and bronchitis; make cough syrup from Watercress and honey. Culpeper advises the bruised leaves to be placed directly on the skin to combat freckles, pimples and other skin ailments. Watercress is an excellent diuretic, but large doses are purgative. Like Niflheim, Watercress can have its dangers; in the wild, it sometimes carries liver flukes.
Culinary Uses: Leaves are edible and Mustard-flavored.
Magical Uses: Watercress is associated with fresh-water elementals—the *näckar* (nixies), the *Sjörar* (lake-spirits), the *forskarlar* (falls-men). These creatures are often dangerous, and making an offering of Watercress can sweeten their disposition towards you. It has also been used as a protective spell for passing over water of any kind. Eating it regularly is supposed to help with precognitive gifts.
Shamanic Uses: This is the plant of Niflheim, land of water and ice and mists. Niflheim is one of the two primal worlds (the other being Muspellheim) and in its case "primal" has the connotation not just of "first" but of "unfinished". There is something shifting and malleable about Niflheim, and not just because a significant portion of it is ice floes and water. Solidity sometimes shifts there....not quickly, but slowly. Watercress can be used to do this kind of slow shifting of reality, seeing its icy solidity become watery and then as misty as the Land of Mists, and then, hopefully, you can shape it little by little.

If you place it under your tongue, you'll notice that it is peppery, even burns a little. Stay with the sensation. Breathe through it. See your breath come out as mist. Keep breathing, and working with the spirit of the plant, until reality starts to blur a little. This will not happen due to some psychedelic experience—Watercress is certainly not psychoactive—but only due to the work of the plant spirit. Conjure the problem that needs to be changed as if it was a solid object in front of you. Reach out and touch it. If your fingers slip off it, it is still ice—Isa, a blockage—and cannot be changed. Breathe and work at it longer. Sometimes it won't change—you aren't a god, some things are beyond your power—but sometimes it will start to become more malleable. Shape it quickly, and accurately, with a clear idea in your mind of what it should look like. Sometimes it shifts back on you, and you have to do it again. If three tries fail, give up.
Affinity: Fire (warming). Use on Earth conditions.

Point: LU 1

Plant-wight's Nature: Watercress came to me as an aquatic creature, almost dragonlike, swirling through the deep waters. While it was submerged, it glowed orangey in the water, but as it lifted into the air it darkened to blue. *I am fire of water*, it communicated to me. Indeed, Watercress is warm and spicy in spite of its cold aquatic tendencies—the fire that is fed by water instead of being doused by it. It scales were round and overlapped like the leaves of the plant. This tiny plant is more magically powerful than one would think, sending out tendrils of dragony energy into the rivers and swamps where it abides. It communicated that it should be eaten before swimming, in order to drown-proof yourself, and then mysteriously vanished back into the stream.

Medicinal Charm: Dragon's Breath

During the summer, gather Watercress and freeze it in ice cubes with a little water. When the winter cold has scalded your lungs and bronchitis has set in, thaw and gently heat a few of these, and add honey until it has thickened, reciting the charm below as you stir. Sip slowly to warm the lungs.

> *Land of Mists and Ice and Cold,*
> *Take back your chill, your bitter breath*
> *With each I draw, let dragon's fire*
> *Sweep the sky with summer's warmth.*

Weld

Botanical Name: *Reseda luteola*
Folk Names: Dyer's Yellowweed
Anglo-Saxon Name: Wealde
Middle Germanic Name: Walde
Modern German Names: Färber-Wau, Färber-Resede
Modern Swedish Names: Färgreseda, Vau
Modern Danish Names: Farvevau, Farvereseda
Modern Norwegian Name: Fargereseda
Deity Association: Frigga
Height: 1'
Season: Biennial
History: Weld is native to all of Europe and central Asia; examples of Weld-dyed cloth have been found is Swiss archaeological sites dating to well before the Greeks recorded it as a dye plant. It is a close sister to Mignonette (*Reseda odorata*), a well-loved medieval strewing herb known for its fragrance.

Medicinal Uses: Both Weld and her sister Mignonette have mild sedative qualities, and can be put in calming teas.

Household Uses: Classic yellow dye plant of our ancestors.

Magical Uses: Weld's yellow dye can be used to charge items to bring luck to women, especially young mothers and homemakers.

Shamanic Uses: As Woad seems to be Odin's, so Weld seems to be Frigga's. The two were dyed one over the other to make the famous Lincoln Green of Robin Hood's men. If you are up to making magical dyes, you can make both and ritually dye a natural-fiber garment, invoking them as a pair. Lincoln Green might be a good dye for a wedding-gift garment, as they are a long-married couple.

Affinity: Stone (sedative). Use on Fire conditions.

Point: GV 27

Plant-wight's Nature: Weld, like her sister Mignonette, appeared as a pale Willowy girl in her teens. Mignonette seemed shorter and more delicate, gowned in white; Weld was taller and a bit more sturdy and wore her famous yellow. Like Madder, both are household herb spirits in the sense that they will bless a home, and especially the makers of domestic crafts—cooking, basketry, fiber arts, etc. Weld is a woman's herb in the sense that she is most interested in women and rather ignores men entirely. She is especially interested in homemakers and mothers.

Magical Charm: Frigga's Fibers

For a blessing on a marriage, dye wool to a yellow color with Weld, and then weave or knit it into something that can be hung. When this is done, embroider the charm below onto the piece and give it to a newlywed couple to be hung above their bed.

> *Fensalir's Mistress, bless this bed*
> *And those who bind this bond together,*
> *And those who hold this hearth together,*
> *And those who ride this road together,*
> *May contentment haunt their days.*

Wheat

Botanical Name: *Triticum spp.*
Anglo-Saxon Name: Hwæte
Old Norse Name: Hveiti
Old High Germanic Name: Weizzi
Modern German Name: Weizen
Modern Swedish Name: Vete
Modern Danish Name: Hvede
Modern Norwegian Name: Hvete
Deity Association: Frey
Height: 3'
Season: Annual
History: Wheat, the highest gluten-producing grain of Europe, developed in the Near East and spread north during the Neolithic era. Many folk rituals grew up around the harvesting of Wheat, and the sacrifice of the Corn god; the last Wheat sheaf was made into a corn dolly and placed on the community altar. Einkorn Wheat (*Einkhorn hornemanii*), the Wheat of our Neolithic ancestors, is still available through specialty herb catalogs and can be grown in small patches for a celebration of or an offering to the remote ancestors.
Household Uses: Wheat flour and water makes the best flour paste.
Culinary Uses: The ultimate bread grain of Europe.
Magical Uses: Spells of fertility and money.
Shamanic Uses: Sacred to Frey, Wheat is the traditional sheaf on the harvest altar. It can be used with the runes Ing (which is the pictograph of a bound grain sheaf) and Fehu, indicating that one would like some money and that one is willing to sacrifice the labor necessary for it. Jera, the harvest rune, may also be added as one wishes. Ask Frey's blessing on such abundance.
Affinity: Harvest (nourishing), Stone (sedative), Earth (cooling). Use for Air conditions.
Point: CV 8
Plant-wight's Nature: Father Wheat is the last of the four Ancestral Fathers dealt with in this book. In contrast to Father Barley, Father Rye, and Father Oat, he seems much more youthful in spite of his long history—the archetypal young farmer with his first patch of land, fair and tanned and slender, generous and open-handed, with a new bride at home whose first child is swelling her belly. There is

something softer about him than about the other, tougher Fathers. He is a bringer of luck and wealth with his hair in long golden braids. While he dresses plainly in amber colors, gold occasionally drops from his fingers. He has the air of one who has been propitiated for so long that he doesn't pay much attention any more to individuals, unless they really catch his eye.

Magical Charm: Wheat's Wealth

Make whole Wheat homemade bread with any recipe; it doesn't matter so much what else is in it, although you might want to put in some honey for Frey. While kneading, sing: "Ancient Father who gives his life, heap our hold with gold and gifting." Very simple. The important part is afterwards: before baking, mark a double Fehu on the top of the loaf. This is two Fehu runes, one facing forward and one backward, with the vertical lines superimposed so that the "cow horns" are coming off both sides of the same shaft. Then bake and eat to bring wealth into the home.

Wild Rose

Botanical Name: *Rosa canina*

Folk Names: Dog Rose

Anglo-Saxon Name: Rosa

Modern German Names: Hunds-Rose, Hagebutte, Gewöhnliche Hecken-Rose

Modern Swedish Name: Nyponros, Stenros

Modern Danish Name: Rose

Modern Norwegian Name: Steinnype

Deity Association: Holda

Height: To 18'

Season: Perennial shrub

History: Wild Roses are native to all parts of Europe and Asia. Cultivated Roses, on the other hand, originated in ancient Persia and traveled across Asia Minor to Greece and then to Rome, where the Romans spread them with their empire. Still, the common folk looked to the unaltered, large-hipped Wild Rose as they were less interested in large lavish crimson blossoms for feasts and parades, and more interested in nourishing Rose hips and no necessity for coddling.

Medicinal Uses: Rose hips are cooling and drying, and have been used for bloody coughs (like tuberculosis) and to reduce autoimmune inflammation. Rose also helps the circulatory system. Splash eyes with Rosewater for conjunctivitis. Take the hip syrup as a winter tonic for its vitamin content. Rose hips are used to counteract the effect that antibiotics have on the digestive tract, and also on the vagina—e.g. yeast infections. The leaves, on the other hand, are used to ameliorate chemotherapy. Rose hips are often added to other herbal compounds for diarrhea, colic, or coughs. It flavors medicine and adds Vitamin C. Rose oil (the real thing, not fake stuff) is an antidepressant; use in baths or steam.

Household Uses: Rosewater is used for cleaning, cosmetics, and some cooking.

Culinary Uses: Rose hips are made into syrups, jam, and wine, petals into jams and jellies.

Magical Uses: Spells of love, calm, and luck.

Shamanic Uses: Sacred to Holda, it was said that dog Roses could not be picked without her permission, or the bush would attack you. Make offerings to a Wild Rosebush (by fertilizing or watering it, not picking the flowers) in her honor, to gain her aid. Mother Holda is especially kind to travelers lost in a strange place.

Affinity: Earth (cooling), Air (astringent). Use for Fire and River conditions.

Point: CV 12

Plant-wight's Nature: As you might expect, the Rose spirit is proud, haughty and temperamental, and Wild Roses even more so. They bear thorns for a reason, and are perfectly willing to snag you for the fun of it. Use as much sincere flattery as you can bear with the Wild Rose spirit, and be wary of her turning on you out of some pique or imagined slight. Cultivated Roses are more passive and pliable, but still share much of the nature of their wild cousins.

Medicinal Charm: Rosewater

When one has had to resort to modern antibiotics, and they have ravaged your system, bring it all gently back into line with homemade Rosewater. Use it to tone your skin, rehabilitate the vagina, and redecorate your guts with friendly flora again. Pick the petals of Roses—unsprayed, and old-fashioned species are best. Pinch off the bitter white heel of each petal. Then refer to the directions in the Oak entry on making a quick home still; repeat them, but with Rose petals. You have to keep checking the Rosewater that collects, though—there will come a point where it will stop concentrating and start diluting, so it's better to end it sooner than later. While it distills, say this charm:

> Holda's daughter, blossom of beauty,
> Ageless wisdom beyond my ken,
> I am stripped and bare,
> Make my passages fair once again.

Willow

Botanical Name: *Salix alba*

Folk Names: Saille, Osier, Saugh Tree, Tree of Enchantment, Witches' Aspirin, Withy

Anglo-Saxon Names: Welig, Sealh

Old Norse Name: Viker

Old High Germanic Name: Walg

Modern German Names: Silber-Weide, Weiß-Weide

Modern Swedish Name: Pil

Modern Danish Name: Pil

Modern Norwegian Name: Hvitpil

Deity Association: Jormundgand, Laufey

Height: To 80'

Season: Perennial tree

History: Willow trees are native to temperate wetlands all over Europe and western Asia. White Willow bark is a very old remedy; Willow and Meadowsweet were the best sources of salicylin. The Willow's name has a roundabout connection with witchcraft; it comes from the Indo-European root *wik*, meaning flexible, and gives us also *wicker*. Eventually, during the Catholic medieval period, flexible became associated with morally flexible, and thus *wicked*. In old British country slang, *wick* still means green and alive. Green George, a central European Green Man figure, is personified by a man dressed in Willow boughs who drives three nails into a large Willow and then tosses them into a river, thus driving out all evil from the people.

Medicinal Uses: The stem bark of the White Willow is the original aspirin: painkiller and fever-reducer. It is an anti-inflammatory and antiseptic. The active ingredient, salicin, is converted into salicylic acid by the kidneys and as such is a good purifier of urinary tract infections when excreted. Unlike commercial aspirin, Willow tea does not assault the stomach and is easier to take over a longer period of time.

Household Uses: Makes the best quality artist's charcoal. Used for fine basketry.

Magical Uses: Lunar magic and healing magic. Willow wands were a favored amulet against thunder and disease. Willow was considered a plant of immortality because the tiniest cutting can be used to bring forth another plant. Among the Greeks, it is sacred to Hecate and Hermes Psychopompus, as well as Persephone, and is supposedly a gateway to the Underworld (that would be Hades, not Helheim). The Celts linked it with the moon, and women's magic. It has been associated with rock crystal.

Shamanic Uses: Willow trees are much liked by the third child of Loki and Angrboda, the great Midgard Serpent. Willow is also much liked by Jormundgand's grandmother Laufey, the mother of Loki who loves trees, and Willows can be planted in her honor. She is more linked to the healing rather than the magical side of Willow, and is invoked for healing with its bark.

Affinity: Stone (sedative), Mountain (relaxant), Earth (cooling), Air (astringent). Use on Fire conditions.

Point: GV 14

Plant-wight's Nature: Grandmother Willow is a mysterious singing nymph, feminine-to-androgynous, slender and pointy-faced with long, long fingers and draping hair of palest green. Usually she appears young, but sometimes comes as a very thin, gnarled old woman. She sings and hums a great deal, with a voice that sometimes sounds as if it is coming through water, and always moves as if she is dancing. She has appeared to some people as blind, with skin over her eye sockets, feeling them up with her long fingers; to others she has large green eyes that do not focus on you. Either way, she likes to touch people and seems to get most of her information about them that way. She communicates more through stroking than through her voice. Grandmother Willow is watery and cool, but there is something vaguely dangerous, like the water-nymph who might drag you down and drown you, about her. However, she is helpful more often than not.

Magical Charm: Boundaries

Jormundgand's protection can be invoked by making a talisman of Willow wood with Ior, the Rune of the Serpent, on it. This charm will create clear boundaries in one's life. It is also a good charm for walkers between worlds, those who travel in liminal spaces between one thing and the next, and need not to get lost or confused as to which is what reality. As the living boundary between Midgard and the other worlds, Jormundgand can give that gift. Carve a ring of Willow wood, put the rune Ior on it, and pour salt water over the Willow charm to seal the magic. Say the following charm over it:

> *Serpent separate, lay the lines clear,*
> *Be boundary between in the Willowy water.*

Medicinal Charm: Ache Tea

For all your pains, but especially for headache. Pour a pint of cold water over two heaping spoonfuls of Willow bark, and let stand for 12 hours, preferably overnight. Say the following charm over it:

> *Lady of the Leafy Isle,*
> *Water-Woman, Fire-Bearer,*
> *Drive the fire from my nerves*

As you cooled Cruel-Striker's brow.

In the morning, strain and drink. You will probably want to sweeten it with honey or sugar, as it's pretty bitter. This is the equivalent of one to two aspirin, but will not harm your stomach in the way that concentrated aspirin might.

Woad

Botanical Name: *Isatis tinctoria*
Folk Names: Isatan, Blueweed
Anglo-Saxon Name: Wad
Old Norse Name: Weede
Old High Germanic Names: Waido, Wede, Weit
Modern German Name: Färberwaid
Modern Swedish Name: Vejde
Modern Danish Name: Vajd
Modern Norwegian Name: Vaid
Deity Association: Woden, Odin
Height: To 3'
Season: Biennial
History: Woad is native to western continental Europe and the British Isles; it was first cultivated by the Celts—Gauls and Britons—who smeared themselves with Woad-dyed paste before going into battle, in the hopes that it would put them into a berserker rage. After the Romans drove the Celts back, the Germanic peoples moved in, and picked up the cultivation of Woad from the surviving Celts, dedicating it to the leader of the berserk soldiers, Woden. (His name is not etymologically related to Woad per se, as it comes from a root-word meaning "blue", but it might have seemed awfully appropriate to the Germans, who were as fond of word-play as the Celts.) Woad was the primary blue dye of northern Europe until the seventeenth-century indigo trade took over.
Medicinal Uses: Woad is mildly toxic when taken internally (although not hallucinogenic, as some have claimed). On the surface of the skin, however, it is reasonably safe, and the leaves are used as a poultice to stop bleeding and heal wounds, which may have been part of the reason why warriors in some cultures smeared it on their bodies before going into battle.
Household Uses: Classic blue dye plant of the northern peoples. As its indocin content is lower than that of indigo or Japanese indigo, its blue is greyer and dustier.
Magical Uses: Smeared on the body as a charm for courage. Woad dye can be mixed with any floury base, or paste of dried plant material. It is the mark of warriors.
Shamanic Uses: Sacred to Odin and his warriors, Woad was used by the fighting men of many cultures for their pre-battle ritual body paint. It can be used again in this way, on body or cloth, for any sort of battle where courage is needed, not just one where blood is shed.
Affinity: Air (astringent). Use on River conditions.
Point: SP 13
Plant-wight's Nature: I expected Woad to come to me as a warrior, but instead he was a short, squat man covered in rattling charms, with a drum which he struck with the butt of a spear. His hair stood stiffly upright with yellow mud, and he was covered in sigils of blue. Woad is a war-shaman, the one who smeared the blue paint onto the warriors and blessed them with strength and skillful swords, and luck enough not to get killed. He drummed the arrows away from them, sang curse-songs at the enemy from the sidelines, and hauled the wounded off the field to salve their bodies. Strongly protective, Woad is only interested in warrior types—the other folk have enough spirits to guard them, he says. His definition of who counts as a warrior is unclear to me; if you were other than a traditional

military person (who he would definitely aid and bless) you would have to check with him to see if you counted.

Magical Charm: Battle Woad

If for whatever reason you feel the need for Odin's blessing while battling some enemy, smear some Woad on yourself. The making of Woad is best learned about from herbal dyeing books such are listed in detail in Appendix III; suffice it to say that mixing a small quantity of the liquid dye with any neutral powder (lightweight flour, cornstarch, etc.) will make a paste that can be smeared on. While you are drawing sigils on yourself, say the following prayer:

> *I bind myself today to Woden,*
> *His hand to guide me,*
> *His wisdom to teach me,*
> *His eyes to watch over me,*
> *His ears to hear me,*
> *His words to give me speech,*
> *His will to use me,*
> *My heart always, ever and always, to love Him.*
> *I bind myself today to Woden.*
> *(Written by Galina Krasskova, Odin's woman)*

Wood Sorrel

Botanical Name: *Oxalis acetosella*

Folk Names: Cuckoo Bread, Cuckowe's Meat, Fairy Bells, Sourgrass, Sour Trefoil, Stickwort, Stubwort, Surelle, Three-Leaved Grass, Wood Sour

Anglo-Saxon Name: Geaces Sure ("Cuckoo Sorrel")

Old Norse Name: Skósúra

Modern German Names: Wald-Sauerklee, Kuckucks-Klee

Modern Swedish Names: Harsyra, Surklöver, Gökmat, Harväppling

Modern Danish Name: Skovsyre

Modern Norwegian Name: Gjøkesyre

Deity Association: Walburga

Height: 6"

Season: Perennial

History: Found in shady woodlands throughout the northern hemisphere, Wood Sorrel has always been a common woodland foraging plant.

Medicinal Uses: The astringent diuretic infusion treats fevers and urinary problems and is prepared as a soothing external wash for rashes and boils. Wood Sorrel is dangerous in large quantities, and should not be used for patients with rheumatoid arthritis, gastritis, colitis, or chronic water retention.

Household Uses: The leaf juice is use to remove stains.

Culinary Uses: Young leaves are added to salads.

Magical Uses: Placed in sickrooms to clear the air of evil spirits.

Shamanic Uses: The unnamed goddess that we call Walburga, who may also be Ostara the goddess of spring, is associated with the tiny humble Wood Sorrel, and carrying or eating it can bestow her protection. She is especially good at hiding people in the woods.

Affinity: Earth (cooling), Stone (sedative), Air (astringent). Use on Fire, River, and Swamp (it's a non-bitter alterative).

Point: UB 10

Plant-wight's Nature: Cuckoo-Bread is a tiny wood-sprite, giggling and hiding behind trees, bouncing about, so unformed as to be largely genderless. Cuckoo-Bread-wight isn't very bright, but is extremely cheerful. If you can cope with the short attention span, Cuckoo-Bread-Wight can be asked to call out to you when you are traipsing through the woods, and intend to pass one of its plants on the way back (preferably one in a prominent place) and want to make sure you're on the right path. On the other hand, you might not want to entrust such an important thing to such a scatterbrained wight. Another use for Cuckoo-Bread-Wight is to point out faeries; if you think that you are being followed or spied upon by Fey Folk, you can ask Cuckoo-Bread, who can not only see faery-folk, but will innocently and cheerfully point them out—"Why, of course, can't you see that elf hiding behind that tree, silly?" Don't worry about repercussions from faery to plant-wight; the Alfar are all aware of Cuckoo-Bread's nature and will simply sigh, grind their teeth, and shrug it off.

Magical Charm: Woods Hiding

Take a bit of Wood Sorrel and place it over your heart, under your clothing. Then silently explain to Cuckoo-Bread that you need to hide quietly in the woods or you will be caught. This is one of the few things that he understands, and he will be silent. Then say the following charm, and Walburga will work through Cuckoo-Bread to hide you.

> *Walburga's wight, hide me from now*
> *To Walburga's Night, when I shall come forth*
> *And fairly find my enemies fled.*
> *Guard me, gentle Cuckoo-Bread.*

Wormwood

Botanical Name: *Artemisia absinthium*

Folk Names: Absinthe, Old Man, Old Woman, King's Crown, Wermod, Green Ginger

Anglo-Saxon Name: Wermod, Wyrmwyrt ("Worm Plant")

Old High Germanic Name: Werimuota

Modern German Name: Wermut

Modern Swedish Names: Malört, Maerta, Mallukt, Mårta

Modern Danish Name: Malurt

Modern Norwegian Name: Malurt

Deity Association: Hel, Mordgud

Height: To 5'

Season: Perennial

History: Wormwood is found in some form all over the entire northern hemisphere, from Mexico to Siberia. It is the bitterest common herb known. It has religious significance in Greek and Hebrew custom, and was said to have been given to human herbalists by the centaur Chiron, who was taught in turn by Artemis (thus Artemisia).

Medicinal Uses: As its name suggests, Wormwood expels intestinal worms from humans and animals, and the decoction has been used as a wash for external parasites such as lice and scabies. It is also a uterine stimulant, and is used in stalled labor, so don't give to pregnant women in any other situation. Breastfeeding women should also avoid it, as the thujone can be passed on through their milk. It is a tonifying bitter, and has been used for liver problems, specifically a cold, low-functioning liver as opposed to a hot overworked one. A classic Wormwood liver symptom is a constant bitter taste in the mouth that interferes with eating. A very light infusion of Wormwood is used as a digestive tonic against flatulence and indigestion, in cases of a cold stomach. However, too much "deranges the stomach" and a strong infusion can produce nausea. Matthew Wood recommends a dose of two drops of tincture twice a week.

Wormwood can soothe nervousness and irritability, but don't take it often—it can create problems if a habit is formed. The Wormwood plant-wight doesn't like being used often, and is offended by habituation. There is really no way to get past the horrid taste, either; that's the price you pay for working with this herb. Emotionally, Wormwood is said to help those who are cold and deadened by their bad life experiences.

Household Uses: Powder for moth repellent, infuse and spray for disinfectant and herbal pesticide on plants. Wormwood is antiseptic; the leaves resist rot, and food can be wrapped in them to keep it longer without refrigeration (although it may smell like Wormwood).

Magical Uses: Burned in an incense, it aids in psychic powers and protects from snakebite. Supposedly, Wormwood counteracted the effects of poisoning by Hemlock and Toadstools, but I wouldn't bet your life on that. The Greeks considered it, as with all the Artemisia, to be sacred to Artemis; supposedly she presented it to Chiron the centaur to teach him healing herbs, and it became the sign of the herbalist from then on.

Shamanic Uses: Wormwood is burned to call on the spirits of the Dead. It is a useful Helheim recaning herb; Mordgud has a special liking for it, and it can be burned to please her and propitiate her into letting you enter. Of course, if her mistress doesn't want you in, you're out of luck, but it can be worth trying. In or out of Helheim, burn it to get the attention of the dead.

Wormwood can also be used as a mildly hallucinogenic drug in tincture form, due to its levels of thujone; the process and effects are described below. If you use it, you might want to ritually call on Hela for protection first. As with any plant that you are using as an entheogen, get on good terms with the plant spirit first, and obey any rules that they give you about the plant's usage.

Affinity: Storm (very bitter alterative tonic), Mountain (relaxant), Fire (pungent). Use for Swamp and Earth conditions.

Point: LV 3

Plant-wight's Nature:

The first plant spirit I had a firm working relationship with, Grandfather Wormwood is an earthy practical spirit who taught me the correct way to approach and work with entheogenic plants and their spirits. Wormwood is a true patriarch in the way Grandmother Henbane is a matriarch; he is very wise and knows much more than he lets on. I have seen him as a bearded, green-tinted, "tree-man" that reminds me a little of the Green Man images appearing in art and architecture. He likes people to know their place in his rather ordered, hierarchical view of the world. He is not against teaching people who come to him, but he will not directly come out and say so; you have to allow him time to come around to the point. He knows what he's doing and will test your patience to see how serious you are about learning from him. He, more than the other plants I've worked with, likes ritualistic behavior; there are things to say when gathering the herb, things to say when brewing, things to say when watering, all kinds of little prayer songs for him and his children. He is a stable presence to have in your life, no-nonsense and grounding.

Most entheogenic plants aren't tasty, but Wormwood is in a class of its own; it is one of the most bitter plants known, second to Rue, and even a few sips of weak tea brewed from the dried herb can be almost too much to handle. This bitterness is part of Grandfather's lessons; life isn't always very pleasant, but sorrow and bitterness have to be accepted as part of the experience. Wormwood has purgative qualities, serving much the same function as grief does by clearing out what no longer belongs in the body; continuing the comparison with grief, Wormwood has toxic qualities that aggravate the body when too much has been ingested in too short a space of time. It is an herb with moderate physical effects and potent spiritual ones.

Though generally practical almost to a fault, Grandfather Wormwood has a joyful and healing side that is evidenced in Wormwood's inclusion in Absinthe; Wormwood is the ingredient that gives the drink its (in)famous effects, carried by thujone, a constituent also found in varieties of Sage and a few other plants. Absinthe drinkers were featured in many works of art in the first part of the twentieth century, often depicted sitting and staring into space. Drinking Wormwood tea, it becomes clear why they were depicted thus. Wormwood enhances the senses just enough that everything seems brighter and richer; you just want to relax and take it all in. It is quite different from the heightened senses brought on by marijuana; Wormwood gives me a feeling of well-being, peace, and down-to-earth contentment; it makes me wonder why I haven't thought to sit still and just look at things before.

Wormwood, both plant and spirit, are beneficent, healing, and above all practical; beneath the apparently straightforward personality is a deeper and more complex being that will always be many steps ahead of you.   *-Silence Maestas*

Magical Charm: Divination Tea

Before a major divination, one can call upon the power of Wormwood to aid the endeavor. We would caution against using this for client-based on-the-spot divination; it is better for divining done on one's own time, when there are no time limits or the distractions of other people. If this is done for another person, do it on your own time and tell them about it later. Brew a very mild tea of Wormwood—a few teaspoons infused in a pint of boiling water for only about ten minutes—and take a few sips. Then say the following charm, taking a sip between each line:

> *Wermod, Wyrmwyrt, weave the way,*
> *Open the path and point me on,*
> *I dive into the dark of fate,*
> *Rend the veil and let darkness be gone.*

Make sure to have the rest of the tea with you while you read, and keep sipping it. If you begin to feel nausea, stop. Take the reading slowly; ponder thoroughly on each part of it.

Yarrow

Botanical Name: *Achillea millefolium*
Folk Names: Milfoil, Achillea, Bad Man's Plaything, Carpenter's Weed, Devil's Nettle, Eerie, Field Hops, Gearwe, Hundred-Leaved Grass, Knight's Milfoil, Knyghten, Nosebleed, Old Man's Pepper, Sanguinary, Seven Year's Love, Soldier's Woundwort, Stanch Weed, Thousand-Seal, Herbe Militaris, Yarroway
Anglo-Saxon Name: Gearwe
Old High Germanic Name: Yeru, Garawa
Modern German Name: Gemeine Schafgarbe
Modern Swedish Names: Rölleka, Backhumle, Farfars Tobak, Flengräs, Fraggört, Karibacka,

Per i backe, Olsmässgräs, Ölgräs

Modern Danish Name: Røllike

Modern Norwegian Name: Ryllik

Deity Association: Hel

Height: 12"

Season: Perennial

History: Yarrow is native to all of Eurasia. During medieval times, it was thought to be one of the plants of the Devil; the association with Hel became an association with "hell" in the eyes of the now-Christian populace, and growing Yarrow in one's garden could be cause for accusation of witchcraft. The botanical name comes from a legend about Achilles, who supposedly used it to stanch the wounds of his soldiers.

Medicinal Uses: A wonderful multi-purpose medicinal herb, Yarrow cleanses the system and is good before fasting. Use the infusion as a mouthwash for toothache, a phlegm reducer for colds, and inhale steam for asthma and hay fever. The leaves encourage clotting of blood, and can be used to stanch nosebleeds in an emergency. A poultice or powdered herb on cuts and wounds encourages blood-stanching, including cuts deep enough to involve some arterial blood, and taking it internally in tea helps with hemorrhaging of the lungs, intestines, and uterus.

A Yarrow tea enema will aid in drying up hemorrhoids and chronic low-grade rectal or colonic bleeding. It is also an anti-spasmodic for stomach cramps, and aids digestion. Yarrow is an anti-inflammatory, promotes perspiration, and has been used to break fevers. It is a peripheral vasodilator, opening up surface blood vessels and enabling more blood to be circulated. The oil is used to massage inflamed joints, or put into a chest rub with Thyme, Hyssop, Mint, and eucalyptus. It will heal burns, including radiation burns, and has been used to bring people out of comas from brain aneurysm—checking the internal cerebral hemorrhaging.

Yarrow is a uterine stimulant and can be used in combination with other herbs to bring on delayed menstruation; however, since it also retards bleeding, menses brought on in this way may have extra cramping until the Yarrow is discontinued. It has also been used to get menstrual blood out quicker and prevent over-hemorrhaging, sometimes along with Shepherd's Purse. It should not be taken by pregnant women.

Household Uses: Chopped leaves added to the compost pile will speed decomposition. Planted next to other plants, it stimulates their immunities. In Sweden, it is used to beer, and legend says that such beer is extra intoxicating, although Yarrow is not an entheogen/hallucinogen.

Magical Uses: Yarrow aids in heightening psychic powers, is used in love spells, and brings knowledge. This plant is so associated with divination around the world that it can be found both in divinatory folk spells in Britain, and as the I Ching plant in China. The leaves are used in spells to dispel melancholy, and it is also a funereal herb. It has been used for psychic protection, and in a peculiarly modern twist, as protection of the subtle senses from the effects of electromagnetic energy in the environment. Its names of Soldier's Woundwort and Herba Militaris have also given it a reputation for a good talismanic herb for veterans suffering from PTSD. As a blood-stancher, it has been used magically to prevent accidents; Matthew Wood suggests putting a sprig in the toolbox to bless tools for this purpose.

Shamanic Uses: It is said that "where the Yarrow grows, there be one who knows." Yarrow is much loved by Hel, and seems to be one of her herbs. Its ability to speed decomposition reminds us of her modern title, "Mother Rot". Yarrow is used to ask a boon of knowledge from Hel, whether from one of her dead folk or from her own stores of wisdom. It can be eaten, drunk, burned, or asperged. One can also use Yarrow to call on Hel during battle circumstances to preserve one's life, but in return if you are allowed to live, you must give up all hope of Valhalla and dying in battle, and return home to die a straw death and go to her realm.

Affinity: Storm (bitter alterative), Fire (stimulant, but an weird anomalous one that actually cools the body by pulling blood away, so it's a Cold Fire herb), Air (astringent), Stone (sedative). Use on Fire, Earth, River, and Swamp conditions.

Point: UB 17

Plant-wight's Nature: Grandmother Yarrow is one of the Wisewoman plants. A sorceress among plant-wights, she appears as a slight woman with long white hair in many thick plaits, old but somehow ageless, dressed in white. Her eyes are luminous grey; moonlight falls about her. She holds many wisdoms about all sorts of magics, but will not tell just anyone; even more than being an acquaintance or a friend, you must formally apprentice yourself to her for a time before she will impart her knowledge. It will be intuitive and mysterious, so if you're the sort who likes things cut-and-dry, don't bother her. For those with the talent, she is especially good at training her apprentices to intuitively learn the healing qualities of a plant by merely touching them. If you offend her, she will simply withdraw and not speak to you again.

Medicinal Charm: High Blood Pressure Tea

Infuse 1ounce of Yarrow flowers, half an ounce of Nettles, and half an ounce of Linden flowers in a quart of boiling water. Drink a cup morning and evening, saying the following charm:

> *Sanguinary, Seven Years, slow the red stampeding flow*
> *Needlewort and lovely Lind, run the rivers in their rows,*
> *Eerie, Eerie, Yarroway, let them never burst their banks,*
> *Devil's Nettle, Fire Nettle, Lady Tree, I give my thanks.*

Magical Charm: Spouse-Finder Pillow

This is a traditional British charm. Dry an ounce of Yarrow and sew it up in a bit of flannel, and place it under the pillow before sleeping. Recite the following charm and one's dreams will be of one's future lover:

> *Thou pretty herb of Venus's tree,*
> *Thy true name it is Yarrow;*
> *Now who my bosom friend must be,*
> *Pray tell me thou tomorrow.*

Yew

Botanical Name: *Taxus baccata*
Folk Names: Idho, Eoh, Eow
Anglo-Saxon Name: Yr, Eoh
Old Norse Name: Ýr, Eih
Old High Germanic Name: Iwa
Modern German Name: Eibe
Modern Swedish Name: Idegran
Modern Danish Name: Taks
Modern Norwegian Name: Barlind
Deity Association: Ullr, Hel
Height: To 80'
Season: Perennial tree

History: Native to all parts of Europe, the Yew-tree was prized for bows, quarterstaves, and axe handles. The tools of Otzi the Iceman, over 5000 years old, were handled with Yew wood. As it is poisonous and used generally for weapons of killing and tools3 of cutting, it was always associated with death.

Medicinal Uses: Yew is generally poisonous, and should not be used without the supervision of an experienced herbalist. A very mild decoction is sometimes used topically as a sedative for nervous anxiety and hysteria.

Household Uses: Smoldering Yew leaves will keep away flying insects.

Magical Uses: Raising the Dead.

Shamanic Uses: Sacred to both Hel and Ullr, whose hall was "Yew-Dale". A Yew talisman will bring his blessing upon a hunting venture, especially if it is carved with the rune Eihwaz, the Yew staff. With the rune Ear upon it, it can be used to propitiate Hela and allow you to speak with dead people.

Affinity: Mountain (relaxant), Stone (sedative), Earth (cooling). Use on Fire and Storm conditions, but only under the care of an experienced herbalist who knows this tree.

Point: ST 45

Plant-wight's Nature: Grandfather Yew looks at you through slitted eyes and says little. In fact, silence is his nature. Tall and dark-bearded, with streaks of silver in his hair, his glare can freeze you in your tracks. He is stern and grim, but a relentless protector if you can gain his friendship, which is difficult. As a wight of war and death, he is comfortable in cemeteries and enjoys being made into weapons of any kind. He likes to be propitiated with the deaths of actual small animals—he is rather old-fashioned that way. If you make or buy a bow of Yew-wood and actually use it for hunting, and wish his blessing on it, make sure to give him part of the kill—perhaps a bone buried at the base of a Yew tree, or if you have one on your property, nail the skull to it.

Magical Charm: Bow Blessing

Grandfather Yew is not to be called upon by beginners. First, if you want his blessing for hunting, you had best prove yourself competent. He isn't interested in someone who is just going to hang a bow on the wall and brag. Bring him an actual sacrifice of some kind, if only a squirrel or bird—he seems partial to birds—that you have hunted yourself, with any weapon. Mark the bow with its blood, and say:

> *Yr, Yr, here I blood you,*
> *Deadly my draw with you in my hand,*
> *Eoh, Eoh, here you bless me,*
> *On track and trail across the land.*
> *Ullr lend me luck and skill,*
> *My sight be keen, and clean my kill.*

Entheogenic Plants

Here we have to address those herbs that our ancestors used to put themselves into altered states, both for religious and for shamanic work. This is a controversial subject, but there is really no way to avoid it in a Northern Tradition herbal. These plants were among the most sacred of all, and to dishonor them is to dishonor the ancestors that used them.

Today, many of these plants are illegal, and all are looked at askance by mainstream society. The ancestors put a much lower value on immediate physical safety than we do, and considered it reasonable to take a certain amount of risk for many of the important things in their life. They also had a higher death rate, and they considered that to be merely part of the package. The values of our society are somewhat different now, and protecting people from their own stupidity is more acceptable; thus, entheogens (the word means *those substances that connect us with the Gods*) are deemed too dangerous. And for most people, they probably are.

On the other hand, shamans the world over have used them to visit other worlds, and they are one of the legitimate branches of the Eightfold Path to altered states. They continue to do so today, regardless of what society or the law thinks, because shamans tend to be a cussed lot, and if it works—or if your gods and spirits tell you that this is part of your path- then you do it. It's also fashionable right now for anyone who writes about shamanic paths to immediately disclaimer that they never use entheogens, they don't approve of using entheogens, and that today's shamans don't need to use them, and oughtn't to. Perhaps they're all worried that the DEA will start raiding their houses ... or perhaps their publishers are all afraid of getting sued.

Either way, I am not good enough at hypocrisy to do that. I could, of course, just skip the entire controversy, but I don't think that would fool anyone for a minute. The personal truth is that I don't do entheogens because Hela forbids me to. On the other hand, some magical workers may—certainly not always, but sometimes—get told to use such things. It can happen, and if those are the plant allies that call to you, and they specifically want you to ingest them, then it's between you and them and no one else has a say. I have a great deal of respect for those who use this technique skillfully and respectfully.

Of course, most people have no idea how to properly respect the plant spirits. Part of working with them is being taught, by someone who is spiritually skilled with such things, how to utilize them properly. To approach them with an attitude of experimentation is to disrespect their power, and you deserve to end up in the emergency room or worse. If you can't find someone who is skilled, reputable, and stable to train you in how to deal with them, don't do it. If you must learn it from a book, I recommend checking out the Greenwights chapter in the fourth book in this series, *Wightridden: Paths of Northern Tradition Shamanism*. It is a basic primer for how to work with these rather dangerous plant spirits in ways to don't get you killed, arrested, or otherwise in deep trouble.

For the record, it is disrespectful to approach these plants with an attitude of recreation. If you use a mind-altering plant for sacred purposes, you should never be using it for recreational purposes, because it is an offense to the plant spirit. That means that if you use a tobacco pipe for spirit work, you can't recreationally smoke cigarettes, and you certainly can't be addicted or habituated. (That goes as well for Hemp and its byforms.) If you are going to use them for sacred purposes, you are forming a relationship with them that will last the rest of your life, whether or not you ever partake of them a second time. You will be in working partnership with their spirits, not merely exploiting their alkaloids for a good time, and they will hold you to that. Once you make that decision, You Know Better. You don't get to be blithely blinded to their real purpose on this earth, which is not to let people have cool trips and talk to light fixtures for fun.

There's also the slippery-slope effect; sometimes, once you enter into a deal with one of these sly and powerful plant allies, you may find yourself unable to be recreational about any others that you might be taking. This may require you to quit addictions, or at least not take some or all mind-altering substances socially. It's all part of that "you know better" thing. If this sounds like it might cramp your style, and it makes you nervous, then stay out of the ring and stick to drumming or dancing or fasting or whatever works for you.

That said, here are the entheogens which we have evidence of the northern ancestors using for religious purposes.

Aconite

Botanical Name: *Aconitum napellus*

Folk Names: Monkshood, Wolfsbane (also used to refer to *A. vulparia*), Tyr's Helm, Aulde Wife's Hood, Dumbledore's Delight, Leopard's Bane, Wolf's Hat

Anglo-Saxon Name: Þung (general name for a poisonous plant, but most often applied to Aconite)

Modern German Names: Blauer Eisenhut, Sturmhut, Wolfswurz

Modern Swedish Name: Stormhatt

Modern Danish Name: Stormhat

Modern Norwegian Name: Storhjelm

Deity Association: A herb of Jotunheim, sacred to the clans of the Iron Wood, among whom are many werewolves.

Height: 5-6'

Season: Perennial

History: Aconite is native to continental Europe, and was brought to the British Isles by the Saxon invasion; it was already naturalized by the time of the Anglo-Saxon herbals, but it had been used as wolf poison on the continent for millennia before. It is one of the last plants to bloom in the fall, providing color when everything else is withered.

Medicinal Uses: All parts of Monkshood are extremely poisonous, and it is only used externally medicinally, as a salve for nerve-related pain such as rheumatism, neuralgia, and sciatica. It paralyzes nerve centers and is a sedative and painkiller. Since the dosages, even for external use, can kill, we strongly suggest that this plant be used only under the supervision of experienced herbalists. Historically, tiny and precise doses of Monkshood were used for fevers where the pulse was "gazelling"—bounding as if to try and leave the blood vessel. It is still used homeopathically for this purpose.

Magical Uses: Once an arrow-tip poison and an execution method for condemned criminals, Wolvesbane has long been used as a spell of binding and protection. Medea used it in Greek lore to take vengeance upon Theseus when he rejected her. It was said both to cause and to cure lycanthropy. It has been used as a wash and a smoke to clean ritual knives. When used for euthanasia, the flower was traditionally planted on the grave.

Shamanic Uses: This extremely poisonous plant has a special relationship with Tyr, the warrior god of honor, whose bravery chained the great wolf Fenris. Use it to find him, call him, or make offerings to him. To do the latter, lay it on an altar out of the reach of children, pets, and irresponsible housemates, and bury it when it was withered. (Don't burn or eat it.) Carry it when traveling in Jotunheim, especially in the area of the Iron Wood, to keep were-creatures and other aggressive folks away from you. This plant also helps with folks who are shapeshifters and are having trouble with the shifting getting out of control; carrying a small pouch of wolvesbane will keep you human. It also works well as a charm for those humans with Jotun bloodlines who have anger-management problems from lack of self-control in managing their own internal beast; it can be used in binding spells for this purpose.

Affinity: Earth (sedative and relaxant) . Theoretically for Stormand Fire conditions, but the only one we can recommend is external use for inflammation, and even then only under the aegis of a trained herbalist.

Point: PC 9

Plant-wight's Nature: There is something very doglike about this plant spirit; it reminds one of the sort of large guard dog set out with the sheep to protect them—solitary, quiet until angered but then exploding in danger and teeth. Lydia Helasdottir refers to him as "a male figure, stern and upright, with chiseled features." Grandfather Wolvesbane is a protector rather than an offensive warrior, although like his plant-body, he is deadly and has no mercy. I perceive him sometimes as a lone cloaked and hooded figure with a sword, and sometimes as the guard dog. He is willing to sit and hold a quiet, taciturn conversation, but doesn't like you to distract him from his task.

Magical Charm: Binding the Wolf

This is for those whose nature is one of violence and rage, and who are having trouble controlling it. This is not a spell for one person to cast on another; Grandfather Aconite's reaction to someone asking for that is to kill the one who has run amok, thus removing the problem. While effective, this is not recommended for the sake of the stain on one's own Wyrd. The binding spell must be done by the one themselves, when they have come to the point of honestly wanting it. However, they must take care; if they speak without a whole heart, secretly wishing to continue their behavior, he will strike them down in some painful way. This spell must be done with the greatest sincerity, or not at all. At sunset, while wearing gloves, pick six large leaves of Aconite and bind them together with black thread, saying the following charm:

> In the name of the Lord of Swords,
> I bind you with the roots of mountains.
> In the name of the One-Handed God,
> I bind you with a woman's beard.
> In the name of the Lord of Honor,
> I bind you with the footfall of a cat.
> In the name of the sorrowing God,
> I bind you with the breath of a fish.
> In the name of the One who failed and sacrificed,
> I bind you with the spittle of a bird.
> In the name of the Great God Tyr,
> I bind you with the nerves of a bear.
> In the name of one who loved the Wolf and yet bound him,
> I who love you accept that you must be bound,
> And I will not forsake you in your prison,
> Even though I must wear these chains forever.
> Be it so, be it so, it is so. Hail Tyr.

Then place the bunch of leaves into a plastic bag, so that they might not flake off and rub on everything, and place them into a fabric bag, and leave this under your pillow while sleeping for one turn of the moon, and then hang it above your bed.

Belladonna

Botanical Name: *Atropa belladonna*

Folk Names: Tolkirsch, Wutbeere, Banewort, Black Cherry, Deadly Nightshade, Death's Herb, Devil's Cherries, Dwaleberry, Fair Lady, Sorcerer's Berry

Anglo-Saxon Name: Dwale

Old Norse Name: Dvale

Modern German Name: Tollkirsche

Modern Swedish Names: Dvalbär

Modern Danish Name: Galnebær

Modern Norwegian Name: Belladonnaurt

Deity Association: The Norns (especially Skuld) and Hela, and assorted Valkyries

Height: Climbing vine to 8'

Season: Perennial

History: Belladonna has grown wild all over Europe for millennia, and has been used as an anesthetic, a poison, and a magical plant for likely that long as well.

Medicinal Uses: Leaves and root are narcotic and sedative, and have been used as an anesthetic. However, dosage is difficult and mistakes could be deadly, so we do not recommend this plant for internal use except under the guidance of a skilled herbalist. Like Monkshood, Belladonna has been used in tiny and precise doses for high fever when the pulse is bounding, the tongue is like a Strawberry, and the eyes are dilated and light-sensitive; it is still used homeopathically in this way. As it is drying as well as sedating, it has been used for situations where other sedatives have increased sweating, drooling, or incontinence. Belladonna has the opposite action of both Opium Poppy and Foxglove, and can be used as an antidote to either.

Magical Uses: Faring forth. Lady Belladonna is one of the classic plants for journeying.

Shamanic Uses: This is the plant of the Valkyries, who answer to Freya and Odhinn. Belladonna is said to open the gateway to Valhalla, so that one may be let in whilst still alive (and presumably stay that way). However, I would strongly suggest getting Odhinn's permission to go before attempting it. Belladonna is also a plant of Death, and sometimes works with Hela and the Norns; she is partial to Lady Death. If you work with Foxglove or Poppy, you are unlikely to make an ally of Belladonna, and the reverse is also true.

Affinity: Earth (sedative and relaxant), Air (astringent). Theoretically for Storm, Fire and certain River conditions as noted above.

Point: LI 1

Plant-wight's Nature: Lady Belladonna is feminine, sleek, wily, and dangerous. She is La Belle Dame Sans Merci, a capricious femme fatale who will indulge you one moment and lash out at you the next. She should be resorted to only rarely and for short periods of time. Songs written to work with her should flatter her and stress her beauty and power, but not be too blatant toadying; she's not stupid. Never turn your back on her.

On the other hand, Lady Belladonna is one of my watch-wights, along with Dame Ellhorn. One or the other or both of them has grown wild wherever I have lived in my life, from childhood on; it got to the point where I wouldn't rent an apartment unless I saw one of them growing around the building. The farm where I live now, and where I will be buried, sports them both in wild profusion, and I will never cut down either of them. They may grow where they will. Lady Belladonna has watched my back, at the request of my patron goddess Hela, Lady Death, for my whole life. My respect for her may be tinged with a little fear, but that's only because I know what she's capable of.

"Grandmother Belladonna has appeared as a slight fae woman with a dark purple gown, dark brown hair and pale white skin, colors that seem proper as she exists somewhere in the flux between life and death. A spirit with watery and Saturn energies, her relative quiet should not be mistaken for a retiring nature; she is dangerous because she is seductive and tempting, relaxing away defenses and good sense until death closes in. Most people are safely able to approach Belladonna, though she seems to have her own ideas about who she is willing to work with, when, and in what way. When angered, she expresses her displeasure very clearly; such experiences leave a lasting impression. (I speak from experience; she was unhappy about my attempts to sprout Belladonna seeds this season. There is nothing quite like having a plant spirit yell at you.)"

-Silence Maestas

Magical Charm: Guarding Your Death

Carefully pick and dry some Belladonna leaves. On the night of the dark moon, light a black and a white candle, and lay the leaves out on a small black cloth. Ask Belladonna to be your emissary to Hela, and to the Norns. Ask that your death be guarded, so that you will die only when it is your time as appointed by the Ladies who cut your thread, and not before. In return, promise that you will not be stupid or reckless with this gift. There is no spoken charm for this; you must find your own words. Burn one of the leaves in the flame of the black candle, and one in the white; tie up the rest in the black cloth and bind it with three threads—black, white, and grey—and keep it in a safe place. When you die, it must go into your grave with you.

Black Hellebore

Botanical Name: *Helleborus niger*
Folk Names: Christmas Rose, Melampode, Hammerwort
Anglo-Saxon Names: Wedeberge, Homorwort
Modern German Names: Schwarze Nieswurz, Christrose
Modern Swedish Names: Julros, Svart Prustrot
Modern Danish Name: Nyserod
Modern Norwegian Name: Julerose
Deity Association: Hel
Height: 12"
Season: Perennial
History: Black Hellebore hails originally from the subalpine mountains of central and southern Europe, and was imported into Germany during Roman times. It came much later to the British Isles. It was primarily used as a narcotic, an abortifacient, and as a poison; the level of dosage for one is perilously close to the other. Its association with Christmas came from its later widespread use as an ornamental that blooms late in winter in more temperate climates. Strangely enough, it has recently been discovered that pregnant sheep who eat wild Hellebore (and don't die from it) can bear lambs with an odd deformity: either one single eye in the middle of their heads, or two eyes crowded into one central socket. Hellebore was used to induce berserk altered states, and also to cure people of them—what can give can take away, in magical theory, and the Anglo-Saxon name Wedeberge meant "Berries

of Wod (madness)". Its other name, Homorwort (also used to refer to Pellitory), meant "rock-herb", referring to its habit of protruding from stone walls.

Medicinal Uses: Hellebore is extremely poisonous. Although it was used in abortifacient potions in ancient times, we do not have entirely safe dosages for it, and there are safer herbs to use. The root tincture is a narcotic, but we strongly suggest that this plant should only be used under the tutelage of a trained herbalist who has worked with it. It causes irritation and inflammation of tissue, and while it can heat up a sluggish heart, it can just as easily cause it to spasm and die.

Magical Uses: Powdered Hellebore was used as an invisibility spell. It was often used to "draw out" other poisons by laying the plant on the afflicted part, or in the case of livestock, by slitting their ear and slipping in a piece of Hellebore for an hour or so. It has been used as an antidepressant magic.

Shamanic Uses: Hellebore was used for magically treating both mania and melancholy, and, one might assume, the manic-depressive combination. This winter-blooming plant is one of Hela's death-herbs, and it can be used both to kill and also magically to work on someone's mental illness.

Affinity: Fire (irritation) , Earth (sedative and relaxant). Theoretically for Storm and cardiac Earth conditions, but we advise against it.

Point: GV 18

Plant-wight's Nature: Grandmother Hellebore appears sometimes as a woman in a long white gown, black hair falling all about her, and eyes like black pits in her head. Her voice is like the rushing of winds, and the very air around her is cold. She can sit entirely still for a long time, which makes people mistake her for something more beneficent (like her mask-form as the pretty Christmas Rose) until she lifts her head and you see the unending darkness of her eyes. One of her purposes is to eat melancholy and mania, and if she is properly propitiated, she can do this as an ongoing way of dealing with someone's depression ... but her prices are often high, and sometimes terrifying, so make sure that you can live with the bargain before you make it. Really, she is the line of last defense, when nothing else has worked and the client is ready to give up. She may demand, for example, a discipline of regular physical pain given to her ritually as an offering. However, this is advanced shamanic work and should only be undertaken with the aid of a spirit-worker who has a relationship with Grandmother Hellebore and can do the negotiating properly.

Magical Charm: Invisibility

Carry dried berries of Hellebore tied up in a cloth when you need to pass invisibly in an area. Remember not to move quickly—part of Grandmother Hellebore's power is in stillness, so walk slowly and unobtrusively so as not to disturb the spell. The following charm should be whispered almost inaudibly; never voice it or it won't work. As with all things to do with this herb, use this spell only occasionally; regular use will begin to cause madness.

Wedeberge, Wedeberge, weave me sheen of shadow,

Helle berry, Hela's herald, drape me deep in darkness,
Silent as a stone I walk, all eyes empty as yours to me.

Fly Agaric

Botanical Name: *Amanita muscaria*
Folk Names: Little Red Man, Rabenbrot, Death Angel, Deathcap, Redcap Mushroom
Anglo-Saxon Name: Feldswamm
Old Germanic Name: Rabenbrot
Modern German Name: Roter Fingerhut
Modern Swedish Name: Röd Flugsvamp
Modern Danish Name: Fluesvamp
Modern Norwegian Name: Rød Fluesopp
Deity Association: Odin
Height: 4"
Season: Perennial fungus
History: Fly Agaric is first referenced linguistically in northern Asia around 4000 B.C., and then appears again in Siberian petroglyphs two millenia later. The Siberian tribal shamans had a long history of using Amanita, and it spread to Europe from there. (Simultaneously, it was growing up independently in Mexico and spreading to the rest of the north and south American continents.) While no one is sure about the extent of Amanita use in pre-migration era Scandinavia and Germany, it is clear that they knew what it was and what it was good for. Further east, the Siberian peoples revere the Little Red Man and will only take the ones that grow locally under their sacred Birch trees. If they have it as a plant ally, they can never drink alcohol. They eat them soaked in blueberry juice for creativity and vision quests. Reindeer will supposedly eat Amanita if they need to travel a long way without stopping.
Medicinal Uses: Siberians use the Amanita as a temporary adaptogen when the body needs a boost of power and energy in emergency situations. It was massaged into the skin to counteract snakebite and gangrene. However, unless you are being watched over by a Koryak shaman, we suggest you not try this by yourself.
Magical Uses: Faring forth, and used to increase fertility.
Shamanic Uses: The name Rabenbrot, or Raven's bread, refers to the tale that Huginn and Muninn, Odhinn's two ravens, ate from this sacred mushroom. It is Odhinn's special fungus, and has been used across Europe and Asia for spirit-journeying. The Little Red Man, as he is generally called in many Northern Traditions, is a harsh master; he has many rules and is quite demanding. Turn to him only with the greatest respect.
Affinity: Fire (stimulating). Used for Earth conditions such as exhaustion and gangrene, but again we suggest great caution.
Point: GV 20
Plant-wight's Nature:

> *The spirits of fungi are different than those of plants—they're older, less complex organisms than chlorophyll-making plants, in the evolutionary and biological sense, and they're much more alien to our human minds, in the spiritual sense. There is a strong feeling of affinity between the Jotnar/Jotunheim and mushrooms.*

The mushroom one sees above ground is generally the fruiting body and not the actual living fungus itself, which as you probably know is a series of connected myceliae under the soil or inside the rotting log or wherever. In my experience, it takes a bit more time and patience to get to know fungus spirits than it does to get to know plant spirits. They are very self-contained, slow-talking spirits, and since they physically feed directly on decay and rot, they're very good helpers with the breaking down of things and with helping one through a death, physical or otherwise. Some mushrooms also have symbiotic biological relationships with certain species of trees.

My impression of Fly Agaric is that he has become quite curmudgeonly towards humans because of all the people who carelessly use him for kicks with no appreciation of his sacredness. He chooses who he will and will not work with, and those who he's not interested in, yet who come across some Amanita muscaria and ingest it, will probably not get much more out of the experience than extreme nausea and a bad trip. Fly Agaric has a very poisonous look-alike in the genus, and mushrooms are much easier to mix up than plants. Amanita pantherina is a mushroom that, instead of having a red cap with white spots, has a brown to yellowish-brown cap with white spots, and is easily mistaken for Fly Agaric, but ingesting it can potentially be deadly. People who want to be certain they have Amanita muscaria should use only those with scarlet/red caps—not orange, not yellow, not brownish or any other shade, even though the Little Red Man can come in those colors as well.

-Elizabeth Vongvisith

Father Redcap (he told me he didn't like the distinction of Grandfather, and corrected me) is the direct ancestor of our modern image of the red-capped gnome. A diminutive spirit with a merry animated face, bright eyes, and possessing a distinctive red hat, Redcap is one of humanity's oldest plant allies. He is tricky and very clever, sometimes racing on ahead, sometimes sitting still and considering you with a mind that can find just about anything you wish to know; I think of him as a spiritual search engine or research librarian. He won't just give you the answers you seek, but he will help you find the path to locate them yourself.

Like all mushrooms, Fly Agaric exists in a twilight space between life and death (or, as I think of it, between death and rebirth). He embodies the transition and that which transitions; it is this power that associates him with Odin. Redcap's powers suspend a person between the Worlds and cause the body and everything relating to it to be entirely forgotten for a few hours. Or a few years. You never know with Redcap. The spirit can be quite kinetic, contrasting with the physical chemistry of the mushroom, which totally removes the desire to move, and even the recollection of movement. It's the mind that accelerates and amazing things can happen under the touch of Father Redcap.

Father Redcap can be very friendly and outgoing, and it is tempting to let him convince you that he's not dangerous, but any force that can lead you to forget yourself as completely as Fly Agaric can is not to be ever underestimated; he is a true trickster in the most classic sense—a beguiling teacher who will lead you wide-eyed into territory beyond your control and then laugh at your struggles to go back the way you came. But he is a teacher and is willing to educate some people in the proper ways to work with his powers; keep in mind that even his willingness to help you won't keep you safe from his tricks and teasing.

-Silence Maestas

Magical Charm: Little Red Man's Praise Song

My dear Red Man wasn't willing to give me a charm for this book and, to be honest, I'm not really surprised. Red Man didn't like the idea of having too many ways for people to catch his attention. He's really just a curmudgeon so I can't expect anything else out of him—I wouldn't want people having too many ways to knock on my door if I were him. Instead, I asked Red Man if he'd allow me to create a charm in his praise, instead of getting a charm from him, and here it is.

> *Red Man, you've walked before me,*
> *pushed me from behind, dragged me*
> *across the dark plains and up again*
> *to heights of giddiness (or to ruin).*
> *Red Man, the glint in your eye*
> *tells me to beware. I'm drawn in*
> *caught fast in your presence, spots*
> *on all sides, colorful, quick,*
> *then gone.*
> *Red Man, you'll be my disaster*
> *before long. You'd bring me crashing*
> *to knees, to hands, I'd fall out of the Tree*
> *if you weren't there*
> *teaching me how to stand.*
> —Silence Maestas

Hemlock

Botanical name: *Conium maculatum*
Folk names: Beaver Poison, Keckies, Kex, Musquash Root, Poison Hemlock, Poison Parsley, Spotted Corobane, Spotted Hemlock, Water Parsley, Winter Fern, Kecksies
Anglo-Saxon Name: Hemleac, Hymlic, Hemlic, Wodwistle
Modern German Name: Gefleckter Schierling
Modern Swedish Name: Odört
Modern Danish Name: Skarntyde
Modern Norwegian Name: Skarntyde, Giftkjeks
Deity Association: Hel, Odin
Height: To 6'
Season: Biennial
History: In ancient Greece, Hemlock was the upper-class execution drug. In northern Europe, it was associated with toads, who were thought to eat it safely but absorb its poison and become poisonous themselves. During the Middle Ages, it was used occasionally as a sedative for epilepsy and St. Vitus's Dance. Small amounts were used in "flying ointments", acting as a giddy-making tranquilizer, although of course the dosage for such is iffy and dangerous. Its use in entheogen potions (almost always as one of several such ingredients) led to one of its Anglo-Saxon names, Wodwistle (whistle of

inspiration or whistle of Woden). The Latin name comes from the Greek *Konas*, meaning "to whirl about", as it brings on vertigo before killing. Its Anglo-Saxon name comes from Hemleac, meaning "shore-leek", as it is often found on riverbanks.

Medicinal Uses: Euthanasia, mainly. The toxic ingredient coniine causes death by respiratory paralysis. As its actions are the opposite of strychnine, it has been used as an antidote for strychnine poisoning. Hemlock is a sedative, pain-killer, eases spasms such as those in whooping-cough or asthma, and was used to treat the pain of hemorrhoids in a salve, but as it is highly fatal and dosages are tricky, we cannot recommend it for any treatment where you are trying to keep the patient alive. It's just too dangerous.

Magical Uses: Deathspells. Not recommended.

Shamanic Uses: This is one of Hel's plants, as it brings a quick and relatively painless death. It is used in ritual suicide, which should not be undertaken without her approval. The plant is also honored by Odin in his form as Master of Entheogens. (You'll notice that the Swedish name looks a lot like "Odhinn/Odin/Woden's Herb". Basically, its death uses are Hel's and its entheogenic uses are Odin's, although the one can easily become the other.

Affinity: Earth (sedative, relaxant).

Point: GV 1

Plant-wight's Nature: Hemlock is cold and wet like a bog, and indeed that's what its energy feels like—sinking into a swamp. Connecting with it gives one's vision a greeny-brown-olive cast, and one feels like one is sinking slowly. Hemlock-wight is not cruel or malicious in any way; indeed s/he is rather solicitous in a strangely cold way, and s/he feels that sinking you into a deep (and permanent) sleep is probably the best thing for you. After all, isn't it peaceful here? It's not easy to get hold of Hemlock without ingesting the plant; I tried sitting with that pretty lacy Parsley-like creature for some time, and it wasn't interested in coming out just for a tourist, as it were. Indeed, the plant felt somewhat "empty" of overarching spirit, until Hemlock-wight deigned to show his/her face from its bog.

Spells: I have neither a medicinal nor a magical spell for Hemlock at this time; at least, we couldn't find one of either (through research or through talking to the spirits) that I felt comfortable writing here. Sorry. Maybe you can do better.

Hemp

Botanical Name: *Cannabis sativa*

Folk Names: Pot, Weed, Marijuana, Chanvre, Gallowgrass, Ganeb, Bhang, Ganja, Hanf, Kif, Neckweede, Tekrouri

Anglo-Saxon Name: Hænep

Old Norse Name: Hampr

Old Germanic Name: Hanf

Modern German Name: Hanf, Haschischpflanze, Marihuana, Kultur-Hanf

Modern Swedish Name: Hampa

Modern Danish Name: Hamp

Modern Norwegian Name: Hamp

Deity Association: Frey, Freya, and sacred to the Vanir deities in general.

Height: To 8'

Season: Perennial

History: Hemp is a plant of ancient cultivation, native to India (from whence it spread to the Far East), central Asia, and Siberia (from whence it spread to Europe). The spreading was fairly early; it was cultivated northern Europe in preliterate times and was already a staple fiber crop by the time of the Anglo-Saxon herbals.

Medicinal Uses: Eases asthma, glaucoma, nausea, migraine, and general pains. It stimulates the appetite and relieves muscle spasms. Although it is generally smoked, tincture, tea, or cooking in food may be a better delivery method. To cook with cannabis, saute in any oil until it turns brown (THC is soluble in fats), then strain and keep the oil and use it sparingly in any recipe that uses oil or butter.

Household Uses: The plant fiber is made into rope, twine, and durable cloth. Hemp plants make excellent paper, and are more renewable for that purpose than trees. The modern plants bred for their smoke are not as good for fiber; separate fiber types exist that aren't much good for any kind of psychoactive effect.

Magical Uses: Seeds were often sown as part of love spells. One particularly potent love spell involved a young woman sowing a full circle of Hemp seed all around a church. (Definitely try this one, ladies.)

Shamanic Uses: Hemp was smoked by shamans across Europe and Asia; one can still find antique-to-ancient ritual Hemp smokers in Siberia and Mongolia. It is associated with Freya, in her role as Mistress of Seidhr, although most modern seidhr-workers tend to avoid its ritual usage for a number of reasons. Since Hemp and its bred byform, marijuana, is a testosterone reducer, and Freya is known to be fond of effeminate men, I can see the connection. Since it is currently illegal in the USA, you may take your freedom into your hands if you decide to use it as a mind-altering substance for shamanic work.

Affinity: Earth (sedative, relaxant), Fire (stimulant), Swamp (oily). Use for Storm, Fire, and Air conditions. Hemp can either sedate or stimulate, depending on what she thinks is the right thing to do to that person.

Point: GB 20

Plant-wight's Nature:

The Marijuana spirit ... she seems to be very diffuse, because so many people are smoking without knowing that she's there, or caring, which is a shame, so she seems to be very shy. But I've experienced her as a kind of late-teenage, early-twenties, beautiful flitting fey-like entity that could wear a thousand different dresses, always different. She's aloof, and vexed with the way it's being used these days. So sometimes she just drops a really bad one on someone, just for the sake of it, who wasn't expecting it. It is one of the classic plants that I would consider energy-awareness-expanding. Marijuana, which isn't strong enough to be that visionary, unless you live in Holland; it tends to take a lot of the filters off, depending on how much radiation you are receiving. Having lived in Holland where things are legal, we find that up to a certain point you have automatic safeties. You can only go so high, and you don't really get any radiation damage from being there. You do get a guided tour a little closer to the Source, and some of the natural radiation-dampening effects that you get from living quite close to the material plane are diminished. You get increased awareness of energy and such—for us it's pretty real. You can experience this state in a variety of ways, but we consider it valid.

When you've passed certain ring-pass-nots in your development, that safety isn't there any more, so you really can get burnt. It can certainly trigger a Kundalini-like experience with all the disadvantages and pains that go with that. You can get burned by the radiation up there, and it can really crisp your organs. So if you read the literature about the things that can happen if you get an uncontrolled Kundalini experience, all that damage can happen to you. It's as if suddenly your 110-volt system is running on 220, or 440, even. We have seen a lot of cases of wires burnt out in people's energy bodies from smoking.

-Lydia Helasdottir

It is a bit strange to call the marijuana spirit "Grandmother" because she has appeared to me in such a youthful form; despite appearances, her aura is ancient and there is no question in my mind that she is one of the most powerful plant spirits known to us. With kaleidoscopic eyes, blond air, and prismatic colors that shift all around her form, Grandmother Marijuana is a multifaceted and complex being. Most entheogenic plant spirits dislike addicts and experimental users with feelings that range from Mugwort's indifference to Datura's outright anger, but Grandmother Marijuana seems to treasure her users in a strange way. However, she is offended when those who ought to know better disregard her instead of taking the time to speak with her directly.

Considered against a mentally healthy human, Marijuana may appear a little schizophrenic; she is at once supremely joyful but carries sorrow and paranoia at the same time. She can be flighty or easily distracted, but can also pursue with single-minded focus. Marijuana is complicated and also completely pure in her simplicity. In my mind, she is the flip side of Datura's nature; also personally associated with love Goddesses, Marijuana is the delight that love and passion can bring, as well as the disconnection from the world around us that love can inspire, and the desire to capture that exquisite high one more time. Marijuana is the honeymoon phase of the love affair, with all the advantages and pitfalls thereof.

Marijuana (both spirit and plant) well illustrates the difficulty of the spirit worker who works with sacred plants, at least in the United States. Illegal to grow, possess, and use, marijuana carries legal ramifications the same as heroin and other hard street drugs. It is one of the herbs of choice for those wanting to get high in the name of spirituality, and is included in the debate about what part psychotropics play for serious spiritual practitioners. Marijuana stands somewhere between recreation and spirit work, indulgence and enlightenment; placing it too far on either end of that spectrum ignores the potential it has for the other end as well. Where does one draw the line, especially when acquiring this herb (with whom one has a serious relationship) supports the industry that exploits it? Growing it places us at risk because it can draw the attention of forces we can't control, thus putting that work at high profile. For myself, I am always given the marijuana I need to do my work; I have never purchased any and it is part of my respect to Grandmother Marijuana that I will not support the street drug industry that injures her children. I will not grow it because that would put part of my work under another's control (that of law enforcement). Marijuana has given no instructions about these things and I am satisfied with how I have handled it thus far.

Marijuana, even as dead and dried plant matter, has spiritual properties that bring joy and pleasure. She heals mind and spirit, offering blessings of rest that are uniquely hers. She can open the heart that is weighted with sorrow and brings light to minds that feel dark; she stimulates the senses and calls us to enjoy the world around us for all its complex, imperfect, and confusing beauty. -Silence Maestas

Magical Charm: Smoke of Vanaheim

This is a charm to make one feel worthy of being loved. It is meant to be scattered across coals (or charcoal) and smoked as incense, not as a cigarette. Ideally, all above-ground parts of the plant should be burned, not just the leaf. Use the stems and seeds as well. Consecrate the space, light the burning area, scatter the plant bits, breathe in the smoke, and say:

> *By Hempseed, green gate of gladness,*
> *By the golden glance of the cat's Mistress,*
> *By the gifting gaze of the Boar-rider,*
> *By the fair fields of the Green World,*
> *I speak truth to the Earth: that truly I*
> *Am worthy of wooing and winning,*
> *I am valued and valuable as the Vanadis's nights,*
> *I deserve to set my own true price*
> *In this marketplace of passions,*
> *And I will not shortchange myself for chances*
> *That would have wilted in the heat of honesty.*
> *In token of this value, I shall value others equally*
> *When they show their strength, and value this body*
> *As beauty, and bounty, and worthy of the best care,*
> *As I would have a lover believe.*

You will notice that the charm requires a follow-up. Indeed, once it is done, you are then obligated to take good care of your physical body, whatever that entails, with as much passion as you would hope for a lover to expend on your heart.

Henbane

Botanical Name: *Hyoscyamus niger*

Folk Names: Prophetenkraut, Zauberkraut, Nifelkraut, Belisa, Alsitzerherb, Cassilago, Cassilata, Devil's Eye, Hebenon, Henbells, Hogsbean, Isana, Jusquiasmus, Poison Tobacco, Symphonica, Stinking Nightshade

Anglo-Saxon Name: Hennebelle

Old Germanic Name: Pilsen

Modern German Name: Schwarzes Bilsenkraut

Modern Swedish Name: Bolmört

Modern Danish Name: Bulmeurt

Modern Norwegian Name: Bulemeurt

Deity Association: Thor

Height: 3'

Season: Annual, biennial in warm areas

History: Poisonous Henbane has been in use as a narcotic for at least two millennia. A woman's grave at a Viking excavation in Fyrkat, Denmark, contained a bag of Henbane seeds. It was smoked to relieve toothache during the Dark Ages, but reportedly had a regrettable tendency to bring on delusions and insanity as well. It is native to central and southern Europe, and western and central Asia, but spread to northern continental Europe in preliterate times. It reached the British Isles later, in the early medieval period.

Medicinal Uses: A powerful narcotic, sedative, and antispasmodic, Henbane is poisonous enough that it should not be used except by trained herbalists. It has been used as a muscle relaxant before surgery, and to treat muscle, bowel, and asthmatic spasms. The leaves can reduce pain, ease spasms, and bring on a deep healing sleep in some, but can bring on hallucinations in others.

Magical Uses: Flying ointment plant, said to enable prophecy from its altered state. Burned to attract rain. Used profligately for cursing in the Middle Ages. Used as a charm to pacify children (see below).

Shamanic Uses: Henbane was the plant originally brewed into the ale that we call pilsner, in order to make it psychoactive. Sacred to Thor, it had to be harvested by a naked virgin, tied to her body, and both she and the plant were put in a stream and sprinkled with water. Henbane beer was a libation for Thor, and with his blessing, an aphrodisiac and prophesying potion. Henbane was also used for euthanasia of elders who were tired of living and asked to go out with a lovely dream.

Affinity: Earth (sedative, relaxant), Air (drying). Use for Storm and Fire conditions, but only under a trained herbalist.

Point: GV 26

Plant-wight's Nature:

> This is a spirit with qualities and temperament similar to Mugwort, also appearing like a small elderly woman. Unlike Mugwort, which has some watery, lunar, and secretive elements, Grandmother Henbane is more direct, more bright and solar; Henbane is clear in her wishes and has a precise and discerning nature that expects those wishes carried out exactly. She is a matriarch among the Solanacea plants and expects to be treated as such.
>
> A bit haughty, Henbane has no patience for games or for verbal parlance. She expects to be deferred to, and rightly so. Physically, the Henbane plant has several potent alkaloids present in all parts, including the seeds, which have poisoned children on occasion. The distinct odor keeps most people away, as does Grandmother's attitude; she will be very clear about her willingness to work with you, and without that any work done with the plant risks her displeasure. Some plant spirits can be courted but Grandmother Henbane can't be teased out of her shell or won by sweet words. She does have a dry sense of humor which is expressed through the use of Henbane in the brewing of pilsner beer; she will not punish every fool who

drinks too much of something with her plant children as ingredients, but she will laugh at how much they suffer at their own hands.

Henbane as a plant has a long history of ritual, magical, and shamanic use. The spirit sometimes favors those who work in such disciplines, though without her specific word one way or another, Grandmother Henbane will offer no assistance or protection towards those who experiment; similarly, she will not necessarily seek to punish. Henbane, with the true wisdom of grandmothers, knows that letting children learn on their own is sometimes the best way to teach them.   -Silence Maestas

Magical Charm: Soothing Fits

According to tradition, if a child is given to continual temper tantrums, one can call upon Grandmother Henbane for help. A bit of the plant root is hung on a necklace—we suggest locking it in something small, solid and impenetrable in order to do that, to prevent the child getting to it—and over time, Henbane's effects will help them gain control. If the child can speak well enough, they should be encouraged to say, "Granny Henbell, help me keep my temper," and clutch the herb's container. In addition, the parent can place some of the plant (in its container) under the mattress of the sleeping and child and ask Grandmother Henbane to please help the child gain some control over their fits.

There are many more intense and serious spells to do with this plant, and one might wonder why we chose this one instead of something more arcane. Besides the fact that the arcane ones require more work and study and attainment than simple hedge-spells, any parent with an out-of-control child will tell you that it's not a little thing at all.

Opium Poppy

Botanical Name: *Papaver somniferum*
Folk Names: Blind Buff, Blindeyes, Dream Poppy
Anglo-Saxon Name: Popig
Old Germanic Name: Maga
Modern German Name: Schlafmohn
Modern Swedish Name: Valmo
Modern Danish Name: Valmue
Modern Norwegian Name: Opiumsvalmue
Deity Association: Woden
Height: 1-2'
Season: Annual
History: The Opium Poppy seems to be native to Asia Minor, as records of its use in Sumeria go back 5000 years, and was spread to continental Europe during the Neolithic era. Poppies were cultivated in Germany by the Teutonic peoples, and Poppy seeds are endemic to their cuisine today.
Medicinal Uses: The latex of the unripe seed pod is the source of opium, which is an excellent but highly addictive painkiller.
Household Uses: An artist's oil is made from the second pressing of the seeds.
Culinary Uses: Poppy seeds (which have no entheogenic value) are good in all sorts of baking. A culinary oil is made from the first pressing of the seeds.
Magical Uses: Poppy seeds are carried for wealth, used in invisibility charms, and as a charm to bring sleep. In some counties of England, picking poppies was said to bring storms, but placing the flowers on the rooftiles could keep away lightning. Poppy dolls—made from bending back the petals and

securing them with a blade of grass for a sash and another thrust through for arms, making the seed pod into a head—were used as makeshift temporary poppets for spells.

Shamanic Uses: The Germanic peoples planted fields of poppies that were known as Odainsackr ("field of the living") in Old Norse and Magenfeldern ("stomach fields") in Old Germanic. Just by laying in these fields one could be healed by the earth and by Woden's powers, as poppies were one of his plants. There is some evidence that entheogens were added to mead for ritual purposes, and Poppy is a likely one for this. Poppies are the Dreaming Plants, and they can take you places in your dreams, but don't go without Woden's help and guidance, and don't go often or they will seize you and hold you for ransom, and you will have to worm your way out of their clutches.

Affinity: Earth (sedative, relaxant), Air (astringent) . Use for Storm and Fire conditions.

Point: GV 19

Plant-wight's Nature:

>   In my continuing quest to learn about plant allies (and, let's be honest, legal and quasi-legal ways of altering consciousness, I decided to learn more about he humble Papaver somniferum. Poppies have a long history in spirit-work; they were used by the Sumerians, Minoans, and Greeks, among others. I had some trepidations about this—I'm a recovering alcoholic with an affinity for downers—but I felt that the obvious power of this plant made experimentation worthwhile despite the risk. (Ultimately I discovered that many of my fears were unfounded, as the plant was quite capable of discouraging abuse on its own.)

>   I do not have a ready supply of heroin or laudanum available. While there are lots of heroin users in New York, I don't know where one would go to score, and I had no interest in scoring a street chemical of dubious make and purity. However, those who want to commune with the spirit of the Poppy have yet another route available to them: what the Greeks called mekonium, or tea made with Poppy. (Note: This process is illegal, and opium is highly addictive; people have overdosed on and become addicted to Poppy tea. This is particularly true in Eastern Europe, where Poppy tea is known as "Polish heroin". Experiment at your own risk.) Eight ounces of Poppy tea sent me into a nice reverie, and the Poppy spirit appeared to me as a little girl who wanted to play. I passed in and out of Poppyworld, and finally fell asleep.

>   The problem came the next day, when I woke up still under the influence of Poppy. She wanted me to stay home and play with her; I wanted to go to work. I chose the latter and spent the whole day vomiting off and on in the company bathroom. Staying awake became a Herculean effort, especially with Poppy continually encouraging me to "come and play". Had I done as she asked and stayed home, I doubt I'd have had the bad time that I did at work ... but Poppy is in many ways like a selfish child who wants your attention any way she can get it, and will mess with you in order to get it, one way or another. If you don't give her your full attention for the length of your trip, expect it to get bad. You'll have to ignore her encouragements to "just take a little more", too.

>   My final analysis: While Poppy might be a Deity-send for people with chronic pain and insomnia, and while Poppy is useful for lucid-dream vision questing, this is a powerful spirit ally, and like any powerful ally, must be approached with caution. She can be approached, and you can work with her beneficially, but should always be treated with extreme respect.   -Kenaz Filan

>   Poppy was tricky; her aura draws you in without even being aware of it and pretty soon I was caught in her spell; it was hard to shake myself out of it to work with the other spirits who I had called. She spoke in phrases that strung into sentences, which made for a languid, serpentine conversation. I have no doubt that she can be direct when she wants to be; Poppy is whoever she decides to be whenever she decides to be it. Her faces are myriad and her forms are constantly shifting; she is a supreme shape-shifter and has honed that skill to an art that most plant spirits, generally ambiguous anyway, never bother to cultivate. She demanded that I learn to work with her now. I asked for some time to learn; she told me she'd teach me everything I need to know. She put in my mind the idea of creating a tea from the seeds, since she's not willing to wait for me to start a new batch of seeds. She's very keen on working with me. Just dealing with the spirit was tricky; I look forward to the plant-working being just as difficult.   -Silence Maestas

Magical Charm: Poppy Song

 This charm doesn't rhyme and is unique because the speaker identifies with Opium and invites the spirit to smoke them and take them into herself. Poppy is very clear about the power dynamic one has to be in when working with her. There is music that goes along with this, drawn out melodic tones underneath rhythmic recitation of the words. I'd say that the charm is most effective when paired with music. Poppy seems to like music.

> *Catch me, cautious creeping, fast in your desire*
> *Breathe in my essence, burn me to ash.*
> *Clench me and hold me, oh Poppy most dear*
> *My certainty sacrificed, my rationale dim.*
>   -Silence Maestas

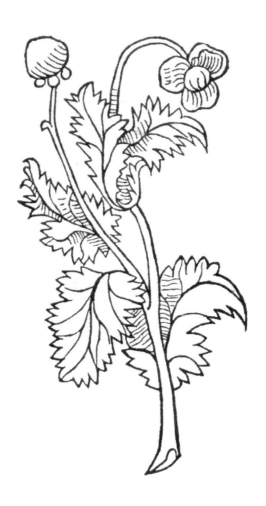

Animal and Metal Substances in Northern Healing

In most modern Western herbalism, the inclusion of animal products or metals raises eyebrows, and sometimes triggers a concerned or even hostile reaction. However, they are used frequently in traditional Chinese and Ayurvedic medicine, and are often included in the early European herbals and medicine texts. Of course, these texts usually neglect to discuss the nature of the animal products used and why they worked, as that information would have been something that was passed on orally.

Because of this, when Mengloth informed me that I would have to look into using some animal products and metals in my remedies, I decided to concentrate on the animal products that were A) easily available to me, B) did not disturb endangered species, and C) could be found both in the old European texts and in Chinese and/or Ayurvedic sources. While different cultural traditions might emphasize different uses of a medicinal product, still, the product is the product and I figured that comparisons might be useful. What I also found useful was the descriptions in Asian medicine of the temperature and uses of some of these substances, which helped me to place them in this elemental system.

According to many old texts—the Anglo-Saxon herbals, the Greek and Roman classics—animal products were frequently included in remedies, as were substances we might think of as food (eggs, butter, milk, cream, bacon fat, etc). Pliny's *Natural History* contains a number of common animal products used in ancient classical medicine, and these were distributed to books all over the continent. The *Old English Herbarium* is often paired with another work of the era—*Medicina de Quadrupedibus*—but this was discarded when animal substances fell out of favor. (*Medicina de Quadrupedibus* is available online at: http://openlibrary.org/b/OL14022035M.) It is impossible to tell, of course, how many of the animal substances used in the old northern herbals were taken from classical sources and how many were "local" remedies, but it's still worth looking into anyway.

Some substances were clearly included entirely for their symbolic and magical value—curing a red spot in the eyes with a splash of pigeon's blood, or making a whip of dolphin hide with which to scourge away madness, or tearing out a raven's eyes (the bird was then drowned alive) and placing them in an amulet around the neck for blindness. (I'm using particularly dramatic, distasteful, and seemingly impractical examples here, but you get the idea.) Other animal parts seem to be included for their actual efficacy as a healing substance, and we will discuss some of those here.

Faunistic medicines (isn't that a great term?) went out of fashion in Europe as the medieval period progressed, largely because they became associated with spells and charms. While plants were (mostly) God's beloved creation and were more defendable by health care practitioners, pounded earthworms and ground antler were harder to discern from "eye of newt and toe of frog", folk magic practices that the medieval Church was determined to root out, with deadly force if necessary. By the Renaissance, animal products had dwindled in usage. Metals, on the other hand, were definitely in, largely due to the influence of alchemist-doctors like Paracelsus. Some of those metals and mineralic chemicals were later found out to be dangerous for human consumption, although their use continued up to the early 20th century. I remember reading an early Jethro Kloss book that still recommended some extremely unsafe metallurgic compounds as medicinal remedies.

Several recipes in the old herbals recommend the use of earthworms (*Lumbricus terrestris*), either pounded to a mush or dried, powdered, and reconstituted to a mush. (The method probably depended on the time of year; remember that in much of northern Europe, finding much of anything in late January would be impossible, and a healer would have to depend on stored supplies. As someone living in snowy New England, I can appreciate this problem.) Earthworm as a substance is cold and salty, very much an Earth substance (of course). In Chinese medicine, earthworms are used for fever and various feverish diseases such as malaria, asthma, skin fungus, arthritis, and stiff neck and shoulders; it is said to be able to relax the airways and prevent convulsions. (This sounds like the mark of a Mountain substance as well.) Ancient European medicine used them for skin eruptions and injured muscles and sinews; they seemed to have used snails interchangeably with worms as well. The worms can simply be mashed and applied, or boiled and drunk for the internal maladies. If they are dried, the internal organs should be removed and the worm spread flat on a screen to dry, and then powdered.

Ants are suggested in *Bald's Leechbook*, powdered and mixed with grease and salved onto shrunken sinews to make them hale. In Chinese medicine, powdered ant is considered an excellent adaptogen and immune tonic, and used to increase virility. Restorative quality, then, is what the two have in common. I was not able to find any information that helped me place ants as an elemental substance as of yet.

Dung-beetles were also used in both European and Asian medicines. It wasn't just the Egyptians who noted them; there was a host of folk beliefs associated with the various species of dung-beetles that affected their use as medicine. May beetles (*Melolontha vulgaris*) were said to be good luck; biting off the head of the first May beetle one saw would supposedly keep one from fever all year. The larvae were pressed for their oil, which was applied topically to wounds and arthritic joints, and the adults were pulverized in wine to treat anemia. Other species were used to treat epilepsy, earache, edema, and bladder stones. (This is all from *Scarab Beetles in Human Culture* by Brett C. Ratcliffe, Coleopterists Society Monograph #5, 2006.) The geotrupid scarab (*Geotrupes stercorarius*) was associated with various storm gods from Finland to Greece; rescuing one would supposedly save your crops from bad weather for the year. (While we don't know which deity it might have been associated with in Germany or Scandinavia, one could probably bet on Thor.) Yet other species were eaten as a diuretic or to prevent cramps. In China, the roasted, pulverized dung-beetles were taken for diarrhea and dysentery, although this practice is being debated today as dung-beetles are carriers for tapeworms, helminths, and pathogenic bacteria that actually cause the symptoms that they are said to alleviate. The use of beetles in various cultures for such things as drying up River conditions (Chinese) and edema (European) suggests an astringent nature at the least, which would be Air. Considering that they were associated with storm gods (like Oak), that's oddly appropriate.

Ground or burnt oyster shells (*Concha ostraea*, which is found on ocean shores all over the world, or the *Arca* family of cockleshell) were used as both a thickener/binder and a medicinal substance. Chinese and Ayurvedic medicines also make use of it; it is antacid and cooling for the stomach (so I would classify it as Earth as well), and an easily absorbed source of calcium. Some varieties have mild astringent (Air) qualities and have been used in Asia for drying up leaking fluids and lung phlegm; others are mildly bitter diuretics used for clearing out edema, which would suggest a Storm nature. Chinese, Ayurvedic and Indian Unani medicine uses it in combination with other herbs for insomnia, irritability, irregular menses, tinnitus, nocturnal emissions, skin conditions, and as a calcium supplement for the teeth.

Horns and antlers, ground to powder, also find a place in the early herbals as well as in Chinese and Ayurvedic medicine. In Chinese medicine, these substances are considered a strong adaptogen and immune stimulant, creating fast growth in reflection of the quick and impressive growth of horns and antlers on herbivores. They are considered warming (Fire) and drying (Air) and are used for cold extremities, fatigue, excessive urination, and a weak lower back and knees. (In comparison, antelope horn is said to be cooling and useful for spasms and convulsions, which would make it Earth and Mountain.) In the Anglo-Saxon herbals, dried hart's antler burned to ash was an early form of "smelling salts", as it contained ammonium salts and would release vapors when mixed with vinegar. It was prescribed for headaches. In *Medicina de Quadrupedibus* it is reputed to be able to "dry up every wet", which would suggest that it has astringent (Air) qualities. It is recommended there for watery eyes, headache (in wine), menstrual cramps, casting out of worms, oozing sores, and loose teeth. Dried, powdered goat's horn was used for skin eruptions, as was powdered ivory from foreign sources. Deerskins and other tanned hides were also scraped with pumice, and the scrapings included in potions.

Certain types of flesh were used in European medicine, but again it is hard to tell whether the use was solely sympathetic magic or had some medicinal property as well. (Not that I'm putting down sympathetic magic, mind you, but it's good to know the mechanism whereby something works, if possible.) Examples of these included pulverized hare's brain in wine for oversleeping, due to the hare's alert energy; or a hound's molar ground and rubbed on teeth to cure their ache. On the other hand, we have the hare's liver being eaten for eye problems as well, which echoes the Chinese idea that the liver affects the eyes. Lungs of rabbit and sheep were sliced thinly and applied to wounds and sores.

Dried animal gall was once a staple in Chinese medicine; its controversial side grew when tradition decreed that the favorite gall was of the now-endangered Asiatic black bear, and bears were promptly overhunted (and today, kept in cages with catheterized gallbladders). Western TCM practitioners have pressed Asian medicine-makers to replace bear gall with common slaughterhouse byproducts such as ox gall and pig gall; chicken and snake gall have also been used. According to them, animal gall is bitter and cold, and alleviates spasms and pain. This would suggest that it is a Mountain substance, and probably Earth as well as it cools hot skin and inflammation when used topically. Gall stimulates the gallbladder and helps with constipation and the digestion of fats, and is applied topically for pain and sprains. It is antiseptic and may have some antibiotic properties.

The ancient Europeans used a wide variety of animal galls, all of them easy for the average peasant to come by: ox, bull, boar, pig, goat, rabbit, fish (usually salmon), fox, raven, and crow. The first several types would have been easily come by during butchering of ordinary food animals. While we may think of ravens and crows as noble birds, European peasantry often considered them pests who attacked the seedling crops, and would send children armed with slings to take out as many as possible. Foxes were an often-hunted scourge of small livestock as well. One recipe does indeed call for bear gall, but this would have been a customarily hunted animal during the cold season. Saami traditions have a long and elaborate ceremony for bear hunting that started days before the hunt and ended days after it, with many taboos intended to show respect for the bear spirit. In European remedies, gall was used for such problems as sore eyes (raven, salmon, rabbit, bull and fox), earaches (fox, goat), toothache (goat), scrotal pain (goat), expelling a placenta (goat), epilepsy (boar), skin eruptions (boar, pig, goat or ox), general external pain (ox), and deworming (several types).

Eggs were often used in such remedies, sometimes as a thickener or binder, and sometimes for their own virtue. As concentrated protein, eggs were nourishing to poorer folk, who might not have enough regular protein for their own good. Eggs are mildly warming (Fire), astringent (Air, and this property made them good for poultice-binding), and oily (Swamp). The combination of those properties reminds me of the gas rising from a hot swamp, which is of course the same sulfur that makes egg yolks yellow and gives them their characteristic smell when rotten. (The contents of a fresh egg are also reasonably sterile, and the white quickly gums over any space, so freshly broken egg whites have been used as sterile wound dressings for millennia, even up to the Civil War for temporary field dressings.) Chinese medicine uses the yolk as a heart medicine, the whites for soothing sore throats, and the ground shells for tuberculosis and organ inflammation. Indian Unani medicine uses egg whites as a sterile wound dressing. In the ancient north, an eggshell was a unit of measurement.

Milk products are oily due to their fat content (Swamp), and generally cooling (Earth), with the exception of yogurt whose fermenting cultures make it warming. Dairy products are much used in Ayurvedic and Unani medicines, but Chinese culture has no use for them. *Medicina de Quadrupedibus* lists several uses for new goat cheese (which, having made cheese, I assume is largely unpressed and still in a gelatinous tofu-like state), including inflamed eyes, headache, and foot sores. The whey was drunk to cleanse the innards and clear obstructions. Cow milk, goat milk, and even human milk figure in the old herbals, sometimes as a medium for herbs and sometimes on its own merits; as far as the latter goes, we must remember that women were less modest about such things then, and babies were nursed for a much longer time.

Probably the most common (and least objectionable) animal substance used in ancient European medicine was honey. Not only is honey a natural preservative and excellent binder of dry matter, it makes horrid potions much more tolerable. As an all-purpose medium, it finds its way into many recipes simply for that reason. However, it was also given as a medicine in and of itself. Honey is anti-microbial when at full strength, and interestingly enough, when diluted it fosters the growth of beneficial microbes (such as the ones that help digest your food and the ones that ferment it into mead) while still fending off destructive ones. It functions as an anti-inflammatory, antifungal, and helps prevent scarring. It helps to heal raw flesh throughout the intestinal tract, from sore throats to internal ulcers. Its ancient uses as a wound-healer were legendary, and it was (and is) especially good in healing diabetic ulcers.

While silver and copper are sometimes seen in ancient European herbal remedies, gold is not, unlike Chinese and Ayurvedic medicine. This may have had to do with the comparative poverty of European peasantry; gold was something that lords hoarded, and it was not wasted on medicine for the people. The Sun's metal didn't make its way firmly into the pharmacopoeia until the alchemists arrived with their gold-obsession.

Sometimes metals were actually used deliberately—such as silver filings being used on wounds—and sometimes cooking vessels of particular materials were recommended for specific potions, thus taking in the virtues (and chemical taint) of that metal. There are references to copper, bronze, brass, and iron vessels used in this way. The first three might have been used to encourage the formation of copper acetates and tartrates, which have some antibiotic compounds. However, the most common metal used in this rather sideways manner was iron. Most cooking pots and kettles were iron, so food cooked in them would absorb and transfer minute amounts of the metal, possibly preventing iron deficiency.

When metals or minerals were used in a prescription in other ways, they might be ground or filed, or simply rubbed. One salve recipe from the *Lacnunga* suggests rubbing butter against copper and then melting it for the salve (in a bronze pot, of course, for dual-density copper flavor). The silver filings mentioned above were used in a cure for burns. In Asian medicines, copper and silver are used as topical painkillers.

Salt, as a food substance, was also a medicinal one and many recipes call for it. Salt is especially popular in salves for its ability to draw infection to the surface of the skin; poultices of salt are still used in this way today. In Chinese medicine, "salty" is one of the tastes associated with their own five-element system which associates it with the watery kidneys; in Ayurvedic medicine it is associated with the *kapha* or watery type and is prescribed for poor digestion, constipation, and lack of appetite. It was not lost on the ancestors anywhere in the world that salt helped to keep in the water in the body. Salty herbs are often emollient, reminding us of the age-old original connection of salt and Water, and yet salt is drying like Air. It may be that salt balances out the watery essence of "wet" herbs, adding a complementary note.

Sulfur was found in many ancient northern medicines, both external as a salve (often for worms or fungus) and internally as a cure for stomach pains. In one recipe, it is burned and inhaled for coughs. It is remarkably often combined with vinegar, perhaps for a reaction that I am not aware of. Chinese medicine has used sulfur since its discovery in the 6th century B.C. According to them, sulfur is sour and hot, making it a Fire substance. Which, considering its association with hot mythical places, is somehow appropriate. I find it to definitely have the feel of Muspellheim. When ingested, it is a purgative that clears fats from the system (largely by inducing diarrhea). Topically it kills skin parasites and alleviates itch, but needs to be used carefully or it will burn. It is rarely used internally today.

Gypsum was used as a way to preserve Rose petals for medicinal use in northern medicine; we don't know if the gypsum itself was considered to have qualities beyond preservation, but the combination was noted to work as a styptic. Chinese medicine uses gypsum internally for fevers, headaches, coughs, and bronchitis; and externally for skin disorders. We do tend to forget that one form of gypsum is alabaster, which was a fairly valuable stone; some researchers believe that alabaster/gypsum was the famous "white stone" which is mentioned in *Bald's Leechbook*. It was to be scraped, and the scrapings watered with red ochre. The two together would supposedly heal "stitch and flying venom and all unknown afflictions". The combination of red and white minerals figures frequently in a variety of European cultures as a symbol of the sacred marriage of male and female (semen and menstrual blood). The one that comes quickest to mind are the two springs at Chalice Well in Glastonbury, one of which is red with iron ore and the other white with chalk, and which supposedly flow together to create a sacred well.

Another substance used in both areas which will be familiar to the modern Northern Tradition practitioner is powdered amber. We don't know exactly what conditions it was used for in northern medicine, but Chinese medicine considered it very neutral in temperature and feel. They use it to arrest tremors and palpitations, making it a Mountain substance. It is applied topically to heal skin quickly and used internally to break up blood clots and clear the blood, but it is slightly sweet rather than bitter.

Unlike the rest of this book, this section does not have practical and specific uses for many or most of these substances, and that's because I don't know enough about them to give proper tested formulas. Perhaps those with more free time than me might be interested in a deeper comparison of animal and mineral products as they were used in the various parts of the world, and practical experimentation with clients and/or volunteers to usefully recreate their purposes in western herbalism. I'll be looking forward to the book.

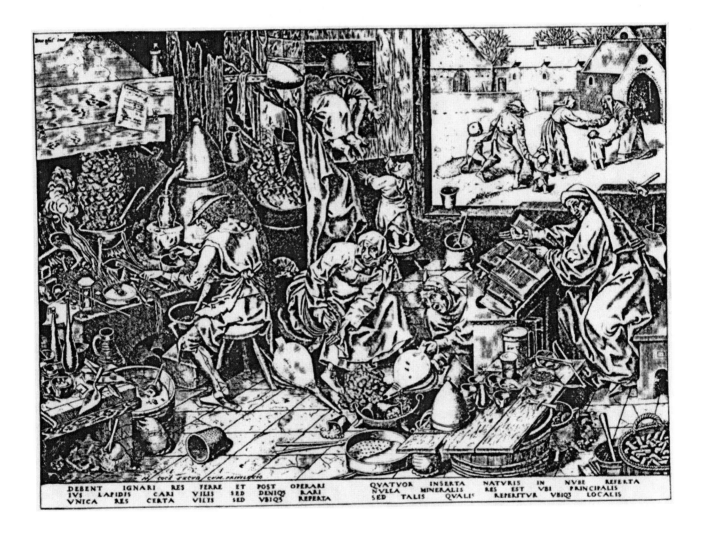

Part III
Songs of Praise

This section includes poetry and a song that I wrote for some of the greenwights that I work with. It may seem odd to some people that I consider these devas to be friends, but I do. The Grandmother and Grandfather spirits of these plants are more than just "allies", they are People that I say hello to when I walk past the plants that are their children and their ears and eyes. (I know that plants don't see or hear per se. But they do sense, and that's the metaphor I'm working with.) Sometimes they share their mysteries with me, and I write them down. Of all the spirits I've worked with, the plants have given me the most joy for the least effort. I praise their names, all of them.

There's also a poem to Gerda, first published in *Honey, Grain and Gold: A Devotional To Frey*, which tells of my herb garden and how it came to be. It's a partner-poem to one I wrote for her husband in that devotional.

Lina's Ordeal

First, the planting.

The silver-haired mother sprinkles her seeds
From a gnarled fist; they are sown thick
That stalks may grow tall rather
Than bushy; thick together to hold up
Each other in wind and rain, not to be
Crushed by the occasional bird
Who mistakes the waving field of blue
For one of Her sacred ponds.
Grow, my children! Reach for the sky,
Says the silver-haired goddess who wakes the apple trees.

Second, the cutting.

The waving stalks crowned like the sky
Are to be cut down, each one at the hand
Of the snaggle-toothed mother with the scythe.
Each flax plant cries out; soft and delicate
As a woman's brow, her spirit is not sturdy
Like that of the waving golden grain. Lina weeps
And lies limply, cut off from the earth.
I am dying! she cries. *This is the end of me!*
Silly girl! Only another beginning,
Says the snaggle-toothed goddess who hangs the elderberries.

Third, the drying.

The stalks dry to brittle fragility, yet
At their core is still a center of stubbornness,
An unwillingness to go where they are
Most needed. *See, I am delicate, I will break*
At your touch! Lina cries, in the hopes
That the silver-haired mother will leave her be.
Oh, you are stronger than you say, my girl,
But I will have you yet. Just wait,
Says the silver-haired goddess who rides in the wagon.

Fourth, the retting.

In her sacred pools the bundles lie,
Waiting in stagnant waters abuzz with flies
And kept company by tadpoles and the
Occasional passing frog. *I shall rot,*
Says Lina with some satisfaction, *and there
Will be an end to me. You'll see. It will serve you right,
For leaving me with such low sorts.* But a practiced
Gnarled finger tests the waters, an old nose
That was old when the Duergar first hollowed hills
Across the border of the world, sniffs the scum
And just in time, lifts Lina from her bed of slime.
I will cleanse you in clear lake waters,
Says the gnarled-handed goddess whose washing-day is the summ

Fifth, the breaking.

The wooden brake lies in the hut's
Darkest corner; those gnarled hands
Life it out, dust off the elderberry dreams
And prepare the victim. Crack! and the shell breaks.
Crack! Crack! and Lina cries, *Enough!
My hard stem is broken, old woman,
Are you not satisfied?* But the grinning hag
Knows better. *Your core is still untouched,
And thus you seek to hide it from me. I'll not have it!
And I'll break you still, my girl.* Crack! and Lina
Yields to the hag who steals bad children, fills their
Dead bellies with straw and dirt from the cottage floor.
I will break you and remake you,
Says the tangled-haired goddess who leads the Wild Hunt.

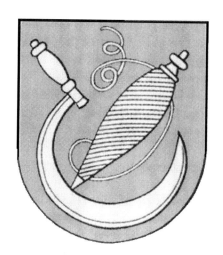

Sixth, the scutching.

Lina is bent backwards in her torment
And the wooden blade scrapes her nerves—
I cannot bear it! she cries. *You can, my chick,
And what is more, you will, for there is
No going back now.* The ghosts of children
Dead aborning flit about that white-clad form,
As she peels away the last of Lina's defenses,
Hanging in tattered scraps from what were
Once stems. *You don't need this any more,*
Says the grey-eyed goddess whose hearth's smoke is the fog.

Seventh, the heckling.

Dragged through a bed of nails,
Lina does not understand why she does not
End, and have it be over. But no, the torment
Goes on, with no mercy in sight. Those hands
Are strong enough to drag her through the hackle
And gentle enough to rock the cradles of babes
Whose exhausted mothers have fallen asleep
At the fire, their fingers bloodied by too-industrious
Spinning. She loves them, the ones who work too hard,
Who push themselves, who are never content
With less than a spotless house, a perfect job,
Who let no discomfort stand in their way. They are
Her children. *You should learn from them, my girl,*
Says the gentle-handed goddess who midwifes dead babes.

Eighth, the combing.

They say that once a man stumbled into a cave
Under a hill, to be met by a jeweled queen
And her maidens who offered him riches.
They say that he asked only for the flowers
She held in her hand—perhaps he was awed,
And humbled, or perhaps he saw the old woman
Beneath, attended by ghostly babes, and thought better
Of any jewels. The flower was Lina, and his wife
Was the first to be taught of the journey, flower to gown.
She sings the tale to herself as she combs Lina,
Laying every hair straight and fine,
And who knows what version she sings?
Do you not like your new form?
Says the white-robed goddess who brings the first flurries.

Ninth, the dressing.

Cradled in the lap of winter, Lina knows comfort
For the first time, and true surrender
As the layers fall, back and forth, back and forth,
And rolled up around the distaff. *But I don't wish
To be bound,* she cries still, rebelling. *Hush, girl,
It will be over soon enough.* A blood-red ribbon
Binds her, for the mother's blood on the spinning.
Like the girl who fell down a well into another country,
Gave everything away, and gained the golden tongue.
Like her sister, who was selfish, and burped toads
Forever. *Which will you be, my chick?*
Says the snowy-haired goddess who guards the deep well.

Tenth, the spinning.

Here is where the magic is made.
The whirl of the whorl, the whirl of the wheel,
The spiral spinning that stretches time
And space. Outside, snow is fluttering
From the feather pillows she shook out this morning
But inside, all comes down to the humming thread.
Lina is silenced by the beauty of it,
Of time, of space, of the web of the Norns
Of which she is now a small part. *I understand, old mother,*
She whispers in the wheel's hum, and truly
It has all been worth it. *See, I have won you, my girl,*
Says the twinkle-eyed goddess who rides on the broom.

Eleventh, the weaving.

From Urd's game to Verdandi's. The threads
Cross back and forth, warp and weft,
Made beautiful, encompassing, a form
Like none ever seen before. The weights
On the loom are the skulls of babies
Too soon spat from their mother's womb.
The old mother works all winter, but not
Every day. There are houses to visit, women
To reward or punish, children to gift or curse,
Larders to inventory, grains of corn to count.
I am beautiful, Mother, Lina says. *I never knew*
I could be this beautiful, even in the days
Of the blue sky. I knew nothing then.
Only death and torment stood between,
Says the blue-cloaked goddess whose lace is the frost.

Twelfth, the wearing.

Stitched together with her own self,
Lina is open and ready, pliant to do the will
Of the broom-bearing mother. Baptized in madder,
Rose as the sunrise she waits. Will I lie
On the shoulders of a maiden, a man, a child?
It matters not—I can dream, but for the first time
I am ready for anything, and glad of it. Only death
And torment could give me this readiness.
I am open to the future, to wrap and caress
Any who will have me, with love.
It's for this you were born, child of the sky,
It's for this that you died, child of the earth,
It's for this that you suffered, child of the summer,
Says the winter-voiced goddess who waits for the spring.

Leac's Watch

The fire burns, the spear-leek
Chopped with an iron knife and put
Into the pot. The first of five men
Gathered around the fire touches the edge
Of the iron pot, remembers the woman
Who put it into his hands, said *Don't lose this,*
You fool, don't lose my pot, don't lose your hands,
Your legs, your arms, your eyes, your guts,
Your head, your life. Thunder-wielder, hear me.
With tears in her voice. The iron burns
His fingers, and he absently puts them
In his mouth, remembering the touch of hers.

Leac scents the air as he cooks, this place of men
Waiting, watching from the hilltop, scenting
The cold air, watching the grey line of dawn
Where the rumor threatened. The second of
Five men wipes his hands. Harsh scent
From the juice on his fingers brings tears to
His eyes, and he wipes them too with one
Woollen sleeve, then remembers the leather brace
On his wrist. He gaze flicks to his bow. Strung. Then
Memory of his small son's voice echoes in his ears
And the tears come further, although he turns
His back to the fire, so that no other can see.

Steam rises from the kettle. The sun peers
Over the horizon like a spear, piercing the gaze
Of the third of five men, the youngest who has
Not yet been tried in battle. Excitement, fear,
Dreams of glory, bold words clench his jaw
Where growth barely covers. When the word came
That they might come, the invaders, carrying
Death by the bucketful, he was the first to raise
His dead father's spear and shout. The others,
Older, wiser, they stood slower, but stood up
Still. It has not yet occurred to him that he
May never return to his old mother's embrace.

The soup of Leac is ladled into wooden bowls.
The fourth of five men shades his eyes
With one rugged hand. The others watch him,
Sideways, covertly, as men are aware of the
Alpha hound, always. He will lead, he has seen
Many battles, although of late he has grown
Very tired of them. *Thunder-wielder, my grandson*

Huddles waiting to be born. I would see him,
Lord who brings rain, lord who blesses my life,
I would sleep at home in my bed next week
And awake to the dawn over my browning fields.

The fifth of five men cleans his knife,
Thinking of throats and bellies waiting
To be sliced. No one waits at home for him.
Silent and lean, with hooded eyes, he tastes
The sharp tang of the spear-wyrt in broth.
He will see blood. He lives for this. No one
Understands this, no one knows the rage
That leads him to live alone, to waste himself
Again and again with sword and spear.

The wind rises. Clouds sweep grey and ragged
Over the sun-spear, and the thunder rolls.
Five men stand up among the first drops
In this place that women do not know,
In this place where bodies are laid down
In sacrifice, where the greatest worth one has
Is to be a living wall, a fence, a gate that will not
Open. A tree to be hacked down.

Blue and sharp, the thunder holds them from above.

Green and sharp, Leac holds them from below.

Garden

Her eyes are like the shadows beneath the spreading mint,
Cool and dark, beneath that which reaches for the light,
But usually downturned upon her busy hands. It is never
That she is shy, merely that the calm darkness of her eyes
Full on is not a gift she shares often. Her gaze is the blessed shade
Of the honeysuckle tree when the sun beats down, unrelenting.
Woodruff spirals at its roots, at her feet, while the braver
Goosegrass bounds across the paving stones of my walled garden.

Her garden. After we put in the short post with her face,
Her wide-lipped mouth and averted gaze, it became hers.
No other northern goddess may have a shrine there, although
She thinks nothing of the clay Buddha and the painted Mariamne
Who were there before her. Gerda's peace lies on my garden,
Even now, when the green is November-withered and dull brown
Like the hems of her undergarments, brushing the stones
Around her ankles. All colors of the earth are kind to her.

Her hair is the color of rich earth, turned with a spade
Before the eager fingers, trembling with anticipation,
Push the seeds, gently, forcefully, into the soil. Its neat plaits
Are like the beds in early spring, when we turn back the straw
Mulch and see the quiescent brown, waiting for a touch,
As she waits patiently in her garden in Jotunheim
For the day when she will methodically make her way
To He whose touch is her yearly awakening. No other
Can rouse her sleeping response, can quicken her breath,
Can make her measured footsteps break into a heedless run.

We wanted the country, the farm, for many reasons, but truth
Be told, the thought of herb gardens made my breath catch
Longing in my throat. Fragrant lemon balm studded with bees,
Hoary sage, spiked motherwort and hyssop, and all the spilling
Mints. Yet I did not expect the bounty of the woods, when I
First walked this land—kinnikinnick, squaw vine, the scarlet
Berries of wintergreen against the December snow. As I built
The garden, bed by bed, my knowledge of the wild ones grew.
Wild and tame, they nourish me now. She loves all, though,
And so do I, as She has taught me.

Her back is broad, her shoulders like rolling hills, her arms
Strong with muscle. She is no delicate gilded thing; she walks
Among the elven people to meet her love, their gazes scandalized
And dwelling on the solidity of her Jotun form, her shape
A grandmother oak among their slender, ephemeral birch
And maple, hard like the oak and elm we split
To feed our kitchen stove, burning long and strong,
Not consumed for the hours it takes to bake

Those fragrant pies. Burning clean and bright, no black
Sludge in the stovepipe like those softer woods.
It is the hardest wood that lights the brightest fires,
A worthy match struck to His gold,
Passion to passion. Her patience is that woodpile, waiting sturdily
To light the coldest winter nights.

*It took me seven years to clear the space. No tiller, no machines
In that rocky, half-sterile hill of patchy lawn, just me
And a garden claw hacking out the weedy turf piece by piece,
Square foot by foot, inch by aching inch. Patience, she said.
There is no deadline here. The magic is in the process,
Not the goal. One by one, the beds went in, stone edgings
Filled with compost dark as Her, rich from the manure piles
Of goat and sheep. One by one, the precious herbs.
If they did not survive, She said, Throw them out.
I want nothing here that is weak, that cannot
Stand up to wind and weather and perishing cold, here in this place
Whose winds and mountains are nothing to the bitter cold of my home.
Her garden is a spell of survival, of hope springing anew in spite of all.*

Her touch is a stone wall, shutting out noise and bustle,
Protecting you from all that would overwhelm and frazzle you.
Her cheek is the paleness of thick roots that grow in the garden,
Buried and eagerly sought. Her body lies hidden beneath
Layers of dresses, plain and dark or brightly embroidered
By giantess-fingers—you would not think them nimble,
Compared to the elves who despise her, and yet her touch is soft,
Sure, and plies a needle well. Dark crescents of soil lie
Under her fingernails, from centuries of plying dirt as well,
On her knees in the gardens she loves, the tiny seedlings twining
Up to kiss those broad fingers, as they know how much
Love is there for them. Her love is the warmth of piled earth
In small mounds about their fragile roots,
Helping them to survive the frosts.

*"It won't survive," I say mournfully, looking at the second black lamb
Whose tiny frame has lived these days only by our driving hands,
Pouring milk down its reluctant throat. Live, we say, like a spell
To give it will to do so, yet sometimes that spell fails. Mother-rejected,
It will not even mewl. That black ewe knows better, her baleful gaze
Protecting its stronger sister, who suckles happily. Sometimes they just
Know. Some life is meant to fail—that is the lesson of Life's profligacy.
Quantity first, then weed for quality. Time to Weed, Gerda says,
And we take the tiny body out in the cold, for the hammer-blow,
For the ceasing of that shallow breath, for the compost heap
That will turn death into more Life, come spring.*

Her rare smile is sweet as elderberries, hanging in dark clusters
On the graceful branches, following the lacy white blossoms
That cure the cough and cold. Her womb is a barred gate;

No young will she bear her beloved, to be hostage to his keepers,
Though tears rack them both on many nights, together and alone,
When they speak of this pain. Her heart is a warm quilt,
Tucked silently over the sobs of the woman whose child
Did not come to fruition, or who had to stop
The child herself. Her tears are the cold rain that falls
On the lovers who cannot speak of something,
Whose words are caught and trapped, yet that rain
Will nourish the seedlings that fight their way upwards.

Because of the weeding, I spend more time kneeling before Gerda
Than any other. I pull, and kill, and kill. It is necessary, she says.
The beams of my kitchen hold bunches of herbs, to find their way
Into savory cooking, or into row upon row of shining glass bottles
For medicine. It was a hobby at first, a way to thwart the high cost
Of the pharmacy, a smug satisfaction ... and then the people came,
Asking for help. The women were the hardest, the girls
With their wombs filled unwanted, fearing the machines
Of the doctors—was there not an easier way? I helped,
And sometimes we were lucky, and the clinic
Not needed. Do what is necessary, Gerda says. And I do.

Her soul is a deep cave under the earth, bored with holes
Like the sacred places under the ancient megaliths.
On sacred days, the sun shines through, and lights the
Bloodied stone table like a miracle. Pain and joy, and I kneel
To deeper wisdom. There must be culling, pruning, weeding
For there to be growth. His growth.
And this is her Mystery.

Tiny Green

Cuckoo-Bread bounces
Toaward me, playful as I rip
Chickweed from the garden. I try
To leave him there, but my care costs
An innocent violet her head. He laughs
Riotously, nothing is funnier. *Enough,*
I say, silence him by stuffing him
In my mouth to eat. Even then,
I can hear the fading of his laughter
Like an echo in my belly.

Clearing the Barn

You're not supposed to be out in the Sun,
She says disapprovingly as I walk past, her leaves
Brushing my shoulder. Not on so little sleep,
Not so soon after being ill. Her white flowers are
Beginning to open, like the lace spilling
From an old woman's velvet dress.
Her emerald brooch flashes. So do her eyes.
The work must be done, I say. Two more loads,
I feel myself sicken, but what would my compatriots
Say if I said, *The tree told me I had to go in.*
Third load, and she loses patience. *Go in, you fool,*
You idiot, you know what will happen. Do you
Expect I'll give comfort once you've ignored me?
Or that you can expect it from anyone else? I'll tell
Them all of your stupidity, and they will just laugh,
No matter how much tea you drink.

A friend, busy with wheelbarrow and fork
Sees me stopped in my tracks. *What's wrong?*
I hesitate, weigh comfortable lies, and then decide.
Friends may come and go. A watch-wight is for life.
The tree told me to go in, I say. And turn for the door.

Liver Combination

Hail the Well of Plenty, heal the Well of Plenty,
May abundance always reign.

Mother Milk Thistle leads.
Only she, with her infinite gentleness, can keep
This band of miscreants together. She moves slowly,
Always with grace, her green gown with its white
Splashes eddying about her ankles. None of the others
Dare to jibe to her face. They would die of shame
At her kind and knowing smile. She lifts her arms
And murmurs her spell at the edge of the Great Well.

Hail the Well of Plenty, heal the Well of Plenty,
May abundance always reign.

Grandfather Burdock next, waddling with his bulk,
Spitting burrs through his teeth like tobacco,
He stoops, tests the water, grunts, eyebrows raised.
A few expletives fall, then with hands surprisingly
Deft for their size, he magics. Old Dock steps up,
Lean and weathered like a stretch of roadside,
His longtime friend, he expressed the same thought
With only a laconic snort. Healing falls from them,
One stream ivory, one saffron, into the dark red well.

Hail the Well of Plenty, heal the Well of Plenty,
May abundance always reign.

Dandelion next, she is there like a ray of Sun
And the old men smile in spite of themselves.
Her smile is sincerity itself, her will a childlike
Hope stronger and more golden than any worn
Grownup. No one *hopes* like Dandelion.
Glimmers of sunlight swim across the surface
Of the clouded water. She prays, she waves,
Looks to the Mother for approval. She gets it,
Steps back, and it is done. Sunlight reaches the
Murky depths of the polluted well, and it is
Washed clean yet again.

Hail the Well of Plenty, heal the Well of Plenty,
May abundance always reign.

Riddle of the Seven Queens

I wrote this as a riddle song for seven herbs that I work with and love. Each year I sing it at Pagan gatherings, and tell people that they should figure out who the seven Queens are. That's all I say, and usually people rack their brains thinking of goddesses or famous historical figures. Few can figure out that they're plants, and of those, fewer still can name them. However, anyone who reads through this book should have no trouble.

Chorus:
I hail the Seven Grandmothers, I praise the Seven Queens,
They dance their way through hill and dell and through the fields of green,
They wend their way through wood and glade and grace the garden round,
Their footsteps left for those with eyes to see,
Making whole and sound,
And I bow before the wisdom of their crowns.

The first Queen flies on wings of smoke, like magic see her rise,
Silver-green her skirts and hair and silver-green her eyes,
The Moon shines silver on her works, she opens up your mind,
Her silver hair floats down from starry skies
And suddenly you'll find
Everything you thought you left behind.

The second Queen's a bitter lass and sorrow is her name,
She's wedded to the brother of the first Queen in her fame,
And she leaves her bitter touch upon each pack of playing cards,
As if to say, You'll curse the day you tried
To leave your frugal yard,
And yet she gives you stomach when it's hard.

Chorus

The third Queen is a cottage-wife all clad in summer's blue,
A sacred well of prophecy, the water falls like dew,
She'll save your breath and soothe your brow and put out fever's flame,
Her cool white hand will clear your inner Sky
Of all its clouds and rain,
The hedge-wife teaches all who call her name.

The fourth Queen is a beauty, with her hair like raven's wings,
As sharp as knives and open eyes, a siren song she sings,
You'll surrender your last breath to her with little but a sigh,
And perhaps she'll snatch your pain and take you high,
On purple wings you'll fly,
Or perhaps she'll snatch your breath and then you'll die.

Chorus

The fifth Queen is a bloody lass whose fame is ever known,
She binds the wounds of warriors cut to the blood and bone,
Her touch is like a feather's kiss, she moves in purity,
And she casts the filth from all the flowing streams,
Lets the rivers all run clean,
And a thousand flowers curl around her feet.

The sixth Queen is an angel wreathed in towers of golden light,
And she guards the road to heaven where the rainbow fills your sight,
She warms the cold, the thin, the old, supports the fragile reed,
A hollow lamp, a holy torch, a hand
To hold you in your need,
The starburst and the sunburst and the seed.

Chorus

The seventh Queen's the Old One crouched beside the swamp and fen,
And she guards the road to Hel where walk a thousand fallen men,
Mistress of the Ancestors, Dame of ancient lays,
Her arms reach out to heal all those who seek
Her hidden tracks and ways,
But never touch her hand without her say,
And you'd best bow down your head before you speak.

Chorus

Riddle of the Seven Queens

Raven Kaldera

I hail the Se-ven Grand-mo-thers, I praise the Se-ven Queens, They dance their way through hill and dell and through the fields of green, They wend their way through wood and glade and grace the gar-den round, Their foot-steps left for those with eyes to see, Ma-king whole and sound, And I bow be-fore the wis - dom of their crowns.

Part IV
Appendices

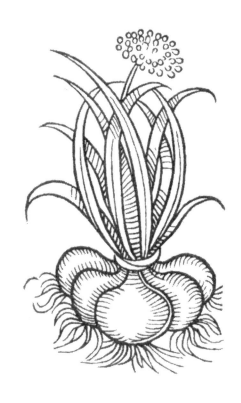

Appendix I: Greenwights

These categories are purely experiential, and others may connect with these plants in different ways; that's all right. You don't interact the same way with all the people that you meet, and neither do many spirits. We encourage people to make their own impressions of the greenwights. However, for those who are interested, these are very general categories that I and others perceived the plants as falling into.

Ancestral Fathers
Barley
Oats
Rye
Wheat

Ancestral Mothers
Bean
Pea
Lambsquarters

Magicians
Cinquefoil
Fennel
Vervain
Speedwell
Ash
Little Red Man
Periwinkle

Witches
Belladonna
Hellebore
Apple
Convalilly
Tansy

Servants
Betony
Broom
Shepherd's Purse
Thyme

Faery Plants
Hawthorn
Foxglove
Elecampane
Blackthorn
Sweet Cicely

Wisewoman Plants
Hyssop
Yarrow
Edelweiss
Elder
Mugwort
Gentian
Henbane
Mullein
Rue
Teasel

Wiseman Plants
Sage
Burdock
Horehound
Juniper
Wormwood

Green Children
Dandelion
Daisy
Chamomile
Primrose
Cowslip
Calendula
Chickweed
Cleavers
Ground Ivy
Lady's Bedstraw
Mallow
Poppy
Strawberry
Violet
Viola

Green Woodwights
Centaury
Wood Sorrel
Alder
Celandine
Woodwaxen
Hemlock
Houseleek
Parsley
Sorrel
Woodruff
Tormentil

Animals
Bistort
Catnip
Lupine
Purslane
Watercress

Mother-Healers
Lady's Mantle
Motherwort
Birch
Dill
Feverfew
Goldenrod
Marshmallow
Maple
Milk Thistle
Mint
Pennyroyal
Raspberry
Willow
Linden

Father-Healers
Comfrey
Dock
Herb Bennet
Valerian
Good King Henry

Warriors
Agrimony
Garlic
Gorse
Nettles
Leek
Holly
Mustard
Yew

Guardians
Aconite
Angelica
Borage
Carline Thistle
Fir
Oak
Onion
Rowan
St. John's Wort
Thistle
Woad

Homemakers
Alecost
Madder
Soapwort
Weld

Dreamers
Aspen
Beech
Cherry
Chicory
Cumin
Flax
Hemp
Hops
Ivy
Lavender
Lemon Balm
Lovage
Meadowsweet
Rosemary
Rose

Wanderers
Caraway
Plantain

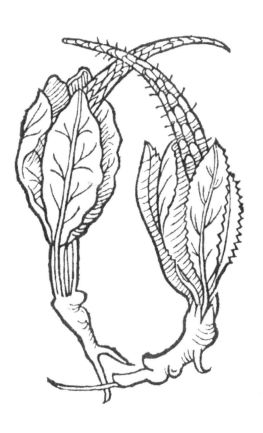

Appendix II:
Sources for Herb Seed

1. Richters Herbs
357 Highway 47
Goodwood, ON L0C 1A0 Canada
Tel. +1.905.640.6677 Fax. +1.905.640.6641
http://www.richters.com

2. Sand Mountain Herbs
321 County Rd. 18 Fyffe, AL 35971
http://www. sandmountainherbs.com

3. Thyme Garden Herb Company
20546 Alsea Highway
Alsea, Oregon 97324
Phone: 541-487-8671
Fax (Call first) 541-487-8671
http://www.thymegarden.com/

4. Fedco Seeds
PO Box 520, Waterville, ME 04903
(207) 873-7333
http://www.fedcoseeds.com
(Primarily vegetable seed, but a really good herb seed section)

5. The Ethnobotanical Catalog of Seeds
J.L. Hudson, Seedsman
Box 337 La Honda CA 94020-0337
www.jlhudsonseeds.net

If you can't find it in any of these, I suggest looking for herbalists who grow it!

Appendix III:
Useful Books on
Herbalism and Herbal Studies

Barber, Elizabeth Wayland. ***Women's Work: The First 20,000 Years.*** W.W. Norton & Co. NY. 1994.
   (*A fascinating trip through the history of fiber arts. Important for the historical fiber artist and dyer.*)

Bartram, Thomas. ***Bartram's Encyclopedia of Herbal Medicine.*** Constable & Robinson, London, 1995.
   (*Good standby with lots of pathology entries.*)

Bremness, Lesley. ***Herbs.*** Dorling Kindersley, NY, London, Stuttgart. 1994.
   (*Full-color pocket handbook with good photos of many herbs. The book to take into the garden to figure out what the heck is that thing coming up in the corner.*)

Bremness, Lesley. ***The Complete Book of Herbs.*** Viking Studio Books, NY. 1988.
   (*A good large full-color photo book of many herbs, including their seed, flower, and immature leaf form. Good info on culinary and household uses.*)

Buchanan, Rita. ***A Dyer's Garden.*** Interweave Press, 1995.
Buchanan, Rita. ***A Weaver's Garden.*** Dover Books, 2000.
   (*These are the ultimate guides to growing and using dye plants and fiber plants.*)

Buhner, Stephen Harrod. ***Herbal Antibiotics*** (1999), ***Herbs for Hepatitis C and the Liver*** (2000), ***Healing Lyme*** (2005). Storey Publishing, North Adams, MA.
   (*These are three of my favorites in a series of disorder-specific herbal guides. They are clear, hard-hitting, and eminently practical. He's written others too.*)

Buhner, Stephen Harrod. ***The Lost Language of Plants.*** Chelsea Green Publishing, White River Junction VT. 2002.
   (*One of the best and most moving descriptions of dealing with plant spirits for healing. After years of reading herbals that attempted to push herbalism in the direction of cold scientific modern medicine, this book was a joy to my heart. It showed me that I wasn't alone in the way I saw plants.*)

Clarkson, Rosetta E. ***Herbs and Savory Seeds.*** Dover Publications Inc. NY 1972.
   (*An old classic of the stillroom, with lots of antique household uses.*)

Cruden, Loren. *Medicine Grove.* Destiny Books, Rochester VT. 1997.
(While it has a Native American traditional context, this book has a lot of good descriptions of the author's dealing with greenwights.)

Garland, Sarah. *The Herb Garden.* Viking Penguin Books, NY. 1994.
(A great book for creating a herb garden, including many really nice layouts, and photos that will make you envious—and inspired. Includes medieval monastery layouts.)

Green, James. *The Herbal Medicine-Maker's Handbook.* The Crossing Press, Berkeley CA. 2000.
(The textbook manual for the California School of Herbalism, this book is the best and clearest guide to home manufacture of almost any kind of whole-plant herbal medicine. If you're making your own, you need this one.)

Grieve, Maude. *A Modern Herbal.* Dover Books, NY. 1971.
(A reprint of an early classic, first published in the early 1900s. Available online at botanical.com.)

Landsberg, Sylvia. *The Medieval Garden.* The British Museum Press, London.
(A terrific book if you're into designing medieval gardens. This goes into everything from fencing to trellising to the layouts of monasteries, and includes lists of period herbs. Examples of current historical recreation gardens are described.)

Montgomery, Pam. *Plant Spirit Healing.* Bear & Co. Rochester VT. 2008.
(While it comes from a more New Age perspective, the book clearly indicates that Pam Montgomery knows her plant spirits. In fact, she teaches budding herbalists how to contact and work with them. In a phone call, she told me about using burning herbs to smudge a particular meridian.)

Ody, Penelope. *The Complete Medicinal Herbal.* Dorling Kindersley, NY, London, Stuttgart. 1994.
(Another beautiful full-color book that's worth having, especially as it has pictures of herbal preparations as well as plants.)

Phillips, Nancy and Michael. *The Herbalist's Way.* Chelsea Green Publishing, White River Junction VT. 2005.
(If you're a practicing herbalist, this is one to pick up. There are interviews of famous herbalists and discussion of every part of the business and ethical aspects of professional herbalism. Inspiring, too.)

Phillips, Roger, and Foy, Nicky. *The Random House Book of Herbs.* Random House, NY. 1990.
(Good pictures, good medicinal information, especially about obscure British wild herbs not generally found in American books.)

Pollington, Stephen. *Leechcraft.* Anglo-Saxon Books, Trowbridge UK. 2000.
(The definitive guide to the Anglo-Saxon herbals. Includes translations of all of them. The downside of this book is that the author is not a herbalist and the medicinal aspects of herbs listed are sketchy at best. However, it has reams of info on charms and non-herb healing substances of ancient England.)

Polunin, Miriam, and Robbins, Christopher. *The Natural Pharmacy.* Collier Books NY. 1992.
(Another beautiful full-color book, but this one doesn't just have identification pictures of herbs. Animal products and minerals also appear. The front part is a comparison of world medicinal systems. Fascinating and gorgeous.)

Walter, Eugene. **Hints & Pinches.** MJF Books, NY. 2002.

(*For the culinary herbalist. Describes what to do with all manner of herbs and spices. The recipes alone are worth it.*)

Weed, Susun. **The Wise Woman Herbal for the Childbearing Year.** Ash Tree Publishing, Woodstock NY. 1986.

(*A classic for treating pregnant women, and women who don't want to be pregnant, and women with new babies. The midwife hedge-witch's best friend.*)

Wood, Matthew. **The Book of Herbal Wisdom.** North Atlantic Books, Berkeley CA. 1997.

(*An awesome book by Matthew Wood. Goes deeply into the spiritual and emotional uses of herbs, largely from a Native American perspective.*)

Wood, Matthew. **The Earthwise Herbal: The Complete Guide to Old World Medicinal Plants.** North Atlantic Books, Berkeley, CA. 2008.

(*The first in a two-book series, this is the one that most NT herbalists will want. It goes into the many uses of European herbs. The second book covers New World herbs. An absolute must in the herbalist's library.*)

Wood, Matthew. **The Practice of Traditional Western Herbalism.** North Atlantic Books, Berkeley, CA. 2004.

(*A brilliant book, the one that made all of Mengloth's imagery around herbs click properly in my mind.*)

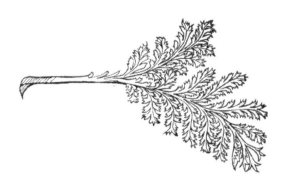

Part IV
Index

General Index

Please note that herbal properties (such as analgesic, antiseptic, vermifuge, etc.) will be found in the Properties Index. For preparations - poultices, candies, capsules, etc - look up the relevant herb, affliction, body system, property, household use, or magical purpose.

Affinities Index

Conditions Index

Properties Index

Artistic Contributions

I would like to thank and acknowledge all the wonderful artists who drew my green friends for me and donated their work to this book. May your names be praised.

P. 34 "Agrimony" by Alicia Stychek
P. 35 "Alder-Man" by Corey Nicol http://coreythorn.deviantart.com/
P. 38 "Angelica" by Fire Tashlin
P. 39 "Ash" by Seawalker
P. 42 "Father Barley" by Raven Kaldera
P. 44 "Mother Bean" by Raven Kaldera
P. 47 "Birch Lady" by Ellen http://www.ellenmillion.com/
P. 49 "Bistort" by Raven Kaldera
P. 51 "Lady Borage" by Raven Kaldera
P. 60 "Master Catnip" by Corey Nicol http://coreythorn.deviantart.com/
P. 64 "The Maythen Chidren" by Raven Kaldera
P. 66 "Cherry" by Raven Kaldera
P. 70 "Master Cinquefoil" by Seawalker
P. 72 "Master Clover" by Raven Kaldera
P. 77 "Cowslip and Primrose" by Raven Kaldera
P. 80 "Apple-Maiden" by Pia Van Ravenstein http://piavanravestein.com/
P. 81 "Cumin" by Corey Nicol http://coreythorn.deviantart.com/
P. 84 "Mother Dill" by Raven Kaldera
P. 86 "Dittany" by Seawalker
P. 90 "Dame Ellhorn" by Raven Kaldera
P. 92 "Elecampane" by Raven Kaldera
P. 96 "Mistress Feverfew" by Raven Kaldera
P. 99 "Lina" by Seawalker
P. 101 "Foxglove" by Sade Wolfkitten
P. 103 "Garlic" by Seawalker
P. 113 "Herb Bennet" by Raven Kaldera
P. 117 "Horehound" by Raven Kaldera
P. 121 "Hyssop" by Raven Kaldera
P. 123 "Ivy" by Corey Nicol http://coreythorn.deviantart.com/
P. 125 "Juniper" by Seawalker
P. 128 "Lady's Bedstraw" by Pia Van Ravenstein http://piavanravestein.com/
P. 129 "Lady's Mantle" by Raven Kaldera
P. 130 "Lambsquarters" by Seawalker
P. 131 "Lambsquarters" by Pia Van Ravenstein http://piavanravestein.com/
P. 132 "Lavender" by Mara
P. 133 "Lavender" by Faye Estrella
P. 134 "Leac" by Seawalker
P. 135 "Balm-Wight" by Raven Kaldera
P. 136 "Reindeer Moss" by Pia Van Ravenstein http://piavanravestein.com/
P. 145 "Marshmallow" by Raven Kaldera
P. 147 "Mistress Bridewort" by Seawalker
P. 149 "Mint" by Faye Estrella
P. 154 "Motherwort" by Raven Kaldera
P. 156 "Mugwort" by Raven Kaldera
P. 160 "Nettles" by Raven Kaldera

Coats of arms on pp. 250-254 designed by:

1. Oberflachs by Voyager
2. Karcunovce by Peter Zeliznak
3. Frankfurt-Fechenheim by Enslin
4. Unterhausen by Enslin
5. Mark by Lokal Profil
6. Blason de la ville Fleurs by Bruno Villette
7. Kiikka by Care
8. Ivanovo by Panther

All others public domain.

CPSIA information can be obtained at www.ICGtesting.com
Printed in the USA
BVOW04s0848040516

446713BV00004B/66/P

9 780982 579848